You Can
Find *Anybody!*

JOSEPH CULLIGAN

Licensed Private Investigator

YOU CAN FIND

Anybody!

JODERE GROUP

Jodere Group, Inc.
San Diego, California

Library of Congress Catalog Card Number: 00-062780
ISBN: 1-58872-000-4
Printed in the United States of America

Culligan, Joseph
        You Can Find Anybody
        p. cm.
        Includes directories

        1. Missing persons—Investigations.   I. Title.

HV6762.A3C8 2000   362.233'6
                        QB192-10608

*This book is dedicated
to the readers of this book,
who, after their search is complete,
go on to help others.*

Contents

Preface

This reference manual is being published because of the overwhelming response received due to television shows featuring cases of mine, in which regular, everyday people were able, with a minimal amount of guidance from me, to locate loved ones by simply searching public records.

You Can Find Anybody! will show everybody, professional and amateur alike, that public records are available to all, and it will clearly demonstrate how easy it is to locate a person using legal sources of information. In an investigation, there is no reason to employ surreptitious, covert, or clandestine methods to locate your subject.

The reader of this manual will be able to access a myriad of public records with the aplomb and dexterity of an experienced investigator. A subject missing for 40 years will be found using different sources from those applied when attempting to find an individual missing for four months, and the reader will instinctively know which sources are to be utilized.

As many of you know, I work for the media and government, and my cases are routinely dissected as the result of being subpoenaed. The reason that my cases are subpoenaed is because in high-profile cases, there are lawsuits where one party accuses the other of invading their privacy and employing illegal methods to get information. The plaintiff usually says that the information that came out on television and in print has caused much embarrassment, diluted the plaintiff's earning power, and has created a hostile living environment. If the plaintiff can prove that anything but public records were used to get information, there is a real possibility that they will be awarded damages. This is a situation of liability and litigation that I can never allow a client to undergo. Neither can you allow yourself to be exposed to civil and criminal penalties. Hence, the use of public records.

Because you may not have access to information brokers, on page 3-17, I give the address of a company that investigators and governments have used for years to run Social Security Numbers, Death Master File records, and other important support searches. If you find the person you are looking for using this book and you think that your case would translate into good television, then write to me immediately. I do not want to delay your reunion, and I cannot promise you that your story will fit in to a television show's schedule at that moment, but as I'm sure you are aware, I do many programs each month on national television where I reunite families who did the finding themselves. They have appeared with me on the *Montel* show, *Maury Povich*, and many other programs.

Best of luck in your search, and please visit me on the Web at: **www.josephculligan.com.**

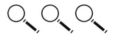

Driving Records, Registrations, and Titles

Driving Records, Registrations, and Titles has always been the first chapter in my books, and I will make it the first chapter once again, but not for long. The reason I will relegate this chapter farther back in my books in the future is that because of new anticipated laws and restrictions on their access, I will not be able to say, "Many readers of this book will be able to locate their subjects by simply contacting motor vehicle departments," which is something I have said for many years.

The history behind the new restrictive laws is quite simple. In 1991, an individual was able to locate a young actress through her California driving record. The individual then went to her house and shot and killed her when she answered her front door. California immediately put restrictions on the access by the public to driving records, registrations, and titles.

Over the next several years, there was a movement by privacy advocates to have more states restrict access to these records. In 1994, President Clinton signed into law the Driver's Privacy Act. This made it mandatory for all states to restrict their driving and motor vehicles records to the public. Since driving records, registrations, and titles are the type of records that are state records and cannot be controlled or restricted by the federal government, the law ordered that federal highway funds would be withheld to states that did not close up access.

Since all states still do not have in place any new program of restrictions, it is important that I include this chapter first, because driving records, registrations, and titles are an excellent source of information. Many readers of this book will be able to locate their subject by simply contacting motor vehicle departments.

The best hit rate will be for males, since they do not change their name as often as females do. Motor vehicle departments maintain license records for females with their previous surname(s) for years, so you will want to write to them, even though you believe that your female subject has had a name change. Many of my "impossible" cases have been solved because I simply requested the subject's driving record.

You will, no doubt, want to start with the last known state of the subject. Even if the subject has moved to another state, each motor vehicle department maintains a record going back from two years to thirty years (each state varies) indicating what state the subject's license was surrendered to. When writing to request a copy of the subject's driving record, include their date of birth. If you do not have an exact date of birth for the subject, write and ask for an alpha search.

Here is a sample letter requesting a driving record when you do not have a date of birth.

Date
John Anyone
123 Anywhere Drive
Anytown, New York 12345
Telephone: (212) 555-1234

Dear Commissioner of Motor Vehicles:

Kindly send me the driving record of Robert Hamilton. I am sorry I do not have a date of birth, but please do an alpha search for the year of 1943. Find attached a check for the appropriate fee. I am also submitting an additional check for $15.00. This fee will cover any additional costs should there be more than one Robert Hamilton.

If your search reveals that there are numerous Robert Hamiltons, please advise me, and I will decide on what course of action I wish to pursue.

Sincerely,
John Anyone

The previous letter does wonders. If the driving-record division writes to you and says there are many individuals who have your subject's name with that year of birth, you will want to write back and give the area of the state where you feel the subject may now reside or had resided in. If you receive several driving records and do not know which is your subject, don't despair. Driving records may contain some or all of the following, which will assist you in determining which of the licensees is your subject.

Address	**Social Security Number**
Height	**Date of Birth**
Weight	**Dates and Locations of Accidents**
Hair Color	**Dates and Locations of Traffic Tickets**
Eye Color	**Restrictions—i.e., Eyeglasses**

DRIVER'S LICENSES

ALABAMA

Driver's Licenses
State of Alabama
P.O. Box 1471–H
Montgomery, Alabama 36192

ALASKA

Driver's Licenses
State of Alaska
P.O. Box 20020–E
Juneau, Alaska 99802

ARIZONA

Driver's Licenses
State of Arizona
P.O. Box 2100–L
Phoenix, Arizona 85001

ARKANSAS

Driver's Licenses
State of Arkansas
P.O. Box 1271–L
Little Rock, Arkansas 72203

CALIFORNIA

Driver's Licenses
State of California
P.O. Box 944231–O
Sacramento, California 94244

COLORADO

Driver's Licenses
State of Colorado
140 West 6th Avenue
Denver, Colorado 80204

CONNECTICUT

Driver's Licenses
State of Connecticut
60 State Street
Wethersfield, Connecticut 06109

DELAWARE

Driver's Licenses
State of Delaware
P.O. Box 698–R
Dover, Delaware 19903

DISTRICT OF COLUMBIA

Driver's Licenses
District of Columbia
301 C Street, N.W.
Washington, DC 20001

FLORIDA

Driver's Licenses
State of Florida
Neil Kirkman Building
Tallahassee, Florida 32399

GEORGIA

Driver's Licenses
State of Georgia
P.O. Box 1456–E
Atlanta, Georgia 30371

HAWAII

Driver's Licenses
State of Hawaii
530 South King Street
Honolulu, Hawaii 96813

IDAHO

Driver's Licenses
State of Idaho
P.O. Box 7129–I
Boise, Idaho 83707

ILLINOIS

Driver's Licenses
State of Illinois
2701 South Dirksen Parkway
Springfield, Illinois 62723

INDIANA

Driver's Licenses
State of Indiana
State Office Building
Indianapolis, Indiana 46204

IOWA

Driver's Licenses
State of Iowa
100 Euclid Avenue
Des Moines, Iowa 50306

KANSAS

Driver's Licenses
State of Kansas
Docking Office Building
Topeka, Kansas 66626

KENTUCKY

Driver's Licenses
State of Kentucky
State Office Building
Frankfort, Kentucky 40622

LOUISIANA

Driver's Licenses
State of Louisiana
P.O. Box 64886–D
Baton Rouge, Louisiana 70896

MAINE

Driver's Licenses
State of Maine
State House, Room 29
Augusta, Maine 04333

MARYLAND

Driver's Licenses
State of Maryland
6601 Ritchie Highway, N.E. Room 211
Glen Burnie, Maryland 21062

MASSACHUSETTS

Driver's Licenses
Commonwealth of Massachusetts
100 Nashua Street
Boston, Massachusetts 02114

MICHIGAN

Driver's Licenses
State of Michigan
7064 Crowner Drive
Lansing, Michigan 48918

MINNESOTA

Driver's Licenses
State of Minnesota
Transportation Building, Room 108
St. Paul, Minnesota 55155

MISSISSIPPI

Driver's Licenses
State of Mississippi
P.O. Box 958–J
Jackson, Mississippi 39205

MISSOURI

Driver's Licenses
State of Missouri
P.O. Box 200–O
Jefferson City, Missouri 65105

MONTANA

Driver's Licenses
State of Montana
303 North Roberts
Helena, Montana 59620

NEBRASKA

Driver's Licenses
State of Nebraska
301 Centennial Mall South
Lincoln, Nebraska 68509

NEVADA

Driver's Licenses
State of Nevada
555 Wright Way
Carson City, Nevada 89711

NEW HAMPSHIRE

Driver's Licenses
State of New Hampshire
10 Hazen Drive
Concord, New Hampshire 03305

NEW JERSEY

Driver's Licenses
State of New Jersey
25 South Montgomery Street
Trenton, New Jersey 08666

NEW MEXICO

Driver's Licenses
State of New Mexico
P.O. Box 1028–E
Santa Fe, New Mexico 87504

NEW YORK

Driver's Licenses
State of New York
Empire State Plaza
Albany, New York 12228

NORTH CAROLINA

Driver's Licenses
State of North Carolina
1100 New Bern Avenue
Raleigh, North Carolina 27697

NORTH DAKOTA

Driver's Licenses
State of North Dakota
Capitol Grounds
Bismarck, North Dakota 58505

OHIO

Driver's Licenses
State of Ohio
P.O. Box 7167–Y
Columbus, Ohio 43266

OKLAHOMA

Driver's Licenses
State of Oklahoma
P.O. Box 11415–C
Oklahoma City, Oklahoma 73136

OREGON

Driver's Licenses
State of Oregon
1905 Lana Avenue, N.E.
Salem, Oregon 97314

PENNSYLVANIA

Driver's Licenses
State of Pennsylvania
P.O. Box 8695–O
Harrisburg, Pennsylvania 17105

PUERTO RICO

Driver's Licenses
Commonwealth of Puerto Rico
P.O. Box 41243–L
Santurce, Puerto Rico 00940

RHODE ISLAND

Driver's Licenses
State of Rhode Island
345 Harris Avenue
Providence, Rhode Island 02909

SOUTH CAROLINA

Driver's Licenses
State of South Carolina
P.O. Box 1498–U
Columbia, South Carolina 29216

SOUTH DAKOTA

Driver's Licenses
State of South Dakota
118 West Capitol Avenue
Pierre, South Dakota 57501

TENNESSEE

Driver's Licenses
State of Tennessee
P.O. Box 945–C
Nashville, Tennessee 37202

TEXAS

Driver's Licenses
State of Texas
P.O. Box 4087–C
Austin, Texas 78773

UTAH

Driver's Licenses
State of Utah
1095 Motor Avenue
Salt Lake City, Utah 84116

VERMONT

Driver's Licenses
State of Vermont
120 State Street
Montpelier, Vermont 05603

VIRGINIA

Driver's Licenses
State of Virginia
2300 West Broad Street
Richmond, Virginia 23269

WASHINGTON

Driver's Licenses
State of Washington
211 12th Avenue, S.E.
Olympia, Washington 98504

WEST VIRGINIA

Driver's Licenses
State of West Virginia
1800 Washington Street, East
Charleston, West Virginia 25317

WISCONSIN

Driver's Licenses
State of Wisconsin
P.O. Box 7918
Madison, Wisconsin 53707

WYOMING

Driver's Licenses
State of Wyoming
122 West 25th Street
Cheyenne, Wyoming 82002

Note: If your subject appears to be a person who will not give proper information on any licenses or other documents, then the traffic ticket will possibly be able to lead you to the subject's location. If your subject's driving record indicates traffic violations, take note of the jurisdiction or location that issued the ticket. Write to that authority, and request a photocopy of the ticket.

On the ticket will be the make, model, and license number of the vehicle the subject was driving when stopped for the citation.

Write to the motor vehicle registration department, supplying the license plate number of the vehicle. Many times the registration that you receive to the vehicle will indicate ownership of a person other than your subject. You will now have a new address to check and a new person that may be questioned as to the whereabouts of your subject.

Accident Reports

If your subject's driving record indicates an accident, then you will want to order a copy of the accident report. This report will, of course, contain much information such as address, vehicles involved in the accident, location of the accident, etc., but what I use this report for is primarily to find out about the other party in the accident. You will have the name, address, driver's license number, vehicle information, and other important details listed in the report.

If the accident report indicates that your subject was at fault and there was damage to the vehicles, and injuries, then your subject may have been sued or will be facing a court date in the near future. You will need the other party's information because you will want to search the public records for a suit filed by this party. The address of this other party is important because this person may file suit where they reside, which may not be necessarily in the same court jurisdiction where the accident occurred or where your subject lives.

Pay particular attention to the subpoena the subject was served, and the address they were served at. If any damages were awarded that exceeded the subject's insurance coverage, then there will be numerous records indicating the liens and attachments that have been filed. You may be able to glean numerous addresses for the subject by reviewing these public records.

If your subject was not at fault, then they may have filed suit. You will want to review the files of any litigation. You can be assured that any address listed for your subject will be accurate because the subject had filed this suit with the intent of collecting damages, and, of course, a correct address would have been supplied by the subject so they would be able to collect any damages.

You may order the accident report from the jurisdiction that is noted on the driving record. The following list of state police agencies is included in this chapter because the state will usually have a copy of every accident involving damage and injuries. If the jurisdiction on the accident report is unclear, then the state police will be able to either provide you a copy of the accident report or will evaluate the accident location from the information on the driving record and advise you exactly where to make your inquiry.

STATE POLICE AGENCIES

ALABAMA

Alabama Department of Public Safety
State of Alabama
P.O. Box 1511
Montgomery, Alabama 36192

ALASKA

Department of Public Safety
State of Alaska
P.O. Box N
Juneau, Alaska 99811

ARIZONA

Department of Public Safety
State of Arizona
2102 West Encanto Boulevard
Phoenix, Arizona 85005

ARKANSAS

Department of Public Safety
State of Arkansas
Three Natural Resources Drive
Little Rock, Arkansas 72215

CALIFORNIA

State Department of Justice
State of California
P.O. Box 944255
Sacramento, California 94244

COLORADO

Colorado Bureau of Investigation
State of Colorado
690 Kipling Street
Lakewood, Colorado 80215

CONNECTICUT

State Police Department
State of Connecticut
294 Colony Street
Meriden, Connecticut 06450

DELAWARE

Delaware State Police Department
State of Delaware
P.O. Box 430
Dover, Delaware 19903

DISTRICT OF COLUMBIA

Department of Public Safety
District of Columbia
P.O. Box 1606
Washington, DC 20013

FLORIDA

Department of Law Enforcement
State of Florida
P.O. Box 1489
Tallahassee, Florida 32302

GEORGIA

Department of State Police
State of Georgia
P.O. Box 370748
Decatur, Georgia 30037

HAWAII

Department of Public Safety
State of Hawaii
465 South King Street
Honolulu, Hawaii 96813

IDAHO

Department of State Police
State of Idaho
6083 Clinton Street
Boise, Idaho 83704

ILLINOIS

Department of State Police
State of Illinois
260 North Chicago Street
Joliet, Illinois 60431

INDIANA

Indiana State Police
State of Indiana
100 North Senate Avenue
Indianapolis, Indiana 46204

IOWA

Department of Public Safety
State of Iowa
Wallace State Office Building
Des Moines, Iowa 50319

KANSAS

Kansas Bureau of Public Safety
State of Kansas
1620 Southwest Tyler
Topeka, Kansas 66612

KENTUCKY

Kentucky State Police
State of Kentucky
1250 Louisville Road
Frankfort, Kentucky 40601

LOUISIANA

Department of Public Safety
State of Louisiana
P.O. Box 66614
Baton Rouge, Louisiana 70896

MAINE

Maine State Police
State of Maine
36 Hospital Street
Augusta, Maine 04330

MARYLAND

Maryland State Police
State of Maryland
1201 Reisterstown Road
Pikesville, Maryland 21208

MASSACHUSETTS

Department of Public Safety
Commonwealth of Massachusetts
One Ashburton Place
Boston, Massachusetts 02108

MICHIGAN

Department of State Police
State of Michigan
714 South Harrison Road
East Lansing, Michigan 48823

MINNESOTA

Department of Public Safety
State of Minnesota
1246 University Avenue
St. Paul, Minnesota 55104

MISSISSIPPI

Department of Public Safety
State of Mississippi
P.O. Box 958
Jackson, Mississippi 39205

MISSOURI

Department of Public Safety
State of Missouri
1510 East Elm Street
Jefferson City, Missouri 65102

MONTANA

Department of State Police
State of Montana
303 North Roberts
Helena, Montana 59620

NEBRASKA

Nebraska State Police
State of Nebraska
P.O. Box 94907
Lincoln, Nebraska 68509

NEVADA

Department of Public Safety
State of Nevada
555 Wright Way
Carson City, Nevada 89711

NEW HAMPSHIRE

New Hampshire State Police
State of New Hampshire
10 Hazen Drive
Concord, New Hampshire 03305

NEW JERSEY

New Jersey State Police
State of New Jersey
P.O. Box 7068
West Trenton, New Jersey 08628

NEW MEXICO

Department of Public Safety
State of New Mexico
P.O. Box 1628
Santa Fe, New Mexico 87504

NEW YORK

New York State Police
State of New York
Executive Park Tower
Albany, New York 12203

NORTH CAROLINA

Department of Public Safety
State of North Carolina
407 Blount Street
Raleigh, North Carolina 27602

NORTH DAKOTA

North Dakota Bureau of Investigation
State of North Dakota
P.O. Box 1054
Bismarck, North Dakota 58502

OHIO

Department of Investigations
State of Ohio
P.O. Box 365
London, Ohio 43140

OKLAHOMA

Department of Public Safety
State of Oklahoma
P.O. Box 11497
Oklahoma City, Oklahoma 73136

OREGON

Oregon State Police
State of Oregon
3772 Portland Road
Salem, Oregon 97310

PENNSYLVANIA

Pennsylvania State Police
Commonwealth of Pennsylvania
1800 Elmerton Avenue
Harrisburg, Pennsylvania 17110

RHODE ISLAND

Department of Public Safety
State of Rhode Island
72 Pine Street
Providence, Rhode Island 02903

SOUTH CAROLINA

Department of Law Enforcement
State of South Carolina
P.O. Box 21398
Columbia, South Carolina 29221

SOUTH DAKOTA

Division of Criminal Investigation
State of South Dakota
500 East Capitol Avenue
Pierre, South Dakota 57501

TENNESSEE

Department of Public Safety
State of Tennessee
1150 Foster Avenue
Nashville, Tennessee 37224

TEXAS

Texas State Police
State of Texas
P.O. Box 4143
Austin, Texas 78765

UTAH

Department of Public Safety
State of Utah
4501 South 2700 West Avenue
Salt Lake City, Utah 84119

VERMONT

Vermont State Police
State of Vermont
103 South Main Street
Waterbury, Vermont 05676

VIRGINIA

State Police of Virginia
State of Virginia
P.O. Box 27272
Richmond, Virginia 23261

WASHINGTON

Washington State Police
State of Washington
P.O. Box 2527
Olympia, Washington 98504

WEST VIRGINIA

West Virginia State Police
State of West Virginia
725 Jefferson Road
South Charleston, West Virginia 25309

WISCONSIN

Wisconsin Law Enforcement Bureau
State of Wisconsin
P.O. Box 2718
Madison, Wisconsin 53701

WYOMING

Criminal Investigation Bureau
State of Wyoming
316 West 22nd Street
Cheyenne, Wyoming 85002

After you have the subject's driving record and address, you may discover that the address is not the current one. Of course, there are many ways to receive a person's new address, but you may want to write to the appropriate motor vehicle department, and, armed with the subject's date of birth from the driving record, request a list of all motor vehicles listed in the subject's name. Many times the search will reveal that the subject is co-owner of a vehicle with a spouse, friend, or business associate.

Motor vehicle registrations are important to request in the event that the address on the subject's driving record is not current. A driver's license may be **renewed as infrequently as every eight years**. Since motor vehicle registrations are **renewed every year**, you will obtain a more current address.

Here is a sample of a letter:

Date
John Anyone
123 Anywhere Drive
Anytown, New York 12345
Telephone Number: (212) 555-1234

Dear Commissioner of Motor Vehicles:

Kindly send me the motor vehicle information for vehicles owned by: Robert Hamilton, date of birth: 03/04/1943. Please find attached a check to cover the costs of the requested registration information for up to five vehicles. If there are more than five vehicles, please contact me, and I will be glad to remit the amount requested.

Sincerely,
John Anyone

Fees were not included in this chapter because most of the states will adjust prices periodically. Write to the states for their current price structure. Please note that all government agencies, including driving and motor vehicle records departments, are constantly changing policies insofar as what access to records and files will be accorded the public.

For instance, a marriage record is public record in Dade County, Florida, whereas a marriage record is *not* public in any of the five boroughs of New York City. Also, for example, California restricts access to driving records. However, Florida will not only send you the driving record you requested, but will give the individual's Social Security Number as part of the record.

Now that you have the registration information, you may want to do additional research. Every state keeps a record of all transactions regarding the sale of a motor vehicle because of the need to ensure continuity of odometer readings and to prove that the records followed a specific sequence in case the validity of a vehicle identification number is questioned in the event of tampering.

You may want to request a "body file" or "vehicle history" of a particular motor vehicle of the subject. You will receive a packet that may occasionally include up to 30 pages.

The photocopies will include paperwork with the subject's signature. This may help you to compare what you have on record as positive proof that you are on the right track, pursuing leads for the location of the correct subject.

You will also see that the history of that particular motor vehicle will indicate what previous addresses were contained on the yearly registrations. You may need these addresses so that you can contact the current occupants and inquire as to where your subject may have moved.

The information will indicate the name and address of the previous owner. This individual may have known the subject and may be able to provide you with more information. Even if the previous owner did not know the subject, ask (through casual conversation), if, when the sale of the vehicle was being consummated, there was any mention of employment or other personal information. If you recall the last time you bought or sold a vehicle, look how much information you and the other person exchanged just chatting.

If you write and request the file on a vehicle that the subject does not own anymore, this may provide new information relating to the location of the subject. The packet of information you will receive about the sold vehicle will indicate the new owner's address. Your subject may have sold the vehicle to this person because the subject needed money from the sale so that they could buy a new vehicle, etc. The point is that the subject, like all of us, had to explain to the buyer why the vehicle was being sold. There will be many possibilities for new information regarding the location of your subject from this simple method of inquiry.

Here is a sample letter to order a "body file" or "vehicle history."

Date
John Anyone
123 Anywhere Drive
Anytown, New York 12345
Telephone Number: (212) 558-1234

Dear Tag Department:

   Kindly send the complete vehicle history of the following vehicle:
   Title number: 74651201
   Vehicle Identification Number: 23988UTG670KR453H6

   I have attached a check for $8.00. If this is not sufficient, please contact me and I will remit the requested amount.

Sincerely,
John Anyone

REGISTRATION AND TITLES

ALABAMA

http://www.ador.state.al.us/motorvehicle/MVD_MAIN.html
Department of Motor Vehicles
State of Alabama
P.O. Box 104–I
Montgomery, Alabama 36101

ALASKA

http://www.state.ak.us/local/akpages/ADMIN/dmv/dmvhome.htm
Department of Motor Vehicles
State of Alaska
5700 Todor Road
Anchorage, Alaska 99507

ARIZONA

http://www.dot.state.az.us/MVD/mvd.htm
Department of Motor Vehicles
State of Arizona
1801 West Jefferson Street
Phoenix, Arizona 85001

ARKANSAS

http://www.ark.org/revenue/motorv.mvfaq.html
Department of Motor Vehicles
State of Arkansas
P.O. 1272–I
Little Rock, Arkansas 72203

CALIFORNIA

http://www.dmv.ca.gov
Department of Motor Vehicles
State of California
P.O. Box 932328–S
Sacramento, California 94232

COLORADO

http://www.state.co.us/gov_dir/rev-
enue_dir/MV_dir/mv.html
Department of Motor Vehicles
State of Colorado
140 West 6th Street
Denver, Colorado 80204

CONNECTICUT

http://dmvct.org
Department of Motor Vehicles
State of Connecticut
60 State Street
Wethersfield, Connecticut 06109

DELAWARE

http://www.state.de.us/pubsafe/index.htm
Department of Motor Vehicles
State of Delaware
State Office Building
Dover, Delaware 19903

DISTRICT OF COLUMBIA

http://www.washingtondc.gov/
Department of Motor Vehicles
District of Columbia
301 C Street
Washington, DC 20001

FLORIDA

http://www.hsmv.state.fl.us
Department of Motor Vehicles
State of Florida
2900 Apalachee Parkkway
Tallahassee, Florida 32399

GEORGIA

http://www.state.ga.us/
Department of Motor Vehicles
State of Georgia
104 Trinity Washington Building
Atlanta, Georgia 30334

HAWAII

http://www.hawaii.gov/index/transporta-
tion.htm
Department of Motor Vehicles
State of Hawaii
896 Punchbowl Street
Honolulu, Hawaii 96813

IDAHO

http://www.state.id.us/itd/overorg.htm#mvb
Department of Motor Vehicles
State of Idaho
P.O. Box 34–G
Boise, Idaho 83731

ILLINOIS

http://www.sos.state.il.us:80/depts/driv-
ers/mot_info.html
Department of Motor Vehicles
State of Illinois
Centennial Government Building
Springfield, Illinois 62756

INDIANA

http://www.state.in.us/bmv
Department of Motor Vehicles
State of Indiana
State Office Building, Room 416
Indianapolis, Indiana 46204

IOWA

http://www.state.ia.us/government/dot/-
index.html
Department of Motor Vehicles
State of Iowa
Park Fair Mall, Box 9204
Des Moines, Iowa 50306

KANSAS

http://www.ink.org/public/kdor/dmv/
Department of Motor Vehicles
State of Kansas
P.O. Box 12021-L
Topeka, Kansas 66616

KENTUCKY

http://www.kytc.state.ky.us
Department of Motor Vehicles
State of Kentucky
State Building, Room 204
Frankfort, Kentucky 40622

LOUISIANA

http://www.dps.state.la.us/omv/home.html
Department of Motor Vehicles
State of Louisiana
P.O. Box 64886-A
Baton Rouge, Louisiana 70896

MAINE

http://www.state.me.us/sos/bmv/bmv.htm
Department of Motor Vehicles
State of Maine
State Building
Augusta, Maine 04333

MARYLAND

http://mva.state.md.us
Department of Motor Vehicles
State of Maryland
6601 Ritchie Highway, N.E.
Glen Burnie, Maryland 21062

MASSACHUSETTS

http://www.state.ma.us/rmv/index.htm
Department of Motor Vehicles
Commonwealth of Massachusetts
100 Nashua Street, Room 100
Boston, Massachusetts 02114

MICHIGAN

http://www.sos.state.mi.us/dv/index.html
Department of Motor Vehicles
State of Michigan
Mutual Government Building
Lansing, Michigan 48918

MINNESOTA

http://www.dps.state.mn.us/dvs/index.html
Department of Motor Vehicles
State of Minnesota
Transportation Building, Room 159
St. Paul, Minnesota 55155

MISSISSIPPI

http://www.mmvc.state.ms.us
Department of Motor Vehicles
State of Mississippi
P.O. Box 1140-D
Jackson, Mississippi 39205

MISSOURI

http://www.dor.state.mo.us
Department of Motor Vehicles
State of Missouri
P.O. Box 100-T
Jefferson City, Missouri 65105

MONTANA

http://www.doj.state.mt.us/mvd/index.htm
Department of Motor Vehicles
State of Montana
925 Main Street
Deer Lodge, Montana 59722

NEBRASKA

http://www.nol.org/home/DMV/
Department of Motor Vehicles
State of Nebraska
P.O. Box 94789-O
Lincoln, Nebraska 68509

NEVADA

http://www.state.nv.us/dmv_ps
Department of Motor Vehicles
State of Nevada
State Building
Carson City, Nevada 89111

NEW HAMPSHIRE

http://www.state.nh.us/dot/
Department of Motor Vehicles
State of New Hampshire
James H. Hayes Building
Concord, New Hampshire 03305

NEW JERSEY

http://www.state.nj.us/mvs
Department of Motor Vehicles
State of New Jersey
135 East State Street
Trenton, New Jersey 08666

NEW MEXICO

http://www.state.nm.us/tax/mvd/mvd_home.
htm
Department of Motor Vehicles
State of New Mexico
P.O. Box 1028–B
Santa Fe, New Mexico 87504

NEW YORK

http://www.nydmv.state.ny.us
Department of Motor Vehicles
State of New York
State Office Building North
Albany, New York 12228

NORTH CAROLINA

http://www.dmv.dot.state.nc.us
Department of Motor Vehicles
State of North Carolina
1100 New Bern Avenue, Room 124
Raleigh, North Carolina 27697

NORTH DAKOTA

http://www.state.nd.us/dot
Department of Motor Vehicles
State of North Dakota
806 East Boulevard
Bismarck, North Dakota 58505

OHIO

http://www.dot.state.oh.us/
Department of Motor Vehicles
State of Ohio
P.O. Box 16520
Columbus, Ohio 43266

OKLAHOMA

http://www.oktax.state.ok.us/oktax/-
motorveh.html
Department of Motor Vehicles
State of Oklahoma
409 Northeast 28 Street
Oklahoma City, Oklahoma 73105

OREGON

http://www.odot.state.or.us/dmv/index.htm
Department of Motor Vehicles
State of Oregon
1905 Lana Avenue, NE
Salem, Oregon 97314

PENNSYLVANIA

http://www.dmv.state.pa.us/home/index1.asp
Department of Motor Vehicles
Commonwealth of Pennsylvania
P.O. Box 8691-W
Harrisburg, Pennsylvania 17105

PUERTO RICO

http://www.dtop.gov.pr/english/DISCO/Di
schome.htm
Department of Motor Vehicles
Commonwealth of Puerto Rico
P.O. Box 41269-I
Santurce, Puerto Rico 00940

RHODE ISLAND

http://www.dmv.state.ri.us
Department of Motor Vehicles
State of Rhode Island
State Office Building
Providence, Rhode Island 02903

SOUTH CAROLINA

http://www.state.sc.us/dps/dmv
Department of Motor Vehicles
State of South Carolina
P.O. Box 1498–T
Columbia, South Carolina 29216

SOUTH DAKOTA

http://www.state.sd.us/state/executive/revenue/motorvcl.htm
Department of Motor Vehicles
State of South Dakota
118 West Capitol Avenue
Pierre, South Dakota 57501

TENNESSEE

http://www.state.tn.us/safety
Department of Motor Vehicles
State of Tennessee
500 Deaderick Street
Nashville, Tennessee 37242

TEXAS

http://www.dot.state.tx.us/insdtdot/orgchart/vtr/vtr.htm
Department of Motor Vehicles
State of Texas
5805 North Lamar Boulevard
Austin, Texas 78773

UTAH

http://www.dmv-utah.com
Department of Motor Vehicles
State of Utah
1095 Motor Avenue
Salt Lake City, Utah 84116

VERMONT

http://www.aot.state.vt.us/dmv/dmvhp.htm
Department of Motor Vehicles
State of Vermont
120 State Street
Montpelier, Vermont 05603

VIRGINIA

http://www.dmv.state.va.us
Department of Motor Vehicles
State of Virginia
P.O. Box 27412–H
Richmond, Virginia 23269

WASHINGTON

http://www.wa.gov/dol/main.htm
Department of Motor Vehicles
State of Washington
P.O. Box 9909–H
Olympia, Washington 98504

WEST VIRGINIA

http://www.state.wv.us/dmv
Department of Motor Vehicles
State of West Virginia
State Office Building
Charleston, West Virginia 25305

WISCONSIN

http://www.dot.state.wi.us/dmv/dmv.html
Department of Motor Vehicles
State of Wisconsin
4802 Sheboygan Avenue
Madison, Wisconsin 53707

WYOMING

http://wydotweb.state.wy.us/
Department of Motor Vehicles
State of Wyoming
122 West 25th Street
Cheyenne, Wyoming 82002

DRIVING RECORDS, REGISTRATIONS, AND TITLES— CANADA

ALBERTA
Department of Motor Vehicles
10365 97th Street
Edmonton, Alberta T5J 3W7

BRITISH COLUMBIA
Department of Motor Vehicles
2631 Douglas Street
Victoria, British Columbia V8T 5A3

MANITOBA
Department of Motor Vehicles
1075 Portage Avenue
Winnipeg, Manitoba R3G 0S1

NEW BRUNSWICK
Department of Motor Vehicles
P.O. Box 6000–A
Fredericton, New Brunswick E3B 5H1

NEWFOUNDLAND
Department of Motor Vehicles
P.O. Box 8710–Y
Saint John's, Newfoundland A1B 4J5

NORTHWEST TERRITORIES
Department of Motor Vehicles
P.O. Box 1320–H
Yellowknife, Northwest Territories,
X1A 2L9

NOVA SCOTIA
Department of Motor Vehicles
P.O. Box 54–O
Halifax, Nova Scotia B3J 2L4

ONTARIO
Department of Motor Vehicles
2680 Keele Street
Downsview, Ontario M3M 3E6

PRINCE EDWARD ISLAND
Department of Motor Vehicles
P.O. Box 2000-U
Charlottetown, Prince Edward Island,
C1A 7N8

QUEBEC
Department of Motor Vehicles
1037 de la Chevrotiere Street
Quebec, Quebec G1R 4Y7

SASKATCHEWAN
Department of Motor Vehicles
2260 11th Avenue
Regina, Saskatchewan S4P 2N7

YUKON
Department of Motor Vehicles
P.O. Box 2703–S
Whitehorse, Yukon Y1A 2C6

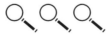

Births, Deaths, Marriages, and Divorces

Birth Records

irth Records will usually contain the following information:

Complete name
Subject's exact date of birth
Place of birth
Name of the father and mother
Age of the father and mother
Occupation of the father and mother
Mother's maiden name
Address of the father and mother
Place of birth of the father and mother

Complete Name: You will need an exact name when checking the motor vehicle records. A middle name is of importance because many individuals use a middle name prominently later on. For example: G. Gordon Liddy, J. Edgar Hoover, F. Scott Fitzgerald, H. Norman Schwartzkopf.

Subject's exact date of birth: If you did not have the exact date of birth of your subject, you would have ordered a search for a particular year or a span of several years. Now that you have the birth record, you now have the exact date of birth.

Place of birth: There is much research that can be done when you are aware of the place of birth of your subject. You may want to search for other relatives at the city of birth. You will see elsewhere in this book (page 3-17) a firm mentioned that does specialized computer work called *Research Is*. They will run on a city, state, or nationwide basis any name for a listing for a telephone number, so if the birth certificate of your subject lists the name Robert Rowland of Hialeah, Florida, as the father, you may run the name Robert Rowland nationwide or have *Research Is* run all the Robert Rowland names in the southern part of Florida. You may also run just the last name Rowland with no first name for southern Florida or Hialeah. You will probably be able to contact a sibling, cousin, uncle, aunt, or a grandparent who may be able to give you the location of your subject. Of course, the leads that can be provided by relatives of the subject speak for itself, and you can be assured that the information is accurate because of the source.

Name of father and mother: From the birth record, you now have the complete name of the father and mother. If you feel that the subject's parents may be alive, then you can conduct a search of the motor vehicle records for their location. They may be able to provide information.

Age of the father and mother: Birth records will usually contain the age but not the exact date of birth of the parents. The age of the parents at the time of birth of the subject will give you an approximate year of birth.

Occupation of the father and mother: The occupations, professions, or trades of both parents are listed on the birth certificate. If you have a problem with finding the parents of the subject, you may want to check trade associations and unions if the parents had occupations that required participation or membership in an organization. The occupation listing may list physician, attorney, barber, taxi driver, certified public accountant, or any of a myriad of professions that necessitate licensing, which generates records that are public information. You will want to inquire if the parent is still licensed, or order a record from the archives if many years have passed. Again, contacting a parent of the subject is another avenue you will want to evaluate.

Mother's maiden name: The mother's name is of importance because this will be one of the only records you will be able to retrieve to access the mother's maiden name. You may want to conduct a search for the family of the mother and question them on the whereabouts of your subject, who, of course, is their relative.

Address of father and mother: The address of the parents at the time of birth may be different from the place of birth of your subject. You may want to check property records. The family may still own the residence, or, as has happened before, the subject may own property through an inheritance. If you discover that the property the address matches was a rental by the parents, you may want to inquire through the real estate records who owned the property then and who owns the property now. An inquiry to the owner may provide information as to the whereabouts of the parents.

Place of birth of the father and mother: Because of the need to contact the parents in certain cases, the place of birth of the parents is of value. Remember that the parents may be divorced, and together with the fact that many years may have passed, a place of birth of either parent will yield a starting point for a search for each parent.

In difficult cases where the subject simply can't be located, I have found that contact with the family will provide information that could not have been developed independently. To locate a missing person requires a coalition of resources. If every avenue fails in the search for your subject, the contact with the family is a key that many do not utilize because their location at the present time seems hopeless to ascertain. But as you see from the birth record, you have enough information regarding the parents to conduct a search.

Death Records

Death records provide the following:

> **A person's complete name**
> **Date of death**
> **Date of birth**
> **Social Security Number of the deceased**
> **Place of birth of the deceased**
> **Occupation of the deceased**
> **Place of death**
> **Cause of death**

Name of the father and mother of the deceased
Mother's maiden name
Name and address of cemetery or crematory
Name of physician that certified cause of death

Death records are of value because you may want to order a search to be conducted on the parent or a relative of the subject you are trying to find. From the death record, you will be able to have enough information to possibly contact persons who know your subject.

Step one was to order a sweep done on several years if you do not know when a parent or sibling died. Now that you have the death record, you will see that there are several avenues to explore. You may want to contact the funeral home listed on the death record. The funeral home maintains records in hard copy form. On record will be the person responsible for making and paying for the arrangement of internment. Many times, as you can imagine, this person may be your subject, or at the very least, a relative who may know where your subject is.

Cause of death is important because one of the most successful methods of locating a subject is through autopsy records. Check to see if a parent, sibling, or relative has died. If the cause of death is homicide, automobile accident, industrial accident, etc., an autopsy is performed. In many locales, the autopsy is public record. The routine entries in the files will provide very specific information. The medical examiner makes notes regarding who was contacted to make arrangements for disposition of the body. The full names, telephone numbers, and addresses of relatives are entered on the record.

If you do not have an autopsy to review, you may want to contact the probate court. If the parent of the subject died without a will (intestate), there will be a wealth of information in the probate court files. Information in the file will contain the names, addresses, and amounts of monies of each of the persons who are recognized by the court as heirs. If your subject's whereabouts are unknown at the time the estate is distributed, there will be a note in the file under distribution of assets that reads: "Registry of the County Probate Court will hold for John Doe (subject's name), son of decedent, all monies in escrow until whereabouts of this heir has been determined." When you see this written, search through the entire file, because professional heir finders have most likely located the subject, and the release forms and other information are in the file.

Marriage Records

Marriage records will provide the following information about the bride and groom:

Name
Address
Date of birth
Place of birth
Previous marriage status (married or never married)
Last marriage status (married or never married)
Last marriage ended by: (death, divorce or annulment)
Number of previous marriages
If divorced, where
Name of person performing the ceremony
Signatures of bride and groom
Names of the witnesses

There are a myriad of uses for the information gleaned from the marriage record. If you do not know if your male or female subject is married, order a search conducted for a span of several years. If you do locate a marriage record, then review the certificate for the above noted information. If there is a divorce indicated, you may want to order a copy of the divorce file. The witnesses and person who performed the ceremony may be contacted. They may know obscure details about the bride and groom, and may even know the whereabouts of your subject.

Marriage records are one of the best ways to find the changes in a female name. Start with an age at which you believe the first marriage occurred. You will have the first marriage searched by the maiden name. After you have that record, you may want to now search the marriage records with the new name. Then, of course, this can be done until you are satisfied that you have the current name.

Divorce Records

A review of a complete divorce file will yield information that is unattainable anywhere else. The file will contain the names and ages of the children of the subject. If time has passed and the children are of age, they may be of assistance in locating the subject. You may, of course, use all the regular means of locating one or all of the children.

The divorce file will contain a list of vehicles owned by the couple and will include the vehicle identification number (VIN) in many instances. See which vehicle your subject took possession of. Even if this case is years old, the VIN will never change on a vehicle, so you may want to order a body history on the vehicle. If your subject does not own the vehicle anymore, you will be able to see all the documentation that will include the name of the person who purchased it. You will then contact that individual, and they may be able to provide information about your subject.

Many times the divorce file will specify what boats or vessels the couple owned. You will want to follow the course outlined in the above paragraph.

The divorce file will contain a listing of property owned. You will learn what real estate your subject retained. If your subject keeps even a small undeveloped piece of land, this will be of help. The mailing address for the tax bill will be public record and may lead you to your subject.

Vital Records
(Birth, Death, Marriage, and Divorce)

It is important for me to include the Website addresses of the following Departments of Vital Records. As we all know, the prices, costs, and fees of all public records change constantly. I ask that you visit the state's Website for several reasons, the first being that you will have the most updated prices. The second reason is that many of these state Websites now will let you order birth, death, marriage, divorce, and other records online by using a credit card. When you visit the state's Website, take a look around the Website to see if there is an e-mail address to contact the Vital Records Department directly. The reason for this is that many times you will need the records you seek immediately, and you will be able to ask, by e-mail, whether the department provides overnight mail service.

PLACE OF EVENT: ALABAMA

EVENT: BIRTH OR DEATH

COST OF COPY: $12.00

ADDRESS: Alabama Vital Records, 201 Monroe Street, Suite 1150, Montgomery, Alabama 36104

WWW: http://www.alapubhealth.org/vital/vitalrcd.htm

REMARKS: The state office has had records since January 1908. Prior to 1908, there are no birth certificates in Alabama; however, most counties did register births in ledgers. The best source is the Department of Archives and History, 624 Washington Ave., Montgomery, Alabama 36130 • (334) 242-4363.

For birth records less than 125 years old and death records less than 25 years old, you have to be immediate family or have written permission from the next of kin in order to obtain these records. Marriage and divorce records have no restrictions and may be obtained by any individual upon payment of proper fee.

Additional copies ordered at the same time are $4.00 each. Fees are not refundable. Money order or certified check should be made payable to: **Vital Records** and mailed to Alabama Vital Records, P.O. Box 5625, Montgomery, Alabama 36103-5625. Personal checks are not accepted.

FAST SERVICE: Call (334) 206-5418 and pay by major credit card.

To verify current fees, the telephone number is: (334) 206-5418.

EVENT: MARRIAGE

COST OF COPY: $12.00

ADDRESS/WWW: Same as Birth or Death

REMARKS: State office has had records since August 1936.

EVENT: DIVORCE

COST OF COPY: $12.00

ADDRESS/WWW: Same as Birth or Death

REMARKS: State office has had records since January 1950.

PLACE OF EVENT: ALASKA

EVENT: BIRTH OR DEATH

COST OF COPY: $10.00

ADDRESS: Alaska Bureau of Vital Statistics, 350 Main St., Rm. 114, Juneau, Alaska 99811-0675.

WWW: http://health.hss.state.ak.us/

REMARKS: State office has had records since January 1913.

Births records are not available until 100 years after the event, except to the person involved or parents. Death records are sealed for 50 years, as are marriage and divorce records.

Money order should be made payable to: **Bureau of Vital Statistics** and mailed to Alaska Department of Health and Social Services, P.O. Box 110675, Juneau, Alaska 99811-0675. Personal checks are not accepted.

FAST SERVICE: Fax: (907) 465-3618. Payment by credit card is an additional $10.00. Express mail is an additional $11.75.

To verify current fees, the telephone number is: (907) 465-3392 (direct line).

EVENT: MARRIAGE

COST OF COPY: $10.00

ADDRESS/WWW: Same as Birth or Death

REMARKS: State office has had records since 1913.

EVENT: DIVORCE

COST OF COPY: $10.00

ADDRESS/WWW: Same as Birth or Death

REMARKS: State office has had records since 1950. If the records are not available at the state office, they should be available from Clerk of the Superior Court in judicial court where divorce was granted.

PLACE OF EVENT: AMERICAN SAMOA

EVENT: BIRTH OR DEATH

COST OF COPY: $5.00

ADDRESS: Registrar of Vital Statistics, Vital Statistics Section, Government of American Samoa, Pago Pago, American Samoa 96799.

WWW: http://www.government.as/

REMARKS: Registrar has had records since 1900.

Personal identification required before record will be sent.

Money order should be made payable to: **ASG Treasurer.** Personal checks are not accepted.

To verify current fees, the telephone number is: (684) 633-1406.

EVENT: MARRIAGE

COST OF COPY: $5.00

ADDRESS/WWW: Same as Birth or Death

EVENT: DIVORCE

COST OF COPY: $1.00

ADDRESS/WWW: Write to: High Court of American Samoa, Tutuila, American Samoa 96799

PLACE OF EVENT: ARIZONA

EVENT: BIRTH OR DEATH

COST OF COPY: Birth: $9.00 (July 1903 to 1950)
Birth: $6.00 (1950 to present)
Death: $6.00 (July 1903 to present)

ADDRESS: Vital Statistics Section, Arizona Department of Health Services, 2727 West Glendale, Phoenix, Arizona 85051

WWW: http://www.hs.state.az.us/plan/ohpes.htm

ARIZONA, cont'd.

REMARKS: State office has had records since July 1903 and abstracts of records filed in counties before then.

Only the registrant or an immediate family member may receive copies of birth records. Only immediate family or attorney or funeral director for the immediate family may receive copies of death certificate. Applicants must submit a copy of picture ID (i.e., driver's license), have their request notarized, or provide a family tree sketch to illustrate the family connection and possibly provide proof of family connection, such as birth certificate.

The following information must accompany request: Name of person on certificate, date of event, mother's full maiden name, father's full name, your relationship to the person on the certificate and the reason you are requesting a copy. The request must be signed. You must also print your return address and a daytime phone number where you can be reached.

Check or money order should be made payable to: **Office of Vital Records** and mailed to Office of Vital Records, P.O. Box 3887, Phoenix, Arizona 85030. Personal checks are accepted but will delay your request by 30 days. Money orders and certified checks received by mail will be processed in two to four weeks.

FAST SERVICE: Order by fax using a major credit card. Fax: (602) 249-3040. A $5.00 processing fee is added. If you want the certificate sent via Federal Express, there is an additional $12.50 charge.

To verify the current fees, the telephone number is: (602) 255-3260.

EVENT: MARRIAGE

COST OF COPY: Varies

ADDRESS/WWW: Same as Birth or Death

REMARKS: Records available from Clerk of Superior Court in county where license was issued.

EVENT: DIVORCE

COST OF COPY: Varies

ADDRESS/WWW: Same as Birth or Death

REMARKS: Records available from Clerk of Superior Court in county where divorce was granted.

PLACE OF EVENT: ARKANSAS

EVENT: BIRTH OR DEATH

COST OF COPY: Birth: $5.00
Death: $4.00

ADDRESS: Division of Vital Records, Arkansas Department of Health, 4815 West Markham St., Slot 44, Little Rock, Arkansas 72205

WWW: http://health.state.ar.us/

REMARKS: State office has had records since February 1914 and some original Little Rock and Fort Smith records from 1881.

There are restrictions on who can have copies. Family members must complete and sign an application.

Extra copies of death record are $1.00 each when requested at same time.

Personal check or money order should be made payable to: **Arkansas Department of Health.**

FAST SERVICE: To expedite service, you may call (501) 661-2726. There is a $5.00 handling fee for credit cards.

To verify current fees, the telephone number is: (800) 637-9314 or (501) 661-2726.

EVENT: MARRIAGE

COST OF COPY: $5.00

ADDRESS/WWW: Same as Birth or Death

REMARKS: Marriage coupons since 1917. Full certified copy may be obtained from Circuit or Chancery Clerk in county where license was issued.

EVENT: DIVORCE

COST OF COPY: $5.00

ADDRESS/WWW: Same as Birth or Death

REMARKS: Coupons since 1923. Full certified copy may be obtained from Circuit or Chancery Clerk in county where divorce was granted.

PLACE OF EVENT: CALIFORNIA

EVENT: BIRTH OR DEATH

COST OF COPY: Birth $12.00
Heirloom Birth Certificate (decorative):$30.00
Death $8.00

ADDRESS: State Department of Health Services, Office of Vital Records, 304 'S' Street, P.O. Box 730241, Sacramento, California 94244-0241

WWW: http://www.dhs.cahwnet.gov/hisp/chs/OVR/Ordercert.htm

REMARKS: State office has had records since July 1905. For earlier records, write to County Recorder in county where event occurred.

Birth record request: Include full name, father's full name, mother's full maiden name, date of birth, and city or county of birth.

Death record request: Include full name of decedent, date of death, city or county of death, date of birth (if known), and Social Security Number (if known).

Processing time for copies of vital records is 3–4 weeks if request with all information is submitted on state form; 5–7 weeks if request with all information is submitted in a letter; and 6–8 months for requests with incomplete information, multiple records, or multiple years to search.

Personal check or money order should be made payable to: **Office of Vital Records** and mailed to: P.O. Box 730241, Sacramento, California 94244-0241. The fee covers a 10-year period search for the record requested.

FAST SERVICE: Fax: (800) 858-5553. Processing time is approximately 3 weeks for requests by fax, and there is an additional fee of $7.00. Please include the following information when faxing: Credit card number and expiration date, your daytime telephone number, return address where you would like the certificate mailed.

To verify current fees, the telephone number is: (916) 445-2684 (recorded message).

EVENT: MARRIAGE OR DIVORCE

COST OF COPY: $12.00

ADDRESS/WWW: Same as Birth or Death

REMARKS: State office has had records since July 1905.

PLACE OF EVENT: CANAL ZONE

EVENT: BIRTH OR DEATH

COST OF COPY: $4.00

ADDRESS: Panama Canal Commission, Vital Statistics Clerk, Unit 2300, APO AA, CZ 34011-2300

WWW: http://www.zonian.com/

REMARKS: Records available from May 1904 to September 1979.

Make international money orders (a regular money order will be returned) payable to **Treasury, Panama Canal Commission.**

EVENT: MARRIAGE

COST OF COPY: $4.00

ADDRESS/WWW: Same as Birth or Death

REMARKS: Records available from May 1904 to September 1979.

EVENT: DIVORCE

COST OF COPY: $1.00

ADDRESS/WWW: Same as Birth or Death

REMARKS: Certified copies of divorce decree not available. Write for information.

PLACE OF EVENT: COLORADO

EVENT: BIRTH OR DEATH

COST OF COPY: $15.00

ADDRESS: Vital Records Section, Colorado Department of Health, 4300 Cherry Creek Drive South, Denver, Colorado 80246-1530

WWW: http://www.cdphe.state.co.us/hs/certs.asp

REMARKS: State office has had death records since 1900 and birth records since 1910. State office also has birth records for some counties for years before 1910.

The requested certificate must be your own or that of an immediate family member.

COLORADO, cont'd.

Include the reason for your request and your relationship to the person on the certificate. Include an official application form for faster service. Get this form off the Website, or call the number below.

Additional copies of the same record are $6.00 when ordered at the same time.

Check or money order should be made payable to: **Vital Records Section**, and mailed to the above address. Personal checks are accepted.

FAST SERVICE: Order online at above Website. Certificate(s) will be mailed on next work day. Fax your request to: (800) 423-1108. Credit card telephone line is: (303) 692-2224. If you fax your order or telephone your request, you must use your Visa, MasterCard, Discover, or American Express card. There will be an additional charge of $5.00 for the fax or telephone service. Express mail is an additional $11.75, and FedEx is an additional $10.75.

To verify current fees, the telephone number is: (303) 692-2234. To get a recorded message, call: (303) 692-2200.

EVENT: MARRIAGE OR DIVORCE

COST OF COPY: $15.00

ADDRESS/WWW: Certified copies are available from Clerk of the County where marriage license was issued or divorce was granted.

REMARKS: Statewide index of records for 1900–1939 and 1975–present.

PLACE OF EVENT: CONNECTICUT

EVENT: BIRTH, DEATH, OR MARRIAGE

COST OF COPY: $5.00

ADDRESS: Health Department of Vital Records, 410 Capitol Ave., 1st Floor, Hartford, Connecticut 06134

WWW: http://www.state.ct.us/dph/OPPE/vr-birth.html

REMARKS: Please note: Connecticut state records were being microfilmed at the time of printing this reference book. All requests for birth, death, and marriage records are referred to the town or city where event occurred. State office has had records since July 1897.

Must have original signature on your request.

CONNECTICUT, cont'd.

Check or money order should be made payable to: **town or city of birth, death, or marriage,** and mailed to the town clerk. For addresses and verification of fees, please call the Department of Public Health Vital Records customer service representative at: (860) 509-7897. Personal checks are accepted.

EVENT: DIVORCE

REMARKS: Index of records since 1947. Applicant must contact Clerk of Superior Court where divorce was granted. State office does not have divorce decrees and cannot issue certified copies.

PLACE OF EVENT: DELAWARE

EVENT: BIRTH OR DEATH

COST OF COPY: $6.00

ADDRESS: Office of Vital Statistics, Division of Public Health, P.O. Box 637, Dover, Delaware 19903

WWW: http://www.state.de.us/

REMARKS: State office has had death records since 1956 and birth records since 1929. Inquiries will be forwarded to the appropriate office.

Additional copies of the same record requested at the same time are $3.00 each. Check or money order should be made payable to: **Office of Vital Statistics.** Personal checks are accepted.

To verify current fees, the telephone number is: (302) 739-4721.

EVENT: MARRIAGE

COST OF COPY: $6.00

ADDRESS/WWW: Same as Birth or Death

REMARKS: Records since 1930

EVENT: DIVORCE

COST OF COPY: Fee varies

ADDRESS/WWW: Same as Birth or Death

DELAWARE, cont'd.

REMARKS: Records since 1935. Inquiries will be forwarded to appropriate office. Fee for search and verification of essential facts of divorce is $5.00 for each 5-year period searched. Certified copies are not available from state office, but should be available from the county where divorce was granted.

PLACE OF EVENT: DISTRICT OF COLUMBIA

EVENT: BIRTH OR DEATH

COST OF COPY: Birth $18.00—long form
Birth $12.00—short form
Death $12.00

ADDRESS: Vital Records Department, 825 North Capitol St. NE, Washington, DC 20002

WWW: http://www.washingtondc.gov/

REMARKS: Office has had birth records since 1874 and death records since 1855 (except for the Civil War period.).

Cashiers check or money order should be made payable to: **DC Treasurer.**

To verify current fees, the telephone number is: (202) 442-9009.

EVENT: MARRIAGE

COST OF COPY: $10.00

REMARKS: Office has had marriage records since 1980. Prior to 1980, contact Superior Court of the District of Columbia, Marriage Bureau and Special Services, 500 Indiana Ave., NW, Washington, DC 20001. (202) 879-4804.

EVENT: DIVORCE

COST OF COPY: $2.00

REMARKS: For records after September 16, 1956, contact District of Columbia Superior Court Divorce Decrees, Room 4335, 500 Indiana Ave., NW, Washington, DC 20001-2141. (202) 879-1418.

For records prior to September 16, 1956: The United States District Court, Files and Copies Branch, Room 1825-A, 333 Constitution Ave. NW, Washington, DC 20001-2802. (202) 273-0555.

PLACE OF EVENT: FLORIDA

EVENT: BIRTH OR DEATH

COST OF COPY: Birth $9.00
Death $5.00

ADDRESS: Office of Vital Statistics, Department of Health, 1217 Pearl Street, Jacksonville, Florida 32231.

WWW: http://www.doh.state.fl.us/

REMARKS: State office has some birth records dating back to April 1865, and some death records dating back to August 1877. The majority of death records date from January 1917. If the exact date is unknown, the fee is $9.00 (births) or $5.00 (deaths) for the first year searched, and $2.00 for each additional year up to a maximum of $50.00. Fee includes one certification of record if found, or certified statement stating record not on file. Additional copies are $3.00 each when requested at the same time. You can reach the office of death records at: (904) 359-6934.

Check or money order should be made payable to: **Office of Vital Statistics.** Personal checks are accepted. To verify current fees, the telephone number is: (904) 359-6900.

EVENT: MARRIAGE OR DIVORCE

COST OF COPY: $5.00

ADDRESS/WWW: Same as Birth or Death

REMARKS: Records since June 6, 1927.

PLACE OF EVENT: GEORGIA

EVENT: BIRTH OR DEATH

COST OF COPY: $10.00

ADDRESS: Vital Records Service, State Department of Human Resources, Room 217–H, 47 Trinity Avenue, SW, Atlanta, Georgia 30334-5600

WWW: http://www.state.ga.us/

REMARKS: State office has had birth and death records since 1919. Older records may be available in some counties. For county addresses, call: (404) 656-4750. For earlier records, contact the Georgia Division of Archives and History, 330 Capitol Avenue SW, Atlanta, Georgia 30334.

GEORGIA, cont'd.

Georgia law and Department Regulation limits access of these documents to the person named and parents shown on the birth records, and the authorized legal guardian or agent, grandparent, adult child, or spouse.

For a birth certificate, you must fill out a request form (available online at above Website), or write down and mail in all the following information: Full name of person on the birth certificate, date of birth, place of birth, current age, sex, race, full name of mother including maiden name, full name of father, your relationship to person named on the certificate, and the type and quantity of certificate(s) requested.

Two types of birth certificates are available: full and wallet (no parents' names). Additional full-size certificates ordered at same time are $5.00. Additional wallet-size records are $10.00 no matter how many copies are ordered. Special searches cost an additional $10.00.

For a death certificate, you must provide the following information: full name of deceased, date of death, place of death, age of deceased at death, sex, race, and the number of copies you request. Additional death certificates of the same record ordered at the same time are $5.00. Multi-year searches (every ten years of portion thereof) cost $10.00.

Money order or cashiers check should be made payable to: **Vital Records, GA. DHR.** Personal checks are not accepted.

FAST SERVICE: You may telephone VitalChek at: (800) 255-2414 and order a certificate using your MasterCard, Visa, or American Express card for an additional fee of $8.95. Overnight FedEx delivery costs $15.81.

To verify current fees, the telephone number is: (404) 656-4750.

EVENT: MARRIAGE

COST OF COPY: $10.00

REMARKS: Marriage records after June 9, 1952, have been centralized and certified copies are issued at the state office. Inquiries about marriages occurring before June 9, 1952, will be forwarded to appropriate Probate Judge in county where license was issued. Information needed is full name of bride and groom, date and place of marriage, and number of copies requested.

EVENT: DIVORCE

COST OF COPY: $10.00

REMARKS: Fees for search only, no copies issued. Certified copies or divorce records are not issued at state office. Fee is for certification, plus $.50 per page. Inquiries will be forwarded to appropriate Clerk of Superior Court in county where divorce was granted. Fees vary.

PLACE OF EVENT: GUAM

EVENT: BIRTH, DEATH, MARRIAGE

COST OF COPY: $5.00

ADDRESS: Office of Vital Statistics, Department of Public Health and Social Services, Government of Guam, P.O. Box 2816, Hagatna, Guam 96932

WWW: http://ns.gov.gu/government.html

REMARKS: Office has had records since October 16, 1901. Money order should be made payable to: **Treasurer of Guam**. Personal checks are not accepted.

To verify the current fees, please call: (671) 734-7292 or contact via e-mail: cagarri@ns.gu.

EVENT: DIVORCE

COST OF COPY: Fee varies

ADDRESS/WWW: Write to: Clerk, Superior Court of Guam, Agana, Guam 96910

PLACE OF EVENT: HAWAII

EVENT: BIRTH, DEATH, MARRIAGE

COST OF COPY: $10.00

ADDRESS: Office of Health Status Monitoring, Vital Records Section, P.O. Box 3378, Honolulu, Hawaii 96801

WWW: http://www.state.hi.us/health/records/vr_howto.html

REMARKS: State office has had birth and death records since 1853. Cashiers check or money order should be made payable to: **Hawaii State Department of Health.** Fee covers cost of search whether subject is found or not.

To verify current fees, the telephone number is: (808) 586-4533 (recorded message), or e-mail: vr-info@mail.health.state.hi.us.

EVENT: DIVORCE

COST OF COPY: $10.00

REMARKS: If the records are not available at the state office, they should be available from the Circuit Court in county where the divorce was granted. Fees vary.

PLACE OF EVENT: IDAHO

EVENT: BIRTH OR DEATH

COST OF COPY: $10.00

ADDRESS: Idaho Center for Vital Statistics, 450 West State Street, 1st Floor, Boise, Idaho 83720.

WWW: http://www.state.id.us/dhw/hwgd_www/home.html

REMARKS: State office has had birth and death records since 1911. For prior records, write to County Recorder in county where event occurred.

Idaho requires a copy of a picture ID or copies of two forms of ID that have your signature, such as a cancelled check and Social Security card.

Check or money order should be made payable to: **Idaho Vital Statistics.** Personal checks are accepted.

FAST SERVICE: Fax: (208) 389-9096. For $10.00 extra, you can fax your request and pay by credit card. There is an additional $5.00 charge for Special Handling.

To verify current fees, the telephone number is: (208) 334-5988.

EVENT: MARRIAGE OR DIVORCE

COST OF COPY: $10.00

ADDRESS/WWW: Same as Birth or Death

REMARKS: Records since 1947. Earlier records are with County Recorder in county where marriage license was issued or divorce granted.

PLACE OF EVENT: ILLINOIS

EVENT: BIRTH OR DEATH

COST OF COPY: Birth $15.00—long
Birth $10.00—short
Death $17.00—long
Death $10.00—short (uncertified)

ADDRESS: Illinois Department of Public Health, Division of Vital Records, 605 West Jefferson Street, Springfield, Illinois 62702-5079

WWW: http://www.idph.state.il.us/vital/vitalhome.htm

ILLINOIS, cont'd.

REMARKS: State office has had birth and death records since January 1916. For earlier records and for copies of state records since January 1916, write to County Clerk in county where event occurred (county fees vary). Many county records are located at the Eastern Illinois Regional Archives Depository (IRAD), which is in the Booth Library at Eastern Illinois University in Charleston, Illinois, 61920. (217) 581-6093. Hours: 8 A.M.–noon, and 1 P.M.–4 P.M. Also, death records from 1916 to 1943 can be found at the Illinois State Archives, Margaret Cross Norton Bldg, Capitol Complex, Springfield, Illinois 62756. (217) 782-4682.

There is no charge for uncertified photocopies of the records. There is a limit of two names per request.

The fee of $15.00 covers the search of state files—if the record is found, one certification is issued at no additional charge. Additional certified copies of the same record ordered at the same time are $2.00 each.

Make money order, certified check, or personal check payable to **Illinois**. If your request is sent via regular U.S. mail, the turnaround rate is three weeks.

FAST SERVICE: If your request is sent via a speedy service (e.g., overnight, second-day, etc.), then it is processed immediately and the requested document is sent to you within two business days.

To verify current fees, the telephone number is: (217) 782-6554.

EVENT: MARRIAGE

COST OF COPY: $5.00

ADDRESS/WWW: Same as Birth or Death

REMARKS: Records since January 1962. For certified copies, write to the Clerk of the Circuit Court in the county where the marriage license was obtained. Fees vary. Certified copies are *not* available from the state office.

EVENT: DIVORCE

COST OF COPY: $5.00

ADDRESS/WWW: Same as Birth or Death

REMARKS: Records since January 1962. Certified copies are *not* available from state office. For certified copies, write to the Clerk of Circuit Court in county where divorce was granted. Fees vary.

PLACE OF EVENT: INDIANA

EVENT: BIRTH OR DEATH

COST OF COPY: Birth $6.00
　　　　　　　　Death $4.00

ADDRESS: Vital Records Department, Indiana State Department of Health, 2 North Meridian St., Indianapolis, Indiana 46204.

WWW: http://www.state.in.us/

REMARKS: State office has had birth records since October 1907, and death records since 1900. For earlier records, write to the Health Department in city or county where event occurred. For information about the local health departments, call the Indiana State Department of Health at: (317) 233-1325.

There are no indexes to the state death certificates from 1900 through 1918. The specific city or county of death must be provided for searches in this period, and the search is limited to one county for each search fee of $4.00. If the exact date of death is not known, please indicate the five-year period to be searched. An additional $4.00 is required for each additional five-year period or county searched from 1900–1918. Search fees are nonrefundable.

Include a photocopy of personal identification with your request.

Additional copies of the same birth record ordered at the same time are $1.00 each.

Personal check or money order should be made payable to: **Indiana Department of Health.**

FAST SERVICE: To use a major credit card, call: (317) 233-2700. You will be asked for the following information: credit card name, number, and expiration date; type of certificate you are requesting; full name at birth; date and place of birth; full name of father; mother's maiden name; daytime phone number and address where to send the birth certificate.

To verify current fees, the telephone number is: (317) 233-2700.

EVENT: MARRIAGE OR DIVORCE

REMARKS: Marriage index since 1958. Certified copies are *not* available from State Health Department. They are available from the Clerks of the Circuit Court in the county where the marriage license was issued or divorce granted. Fees vary.

PLACE OF EVENT: IOWA

EVENT: BIRTH, DEATH, MARRIAGE

COST OF COPY: $10.00

ADDRESS: Iowa Department of Public Health, Bureau of Vital Records, Lucas Office Building, 321 East 12th Street, Des Moines, Iowa 50319-0075

WWW: http://idph.state.ia.us/pa/vr.htm

REMARKS: The state office has had birth, death, and marriage records since July 1880. Only blood relatives are entitled to receive certified copies of these records. At the county level, records are open to the public, but no certified copies are available. Additional copies cost $10.00.

For written requests, you must complete the Application for Copy of a Vital Record form. This application form is available online or by writing to the above address. Attach a check or money order payable to **Iowa Department of Public Health,** and send to the above address.

FAST SERVICE: Call: (515) 281-4944 and follow instructions. Credit cards currently being accepted include American Express, Discover, MasterCard, and Visa for an additional $5.00 processing fee. FedEx is also available for an additional fee.

To verify current fees, the telephone number is: (515) 281-4944 (recorded message).

Commemorative Birth Certificate, $35.00
All applicants must be immediate family. For Iowa-born citizens only, this parchment certificate, 8-1/2" x 11", with gold-embossed seals, is signed by the Governor and is suitable for framing. The $35.00 fee includes the search for the birth record and one certificate. If the record is not found, a notification of the search results and a $25 refund is sent to you. $10 is retained by the state to cover the cost of the search.

Commemorative Marriage Certificate, $35.00
All applicants must be immediate family. This parchment certificate, 8-1/2" x 11", with gold-embossed seals, is signed by the Governor and is suitable for framing.

EVENT: DIVORCE

COST OF COPY: $10.00

ADDRESS/WWW: Same as Birth or Death

REMARKS: Brief statistical records only since 1906.

PLACE OF EVENT: KANSAS

EVENT: BIRTH, DEATH, MARRIAGE, DIVORCE

COST OF COPY: $10.00

ADDRESS: Office of Vital Statistics, 900 SW Jackson Street, Topeka, Kansas 66612

WWW: http://www.kdhe.state.ks.us/vital

REMARKS: State office has records since July 1911. For earlier records, write to County Clerk in county where event occurred.

Please send the following information with your request for a death certificate: Name of person on record; date and place of event; your relationship to person on record; reason for request; daytime phone number; Social Security Number, or other identifying information.

Additional copy of same birth or death record ordered at the same time costs $5.00.

Personal check or money order should be made payable to: **State Registrar of Vital Statistics.**

To verify current fees, the telephone number is: (785) 296-1400, or e-mail: info@kdhe.state.ks.us.

PLACE OF EVENT: KENTUCKY

EVENT: BIRTH OR DEATH

COST OF COPY: Birth $9.00
　　　　　　　　Death $6.00

ADDRESS: Office of Vital Statistics, 275 East Main Street, Frankfort, Kentucky 40621

WWW: http://ukcc.uky.edu/~vitalrec/

REMARKS: State office has had records since January 1911, and some records for the cities of Louisville, Lexington, Covington, and Newport before then.

Check or money order should be made payable to: **Kentucky State Treasurer.** Personal checks are accepted.

To verify current fees, the telephone number is: (502) 564-4212.

KENTUCKY, cont'd.

EVENT: MARRIAGE

COST OF COPY: $6.00

ADDRESS/WWW: Same as Birth or Death

REMARKS: Records since June 1958.

If records are not available at the state office, they should be available from the Clerk of Circuit Court in the county where the marriage license was issued. Fees vary.

EVENT: DIVORCE

COST OF COPY: $6.00

ADDRESS/WWW: Same as Birth or Death

REMARKS: If the records are not available at the state office, they should be available from the Clerk of Circuit Court in the county where the divorce decree was granted. Fees vary.

PLACE OF EVENT: LOUISIANA

EVENT: BIRTH OR DEATH

COST OF COPY: Birth: (since July 1914)—order from Vital Records Registry. (City of New Orleans records have been available since 1892.) $15.00 (birth certificate), $9.00 (birth card)

Birth: (1790 to 1897) Order city of New Orleans records only from the Louisiana State Archives. $5.00

Death: (since July 1914) Order from Vital Records Registry. City of New Orleans records have been available since 1892. $5.00

ADDRESS: Louisiana Vital Records Registry, P.O. Box 60630, New Orleans, Louisiana 70160. Louisiana State Archives, P.O. Box 94125, Baton Rouge, Louisiana 70804-9125. (225) 922-1208.

WWW: http://www.dhh.state.la.us/oph/vital/index.htm

REMARKS: Personal check or money order should be made payable to: **Vital Records.** Include phone number and SASE in request. To verify current fees, the telephone number is: (504) 568-5152.

LOUISIANA, cont'd.

EVENT: MARRIAGE

COST OF COPY: $5.00

ADDRESS/WWW: Same as Birth or Death

REMARKS: Certified copies are issued by Clerk of Court in parish where license was issued. Fees vary.

EVENT: DIVORCE

REMARKS: Certified copies available from Clerk of Court in the parish where divorce was granted. Fees vary. Call Civil District Court at (504) 592-9100.

PLACE OF EVENT: MAINE

EVENT: BIRTH OR DEATH

COST OF COPY: $10.00

ADDRESS: Office of Vital Statistics, Department of Human Services, State House Station 11, Augusta, Maine 04333-0011

WWW: http://www.state.me.us/

REMARKS: State office has had birth, death, and marriage records since 1892. For earlier records, write to the municipality where the event occurred.

Personal check or money order should be made payable to: **Treasurer, State of Maine.** Search fee includes a record search of files for a time period of two years before and two years after the stated date of the event, and one certified copy of the record if located.

Additional copies of same record ordered at same time are $2.00 each.

To verify current fees, the telephone number is: (207) 287-3181.

EVENT: MARRIAGE

COST OF COPY: $10.00

ADDRESS/WWW: Same as Birth or Death

REMARKS: If the records are not available at the state office, they should be available from the Clerk of the District Court in the county where the event occurred.

MAINE, cont'd.

EVENT: DIVORCE

COST OF COPY: $10.00

ADDRESS/WWW: Same as Birth or Death

REMARKS: Divorce proceedings prior to January 1892 can be found in the court records at the Maine State Archives at: (207) 287-5795.

PLACE OF EVENT: MARYLAND

EVENT: BIRTH OR DEATH

COST OF COPY: $6.00

ADDRESS: Division of Vital Records, Department of Health & Mental Hygiene, 6550 Reisterstown Road Plaza, Baltimore, Maryland 21215-0020.

WWW: http://www.dhmh.state.md.us/html/vitalrec.htm

REMARKS: State office has had birth and death records since August 1898. Birth and death records prior to 1898 may be located at the State of Maryland Archives. City of Baltimore records are available from January 1875. State does not do genealogical research—you must apply to State of Maryland Archives, 350 Rowe Blvd., Annapolis, Maryland 21401. (410) 260-6400.

Only blood relatives or authorized representatives are entitled to birth certificates. You must provide the full name, date and place of birth (city or county), mother's full maiden name, father's full name, your relationship to the person named on the record, and your name and address. Regulations for death records are extensive. Call: (800) 832-3277 for complete list.

Personal check or money order should be made payable to: **Division of Vital Records.** Local health departments will charge an additional fee, per set, for production costs.

FAST SERVICE: Use your credit card and either fax: (410) 358-7381 or call: (800) 832-3277 to make your request. There is an additional fee of $7.00.

To verify current fees, the telephone number is: (410) 764-3038 or (410) 318-6119 (recording).

MARYLAND, cont'd.

Commemorative Birth Certificates, $25.00
The Governor's Office of Children, Youth and Families receives $15 of the proceeds to be used in child abuse prevention programs. Application procedure is the same for regular certificates. This is a legal document, 8-1/2" x 11", suitable for framing.

EVENT: MARRIAGE

COST OF COPY: $6.00

ADDRESS/WWW: Same as Birth or Death

REMARKS: The state has had records since 1973. Provide full name of groom and bride, date and place of marriage, your name and mailing address. Only bride and groom or authorized representative is entitled to certificate. For records prior to 1973, contact the circuit court in county where license was issued. County fees vary.

EVENT: DIVORCE (verification only)

COST OF COPY: No fee

ADDRESS/WWW: Same as Birth or Death

REMARKS: Records since January 1961. Certified copies are not available from state office. Some items may be verified. Certified copies should be available from the Clerk of the Circuit Court in the county where the divorce was granted. Fees vary.

PLACE OF EVENT: MASSACHUSETTS

EVENT: BIRTH OR DEATH

COST OF COPY: $11.00

ADDRESS: Registry of Vital Records and Statistics, 150 Mount Vernon St., 1st Floor, Dorchester, Massachusetts 02125-3105

WWW: http://www.state.ma.us/dph/rvr.htm

REMARKS: State office has had birth and death records since 1905. For earlier records, write to The Massachusetts Archives at Columbia Point, 220 Morrissey Boulevard, Boston, Massachusetts 02125. (617) 727-2816.

Certified copies may be obtained through the Registry in person ($6.00 each), by mail ($11.00), or by phone ($19.00). Regardless of how you request copies, you should be prepared to provide the name of the subject(s) of the record, the date of the event, and, if known, the city or town where the event occurred.

MASSACHUSETTS, cont'd.

FAST SERVICE: For credit card orders of vital records, call: (617) 740-2606. The fee for records ordered by phone is $19.00 per certified copy. Visa, MasterCard, Discover, and American Express are the only acceptable forms of payment. You may request overnight delivery for an additional fee.

Personal check or money order should be made payable to: **Commonwealth of Massachusetts.**

To verify current fees, the telephone number is: (617) 740-2600.

EVENT: MARRIAGE

COST OF COPY: $11.00

ADDRESS/WWW: Same as Birth or Death

REMARKS: Records since 1905. For records prior to 1905, contact the town clerk in the town or city where event occurred. Printed Vital Records prior to 1850, organized by town, are available in many libraries.

EVENT: DIVORCE

COST OF COPY: $10.00

ADDRESS/WWW: Same as Birth or Death

REMARKS: Index only since 1952. Inquirer will be directed where to send request. Certified copies are not available from state office. Copies are available from the Registrar of Probate Court in county where divorce was granted.

PLACE OF EVENT: MICHIGAN

EVENT: BIRTH

COST OF COPY: $13.00 ($5.00 for anyone age 65+ requesting their own record)

ADDRESS: Vital Records Requests, P.O. Box 30721, Lansing, Michigan 48909

WWW: http://www.migov.state.mi.us/

REMARKS: State office has had records since 1867. Copies may also be obtained from clerk in county where birth occurred. Fees vary from county to county. Detroit records may be obtained from the City of Detroit Health Department for births occurring since 1893, and for deaths since 1897.

MICHIGAN, cont'd.

You must be either the person named on the record, a parent, legal guardian or representative, or an heir named on the record. Birth records over 110 years old are available to the public. The appropriate application must be filled out—it is available at the above Website or P.O. Box.

Fee for additional copies is $4.00 and will be refunded if search reveals no state record. Extra years that are paid for but do not have to be searched to locate the record will be refunded. Refunds are mailed within three to four weeks.

Personal checks or money orders should be made payable to: **State of Michigan.** Fee covers the cost of the basic three-year search and includes either one certified copy of the record or an official statement that the record is not filed with the state. A basic search includes the year specified as the birth year, as well as the year before and after.

FAST SERVICE: For turnaround time of two days, fax your request: (517) 321-5884. There is an additional charge of $5.00. The fax request must include your name, credit card number, expiration date, and your signature.

To verify current fees, the telephone number is: (517) 335-8666.

EVENT: DEATH

COST OF COPY: $13.00

ADDRESS/WWW: Same as Birth

REMARKS: State office has had records of deaths since 1867.

Anyone is eligible to request a copy of a Michigan death record. Fee covers basic three-year search.

EVENT: MARRIAGE

COST OF COPY: $13.00

ADDRESS/WWW: Same as Birth or Death

REMARKS: Records since April 1867. Search fees and additional fees are same as Birth.

EVENT: DIVORCE

COST OF COPY: $13.00

ADDRESS/WWW: Same as Birth or Death

REMARKS: Records since April 1867. Search fees and additional fees are same as Birth.

PLACE OF EVENT: MINNESOTA

EVENT: BIRTH OR DEATH

COST OF COPY: Birth $14.00
                            Death $11.00

ADDRESS: Minnesota Department of Health, Birth and Death Records, 717 Delaware Street, SE, P.O. Box 9441, Minneapolis, Minnesota 55440

WWW: http://www.state.mn.us/

REMARKS: State office has birth records since 1900 and death records since January 1908. Copies of earlier records may be obtained from the Local Registrar in the county where event occurred or from the St. Paul City Health Department, if the event occurred in St. Paul.

Additional copies of the birth record when ordered at the same time are $5.00 each. Additional copies of the death record when ordered at the same time are $2.00 each.

Personal check or money order should be made payable to: **Minnesota Department of Health.**

To verify current fees, the telephone number is: (612) 676-5120.

EVENT: MARRIAGE

COST OF COPY: $8.00

ADDRESS/WWW: Same as Birth or Death

REMARKS: Statewide index since January 1958. Inquiries will be forwarded to the appropriate office. Certified copies are not available from State Department of Health. They should be available from the Local Registrar in the county where license was issued.

EVENT: DIVORCE

ADDRESS/WWW: Same as Birth or Death

REMARKS: Index since January 1970. Certified copies are not available from state office.

PLACE OF EVENT: MISSISSIPPI

EVENT: BIRTH OR DEATH

COST OF COPY: Birth $12.00— long form
Birth $7.00—short form
Death $10.00

ADDRESS: Vital Records, State Department of Health, 2423 North State Street, Jackson, Mississippi 39215

WWW: http://www.msdh.state.ms.us/

REMARKS: Full copies of birth certificates within one year after the event are $5.00. Additional copies of same record ordered at same time are $2.00 each for Birth, and $1.00 each for Death.

Personal checks accepted from in-state requests only. Make bank or postal money orders payable to: **Mississippi State Department of Health.**

To verify current fees, the telephone number is: (601) 576-7960.

EVENT: MARRIAGE

COST OF COPY: $10.00

ADDRESS/WWW: Same as Birth or Death

REMARKS: Statistical records only from January 1926 to July 1, 1938, and since January 1942.

If records are not available at the state office, they should be available from the Circuit Clerk in county where license was issued.

EVENT: DIVORCE

COST OF COPY: $6.00

ADDRESS/WWW: Same as Birth or Death

REMARKS: Records since January 1926. Certified copies are not available from state office. Inquiries will be forwarded to appropriate office.

PLACE OF EVENT: MISSOURI

EVENT: BIRTH OR DEATH

COST OF COPY: $10.00

ADDRESS: Bureau of Vital Records, 930 Wildwood, P.O. Box 570, Jefferson City, Missouri 65102-0570

WWW: http://www.health.state.mo.us/

REMARKS: State office has had birth and death records since January 1910. Prior to August 1909, records can be obtained from the county clerk of the county where the birth or death occurred, or from Records Management and Archives Service, P.O. Box 778, Jefferson City, Missouri 65102. If the event occurred in St. Louis (city), St. Louis County, or Kansas City before 1910, write to the City or County Health Department.

Birth and death records are not public. Only blood relatives and legal representatives are eligible to receive certificates. Send full name, date and place of birth, father and mother's full name, mother's maiden name, your name, address, telephone number, and relationship to the person whose record is being requested, and explain your reason for requesting the record.

The $10.00 fee covers a basic five-year search. Copies of these records are $3.00 each in St. Louis (city), and $5.00 each in St. Louis County. In Kansas City, the fee is $6.00 for the first copy, and $3.00 for each additional copy ordered at the same time.

Personal check or money order should be made payable to: **Missouri Department of Health.**

FAST SERVICE: Call: (573) 751-6382. They will do an immediate search if you provide them with a Visa or MasterCard number. Cost is $14.95. Results will be mailed the same day request is made.

To verify current fees, the telephone number is: (573) 751-6400.

EVENT: MARRIAGE

COST OF COPY: $10.00

ADDRESS/WWW: Same as Birth or Death

REMARKS: Varies. Indexes since July 1948. Certified copies are *not* available from State Health Department. Inquiries will be forwarded to appropriate office. Copies should be available from the Clerk of the Circuit Court in the county where the divorce was granted.

MISSOURI, cont'd.

All requests must include the following: full names of bride and groom, including maiden name of bride, county issuing license or decree, date or approximate date of marriage or divorce.

To get faster response time, call: (573) 751-6382. They will do an immediate search, if you provide them with a Visa or MasterCard number. Cost with a credit card is $14.95. Results will be mailed the same day the request is made.

PLACE OF EVENT: MONTANA

EVENT: BIRTH OR DEATH

COST OF COPY: $10.00

ADDRESS: Vital Records, State Department of Health and Human Services, P.O. Box 4210, 111 N. Sanders, Helena, Montana 59604-4210.

WWW: http://www.imt.net/~corkykn/vital.html

REMARKS: The state office has had records since late 1907. Both from the standpoint of cost and efficiency, the County Courthouse Records are the best source for records. If you do not know the county, then start with the State Department of Public Health and Human Services. Certified copies are not available from the state; however, some items may be verified. Inquiries about certified copies will be forwarded to the appropriate office.

Birth and death records that are less than 30 years old can be obtained only by the mother, father, spouse, or child of the individual for whom the record is requested. Include a SASE with your request.

Personal check or money order should be made payable to: **Montana Department of Public Health and Human Services**. Fee is for a five-year search.

To verify current fees, the telephone number is: (406) 444-4228.

EVENT: MARRIAGE OR DIVORCE

COST OF COPY: $10.00

ADDRESS/WWW: Same as Birth or Death

REMARKS: Records since July 1943. Some items may be verified. Inquiries will be forwarded to appropriate office. Apply to county where license was issued if known. Certified copies are not available from state office.

PLACE OF EVENT: NEBRASKA

EVENT: BIRTH OR DEATH

COST OF COPY: Birth $8.00
              Death $7.00

ADDRESS: Nebraska Health & Human Services System, Vital Statistics, 301 Centennial Mall South, P.O. Box 95065, Lincoln, Nebraska 68509-5065

WWW: http://www.hhs.state.ne.us/ced/cedindex.htm

REMARKS: The state office has records since late1904. If birth occurred before then, write the county office. They will charge you whether or not they find your subject. Records are available only to immediate family.

Check or money order should be made payable to: **Vital Statistics.** Personal checks are accepted. Walk-in requests take 30 minutes. Basic requests sent by regular mail take 10–15 working days. Credit card requests sent by regular mail take 7 working days.

FAST SERVICE: Call: (402) 471-6440 and use MasterCard or Visa for an additional charge of $8.00. Overnight Express mail is an additional $28.50.

To verify current fees, the telephone number is: (402) 471-2871.

EVENT: MARRIAGE OR DIVORCE

COST OF COPY: $7.00

ADDRESS/WWW: Same as Birth or Death

REMARKS: Records since January 1909. If the record is not available at the state office, it should be available at the county clerk's office in the county where the marriage license was issued. Please send name of bride and groom, date and place where marriage license was issued or divorce granted.

PLACE OF EVENT: NEVADA

EVENT: BIRTH OR DEATH

COST OF COPY: Birth $11.00
              Death $8.00

ADDRESS: Division of Health/Vital Statistics, Capitol Complex, 505 East King Street #102, Carson City, Nevada 89710

NEVADA, cont'd.

WWW: http://www.state.nv.us/

REMARKS: State office has had records since July 1911. For earlier records, write to County Recorder in county where event occurred. Fees vary.

Personal check or money order should be made payable to: **Section of Vital Statistics.**

To verify current fees, the telephone number is: (775) 684-4242.

EVENT: MARRIAGE OR DIVORCE

ADDRESS/WWW: Same as Birth or Death

REMARKS: Indexes since January 1968. Certified copies are not available from State Health Department. Inquiries will be forwarded to the appropriate office.

PLACE OF EVENT: NEW HAMPSHIRE

EVENT: BIRTH, DEATH, MARRIAGE

COST OF COPY: $12.00

ADDRESS: Bureau of Vital Records, 6 Hazen Drive, Concord, New Hampshire 03301

WWW: http://www.state.nh.us/

REMARKS: State office has had records since 1883. Records from 1640 to 1883 may be obtained from the City or Town Clerk where event occurred.

Make personal check or money order payable to: **Treasurer, State of New Hampshire.**

To verify current fees, the telephone number is: (603) 271-4651.

EVENT: DIVORCE

COST OF COPY: $12.00, fees vary.

ADDRESS/WWW: Same as Birth or Death

REMARKS: Copies of records may be obtained from the state office or from the Clerk of Superior Court in the county where divorce was granted.

PLACE OF EVENT: NEW JERSEY

EVENT: BIRTH, DEATH, MARRIAGE

COST OF COPY: Birth $4.00 (1878 to present)
Death $10.00 (1848 to 1923)

ADDRESS: State office has had records since June 1878. New Jersey State Department of Health and Senior Services, Bureau of Vital Statistics, P.O. Box 370, Trenton, New Jersey 08625-0370.

Archives has had records from 1848 to 1923. Archives Section, Division of Archives and Records Management, Department of State, CN307, Trenton, New Jersey 08625-0307.

WWW: http://www.state.nj.us/health/vital/vital.htm

REMARKS: If the exact date is unknown, the fee is an additional $1.00 per year searched. There is a $10 Archival Search Fee, which covers a search of up to five consecutive years for each requested record. Each additional block of five years searched at the same time will cost another $10.00. It can take up to four months to get a vital record from New Jersey.

Personal check or money order should be made payable to: **New Jersey State Department of Health.**

FAST SERVICE: Fax: (609) 392-4292. If you fax your request and are willing to pay by credit card, your order will be processed within seven working days. You will be charged an additional fee of $8.95. For more information, call Vitalchek at: (609) 633-2860.

To verify current fees, the telephone number is: (609) 292-4087.

EVENT: DIVORCE

COST OF COPY: $10.00

ADDRESS/WWW: Make personal check or money order payable to: **Clerk of the Superior Court**, Superior Court of New Jersey, Public Information Center, 171 Jersey Street, P.O. Box 967, Trenton, New Jersey 08625-0967.

PLACE OF EVENT: NEW MEXICO

EVENT: BIRTH OR DEATH

COST OF COPY: Birth $10.00
Death $7.00

ADDRESS: New Mexico Vital Records and Health Statistics, 1105 St. Francis Drive, Santa Fe, New Mexico 87502

WWW: http://www.state.nm.us/

REMARKS: State office has had records since 1920 and delayed records since 1880.

Personal check or money order should be made payable to: **Vital Statistics.**

FAST SERVICE: Call this number to place an order with your credit card: (505) 827-2316. There is an additional $10 handling fee if you use a credit card to order the certificate.

To verify current fees, the telephone number is: (505) 827-2338.

EVENT: MARRIAGE OR DIVORCE

COST OF COPY: $7.00

REMARKS: Available from Clerk of Superior Court in county where license was issued. Fees vary.

PLACE OF EVENT: NEW YORK (EXCEPT NEW YORK CITY)

EVENT: BIRTH OR DEATH

COST OF COPY: $15.00

ADDRESS: New York State Department of Health, Vital Records Section, Empire State Plaza, Albany, New York 12237-0023.

WWW: http://www.health.state.ny.us/

REMARKS: State office has had death records since 1880, and birth and marriage records since 1881. Older records are at the New York State Archives, New York Dept. of Education, Cultural Education Center, Room 11D40, Albany, New York 12230. Call: (518) 474-8955.

For records before 1914 in Albany, Buffalo, and Yonkers, or before 1880 in any other city, write to Registrar of Vital Statistics in city where the event occurred. Birth and

NEW YORK, cont'd.

death records are filed with the Clerk of the city, town, or village in which the event occurred, and normally, with the New York State Bureau of Vital Records. Records are available only to the individual or a member of his or her immediate family.

Personal check or money order should be made payable to: **New York State Department of Health.**

FAST SERVICE: Fax your request to: (518) 474-9168, sending the completed application form (available from the above Website or address); your name, address, and telephone number; credit card type, number, and expiration date; and a copy of your driver's license. Or call the New York Department of Health at: (518) 474-3077. You may use MasterCard, Visa, or Discover. When you order by credit card, your request is sent by Federal Express for a total fee of $35.50 (including $15.00 certificate fee).

To verify current fees, the telephone number is: (518) 474-3077.

EVENT: MARRIAGE

COST OF COPY: $5.00 (no fee for record used for eligibility for social welfare or veteran's benefits)

REMARKS: Submit the application (from the Website or address above), or send a letter including the full name of bride and groom, including bride's maiden name, date of marriage, city or town where license was issued, reason the record is needed, and your relationship to the bride or groom.

EVENT: DIVORCE

COST OF COPY: Varies.

ADDRESS/WWW: County Clerk in county where divorce was granted.

REMARKS: Records since January 1963.

PLACE OF EVENT: NEW YORK CITY

EVENT: BIRTH OR DEATH

COST OF COPY: $5.00

ADDRESS: Bureau of Vital Records, Department of Health of New York City, 125 Worth Street, New York, New York 10013

WWW: http://www.ci.nyc.ny.us/html/doh/html/vr/vr.html

NEW YORK CITY, cont'd.

REMARKS: Office has birth records since 1898 and death records since 1930. For Old City of New York (Manhattan and part of the Bronx), birth records for 1865–1897, and death records for 1865–1929, write to Archives Division, Department of Records and Information Services, 31 Chambers Street, New York, New York 10007. Money order should be made payable to: **New York City Department of Health.**

EVENT: MARRIAGE

COST OF COPY: $10.00, additional copies of same record ordered at same time are $5.00 each.

REMARKS: Bronx Borough—City Clerk's Office, 1780 Grand Concourse, Bronx, New York 10457.

Brooklyn Borough—City Clerk's Office, Municipal Building, Brooklyn, New York 11201.

Manhattan Borough—City Clerk's Office, Municipal Building, New York, New York 10007.

Queens Borough—City Clerk's Office, 120–55 Queens Boulevard, Kew Gardens, New York 11424.

Staten Island Borough (no longer called Richmond)—City Clerk's Office, Staten Island Borough Hall, Staten Island, New York 10301.

Records from 1847–1865 for all boroughs except Brooklyn: Archives Division, Department of Records and Information Services, 31 Chambers Street, New York, New York 10007.

Records from 1847–1865 for Brooklyn: County Clerk's Office, Kings County, Supreme Court Building, Brooklyn, New York 11201.

Records from 1866–1907: City Clerk's Office in borough where marriage was performed.

Records from 1908 to May 12, 1943: New York City residents write to: City Clerk's Office in the borough of bride's residence; nonresidents write to City Clerk's Office in the borough where license was obtained.

Records since May 13, 1943: City Clerk's Office in borough where license was issued.

EVENT: DIVORCE

ADDRESS: See New York State

REMARKS: To verify current fees, for New York City the telephone number is: (212) 669-2400.

PLACE OF EVENT: NORTH CAROLINA

EVENT: BIRTH OR DEATH

COST OF COPY: $10.00

ADDRESS: North Carolina Vital Records, 1903 Mail Service Center, Raleigh, North Carolina, 27699-1903.

WWW: http://www.state.nc.us/

REMARKS: State office has had birth records since October 1913 and death records since January 1, 1956. North Carolina State Archives has had death records from 1913 to 1955. Inquiries may be sent to: State Archives of North Carolina, Archival Services Branch, 4614 Mail Service Center, Raleigh, North Carolina 27699-4614. (919) 733-3952.

Requests sent to Vital Records must include the name of the individual being sought, county of birth or death, approximate year of birth or death, your relationship with this person, and purpose of your request. For birth certificates, the full name of parents, including mother's maiden name, must be given.

Check or money order should be made payable to: **North Carolina Vital Records Section.** Personal checks are accepted.

EVENT: MARRIAGE

COST OF COPY: $10.00

ADDRESS/WWW: Same as Birth or Death

REMARKS: Records since January 1962 are available from the Registrar of Deeds in the county where marriage was performed.

EVENT: DIVORCE

COST OF COPY: $10.00

ADDRESS/WWW: Same as Birth or Death

REMARKS: Records since January 1962 are available from the Clerk of Superior Court in the county where divorce was granted.

PLACE OF EVENT: NORTH DAKOTA

EVENT: BIRTH OR DEATH

COST OF COPY: Birth $7.00
             Death $5.00

ADDRESS: Division of Vital Records, State Capital, 600 East Blvd. Avenue, Bismarck, North Dakota 58505

WWW: http://www.health.state.nd.us/ndhd/admin/vital/

REMARKS: State office has had some records since July 1870. Years from 1894–1920 are incomplete.

Additional copies of birth records are $4.00 each; death records are $2.00 each.

Money order should be made payable to: **Division of Vital Records.**

To verify current fees, the telephone number is: (701) 328-2360.

EVENT: MARRIAGE

COST OF COPY: $5.00

ADDRESS/WWW: Same as Birth or Death

REMARKS: Records since July 1925. Requests for earlier records will be forwarded to the appropriate office. Fees vary. Additional copies are $2.00 each.

EVENT: DIVORCE

ADDRESS/WWW: Same as Birth or Death

REMARKS: Index of records since July 1949. Some items may be verified. Certified copies are not available from State Health Department. Inquiries will be forwarded to appropriate office. Fees vary.

PLACE OF EVENT: NORTHERN MARIANA ISLANDS

EVENT: BIRTH OR DEATH

COST OF COPY: $3.00

ADDRESS: Office of Vital Statistics, Superior Court, Commonwealth of Northern Mariana Islands, P.O. Box 307, Saipan, MP 96950

NORTHERN MARIANA ISLANDS, cont'd.

WWW: http://www.saipan.com/

REMARKS: Birth, death, and marriage records from 1945 to 1950 are incomplete.

Money order or bank cashiers check should be made payable to: **CNMI Treasury.** Personal checks are not accepted.

To verify current fees, the telephone number is: (670) 234-6401, ext 15.

EVENT: MARRIAGE

COST OF COPY: $3.00

ADDRESS/WWW: Same as Birth or Death

EVENT: DIVORCE

COST OF COPY: $2.50 plus $0.50 per page for Divorce Decree

ADDRESS/WWW: Same as Birth or Death

REMARKS: Divorce records since 1960 are available.

PLACE OF EVENT: OHIO

EVENT: BIRTH, DEATH, MARRIAGE, DIVORCE

COST OF COPY: $9.00 (Certified copies)
(3¢ for uncertified copies)
$25.00 (Heirloom Birth Certificate—(614) 466-2703)

ADDRESS: Ohio Department of Health, Vital Statistics, 35 E. Chestnut St., 6th Floor, P.O. Box 15098, Columbus, Ohio 43215-0098

WWW: http://www.odh.state.oh.us/Birth/birthmain.htm

REMARKS: State office has had birth records since December 29, 1908. For earlier birth and death records, write to the Probate Court in the county where the event occurred, or they can be obtained from the Ohio Historical Society, Archives Library Reference Questions, 1982 Velma Avenue, Columbus, Ohio 43211–2497. (614) 297-2510.

If you do not know the date or place of event, you may request a search of the State Vital Statistics office files and records. The fee for a search is $3.00 per name for every

OHIO, cont'd.

ten years searched. Payment must be made in advance. After searching is completed, you will be informed if the record was located.

Birth certificate requests must include: full name at birth and any later name change; date of birth; city and county of birth; father and mother's full name, including mother's maiden name.

Death certificate requests must include: full name of deceased person; date of death; city and county of death.

Marriage licenses and divorce decrees are not on file at the Ohio Vital Statistics Office. Contact the County Probate Court where license or decree was issued. Records have been available since 1949. However, marriage and divorce abstracts are available. Abstracts are nonlegal brief forms that list all basic information. When requesting a marriage or divorce abstract, write "Requesting Marriage (or Divorce) Abstract" on the top of the application. Also include the following information: full name of groom and bride before marriage; date of marriage; city and county of marriage.

Personal check or money order should be made payable to: **Treasury, State of Ohio.** Allow 10 to 12 weeks for regular mail delivery.

FAST SERVICE: Fax your application to: (877) 553-2439. Include credit card number and expiration date on the fax, as well as daytime phone number where you can be reached if there are questions.

To verify current fees, the telephone number is (877) 828-3101.

PLACE OF EVENT: OKLAHOMA

EVENT: BIRTH OR DEATH

COST OF COPY: $5.00

ADDRESS: Vital Records Service—Oklahoma State Department of Health, 1000 Northeast 10th Street, Room 117, Oklahoma City, Oklahoma 73117, or Vital Records Service—Tulsa, 108 N. Greenwood, Tulsa, Oklahoma 74120

WWW: http://www.health.state.ok.us/program/vital/index.html

REMARKS: State office has had records since October 1908.

Oklahoma will only release birth certificates to the person or parent of the person named.

OKLAHOMA, cont'd.

Personal check or money order should be made payable to: **Vital Records Service.**

Vital Records offices (Oklahoma City and Tulsa) are open to the public 8:30 A.M. to 4:00 P.M. Monday through Friday. Copies of records can be picked up in one hour.

To verify current fees, the telephone number is: (405) 271-4040 (Oklahoma City) and (918) 582-4973 (Tulsa).

EVENT: MARRIAGE OR DIVORCE

REMARKS: Clerk of Court in county where license was issued. Fees vary.

PLACE OF EVENT: OREGON

EVENT: BIRTH OR DEATH

COST OF COPY: $15.00
            Heirloom Birth, $25.00

ADDRESS: Oregon Vital Records, P.O. Box 14050, 800 NE Oregon St., Suite 205, Portland, Oregon 97293

WWW: http://www.ohd.hr.state.or.us/

REMARKS: State office has had records since January 1903. Some earlier records for the City of Portland since approximately 1880 are available from the Oregon State Archives, 800 Summer St. NE, Salem, Oregon 97310.

All birth records (including indexes) have a 100-year access restriction. All death records (including indexes) have a 50-year access restriction.

Make money order payable to: **Oregon Health Division.**

To verify current fees, the telephone number is: (503) 731-4108. For a recorded message, call: (503) 731- 4095.

EVENT: MARRIAGE

COST OF COPY: $15.00

ADDRESS/WWW: Same as Birth or Death

REMARKS: State office has had records since January 1906. If not available at state office, they should be available from the County Clerk in the county where the license was issued. County fees vary.

OREGON, cont'd.

EVENT: DIVORCE

COST OF COPY: $15.00

ADDRESS/WWW: Same as Birth or Death

REMARKS: State office has had records since 1925. County Clerks also have some records before 1925. If records are not available at the state office, they should be available from the County Clerk in the county where the license was issued. County fees vary.

PLACE OF EVENT: PENNSYLVANIA

EVENT: BIRTH OR DEATH

COST OF COPY: Birth $4.00
Death $3.00

ADDRESS: Division of Vital Records, State Department of Health, Central Building, 101 South Mercer St. P.O. Box 1528, New Castle, Pennsylvania 16103

WWW: http://www.health.state.pa.us/hpa/apply_bd.htm

REMARKS: State office has had records since January 1906. For earlier records, write to Register of Wills, Orphans Court, in county seat of county where event occurred. For subjects born in Pittsburgh from 1870–1905; or in Allegheny City, now part of Pittsburgh, from 1882–1905, write to Registrar of Wills, City-County Building, Pittsburgh, Pennsylvania 15219. For events occurring in city of Philadelphia from 1860–1915, write to Vital Statistics, Philadelphia Department of Public Health, 401 N. Broad St., Rm. 942, Philadelphia, Pennsylvania 19108.

Access of birth and death certificates is limited to next of kin. You must state your relationship to subject or they will not send a copy.

Personal check or money order should be made payable to: **Division of Vital Records.**

To verify current fees, the telephone number is: (724) 656-3100.

EVENT: MARRIAGE

ADDRESS/WWW: Same as Birth or Death

REMARKS: Make application to the Marriage License Clerks, County Court House in the county where license was issued. County fees vary.

PENNSYLVANIA, cont'd.

EVENT: DIVORCE

ADDRESS/WWW: Same as Birth or Death

REMARKS: Make application to the Prothonotary Court House in the county seat of county where divorce was granted.

PLACE OF EVENT: PUERTO RICO

EVENT: BIRTH, DEATH, MARRIAGE

COST OF COPY: $5.00

ADDRESS: Department of Health, Demographic Registry, P.O. Box 11854, Fernandez Juncos Station, San Juan, Puerto Rico 00910

WWW: http://welcome.topuertorico.org/

REMARKS: Central office has had records since July 22, 1931. Copies of earlier records may be obtained by writing to local Registrar (Registrador Demografico) in municipality where event occurred or by writing to central office for information.

Money order should be made payable to: **Secretary of the Treasury.** Personal checks are not accepted.

To verify current fees, the telephone number is (787) 767-9120.

EVENT: DIVORCE

COST OF COPY: $5.00

ADDRESS/WWW: Same as Birth or Death

REMARKS: Some divorce records are available at the Department of Health. Others can be obtained by contacting the Superior Court where divorce was granted

PLACE OF EVENT: RHODE ISLAND

EVENT: BIRTH, DEATH, MARRIAGE

COST OF COPY: $15.00

ADDRESS: Rhode Island Department of Health, State Vital Records Office, 3 Capitol Hill, Room 101, Providence, Rhode Island 02908–5097.

WWW: http://www.state.ri.us/

REMARKS: State office has had birth and marriage records since 1899. State office has had death records since 1949. For earlier records, write to Town Clerk in town where event occurred.

All vital records from colonial times to the present (except divorce records) are on microfilm at the Family History Center, Church of Latter Day Saints, 1000 Narragansett Blvd., Warwick, Rhode Island, 02888. (401) 463-8150.

Also, the following records are available at the Rhode Island State Archives, 337 Westminster St., Providence, Rhode Island 02903: birth and marriage records for the period 1852–1898; deaths 1853–1948. Alphabetical indices for these records include 1852–1900 (birth and marriage); 1853–1945 (deaths). Additionally, there are also original reported out-of-state deaths recordings for the period 1900–1948 (alphabetical index available); and records of delayed birth filings, 1846–1898 (index available). Aside from these original manuscripts, the archives also maintain an extensive collection of pre-1852 municipal vital record filings (microfilm copies) dating from the earliest recordings in Providence, Westerly, Portsmouth, etc.

Birth, death, marriage, and divorce records from 1853-1900 are available at the Rhode Island Historical Society, 121 Hope St., Providence, Rhode Island 02906. (401) 331-8575.

Additional copies of the same record ordered at the same time are $3.00 each.

Personal check or money order should be payable to: **Rhode Island General Treasury.**

EVENT: DIVORCE

REMARKS: For divorce records 1962 to present, contact the Clerk of Family Court, Garrahy Judicial Complex, 1 Dorrance Plaza, Providence, Rhode Island 02903

PLACE OF EVENT: SOUTH CAROLINA

EVENT: BIRTH OR DEATH

COST OF COPY: $12.00

ADDRESS: Office of Vital Records and Public Health Statistics, South Carolina Department of Health and Environmental Control, 2600 Bull Street, Columbia, South Carolina 29201

WWW: http://www.state.sc.us/

REMARKS: State office has had records since January 1915. City of Charleston births from 1877 and deaths from 1821 are on file at Charleston County Health Department. Ledger entries of Florence City births and deaths from 1895 to 1914 are on file at Florence County Health Department. Ledger entries of Newberry City births and deaths from the late 1800s are on file at Newberry County Health Department. (The fee for these is $13.00.)

Personal check or money order should be made payable to: **Office of Vital Records.**

To verify current fees, the telephone number is: (803) 898-3630.

EVENT: MARRIAGE

COST OF COPY: $13.00

ADDRESS/WWW: Same as Birth or Death

REMARKS: State has had records since July 1950. Records previous to this should be available from the Probate Judge in county where license was issued. County fees vary.

EVENT: DIVORCE

COST OF COPY: $13.00

ADDRESS/WWW: Same as Birth or Death

REMARKS: Records since July 1962. Records previous to this should be available from the Clerk of county where petition was filed. County fees vary.

PLACE OF EVENT: SOUTH DAKOTA

EVENT: BIRTH OR DEATH

COST OF COPY: $10.00

ADDRESS: Vital Records, South Dakota Department of Health, 600 East Capitol, Pierre, South Dakota 57501-2536

WWW: http://www.state.sd.us/

REMARKS: State office has had records since July 1905 and access to other records for some events that occurred before then. If the records are not available at the state office, they should be available from the County Clerk in the county where the event occurred. County fees vary.

You must complete the request form available from the state office or Website above.

For birth certificate, provide name on record, date and place of birth, father and mother's full name, including maiden name. For death certificate, provide name of deceased, date and place of death.

Personal check or money order should be made payable to: **South Dakota Department of Health.**

FAST SERVICE: Call: (605) 773-4961 and be prepared to use your credit card. An additional fee of $10 per request is charged for all credit card, online, and phone orders.

To verify fees and get request form, the telephone number is: (605) 773-4961.

EVENT: MARRIAGE OR DIVORCE

COST OF COPY: $7.00

REMARKS: For marriage or divorce records, provide the names on the record, date and place of event.

PLACE OF EVENT: TENNESSEE

EVENT: BIRTH OR DEATH

COST OF COPY: Birth, long form—$10.00
Birth, short form—$5.00
Death $5.00

TENNESSEE, cont'd.

ADDRESS: Tennessee Vital Records, Central Services Building, 1st Floor, 421 5th Avenue North, Nashville, Tennessee 37247-0450

WWW: http://www.state.tn.us/health/vr/index.html

REMARKS: State office has birth records for entire state since January 1914, and death records from January 1948. Some birth records that occurred in major cities from 1881 to 1913 are also available. To inquire about birth or death records from earlier years, contact the Tennessee Library and Archives in Nashville, Tennessee 37243-0312. (615) 741-2451.

For Memphis birth records from April 1874 through December 1887; November 1898 to January 1, 1914; and for Memphis death records from May 1848 to January 1, 1914, write to Memphis-Shelby County Health Department, Division of Vital Records, Memphis, Tennessee 38105.

Additional copies of the same birth, marriage, or divorce record, requested at the same time, are $2.00 each. Personal check or money order should be made payable to: **Tennessee Vital Records.**

FAST SERVICE: Fax: (615) 726-2559. You may fax your request for a certified copy of a record for an additional fee of $10.00. Charge it to your Visa, MasterCard, Discover, or American Express credit card. Your certificate or other response will be mailed to you within one work day of the day received. Credit card telephone request line: (615) 741-0778.

To verify current fees, the telephone number is (615) 741-1763.

EVENT: MARRIAGE

COST OF COPY: $10.00

ADDRESS/WWW: Same as Birth or Death

REMARKS: State has had records since January 1948. If not available at the state, they should be available from the Clerk of Court in the county where license was issued. County fees vary.

EVENT: DIVORCE

COST OF COPY: $10.00

ADDRESS/WWW: Same as Birth or Death

REMARKS: State has had records since January 1948. If not available at the state, they should be available from the Clerk of Court in the county where petition was filed. County fees vary.

PLACE OF EVENT: TEXAS

EVENT: BIRTH OR DEATH

COST OF COPY: Birth $11.00
Heirloom Birth Certificate $25.00
Death $9.00

ADDRESS: Bureau of Vital Statistics, Texas Department of Health, 1100 West 49th St., P.O. Box 12040, Austin, Texas 78711–2040

WWW: http://www.tdh.state.tx.us/bvs/default.htm

REMARKS: State office has had birth and death records since 1903.

Birth and death certificates are confidential until 25 years after the death and 50 years after the birth. Blood relations and legal representatives qualify to apply for certificates. Requests must include the full names of the subject's mother and father (including mother's maiden name), date and place of event, your reason for obtaining the certificate, and your relationship to the subject.

If you just need to verify that a birth or death occurred, you do not have to qualify to request a Verification of Birth or Death, which includes person's name, date of birth or death, county in which it occurred, and state file number. The nonrefundable fee for verification of certificate of birth is $11.00. The nonrefundable fee for verification of certificate of death is $9.00.

Heirloom Birth Certificates
When the person applying for the certificate is not an immediate family member, it is essential for the application to include the following: a notarized statement from the individual named on the certificate or an immediate family member; a written purpose for obtaining the record; and the relationship of the applicant. Expect to receive your certificate within six to eight weeks.

Additional copies of same record ordered at same time are $3.00 each.

Personal check or money order should be made payable to: **Bureau of Vital Statistics**. The records will be searched without the benefit of the index information, but fees are not refundable, even if no record is found.

FAST SERVICE: Fax: (512) 458-7711. Fax lines are open 24 hours a day. Requests will be processed within one to three business days. Include your MasterCard or Visa card number; expiration date; name on card; a statement with your handwritten signature authorizing charges to the account number; your daytime telephone number with area code; and return address. Specify whether overnight service or regular mail return is requested. Add $5.00 for using your credit card, plus another $5.00 for overnight return, or $11.75 if you use a P.O. Box or rural address.

TEXAS, cont'd.

EVENT: MARRIAGE OR DIVORCE

COST OF COPY: $9.00 (verification only)

REMARKS: For certified copies, contact the County Clerk in the county where license was issued. County fees vary. To authenticate a marriage certificate or divorce decree that will be recognized abroad, you will need an Apostille (this means that the official who signs it must actually use their signature, rather than just stamping it). This is only required when you live abroad, not for ordinary travel.

Complete the Application for Verification of Marriage or Divorce *or* write the following information in a letter: verification of marriage or divorce; husband's and wife's full names (if known); date of birth or age of husband and of wife; date of event (if date unknown, time period to search); county of event; applicant's name; complete mailing address; daytime telephone with area code; your handwritten signature.

PLACE OF EVENT: UTAH

EVENT: BIRTH OR DEATH

COST OF COPY: Birth $12.00
Death $9.00

ADDRESS: Utah State Vital Records Office, Utah Department of Health, P.O. Box 14102, Salt Lake City, Utah 84114-1012

WWW: http://www.state.ut.us/

REMARKS: State office has had records since 1905. If event occurred from 1890 to 1904 in Salt Lake City or Ogden, write to City Board of Health. For records elsewhere in the state from 1898 to 1904, write to County Clerk in county where event occurred. County fees vary.

The Archives Research Center can provide copies of Utah death certificates from 1904 to 50 years from the present. They also have microfilm copies of most of the birth and death registers for Utah counties from 1898 to 1905. Patron Services Archivist, Utah State Archives Research Center, P.O. Box 141021, Salt Lake City, Utah 84114-1021. Telephone (801) 538-3013, or e-mail: research@state.ut.us.

Additional copies, when requested at the same time, are $4.00 each.

Personal check or money order should be made payable to: **Utah Department of Health.**

To verify current fees, the telephone number is: (801) 538-6380.

UTAH, cont'd.

EVENT: MARRIAGE

COST OF COPY: $9.00

ADDRESS/WWW: Same as Birth or Death

REMARKS: State office has had records since 1978. Only short-form certified copies are available. If records are not available from the state, they should be available from the County Clerk in county where license was issued. County fees vary.

EVENT: DIVORCE

COST OF COPY: $5.00

REMARKS: Contact the courthouse in the county in which divorce was granted.

PLACE OF EVENT: VERMONT

EVENT: BIRTH, DEATH, MARRIAGE

COST OF COPY: $7.00

ADDRESS: Vermont Department of Health, Vital Records Section, Box 70, 108 Cherry Street, Burlington, Vermont 05402

WWW: http://www.cit.state.vt.us/

REMARKS: Birth, death, marriage, and divorce records are only available from the Department of Health for 10 years after the event. After 10 years, all records are transferred to the General Service Center, Reference/Research, US Route 2, Middlesex, Drawer 33, Montpelier, Vermont 05633-7601. (802) 828-3286.

For records less than 10 years old, make personal check or money order payable to: **Vermont Department of Health.** For records more than 10 years old, make personal check or money order payable to: **Vermont Public Records Division.**

To verify current fees, the telephone number is: (802) 828-2794.

PLACE OF EVENT: VIRGINIA

EVENT: BIRTH OR DEATH

COST OF COPY: $8.00

ADDRESS: Virginia Department of Health, Office of Vital Records, P.O. Box 1000, Richmond, Virginia 23218-1000

WWW: http://www.vdh.state.va.us/misc/f_08.htm

REMARKS: State office has birth and death records from 1853 to1896, and since June 14, 1912. Only cities of Hampton, Newport News, Norfolk, and Richmond have records between 1896 and June 14, 1912. Write to the Health Department in those cities for records. Also, birth and death records for the period between 1853 and 1896 can be obtained at The Archives Division, The Library of Virginia, 800 East Broad St., Richmond, Virginia 23219-1905.

Any events that occurred in the portion of Virginia that is now West Virginia are recorded in the Archives of the Division of Culture and History, Capital Complex, Cultural Center, 1900 Kanawha Blvd East, Charleston, West Virginia 25305-0300.

You must complete an application form obtained from the Virginia Department of Health. For genealogy purposes, death, marriage, and divorce data becomes public information 50 years from the date of the event, and birth data becomes public information 100 years from the date of event. You must be next of kin to order more recent records.

Check or money order should be made payable to: **State Health Department.** Personal checks are accepted. Allow four weeks for an automated search, and four to six weeks for a manual search.

FAST SERVICE: Call: (804) 644-2537 or (804) 644-2723. Or fax your request to: (804) 644-2550. You will need a major credit card to use this service. In addition to a credit card number and expiration date, the following information is needed: type of certificate you want; your relationship to the person named on the certificate; full name, date and place of event; mother's full and maiden name; father's full name (if requesting birth certificate); full name of husband and wife if requesting a marriage or divorce record; area code and daytime phone number; street address, city/county, state and zip code to send the certificate; fax or send a photo ID of you.

EVENT: MARRIAGE OR DIVORCE

COST OF COPY: $8.00

REMARKS: State has had marriage records since January 1853, and divorce records since January 1918. If not available at the state office, records should be available from the Clerk of court in county or city where marriage license was issued or divorce was granted. County fees vary. To verify current fees, call: (804) 225-5000.

PLACE OF EVENT: VIRGIN ISLANDS

EVENT: BIRTH OR DEATH—ST. CROIX

COST OF COPY: $10.00

ADDRESS: For birth and death records of St. Croix, write to: Department of Health, Vital Statistics, Charles Harwood Memorial Complex, Christiansted, St. Croix, Virgin Islands 00820

WWW: http://www.gov.vi/

REMARKS: Registrar has birth and death records on file since 1840.

For birth and death records make money order payable to: **Department of Health**

EVENT: MARRIAGE OR DIVORCE—ST. CROIX

COST OF COPY: $2.00

ADDRESS: For marriage and divorce records of St. Croix, write to: Chief Deputy Clerk, Family Division, Territorial Court of the Virgin Islands, P.O. Box 929, Christiansted, St. Croix, Virgin Islands 00820.

REMARKS: For marriage and divorce records, make money order payable to: **Territorial Court of the Virgin Islands.**

To verify current fees, for St. Croix, the telephone number is: (340) 773-4050.

EVENT: BIRTH OR DEATH—ST. THOMAS

COST OF COPY: $15.00

ADDRESS: For birth and death records, write to: Vital Statistics, Old Municipal Hospital, St. Thomas, Virgin Islands 00802

REMARKS: Registrar has had birth records on file since July 1906, and death records since January 1906.

Photo identification (i.e., passport, voter registration, driver's license) is now required with the application form.

Money order or business check must be for the exact cost of the certificate and made payable to: **Department of Health.** Personal checks are *not* accepted.

EVENT: MARRIAGE—ST. THOMAS

ADDRESS: For marriage records on St. Thomas, write to: Bureau of Vital Statistics, Virgin Islands Department of Health, Charlotte Amalie, St. Thomas, Virgin Islands 00801

VIRGIN ISLANDS, cont'd.

Certified copies of marriage records are not available. Inquiries will be forwarded to the appropriate office.

To verify current fees for St. Croix, the telephone number is: (340) 774-1734.

EVENT: BIRTH OR DEATH—ST. THOMAS/ST. JOHN

COST OF COPY: $10.00

ADDRESS: For birth and death records on St. Thomas/St. John, write to: Registrar of Vital Statistics, Knud Hansen Complex, Hospital Ground, Charlotte Amalie, St. Thomas, Virgin Islands 00802

EVENT: MARRIAGE OR DIVORCE—ST. THOMAS/ST. JOHN

COST OF COPY: Marriage $2.00
                   Divorce $5.00

ADDRESS: For marriage and divorce records on St. Thomas/St. John, write to: Clerk of the Territorial Court of the Virgin Islands, Family Division, P.O. Box 70, Charlotte Amalie, St. Thomas, Virgin Islands 00801.

REMARKS: Make money order payable to: **Bureau of Vital Statistics.**

To verify current fees on St. Thomas/St. John, the telephone number is: (340) 774-9000, ext 4621.

PLACE OF EVENT: WASHINGTON

EVENT: BIRTH OR DEATH

COST OF COPY: $13.00

ADDRESS: Washington State Vital Records, Department of Health, Center for Health Statistics, P.O. Box 9709, Olympia, Washington 98507–9709

WWW: http://www.doh.wa.gov/ehsphl/chs/cert.htm

REMARKS: State office has had records since July 1907. Most Washington counties offer certified copies of birth certificates from 1954 to present. Select the county where the birth occurred, and contact them directly. To obtain death records before July 1, 1907, or marriage and divorce records before January 1, 1968, contact the County Clerk where the event occurred. Marriage records should be available from the County Clerk where the event occurred. For death, marriage, and divorce records after these dates, contact the state office above.

WASHINGTON, cont'd.

Money order should be made payable to: **Department of Health.** The $13.00 fee is for every 10-year search (death, marriage, or divorce only). In the event no record is found, an $8.00 search fee will be retained for each certificate.

FAST SERVICE: 24 hours a day, call: (360) 236-4313 or fax: (360) 352-2586. Fee is $24.00 plus $10.00 additional for FedEx delivery. You must have EXACT information to order. The Center for Health Statistics will not call you back to verify receipt of your request.

To verify current fees, the telephone number is (360) 236-4300.

EVENT: MARRIAGE OR DIVORCE

COST OF COPY: $13.00

ADDRESS/WWW: Same as Birth or Death

PLACE OF EVENT: WEST VIRGINIA

EVENT: BIRTH OR DEATH

COST OF COPY: $5.00

ADDRESS: Vital Registration Office, Division of Health, State Capitol Complex Bldg. 3, Rm 513, Charleston, West Virginia 25305

WWW: http://www.state.wv.us/

REMARKS: State office has had records since January 1917. For earlier records, write to Clerk of County Court in county where event occurred. County fees vary. Be advised that there was a fire in 1921 that destroyed many records.

Personal check or money order should be made payable to: **Vital Registration.** To verify current fees, the telephone number is (304) 558-2931. Information (304) 558-2931.

EVENT: MARRIAGE OR DIVORCE

COST OF COPY: $5.00

ADDRESS/WWW: Same as Birth or Death

REMARKS: Marriage records since 1921 and divorce records since 1968. If records are not available at the state office, they should be available from the County Clerk in the county where the license was issued or divorce granted. Certified copies are not available from the state.

PLACE OF EVENT: WISCONSIN

EVENT: BIRTH OR DEATH

COST OF COPY: Birth $12.00
Death $7.00

ADDRESS: Wisconsin State Vital Records, Division of Health, 1 West Wilson Street, Rm 158, P.O. Box 309, Madison, Wisconsin 53701-0309

WWW: http://www.dhfs.state.wi.us/vitalrecords/index.htm

REMARKS: State office has scattered records earlier than 1857. Records before October 1, 1907 are very incomplete. For records prior to 1907, you must contact the state office. Not only do counties not have more complete records, they do not have them at all. Prior to 1907, the counties have no records, and the originals are kept with the state.

Only the person named on the birth record, blood relatives, or legal representatives may get a certified copy of a birth certificate. A noncertified copy of a birth certificate is available to anyone who applies. It is similar for a copy of a death record.

Send the following information with your request: a letter noting relationship of person on certificate to person requesting certificate; the reason for requesting the certificate; full name of person on certificate; date of birth or death; city/county of event; parents' name including mother's maiden name for a birth record; for death records, including age at time of death or Social Security Number is helpful but not necessary. Be sure to sign the letter of request, and include a self-addressed stamped envelope. **Note:** Genealogy requests can take up to three months. Other requests will be in the mail within 15 working days.

Additional copies of the same record ordered at the same time are $2.00 each.

Personal check or money order should be made payable to: **Vital Records.**

FAST SERVICE: Fax: (608) 255-2035. Use your credit card, and complete the application form available from above Website or address.

To verify current fees, the telephone number is (608) 266-1371.

EVENT: MARRIAGE

COST OF COPY: $7.00

ADDRESS/WWW: Same as Birth or Death

REMARKS: Records since April 1836. Records before October 1, 1907 are incomplete.

WISCONSIN, cont'd.

EVENT: DIVORCE

COST OF COPY: $7.00

ADDRESS/WWW: Same as Birth or Death

REMARKS: Records since October 1907.

PLACE OF EVENT: WYOMING

EVENT: BIRTH OR DEATH

COST OF COPY: Birth $12.00
Death $9.00

ADDRESS: Wyoming State Vital Records Services, Hathaway Building, Cheyenne, Wyoming 82002

WWW: http://wdhfs.state.wy.us/vital_records/certificate.htm

REMARKS: State office has had records since July 1909. Some counties carry vital records, others do not. Many counties have different offices for handling specific types of vital records. See Appendix for county addresses.

Money order should be made payable to: **Vital Records Services.**

FAST SERVICE: Fax: (307) 635-4103. Credit cards accepted for fee payment by fax are Visa, MasterCard, Discover, and American Express. Requests must include the credit card number and expiration date. There is an additional $5.00 handling charge on each request.

EVENT: MARRIAGE OR DIVORCE

COST OF COPY: $12.00

ADDRESS/WWW: Same as Birth or Death

REMARKS: Records since May 1941. If records are not available at state office, they should be available from the Clerk of District Court in county where marriage license was issued or divorce was granted. County fees vary.

To verify current fees, call (307) 777-7591.

Social Security Administration

The Social Security Administration permits the public to check if a death has occurred for anyone since 1962. Later in this chapter, I will discuss what value knowing the location of death of an individual will have to your search.

Most of you are aware that a Social Security Number is of great use in finding someone. You can find out the Social Security Number of someone through voter's registration records, driving records from certain states, mortgage paperwork that is on file at the county records department, etc. This chapter will contain a source you will be able to use to run Social Security Numbers to obtain an address of an individual. The next two pages will show you that you can find the Social Security Number of your subject by looking through public records, such as a summons and a child-support order.

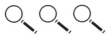

So many times you may find that it is impossible to get someone's Social Security number. Remember, there is no reason to do anything not within the bounds of law to get someone's number. Here is a public document, a subpoena, that contains a subject's Social Security number. Do not overlook this avenue of investigation. Many files contain subpoenas such as divorce files, lawsuits, court appearance summons, and other civil public records.

JUDICIAL CIRCUIT OF
FLORIDA, IN AND FOR
DADE COUNTY.

FAMILY DIVISION: 93-46

CASE NUMBER: _____

State of Florida, Department
of Health and Rehabilitative
Services, Child Support
Enforcement, on behalf of:
PATRICIA COHE
LAURA COHE
by and through LIGIA E COHE
As Custodian and next friend,
Petitioner,

vs.

ALBERTO D COHE
Respondent,
SSN:
271-98-8095

PETITION TO ESTABLISH CHILD SUPPORT AND FOR OTHER RELIEF

COMES NOW the Plaintiff, Department of Health and Rehabilitative Services, et. al., by and through the undersigned attorney, and files this Petition for Child Support and other Relief, and as grounds states as follows:

1. This is an action to establish child support and for other relief for the dependent child(ren):

PATRICIA COHE   BORN ON MARCH 25th 1984 in VENEZUELA
LAURA COHE   BORN ON AUGUST 17th 1982 in VENEZUELA.

2. This Court has personal jurisdiction of the Defendant in that the Defendant is currently or was preceding commencement of this action a resident of the State of Florida.

3. LIGIA E COHE and the child(ren) reside in DADE COUNTY, Florida.

4. Defendant is legally responsible parent of the child(ren).

5. The child(ren) needs and has needed since birth, support from the Defendant who has had the ability to provide support.

6. The Defendant is over 18 years of age and is not a member of the Armed Forces of the United States or its allies.

7. The Department has incurred administrative costs, fees for legal services and court costs in this action which Defendant is able to pay.

8. The child(ren) is or has been a beneficiary of Public Assistance or is otherwise eligible for services of the Department pursuant to Chapter 409, F.S.

9. The participation of the Department and the representation of the undersigned attorney are limited in scope as set forth in s. 409.2564 (5), F.S.

WHEREFORE, the Plaintiff prays that the court will:

1. Determine the Defendant to be a legally responsible parent of the child(ren).

2. Order the Defendant to pay child support pursuant to s. 61.30, F.S., or an amount deemed reasonable by this Court payable through the child support depository plus depository fees.

3. Order the Defendant to pay child support retroactive to date of birth of the child(ren).

4. Determine there is a past period child support in the amount of $1,188.00. as of 12/10/1991, plus any amount paid through the date of the final hearing and require the Defendant to repay the total past period child support.

5. Allow the Department to certify for intercept by the United States Internal Revenue Service any arrears or past period child support owed by Defendant.

When reviewing someone's divorce file, make sure that you look for any Child Support Petitions. These are extremely important documents that contain much information, such as the name of the subject's child. If you are looking for someone and you find an old Child Support Petition, let us say 15 years old, then you may want to look for the children's names and date of births on the Petition because you can find them (remember they are not hiding) using the usual searching means, and they may lead you to your subject. Also note that the Social Security Number is listed on the Petition.

Area Numbers

The following chart may be of assistance to you if you know what your subject's Social Security Number is. The first three digits are *area numbers*. These numbers will indicate what state or territory the subject resided in when they applied for their Social Security card. This information may give you a lead on what area the subject may be in or may have returned to.

001–003	New Hampshire	516–517	Montana
004–007	Maine	518–519	Idaho
008–009	Vermont	520	Wyoming
010–034	Massachusetts	521–524	Colorado
035–039	Rhode Island	525	New Mexico
040–049	Connecticut	526–527	Arizona
050–134	New York	528–529	Utah
135–158	New Jersey	530	Nevada
159–211	Pennsylvania	531–539	Washington
212–220	Maryland	540–544	Oregon
221–222	Delaware	545–573	California
223–231	Virginia	574	Alaska
232–236	West Virginia	575–576	Hawaii
237–246	North Carolina	577–579	District of Columbia
247–251	South Carolina	580	Virgin Islands
252–260	Georgia	581–584	Puerto Rico
261–267	Florida	585	New Mexico
268–302	Ohio	586	Guam, American
303–317	Indiana		Samoa
318–361	Illinois	587–588	Mississippi
362–386	Michigan	589–595	Florida
387–399	Wisconsin	596–599	Puerto Rico
400–407	Kentucky	600–601	Arizona
408–415	Tennessee	602–626	California
416–424	Alabama	627–645	Texas
425–428	Mississippi	646–647	Utah
429–432	Arkansas	648–649	New Mexico
433–439	Louisiana	650–699	Unassigned—for
440–448	Oklahoma		future use
449–467	Texas	700–728	Railroad workers
468–477	Minnesota		through 1963 then,
478–485	Iowa		discontinued
486–500	Missouri	729–799	Unassigned—
501–502	North Dakota		for future use
503–504	South Dakota	800–999	Not valid Social
505-508	Nebraska		Security Numbers
509–515	Kansas		

Social Security Master Death File

I will explain how the Master Death File is accessed because it may prove to be one of the most time-saving and cost-effective techniques you will use.

The Social Security Administration releases an updated list every three months that contains the names of all persons who have died. The information that is available to the public is:

1. **Social Security Number**
2. **First and last name**
3. **Date of birth**
4. **Date of death**
5. **Zip code of exact place of death**
6. **Zip code where the lump sum Death Payment was made**

The total number of persons listed in the Master Death File is currently at 72 million, and includes deaths since 1937. Several companies have bought the magnetic tapes that the Social Security Administration makes available for sale that contain the Master Death File. They have spent $32,000 to convert the tapes over to computer disks, and the quarterly updates cost $1,700.

Here are the various ways in which the Master Death File can be accessed:

1. **By name only**
2. **By name and date of birth**
3. **By Social Security Number**
4. **By name and date of death**
5. **By first name only with date of birth**

If the subject I am trying to find has been missing for more than several years, I will order a check of the Master Death File. If the subject does appear, then I will order a copy of the death record to give to the client as proof that the subject is deceased. Case closed. But the most important use of the Master Death File is to quickly, and with a minimum of information, find a death record of a parent. If I believe that a parent of the subject has died, I will request that a Master Death File record be run on their name. Even though you will usually not have the date of birth, Social Security Number, or even the place of death of the parent, a search can be conducted. Of course, a name like John Smith will not yield good results because of the long list that will be produced. But if you have the year of birth, then the field can be narrowed down considerably.

When I review the Master Death File record of a parent, I look for the zip code that states the place of death. I will order a death certificate and then contact the funeral home that is listed. The funeral home's records will indicate the next of kin, which may be your subject. Even if your subject is not listed, the home address and telephone number of the spouse or other family member will be contained in the funeral home's records. These close relatives may be queried about the location of your subject.

A great way to find your subject is to look for the obituary of a parent. Find out the names of the newspapers that were published at the time of death of the parent. Then check with that newspaper or the public library to order a microfilm copy of the obituary that was printed a few days after the death. The obituary will list the names of the spouse of the deceased and children's names (the female offspring will usually have a married name listed), and the town where they live. Your subject may be listed along with location of residence. If not, then you may have a surviving parent or siblings who may know where your subject is.

Since you now have the place of death of the parent, you may want to contact the probate court of jurisdiction. If the parent had died intestate (no will), there will be a file that contains much information, including the names and addresses of all persons that were paid monies by the probate court for the estate. Since your subject was an offspring, they will be entitled to part of the estate, and the subject's address may be listed along with the amount of money they received.

On many occasions, I have ordered from the probate court a copy of the check that was cashed by a subject. Many times the subject will have their driver's license number listed on the back of the check because they were required to show identification when cashing the check. At the very least, you will know what city the subject's bank is in.

The information that is contained
on the Master Death File is as follows:

St	Soc Sec Num	Last Name	First Name	Birth Date	Death Date	Resi	Zip1	Zip2

St: This indicates what state the subject lived in when they applied for a Social Security Number.

Soc Sec Num: Social Security Number

Last Name: The name that the death benefits list as account holder

First Name: Walt would be Walter, Larry would be Lawrence, and Bob would be Robert—if this is the formal name used by the decedent when they applied for their Social Security Number. A name of Harry could very well be Harry instead of Harold—if this is what was written on the original application.

Birth Date: The full birth date is usually printed on the Master Death File.

Death Date: The exact day is sometimes missing, but the month and year are usually displayed.

Resi: This stands for residence and indicates in which state the death occurred.

Zip1: The zip code in which the death occurred

Zip2: The zip code where the lump sum payment was mailed to

The following sample records of well-known persons will be used to illustrate different information that may or may not appear on the Master Death File.

You can order a copy of a deceased person's Social Security Number Application from the Social Security Administration, which is called an SS-5. As I will discuss below, this document contains much useful information. I have found many fugitives by ordering an SS-5 of the deceased father or relatives of the subject. It gives me information that goes back many years and can lead me to my quarry today. Use the following address to order an SS-5:

> Social Security Administration
> 6401 Security Blvd.
> Baltimore, Maryland 21235

The current fee is $5.00 for a microfilm copy of a person's SS-5 Application. You can supply various types of information to order this application, such as a person's name and date of birth or date of death, or Social Security Number. If you only have the name of the person you want to order an SS-5 Application of, and you are not sure of the person's date of birth, date of death, or Social Security Number, then you may want to order a Master Death File, which I will discuss here.

St	Soc Sec Num	Last Name	First Name	Birth Date	Death Date	Resi	Zip1	Zip2
TN	408-50-1182	Presley	Earl	07/09/1930	03/00/1985	(TN)	38555	
GA	256-48-7374	Presley	Earl	05/08/1936	02/00/1987	(GA)	31904	
MS	428-58-7758	Presley	Eddie	05/25/1934	05/00/1983	(MS)	39501	
WV	232-58-9834	Presley	Edward	01/11/1930	03/00/1983	( )	24830	
AL	424-52-7031	Presley	Edward	07/22/1937	03/00/1980	(AL)	36256	
TN	409-64-5512	Presley	Elmer	08/06/1940	09/22/1990	( )	38134	
* TN	409-52-2002	Presley	Elvis	01/08/1935	*08/16/1977	( )	38116	
MS	425-11-0453	Presley	Elvis	10/24/1957	04/00/1987	(MS)	38858	
TX	455-46-8412	Presley	Ernest	12/24/1930	03/00/1979	( )	76179	

25830 WV Elbert................	38116 TN Memphis..............	38858 MS Nettleton............
31904 GA Columbus...........	38134 TN Memphis..............	39501 MS Gulfport.............
36256 AL Daviston.............	38555 TN Crossville..........	76179 TX Saginaw...............

The above record is a result of a request for all persons with the last name Presley and the first name containing the letter *E* as the first letter. You will notice that in this case, the highlighted Presley does not show a place of death under Zip Code 1, but Zip Code 2 indicates where the lump sum Social Security was sent. For each space on a Master Death File record, there may be no information entered. You can see that there are several spaces above that have no information: death date, Resi, Zip1, and Zip2.

One of the reasons you may want to order an SS-5 of a deceased relative of your subject is to see the real way in which names are spelled. Sometimes you will run into a roadblock where you are trying to find information on the subject's father so that you may be able to track the current location of your subject. Names can be misspelled, and ordering the SS-5 will give you the correct spelling of the names. Remember, when a person applies as a young person for a Social Security Number, they are not thinking of misspelling their name on purpose because they are not hiding from anyone. For example, look at the middle name of Elvis Presley in the following SS-5 application. He spelled it Aron when he was 16 years old. That is the correct spelling of his name.

I did a story about Elvis Presley for a television special years ago. The focus was whether he was truly dead. In my story, I brought out the fact that on the plaque at the top of Elvis Presley's burial site, the name embossed is Elvis Aaron Presley, instead of Elvis Aron Presley. This caused many to speculate that this misspelling was done on purpose by the Presley family to indicate that Elvis was not buried there. Of course, because of autopsy information and medical documentation, we know that he is truly dead. Also, you will note that Elvis got the name Elvis because it was his father Vernon's middle name. And finally, a bit of macabre trivia—you can see from the date of application that Elvis Presley applied for his Social Security Number on Halloween.

St	Soc Sec Num	Last Name	First Name	Birth Date	Death Date	Resi	Zip1	Zip2
MD	215-09-2405	Disney	Walter	03/21/1878	08/00/1967	(MD)	21228	
IL	342-10-3698	Disney	Walter	10/17/1890	05/00/1973	(IL)	61734	
DC	577-07-8270	Disney	Walter	05/31/1894	01/00/1979	(MD)	61734	
NY	110-12-1395	Disney	Walter	08/14/1897	10/00/1980	(FL)	33062	
KY	402-07-4149	Disney	Walter	09/09/1899	06/00/1983	(KY)	40906	
* CA	562-10-0296	Disney	Walter	12/05/1901	*12/00/1966	( )	00000	
TN	413-09-3359	Disney	Walter	03/20/1908	10/00/1972	(TN)	37311	
VA	228-10-8454	Disney	Walter	09/24/1912	03/00/1978	(KY)	40391	24277
KY	401-24-1418	Disney	Walter	09/11/1921	03/00/1972	(KY)	40272	
TN	408-76-5315	Disney	Walter	04/20/1947	09/00/1985	(TN)	37714	

20782 MD Hyattsville.......   37311 TN Cleveland............   40906 KY Barbourville.....
21228 MD Baltimore...........   37714 TN Caryville............   61734 IL Delavan.................
24277 VA Pennington Gap   40272 KY Louisville.........
38062 FL Pompano Beach   40391 KY Winchester.........

The preceding list contains all the Walter Disneys who have died since 1962. When you have a record that does not indicate a place of death, then look at the beginning of the record. The Social Security Number of the highlighted Walter Disney shows that this individual applied for his number in California. This would be where you would start a search for a will that will show the distribution of assets. If this was the father of your subject, in this hypothetical sample, his will would be a good record to review for the address of your subject.

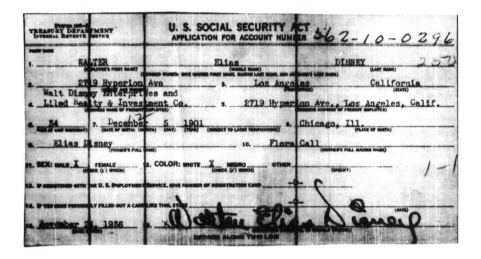

An excellent reason to order your subject's deceased father's or relative's SS-5 Application is because this document will give you all the addresses you may want to investigate. Many times when the hard-to-locate person or fugitive is found, they are located at an old family home. This type of information may not be found on other documents. On Walt Disney's SS-5 Application shown above, you will see that he lived at 2719 Hyperion Avenue in Los Angeles. If this was your subject's father, you would want to see who owned the land, so you would call the Los Angeles County Tax Appraiser's Office. If a relative still owns the house, your subject may be there. This is not far-fetched when you realize that your subject has not been located by you anyplace else. They have to be someplace, and all of your other conventional techniques and methods have failed to this point. Many people who flee (such as persons who owe child support), will go to live with a relative, because they do not have sufficient income and funds to live elsewhere.

You will note on Walt Disney's SS-5 Application that he had listed a business. If this was the SS-5 Application of your subject's deceased father, then you may want to see who owns the company today. It may still be family owned, and the principals of the company, being relatives of your subject, may know of the whereabouts of your subject. Do not overlook what type of business is listed on the SS-5 Application.

In this particular SS-5 Application, please note that a real estate and investment company was put down on the application. This means that your subject's relative had to have licenses to operate the business. Too many times licenses are disregarded as a potential source of information, but they are, in fact, one of the best places to get background information. You know that the applicants for licenses, particularly a real estate license, list much information, including home address, next of kin, names, personal references, business references, criminal arrests and convictions (if any), bank references, schools attended, and much more. Even though this information is not about your subject, it is nevertheless important because it gives you more pieces to the puzzle of where your subject has fled to.

How do you think I find fugitives? *Not* by running driver's licenses, property records, voter's registration records, etc. It is by going deep into the background of my subject and finding out where this person may have felt comfortable enough to return to. The names of relatives of the father will be on license applications, and you may want to contact them. I have located my most impossible-to-find subjects by going back 50 or more years into family history, then talking to people who are second or third cousins who have information no one else has. Remember, *follow the paper trail.* Where do you think I get this information? Yes, from these obscure documents, like the SS-5, which most people do not know exist. Remember, all this information I am discussing here is public information and is available to everyone—not just government officials, attorneys, or private investigators.

There was a book published in 1995 that said that Walt Disney was born in Spain and that the way the Walt Disney signature is written on the Disney logo was a contrived artist's rendering of what the artist thought a Walt Disney signature should look like. There were several other unfounded allegations. I was asked by the media to see if any of the statements in this book about Walt Disney were true. I ordered the SS-5 Application of Walt Disney that you see above. This document clearly demonstrates that Mr. Disney was born in Chicago, Illinois. I know that this had to be good information because Mr. Disney had to provide his birth certificate at the time of application. So the allegation that he was born in Spain was untrue. As is clearly demonstrated on the SS-5 Application on page 3-10, you can see that Mr. Disney did, in fact, sign his name the way you have seen it for years on the Disney logo.

This SS-5 Application was completed by Mr. Disney in 1936, which was well before he became the famous person we know of today. When I say I go back into the past of my subject's father, I also look closely at the maiden name of the wife. Remember, this person is the grandmother of your subject. You now have a new last name to research. The maternal side of a subject's family is overlooked many times because it is difficult to get the maiden name of a person's grandmother. So many people who disappear use, as a hiding place, members of the family that they know searchers will not be aware of. On the SS-5 Application above, Walt Disney's mother's maiden name was Call.

St	Soc Sec Num	Last Name	First Name	Birth Date	Death Date	Resi	Zip1	Zip2
PA	164-09-9984	Eisenhower	David	10/05/1898	02/00/1983	(PA)	19124	33526
PA	185-30-5818	Eisenhower	David	12/25/1914	12/00/1978	(PA)	18102	
PA	204-40-5790	Eisenhower	Dessie	07/29/1881	05/00/1970	(PA)	17044	
PA	205-20-0582	Eisenhower	Dolores	11/01/1906	08/00/1972	(PA)	17834	
PA	182-36-0274	Eisenhower	Dorothy	10/05/1885	12/00/1975	(PA)	19026	
PA	203-20-9135	Eisenhower	Dorothy	09/27/1899	06/00/1979	(PA)	17751	17745
PA	208-18-5794	Eisenhower	Dorothy	10/08/1904	12/00/1981	(PA)	19607	
PA	209-20-7686	Eisenhower	Dorothy	06/17/1927	11/00/1987	(PA)	18201	
OK	440-12-7856	Eisenhower	Dowell	10/16/1903	09/00/1966	(TX)	78401	
* CA	572-64-0315	Eisenhower	Dwight	10/14/1890	*03/00/1969	(PA)	17325	

10504 NY Armonk............	17834 PA Kulpmont............	19607 PA Shillington..........
17044 PA Lewistown............	18102 PA Allentown............	33526 FL Dade City............
17325 PA Gettysburg..........	18201 PA Hazletown............	78401 TX Corpus Christi...
17745 PA Lock Haven.........	19026 PA Drexel Hill..........	
17751 PA Mill Hall................	19124 PA Philadelphia........	

Every Eisenhower with the first name, initial *D*, was requested. If you are not sure of the exact first name of the person you are searching for in the Master Death File list, you may want to use this technique of not giving a first name, but just the first initial of the first name. After you receive the list, then you will be able to review other information and determine the correct decedent. The year of death, state of death, and the issuing state of Social Security Number would have helped find the subject of the search in this hypothetical case.

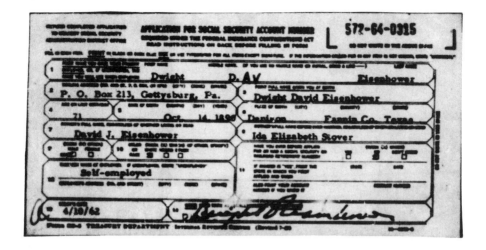

There are many ways that the SS-5 Application will give you more insight into who and what your subject was. In the SS-5 Application shown above of President Dwight Eisenhower, you will note that he was 71 years old when he applied for his Social Security Number for the first time. Now, if this person was the deceased father of your subject, then this would be of interest. Why was a man 71 years old when he first applied for his Social Security Number? Well, the reason is because the subject's father was in the military. That means that if your subject's father was a career military person, then there may be another avenue you can explore to find your subject. Many offspring of military fathers continue the tradition even if for a short period of time. So, if the deceased father was, for instance, in the army, chances are that your subject would have chosen the same branch of service. Please go to the *Federal Records* chapter in this book for addresses of where to write for military records.

St	Soc Sec Num	Last Name	First Name	Birth Date	Death Date	Resi	Zip1	Zip2
KY	402-03-2297	Truman	Harry	10/16/1884	10/00/1966	(KY)	41015	
* MO	448-40-6969	**Truman**	**Harry**	05/08/1884	*12/00/72	(MO)	64050	
PA	170-03-8745	Truman	Harry	05/15/1866	03/00/1973	(PA)	15223	
MI	386-01-1149	Truman	Harry	08/08/1887	07/00/1963	(MI)	00000	
KY	402-20-8745	Truman	Harry	01/27/1890	03/00/1978	(KY)	40205	
WA	535-20-8745	Truman	Harry	10/30/1896	05/00/1980	(WA)	98611	98532
PA	178-05-8291	Truman	Harry	07/04/1897	10/00/1965	(PA)	00000	
MI	367-26-8037	Truman	Harry	03/12/1901	11/00/1978	(OH)	43023	
AZ	527-01-2253	Truman	Harry	02/17/1905	02/00/1968	(CA)	95258	
NY	119-26-6047	Truman	Harry	08/19/1905	02/00/1985	(IN)	47130	

15223 PA Pittsburgh............ 47130 IN Jeffersonville..... 95258 CA Woodbridge........
40205 KY Louisville.......... 49415 MI Fruitport............. 98532 WA Chehalis.............
41015 KY Covington........... 64050 MO Independence... 98611 WA Castle Rock........
43023 OH Granville............. 92646 CA Huntington Beach..

St	Soc Sec Num	Last Name	First Name	Birth Date	Death Date	Resi	Zip1	Zip2
* MO	495-50-5300	**Truman**	**Bess**	02/13/1885	*10/00/1982	(MO)	64050	
WV	234-80-3101	Truman	Bessie	04/18/1889	12/30/1989	(WV)	25276	
IN	305-70-2063	Truman	Bessie	08/07/1889	09/00/1983	(IN)	46806	
OR	542-22-6633	Truman	Bessie	01/15/1893	07/00/1976	(OR)	97034	
OK	445-32-1574	Truman	Bessie	10/05/1936	11/00/1969	(OK)	73502	

27276 WV Spencer..................... 64050 MO Independence.......... 97034 OR Lake Oswego............
46806 IN Fort Wayne............... 73502 OK Lawtow......................

The two Truman Master Death File Records were ordered by name only. There are numerous decedents with the name Harry Truman but if you knew that the person you were searching for was from Missouri, then you would have isolated the focus of your search easily.

You will notice that there is only one Bess Truman who has died since 1962. In this case, you did not need to know what area the person was from.

As I mentioned when discussing the Walt Disney SS-5 Application, employment of the deceased relative is important. You will note that President Truman listed the words *self-employed*. If this was the deceased father of your subject, then you would want to search for occupational licenses so you can review all the information on the license. You are looking for information that will lead you to your missing subject, such as employment and type of business. Also, please remember to check with the probate court to see if the business was handed down through generations—your subject may be the working owner or absentee owner of that business today. The names of other owners of the business will also be listed. You can query them as to the whereabouts of your subject.

It is interesting to note that *Ex-President of the United States* was listed as Harry Truman's former employment. Many times, as I mentioned in my discussion of Elvis Presley, the spelling of the father's name is important. You may have the absolutely most difficult case ever, and you need to research back many years to find out more about the deceased father so you can find your subject today. If you do not have the proper name, your investigation will be hindered.

In the case of President Truman, his real name is Harry, not Harold. If you needed to check the deceased father's past, you would need an exact name. Now after ordering President Truman's SS-5 Application, you can be sure that this was his name. So many times you will be searching records using Harold instead of Harry, or William instead of Bill, or Peter instead of Pete, and you will be searching for the wrong name. You need to be exact, and the SS-5 Application is an excellent source.

As you can see from President Truman's SS-5 Application, he lists *S.* as a middle name. This is incorrect. Harry Truman never had a middle name. When he was a young man he decided to use *S* as a middle name because he believed it made his name more prestigious looking. The *S* is not an initial because it is not an abbreviation for anything. The *S* should stand alone, as a name, without a period, because, as I said, *S* is not an initial. President Truman stated that Harry S. Truman was his full given name at birth, but now you know there was no *S* or *S.* in his name. You will note that Harry Truman was 69 years old when he filled out his first Social Security Application.

St	Soc Sec Num	Last Name	First Name	Birth Date	Death Date	Resi	Zip1	Zip2
PA	203-21-9135	Astaire	Robin	05/05/1898	05/08/1951	(CA)	92008	
CA	563-66-4692	Astaire	Ann	12/22/1878	07/00/1975	(CA)	91202	
* CA	568-05-4206	Astaire	Fred	05/10/1899	*06/00/1987	(CA)	90213	
ME	004-12-2305	Astaire	Theodore	08/12/1913	09/00/1979	(CT)	06503	06511

06503 CT New Haven...........   90213 CA Beverly Hills......

06511 CT New Haven............   91202 CA Glendale...............

The record for the last name Astaire will show that certain names will not produce a lengthy list, which will make your search that much easier. Since 1962, only three people with the name Astaire have died.

It is important to find not only the occupation of the deceased father of your subject, but it is equally important to find out the name of his employer. Many years go by and the names of companies change. As you can see from the SS-5 Application for Fred Astaire, RKO is listed as an employer. If this was the application of the deceased father of your subject, you would want to see if fellow employees remember anything about your subject. You would try to locate the telephone number of RKO through the usual means of telephone books, directory information, and corporation records, etc. But here is the problem: RKO does not exist today. What you would need to do is to check the Tax Appraisers Office for the owner of 780 Gower Street today. This query to the Tax Appraiser's Office will yield the name of Paramount Studios.

The Master Death Record is responsible for the successful resolution of more missing persons cases than any other source. There is no quicker or precise method for ascertaining someone's death. It has been a great tool to use for the past several years. The Social Security Administration will not accept any requests for Master Death File searches. I use a company in Miami that is in the same business I am that charges $33.00 for each name search. This fee covers a list of up to 100 duplicate names returned for each name submitted that you request. The fee for more than 100 duplicate names is $5.00 per hundred.

Research Is Company
P.O. Box 521636
Miami, Florida 33152

Research Is Company does not advertise, as its clients are investigative firms (such as mine), government, and attorneys. However, orders are accepted from the public for the items mentioned here. In fact, you may remember Pam Casey of Northern California who was reunited with her sister after 42 years on *The Maury Povich Show*. She, along with three other families on that particular program, used the Research Investigative Services. Research Is Company has many more services not listed here, such as getting someone's Social Security Number.

Social Security Number Address Update Report

Another service that the Research Is Company provides is the Social Security Number Address Update Report. If you have gleaned your subject's Social Security Number from research, you may submit a request for a search to be conducted on this number.

Any addresses that the subject had used for any dealings with certain businesses, governments, credit card companies, and other entities may be given. This system is perfectly legal because no credit information is given. Research Investigative Services charges a fee of $65.00, and is the only company I know of that will not charge a fee if the computer search fails to return at least one address.

The past few years have brought many investigations that have resulted in the arrests of individuals who had "connections" with persons who worked for the Internal Revenue Service or the Social Security Administration. These individuals had apparently paid money so that they could obtain the Social Security Numbers of people. We cannot stress how important it is that you do not get a subject's Social Security Number by paying a government worker. The federal government considers the person paying money for the Social Security Number of another person guilty of bribery, and prosecutions are handled very aggressively.

Remember, Social Security Numbers can be obtained legally from many sources that are considered public records such as, in many instances, marriage records, divorce records, voter's registration records, driver's licenses in some states, mortgage documents on file in the County Clerk's office, corporate documents on file in the state capitol, fictitious names or DBAs, hunting license applications, fishing license applications, subpoenas, pet licenses, bankruptcy records, FCC license applications, accident applications, arrest records, federal and state tax liens on file in the County Clerk's office, in the documents of lawsuits, worker's compensation files in some states, occupational license applications, etc. Research Is Company will do the research for you and give you the Social Security Number of your subject for $265.00. If they do not provide you with the Social Security Number of your subject, then your money will be refunded. You may prefer to spend the money, but if you have the time, try the many methods that are mentioned here. Getting someone's Social Security Number is just a matter of time and some researching.

If all else fails, Research Is Company will find the person you're looking for, for $325.00 on a *no-trace/no-charge* basis. They will refund your money if your subject cannot be found within 14 days of receiving your check.

Statewide Criminal Checks

The Research Is Company will run a statewide criminal check on your subject for $310.00. If they do not find any record on your subject, the fee will be $95.00, and $210.00 will be refunded to you. Research Is Company will return the results of their investigation to you in approximately 21 days, but they have an expedited service for an additional $125.00 and will mail you the results by overnight mail 48 hours after receiving your order, provided the fee is paid by money order. They cannot do expedited service with personal checks. Each additional state after the first one will be only $140.00, and the fee for no record will be $70.00.

Research Is Company has always done these searches for their clients, but since being listed in books and other publications, they have received so many requests that they have decided to offer their services to the public. Please do not be disappointed if your search comes back with no record, because you can be assured that a complete and comprehensive search is done and the information is only what the state has. **Guarantee:** Research Is Company will refund the money you paid for a statewide criminal check if you ever find that the person had a criminal record in the state they had checked for you and Research Is Company had said there was not a record.

First Name and Date-of-Birth Search

Give Research Is Company a person's first name and date of birth, and they will give you the names of all the people in the United States who have that first name and date of birth, plus they will be giving you their last name and the town they live in. This search is used when you are trying to look for a female from many years ago and you do not know what her married name is. Also, we just did an "impossible" missing persons case for television where we found the twin of a person, and all they had was the date of birth and first name. This is a great search technique that resolves many cases when nothing else will work. Research Is Company will not charge any fee if there are no hits and if they do not give you at least one name with the first name and date of birth you submitted.

Research Is Company makes a nominal charge of $2.00 for 50 names because there are names such as John that will return thousands of results of people with a particular date of birth. They, of course, will contact you and await your instructions if more than 50 same names are returned. A good suggestion for you (if your request is for a common first name) is to pick a state or several states to be run. Of course you do not know where the person is, but with common first names, the list can be extensive.

So, remember when you give the first name and date of birth information to the Research Is Company, they will be giving you the last name and town where your subject lives. They do not furnish street addresses because the sources used by the Research Is Company do not list street addresses. This first name and date-of-birth technique has helped so many people when doing adoption searches because many times the new parents keep the first name of the child. Or if the child is several months old or older, it is often difficult to change the first name. Also, men who want to find their childhood sweetheart use this particular search because they know the name and remember the birthday of the female. Research Is Company charges $360.00 for this service. Try other avenues of searching first, but if there is no other way of finding someone, then you may want to consider using the first name and date-of-birth search.

Active Military Personnel Search

When you cannot find someone and only have a name, no Social Security Number, and no date of birth, you may want to try the Active Military Personnel Roster that Research Is Company has. Just send them the name of your subject, and they will search to see if your subject is currently in the military. You do not need to provide the branch of service. If you look at the following list of names that was run on John Anderson, you will see that this list can sometimes spot a name for you that is not that usual, such as John Campbell Anderson. You will see that at the time this list was run, he was stationed in zip code 92134. You then know there are many records you can run that may lead you to an off-base housing unit he may reside in. He may even be listed in the telephone directory. The important thing is that you may have a child-support order or a legal debt that has to be paid, and now you can contact the branch of service he is in to assist you in your debt collection. Or he may be just an old friend and you can ask the branch of military (which you just narrowed down by this search) to forward a message to him. Sometimes you may have several people with the exact same name, such as John M. Anderson. In this case, you will try to contact both individuals to see which is your subject. Research Is Company's fee for this service is $75.00, and they send the results to you in seven days after receiving your order.

Anderson, John D—Air Force—is stationed in AK 99506

Anderson, John Michael—Army—is stationed in AL 36362

Anderson, John Lewis—Army Guard—is stationed in AL 35611

Anderson, John Dale—Army Reserve—is stationed in AL 35205

Anderson, John E—Air Force—is stationed in AZ 85707

Anderson, John H —Marine Reserve—is stationed in AZ 85009

Anderson, John T—Air Force Reserve—is stationed in AZ 85309

Anderson, John Campbell—Navy—is stationed in CA 92134

Anderson, John F—Air Force Reserve—is stationed in CA 92518

Anderson, John Fitzgerald—Navy Reserve—is stationed in CA 90731

Anderson, John M—Air Force Reserve—is stationed in CA 94535

Anderson, John M—Air Force—is stationed in CA 94535

Anderson, John Miller—Army—is stationed in CA 95813

Anderson, John R—Air Force—is stationed in CA 93524

Anderson, John W—Air Force Guard—is stationed in CA 94545

Anderson John Michael—Navy—is stationed in CT 06349

Anderson, John Edwards—Army—is stationed in DC 20310

Nationwide Telephone Search

Research Is Company has an excellent system for nationwide checks of listed telephone numbers. They charge $42.00 for the first hundred names, and $6.00 for every increment of 100 names thereafter. Research Is Company will run a name such as Robert Hamilton, and the system will respond with every Robert Hamilton who has a **listed** telephone number, plus the address. In some cases, the name will appear with an address and just the area code, indicating an unlisted number, but you now have a location for this person.

This system is of tremendous assistance in cases where people have been missing for a period of time. Many times a subject will move to a different part of the country. After the subject feels comfortable that the search for them is over, they will resume listing their telephone number as they make a move to the mainstream of life. Another use of the nationwide check of a telephone number to a particular name is to find relatives.

Another system that this company offers are files comprising data pertaining to World War II prisoners of war (POWs) from both the Pacific and European theaters. If you know that your subject was a POW, then you may want to access this file or you may want to consider accessing your subject's father's file. The search is run by name. Locating your subject's father is, of course, another technique used in your quest for the location of your subject, and the search will be aided by the information supplied by the POW file. There are more than 175,000 names listed.

World War II POW—European Theater

Morey, Francis R.

Serial Number: (36652216)	Organization: (s53)
Grade Code: (4) Staff Sergeant	Unit Number & Type: (0456-06)
Service Branch: (1) US Army	Area of Casualty: (78) Austria
Service Code #1: (AC) Army Air Corps	Latest Reported Date: 06/06/1945
Residence State: ( ) Unknown	Detained by: (Germany)
Race: ( ) Unknown	Camp Imprisoned: ( ) Unknown location

Francis R. Morey, Staff Sergeant, US Army, was reported taken prisoner in Austria on 12/11/1944. He was imprisoned at a camp in unknown location and was liberated on 06/06/1945.

World War II POW—European Theater

Morey, Howard R.

Serial Number: (06749652)	Unit Number & Type: (0449-06)
Grade Code: (G) Second Lieutenant	Area of Casualty: (72) Germany
Service Branch: (1) US Army	Latest Reported Date: 05/07/1945
Service Code #1: (AC) US Army	Detained by: (Germany)
Residence State: (13) Massachusetts	Camp Imprisoned: (032)
Race: (1) White	Barth-Vogelsang, Prussia
Organization: (215)	

Howard R. Morey, Second Lieutenant, US Army, was reported taken prisoner in Germany on 02/22/1944. He was imprisoned at a camp in Barth-Vogelsang, Prussia, and was liberated on 05/07/45.

World War II POW—Pacific Theater

Wainwright, J.M.

Serial Number: (06002131)
Grade Code: (A) Lt General
Service Branch: (1) US Army
Service Code #1: (USA) Unknown
Service Code #2: (00) Unknown
Date Reported: 05/07/1942
Residence State: (23) New York
Race: (1) White
Organization: (J32)

Unit Number and Type: (7260-41)
Area of Casualty: (45) Philippine
Islands
Latest Reported Date: / /194
Source of Report: (Official)
Status Reported: (8) Was Liberated
Detained By: (Japan)
Camp Imprisoned: (709) Manchuria

J.M. Wainwright, Lt. General, US Army, was taken prisoner on the Philippine Islands on 05/07/1942. He was imprisoned at a camp in Manchuria and was liberated later.

If you are aware of the fact that the subject's father had died in Korea or Vietnam, then a good source is to order a printout of your subject's father's casualty file. This file contains information for every conflict casualty that occurred in the Korean or Vietnam War. There are more than 100,000 listings for these two wars.

Korean Conflict Casualty File

Linton, Robert S.

Military Service: (A) US Army
Country of Casualty: (KR) Korea
Type of Casualty: (A1) Was killed in
Hostile Action
Ref No - Proc Date: (14474L-11/79)
Soc Sec or SVC No: (55079227)
Military Pay Grade: (PVT-E2)
Date of Death: (09/26/51)

Home City: (Cheyenne)
Home State: (28) Nebraska
Date of Birth: (/ /1925)
Cause of Death (') Unknown
Air, Ground, or Sea: (') Unknown
Race: (C) Caucasian
Sex: (M) Male

Robert S. Linton, PVT, US Army was born 1925. His home city was listed as Cheyenne, Nebraska. He was killed in hostile action in Korea on 09/26/51.

Vietnam Conflict Casualty File

Burgess, Stanley Wayne

Military Service: (M) U.S. Marine Corps

Country of Casualty: (VS) South Vietnam

Type of Casualty: (A1) was killed in
    hostile action

Air, Ground, or Sea: (7) Ground Casualty

Ref No-Proc Date: (11256-05/69)

Soc Sec or SVC No: (2412647)

Military Pay Grade: (LCPL-E3)

Date of Death: (05/10/69)

Home City: (Las Vegas)

Service Occupation: (0311)

Date of Birth: (01/24/51)

Cause of Death: (D) Gunshot or Small
    Arms Fire

Race: (C) Caucasian

Religious Affiliate: (00) No Religious
    Preference

Age/Sex/Svc/Marital: (18/Male/01/Single)

Date Tour Begin: (04/25/69)

Body Recovered (') Recovered

Province: (03) Quang Nam

Stanley Wayne Burgess, LCPL, U.S. Marine Corps was born on 01/24/51 and began his tour in Vietnam on 04/25/69. He was killed in hostile action in Quang Nam, South Vietnam, on 05/10/69.

There is much that can be gleaned about the father because you will, in many cases, be able to obtain the father's home city, Social Security Number, marital status, etc., from the printout ordered. Even though the information may be as much as 40 years old, you will be able to contact relatives who may live in the hometown. They may know your subject. This technique is not used, of course, if you know the subject's family.

The World War II POW list of the Pacific and European theaters and the Korean and Vietnam Conflict Casualty Files will all be searched for the one fee for the name you supply. You do not need to furnish a date of birth or Social Security Number. This search is conducted strictly by name. The cost is $40.00 for a list of up to 100 persons with the same name you submit.

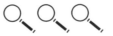

County Records

here are a myriad of public records that can be accessed on the county level. The following is a list of the types of records you will find that may contain your subject's name and address:

Assumption Agreement
Abstract
Affidavit
Agreement
Agreement for Deed
Agreement Not to Encumber
Amended Judgment
Assignment
Assignment of Judgment
Assignment of Lien
Assignment of Mortgage
Assignment of Proprietary Lease
Breach of Agreement
Breach of Contract
Breach of Lease
Certificate
Certificate of Additional
   Intangible Tax
Certificate of Approval

Certificate of Merger
Certificate of Organization
Certificate of Title
Change of Name
Condominium Rider
Corporation
Cost Judgment
Declaration of Trust
Deed
Discharge
Disclaimer
Dismissal
Divorce
Easement
Easement Deed
Eminent Domain
Estate Tax Closing Letter
Estate Tax Lien
Federal Tax Lien

Fictitious Name
Foreclosure of Chattel Mortgage
Guardianship
Incompetency
Incorporation
Involuntary Bankruptcy
Judgment
Lease
Levy
Lien
Modification Agreement
Mortgage Modification
Agreement
Name Restoration
Nontaxable Certificate or Receipt
Notice of Federal Tax Lien
Notice of Lis Pendens
Notice of Tax Lien (State)
Partial Release of Lien
Personal Representative's Deed
Power of Attorney
Public Defender's Claim
Quit Claim Deed
Restrictions (Covenants)

Receipt of Advance
Release of Estate Tax
Release of Federal Tax Lien
Release of Lien (Mechanic's Lien)
Resolution
Restoration of Incompetency
Restored Corporation
Revocation of Power of Attorney
Satisfaction of Final Decree
Satisfaction of Judgment
Satisfaction or Release of Lien
Satisfaction or Release of
    Mortgage
Satisfaction of Tax Executions
Separation
Support Agreement
Tax Warrant
Title Opinion
Trust Agreement
Trustee Resignation
Voluntary Bankruptcy
Warranty Deed
Writ of Garnishment

You may search for any of these records with just the name of your subject. You will note that the list contains public documents that range from federal and state tax liens to writs of garnishment.

For your convenience, a list of 3,200 county mailing addresses are listed in the Appendix at the back of this book.

Voter's Registration

Voter's registration information is available upon written request. Write to the county you believe your subject may have been or is registered in.

The example shown will clearly illustrate how easy it is to ascertain the subject's date of birth and home address. In this case, the only information I had was that the subject named Lub lived in Baldwin, New York, at one time. I was not supplied a first name. I wrote to the Board of Elections of the county of jurisdiction for Baldwin. I sent a nominal fee of $3.00, because this is the average cost of requesting a voter's registration record.

I requested that I be sent the voter's registration information of every person named Lub in Baldwin. In this case, I was fortunate that my request was for an unusual name.

The response I was sent stated that the potential subject, Lub, did not live in Baldwin and had moved in 1985. The potential subject's new address was 140 Larch Street, Wantagh, New York. The response also included the date of birth of the potential subject. Since I was aware that my subject had been in a serious accident on a certain date and at a certain location, I ordered this potential subject's driving record. The accident date and location that I had been supplied with matched what was listed on the driving record.

To be able to write one letter and be provided with a full name for the subject makes this one of the best searching techniques.

OFFICIAL RECEIPT

BOARD OF ELECTIONS   19308

18326

COUNTY OF NASSAU
MINEOLA, NEW YORK 11501

July 25 19 91

$ 3 00/100

Received of _____

_____ three _____ Dollars

For _____ research request _____

COMMISSIONERS OF ELECTIONS

By L. Tabky

Clerk

John W. Matthews, Secretary
Democratic Commissioner

Sinita Walker, President
Republican Commissioner

BOARD OF ELECTIONS
ADMINISTRATION BUILDING
400 COUNTY SEAT DRIVE
MINEOLA, L.I., NEW YORK 11501
(516) 535-2411

July 24, 1991

RE: Lub

To Whom It May Concern:

A letter was received in this office requesting information on the above mentioned, possibly residing in Baldwin, New York.

A search of our official records shows that there was a Kathleen J. Lub who moved out of Baldwin in 1985 and now resides from 140 Larch Street, Wantagh, New York.

Her date of birth is 9/30/56.

Enclosed, is your receipt for research fee. Thank you.

Very truly yours,

Edward chut / lt Rep. Member

_____ Dem. Member
Record Access Officers

EH/NAS: lt
enc.

The following are some other records that may assist you in learning more about your subject, thus making the search for the subject's location easier.

Occupational Licenses

Many counties require that a person who has any type of independent business apply for an occupational or vendor's license. These records are usually filed in three ways:

1. By name
2. By address
3. By company name

You may want to request that a search be done by address or company name if you have this information. The subject may not be listed if you order the search to be conducted by name because the subject could have changed their name by just a few letters or assumed a whole new identity. When accessing by address or company name, you will be able to evaluate if any of the principals of the company fit the profile of the person you believe your subject to be.

Pet Licenses

Persons that arrange many details of their lives to avoid being discovered will overlook the fact that the license they had issued for their pet is public record. Write to the county you believe your subject resides in for a list of all pet licenses issued in your subject's name, or a spouse.

Tax Collector/Property Appraiser

The tax collector will have an alphabetical listing of all persons who paid property taxes. Request that a search be conducted, and specify the years. The tax collector maintains records that go back in time longer than any other record. The necessity of title companies to trace a complete history of property ownership is the reason these records are maintained for perpetuity.

Property may be owned by your subject, and a review of the tax bill may show that the address it is being sent to is out of state or in another country.

You may want to question the present owners of any property your subject had owned at one time. Your subject may hold a mortgage on the property, and there may be constant contact between the present owners and your subject.

Small Claims Court

If a search of county records reveals that your subject had a case filed in small claims court, you will want to order the complete file. The file will contain the address of the subject, any witnesses the subject subpoenaed to court, and details about the court case. You may want to review the subpoena the subject was served if the subject had been a defendant in the case. The subpoena will have noted the address the subject had been served at. If the subject had been trying to conceal their whereabouts, but was found by a process server, then you will want to pay special attention to this address, because it may be different from the listed home address.

When an individual or company has a case decided in their favor in Small Claims Court, they are entitled to file a lien against any property that the defendant owns, if the damages are not paid.

The plaintiff, in many instances, is made aware of the ownership of property by the defendant through a questionnaire that the judge, at the request of the plaintiff, ordered the defendant to answer. The questions ask about property ownership, stocks, bank account locations, etc. You may review this questionnaire, which is part of the court file. You will be able to glean a location of your subject by checking the current address from the aforementioned.

Fictitious Names

Your subject may own a business but did not want to incorporate. Your subject would be required to apply for a fictitious name if they wanted to open a business account at a bank. Your subject could have a house painting, landscaping, accounting, hotdog vending cart, or any type of business, and they will have filed a fictitious name with the county. The application on file will provide you with home and business addresses.

Write to the county asking that a search be conducted. Provide the subject's full name and the years you want searched.

Pending Litigation

If you have information that your subject had been at fault in an automobile accident, then you will want to find out in what county the accident occurred. Write to that county once a month, and eventually a suit may be filed, naming your subject as the defendant. If an action is filed, you will want to order the file. As noted previously, check the file for the address that your subject was served at. Paternity suits, judgments, tax liens, and foreclosures are some actions that may not be listed now, but are public records you may be able to anticipate the filing of.

APPLICATION FOR
REGISTRATION OF FICTITIOUS NAME

Section 1

1. Investments Unlimited
   Fictitious Name to be Registered

2. 5686 36th Street
   Mailing Address of Business
   White Plains,   32801

3. County of _____Westchester_____

4. City of _White Plains_, Florida __32801__
5. FEI Number: _____   Zip Code

This space for office use only

A. Owner(s) of Fictitious Name if Individual(s) (use additional sheets if necessary):

Section 2

1. Rogers, Harold
   Last   First   M.I.

   15672 Emeet Street
   Address

   Orlando, Florida   32801
   City   State   Zip Code

   SS# 251-28-2982

2. Hadesty, Nancy
   Last   First   M.I.

   15672 Emeet Street
   Address

   Orlando, Florida   32801
   City   State   Zip Code

   SS# 325-78-2789

B. Owner(s) of Fictitious Name if Corporation(s) (use additional sheets if necessary):

1. N/A
   Corporate Name

   Address

   City   State   Zip Code

   Corporate Document Number: _____
   FEI Number: _____
   □ Applied for   □ Not Applicable

2. N/A
   Corporate Name

   Address

   City   State   Zip Code

   Corporate Document Number: _____
   FEI Number: _____
   □ Applied for   □ Not Applicable

Section 3

I (we) the undersigned, being the sole (all the) party(ies) owning interest in the above fictitious name, certify that the information indicated on this form is true and accurate. I (we) further certify that the fictitious name shown in Section 1 of this form has been advertised at least once in a newspaper as defined in chapter 50, Florida Statutes, in the county where the applicant's principal place of business is located. I (we) understand that the signature(s) below shall have the same legal effect as if made under oath. (At Least One Signature Required)

Harold H. Rogers
Signature of Owner   Date

Phone Number: 407-982-9276

Nancy Hardesty
Signature of Owner   Date

Phone Number: 407-982-9276

Power of Attorney

Pay special attention to any filing that involves your subject that is listed as Power of Attorney. You will want to know the person's name that your subject gave Power of Attorney to. If you are having difficulty in finding anything under your subject's name, this may be the reason why. Persons that are trying to avoid detection will often give Power of Attorney to a family member or close friend. That person will then conduct all business transactions on behalf of your subject, thus giving the subject the benefit of not having their name listed in public records.

Asset Checks

If you have a judgment against an individual or a business, then you may wish to conduct an asset check to determine if any property exists that can be attached by lien. You may use the addresses in this manual to check for ownership of automobiles, trucks, motorcycles, recreational vehicles, boats, aircraft, real estate, etc.

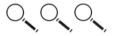

State Records

T he state licenses many professions, trades, and crafts. Write to the Secretary of State (see addresses in Chapter 8), and submit your subject's name to be searched for any licensure by the state. The following are some occupations that may require licensing.

Aircraft Mechanics
Airports
Alarm Contractors
Alarm Installers
Auctioneers
Auto Inspectors
Auto Wreckers
Bankers
Barbers
Bill Collectors
Builders/Carpenters
Building Contractors
Building Wreckers
Carpet Cleaners
Certified Public Accountants
Embalmers
Investigators

Notary Publics
Pawnbrokers
Pest Controllers
Pet Groomers
Pharmacists
Pilots
Real Estate Agents and Brokers
Scrap Dealers
Security Dealers
Security Guards
Stockbrokers
Surveyors
Talent Agents
Teachers
Therapists
Veterinarians
X-ray Technicians

If your subject is licensed by the state for any of the above occupations or any others not listed, then you will be able to receive, at least, the following information from the licensing board: work and home address; length of time the subject has been licensed; the schools attended to be certified (if applicable); date of birth; and any complaints lodged against the subject.

Of course, the most important information will be the addresses that you are given, but you may want to take special note of any complaints filed. If the addresses listed do not prove to be valid, you will want to review the complaint file. A court or hearing date may be scheduled in the near future, and the exact date and location will be listed. You can then meet your subject when he or she appears for the complaint hearing.

The employer of the subject will be part of the information the licensing department will be giving you. You now have a location that you can write to or visit.

Colleges and Universities

There are more than 3,500 colleges and universities in the United States. If you are aware of the institution of higher learning that your subject attended, then inquiring about "directory information" may yield much information. The term "directory information" is used to describe the information that the school will release to the public about the student.

The following is a quote from Florida State University regarding the school's "directory information" policy:

*Prior consent of the student is **not required** for disclosure* of portions of the educational record defined by the institution as *directory information*, which can be released via official media of the University:

Name, date, and place of birth
Local address
Permanent address
Telephone listing
Classification
Major field of study
Participation in official university activities and sports
Weight and height of members of athletic teams
Dates of attendance at the university

Degrees, honors, and awards received
The most recently attended educational institution

Stanford University's *directory information* policy is quoted as follows:

The University regards the following items of information as *directory information*, i.e., information **available to any person** upon specific request:

Student name
Sex
Class status
Major
Local address and/or Stanford Post Office Box number
Local phone number
Permanent or legal address
Summer address
Summer phone number
Residence assignment and room or apartment number
Stanford student identification number
Specific quarters or semesters of registration at Stanford
Stanford degree(s) awarded and date(s), degree major(s)
University degree honors
Institution attended immediately prior to Stanford

The above information that is released is obviously about currently enrolled students. You may contact the alumni association, and you will receive the same information regarding former students.

Even though the permanent address listed may be years old, you may want to check the owner of record with the tax collector to see if the family of your subject is still the owner. Also, do not overlook the summer residence that is listed. The address will, in many instances, prove to be a vacation home that the subject's family still owns.

The date of birth and place of birth is of obvious value. You now have an exact date of birth that can be utilized to access the driving record of the subject. Even though years have passed, you may want to try calling the telephone numbers listed. In many instances, these numbers will still be good numbers that will enable you to contact the family.

Hunting and Fishing Licenses

Even if your subject is trying to avoid detection, the subject will still want to be issued a license for hunting or fishing, if this is their sport. The reason the subject will want to have a current license is to avoid being arrested by a game warden or other law enforcement official when enjoying their sport. Write to the state, and submit a request asking that an alpha search be conducted on your subject so that you may ascertain if they do have a hunting or fishing license.

If you are successful with your inquiry, you will receive the subject's current address, date of birth, and the current status of the license. If the license has been expired for some time, then you will want to use the date of birth that you received and order the subject's driving record.

ALABAMA

http://www.state.al.us/
Hunting and Fishing Licenses
Department of Conservation
State of Alabama
State Administrative Building
Montgomery, Alabama 36130

ALASKA

http://www.state.ak.us/
Hunting and Fishing Licenses
State of Alaska
P.O. Box 6188 Annex
Anchorage, Alaska 99502

ARIZONA

http://www.gf.state.az.us
Hunting and Fishing Licenses
Game and Fish Department
State of Arizona
2221 West Greenway Road
Phoenix, Arizona 85023

ARKANSAS

http://www.agfc.state.ar.us
Hunting and Fishing Licenses
State of Arkansas
2 Natural Resources Drive
Little Rock, Arkansas 72205

CALIFORNIA

http://www.dfg.ca.gov
Hunting and Fishing Licenses
State of California
P.O. Box 11319
Sacramento, California 95853

COLORADO

http://www.dnr.state.co.us/edo/-
wildlife.html
Hunting and Fishing Licenses
Division of Parks and Outdoor Recreation
State of Colorado
13787 South Highway 85
Littleton, Colorado 80125

CONNECTICUT

http://www.state.ct.us/
Hunting and Fishing Licenses
State of Connecticut
165 Capitol Avenue
Hartford, Connecticut 06106

DELAWARE

http://www.dnrec.state.de.us/fandw.htm
Hunting and Fishing Licenses
Division of Fish and Wildlife
State of Delaware
P.O. Box 1401
Dover, Delaware 19903

DISTRICT OF COLUMBIA

http://www.washingtondc.gov/
Hunting and Fishing Licenses
District of Columbia
550 Water Street, S.W.
Washington, DC 20024

FLORIDA

http://www.state.fl.us/gsd/
Hunting and Fishing Licenses
Department of Natural Resources
State of Florida
3900 Commonwealth Boulevard
Tallahassee, Florida 32399

GEORGIA

http://www.state.ga.us/
Hunting and Fishing Licenses
Department of Natural Resources
State of Georgia
270 Washington Street, S.W.
Atlanta, Georgia 30034

HAWAII

http://www.state.hi.us/
Hunting and Fishing Licenses
State of Hawaii
79 South Nimitz Highway
Honolulu, Hawaii 96813

IDAHO

http://www.state.id.us/
Hunting and Fishing Licenses
State of Idaho
2177 Warm Springs Avenue
Boise, Idaho 83720

ILLINOIS

http://dnr.state.il.us/
Hunting and Fishing Licenses
Conservation Department
State of Illinois
524 South Second Street
Springfield, Illinois 62701

INDIANA

http://www.state.in.us/dnr/fishwild/index.htm
Hunting and Fishing Licenses
Department of Natural Resources
State of Indiana
402 West Washington St.
Indianapolis, Indiana 46204

IOWA

http://www.state.ia.us/
Hunting and Fishing Licenses
State Conservation Commission
State of Iowa
Wallace Building
Des Moines, Iowa 50319

KANSAS

http://www.kdwp.state.ks.us/
Hunting and Fishing Licenses
Kansas Department of Wildlife
R.R. No. 2, Box 54A
Pratt, Kansas 67124

KENTUCKY

http://www.kfwis.state.ky.us
Hunting and Fishing Licenses
Department of Natural Resources
1 Game Farm Road
Frankfort, Kentucky 40601

LOUISIANA

http://www.state.la.us/
Hunting and Fishing Licenses
Department of Wildlife and Fisheries
State of Louisiana
P.O. Box 14796
Baton Rouge, Louisiana 70898

MAINE

http://www.state.me.us/ifw/homepage.htm
Hunting and Fishing Licenses
Department of Fisheries and Wildlife
State of Maine
284 State Street
Augusta, Maine 04333

MARYLAND

http://www.state.md.us/
Hunting and Fishing Licenses
Department of Natural Resources
State of Maryland
P.O. Box 1869
Annapolis, Maryland 21404–1869

MASSACHUSETTS

http://www.state.ma.us/
Hunting and Fishing Licenses
Commonwealth of Massachusetts
100 Nashua Street
Boston, Massachusetts 02114

MICHIGAN

http://www.state.mi.us/
Hunting and Fishing Licenses
State of Michigan
7064 Crowner Drive
Lansing, Michigan 48918

MINNESOTA

http://www.state.mn.us/
Hunting and Fishing Licenses
Department of Natural Resources
State of Minnesota
500 Lafayette Road
Saint Paul, Minnesota 55146

MISSISSIPPI

http://www.state.ms.us/its/msportal.nsf?Open
Hunting and Fishing Licenses
Department of Wildlife Conservation
P.O. Box 451
Jackson, Mississippi 39205

MISSOURI

http://www.state.mo.us/
Hunting and Fishing Licenses
Department of Conservation
State of Missouri
2901 West Truman Boulevard
Jefferson City, Missouri 65102

MONTANA

http://www.fwp.state.mt.us
Hunting and Fishing Licenses
State of Montana
1420 East Sixth Avenue
Helena, Montana 59620

NEBRASKA

http://www.ngpc.state.ne.us/fish/fish-ing.html
Hunting and Fishing Licenses
State Game and Parks Commission
State of Nebraska
2200 North 33rd Street
Lincoln, Nebraska 68503

NEVADA

http://colorado.state.nv.us/cnr/nvwildlife
Hunting and Fishing Licenses
Department of Wildlife
State of Nevada
P.O. Box 10678
Reno, Nevada 89520

NEW HAMPSHIRE

http://www.wildlife.state.nh.us
Hunting and Fishing Licenses
State of New Hampshire
10 Hazen Drive
Concord, New Hampshire 03305

NEW JERSEY

http://www.state.nj.us/
Hunting and Fishing Licenses
State of New Jersey
P.O. Box 7068
West Trenton, New Jersey 08625

NEW MEXICO

http://www.state.nm.us/
Hunting and Fishing Licenses
Natural Resources Department
State of New Mexico
P.O. Box 1147
Santa Fe, New Mexico 87504

NEW YORK

http://www.dec.state.ny.us/
Hunting and Fishing Licenses
State of New York
Empire State Plaza
Albany, New York 12238

NORTH CAROLINA

http://www.state.nc.us/
Hunting and Fishing Licenses
Wildlife Resources Commission
State of North Carolina
512 North Salisbury Street
Raleigh, North Carolina 27604

NORTH DAKOTA

http://www.state.nd.us/
Hunting and Fishing Licenses
State Game and Fish Department
State of North Dakota
2121 Lovett Avenue
Bismarck, North Dakota 58505

OHIO

http://www.dnr.state.oh.us/odnr/wildlife/
index.html
Hunting and Fishing Licenses
Department of Natural Resources
State of Ohio
Fountain Square
Columbus, Ohio 43224

OKLAHOMA

http://www.state.ok.us/
Hunting and Fishing Licenses
State of Oklahoma
2501 North Lincoln
Oklahoma City, Oklahoma 73194

OREGON

http://www.dfw.state.or.us
Hunting and Fishing Licenses
State of Oregon
3000 Market Street, N.E.
Salem, Oregon 97310

PENNSYLVANIA

http://www.state.pa.us/
Hunting and Fishing Licenses
Commonwealth of Pennsylvania
3532 Walnut Street
Harrisburg, Pennsylvania 17105

PUERTO RICO

http://fortaleza.govpr.org/
Hunting and Fishing Licenses
Commonwealth of Puerto Rico
GPO Box 2829
San Juan, Puerto Rico 00936

RHODE ISLAND

http://www.state.ri.us/dem/regs.htm#FandW
Hunting and Fishing Licenses
State of Rhode Island
22 Hayes Street
Providence, Rhode Island 02903

SOUTH CAROLINA

http://www.state.sc.us/
Hunting and Fishing Licenses
State of South Carolina
P.O. Box 11710
Columbia, South Carolina 29211

SOUTH DAKOTA

http://www.state.sd.us/state/executive/gfp/
index.htm
Hunting and Fishing Licenses
State of South Dakota
412 West Missouri Street
Pierre, South Dakota 57501

TENNESSEE

http://www.state.tn.us/
Hunting and Fishing Licenses
Tennessee Wildlife Resources Agnecy
Ellington Agriculture Center
Nashville, Tennessee 37204

TEXAS

http://www.state.tx.us/
Hunting and Fishing Licenses
State of Texas
4200 Smith School Road
Austin, Texas 78744

UTAH

http://www.state.ut.us/
Hunting and Fishing Licenses
State of Utah
1095 Motor Avenue
Salt Lake City, Utah 84116

VERMONT

http://www.anr.state.vt.us/fw/fwhome/-
index.htm
Hunting and Fishing Licenses
State of Vermont
103 Main Street
Waterbury, Vermont 05676

VIRGINIA

http://www.state.va.us/
Hunting and Fishing Licenses
Commission of Game and Inland Fisheries
State of Virginia
P.O. Box 11104
Richmond, Virginia 23230

VIRGIN ISLANDS

http://www.virginisles.com/
Hunting and Fishing Licenses
Department of Natural Resources
State of Virgin Islands
Nisky Center, Suite 231
St. Thomas, U.S. Virgin Islands 00803

WASHINGTON

http://www.wa.gov/wdfw
Hunting and Fishing Licenses
Department of Natural Resources
State of Washington
P.O. Box 43135
Olympia, Washington 98504

WEST VIRGINIA

http://www.state.wv.us/
Hunting and Fishing Licenses
Department of Natural Resources
State of West Virginia
1800 Washington Street, East
Charleston, West Virginia 25305

WISCONSIN

http://www.state.wi.us/
Hunting and Fishing Licenses
Department of Natural Resources
State of Wisconsin
P.O. Box 7921
Madison, Wisconsin 53707

WYOMING

http://gf.state.wy.us
Hunting and Fishing Licenses
Game and Fish Department
State of Wyoming
5400 Bishop Boulevard
Cheyenne, Wyoming 82002

South Dakota

GREAT FACES. GREAT PLACES.

DEPARTMENT OF GAME, FISH AND PARKS

Licensing Office
412 West Missouri
Pierre, South Dakota 57501
(605) 773-3393

March 2, 1993

Dear Joseph:

We find no record in our current files of a Robert K. Pavella
having any kind of South Dakota hunting or fishing license.

Sincerely,

Chuck Schlueter
Administrative Asst.

If you are refused public records on the state level, then you will want to write to the Attorney General of that state. Remember, custodians of the records must comply with the public records law, and the Attorney General will enforce it. Always register a complaint when you are not given records. The next time you go in for records, the personnel you complained about will give you good service since you had complained to the Attorney General.

Here is a list of addresses and telephone numbers for State Attorney Generals:

ALABAMA

http://www.ago.state.al.us
State House, 3rd Floor
11 South Union Street
Montgomery, Alabama 36104-3760
(334) 242-7300

ALASKA

http://www.state.ak.us/
123 Fourth Street, 6th Floor
Diamond Court House
Juneau, Alaska 99801
(907) 465-3600

ARIZONA

http://www.state.az.us/
1275 West Washington Street
Phoenix, Arizona 85007
(602) 542-4266

ARKANSAS

http://www.ag.state.ar.us
323 Center Street
200 Tower Building
Little Rock, Arkansas 72201
(501) 682-2007

CALIFORNIA

http://caag.state.ca.us
1300 I Street
P.O. Box 944255
Sacramento, California 94244-2550
(916) 323-5370

COLORADO

http://www.state.co.us/gov_dir/dol/-
index.htm
1525 Sherman Street, 5th Floor
Denver, Colorado 80203
(303) 866-4500

CONNECTICUT

http://www.cslnet.ctstateu.edu/attygenl
55 Elm Street
P.O. Box 120
Hartford, Connecticut 06141-0120
(860) 566-2026

DELAWARE

http://www.state.de.us/attgen
Carvel State Office Building
820 North French Street
Wilmington, Delaware 19801
(302) 577-8338

DISTRICT OF COLUMBIA

http://www.washingtondc.gov/agencies
Office of the Corporation Counsel
441 4th Street, N.W.,
Room 1060 North
Washington, DC 20001
(202) 727-6248

FLORIDA

http://legal.firn.edu/
The Capitol Building
Plaza Level, Suite 01
Tallahassee, Florida 32399-1050
(904) 487-1963

GEORGIA
http://www.state.ga.us/
40 Capitol Square
Atlanta, Georgia 30334-1300
(404) 656-4585

HAWAII
http://www.state.hi.us/ag/
425 Queen Street
Honolulu, Hawaii 96813
(808) 586-1282

IDAHO
http://www2.state.id.us/ag/
700 West Jefferson Street
P.O. Box 83720
Boise, Idaho 83720-0010
(208) 334-2400

ILLINOIS
http://www.ag.state.il.us/
James R. Thompson Center
100 West Randolph Street,
12th Floor
Chicago, Illinois 60601
(312) 814-2503

INDIANA
http://www.ai.org/atty_gen/
Indiana Government Center South,
8th Floor
402 West Washington Street
Indianapolis, Indiana 46204
(317) 233-4386

IOWA
http://www.state.ia.us/government/ag
Hoover State Office Building,
2nd Floor
Des Moines, Iowa 50319
(515) 281-3053

KANSAS
http://www.ink.org/public/ksag/
Judicial Building
301 SW 10th Street
Topeka, Kansas 66612
(913) 296-2215

KENTUCKY
http://www.law.state.ky.us
Capitol Building, Suite 116
700 Capitol Avenue
Frankfort, Kentucky 40601
(502) 564-7600

LOUISIANA
http://www.laag.com
300 Capitol Drive
P.O. Box 94005
Baton Rouge, Louisiana 70804
(504) 342-7013

MAINE
http://www.state.me.us/ag/
Six State House Station
Augusta, Maine 04333
(207) 626-8800

MARYLAND
http://www.oag.state.md.us
200 Saint Paul Place
Baltimore, Maryland 21202-2021
(410) 576-6300

MASSACHUSETTS
http://www.magnet.state.ma.us/ag
One Ashburton Place
Boston, Massachusetts 02108
(617) 727-2200

MICHIGAN
http://www.state.mi.us/
Law Building, 7th Floor
P.O. Box 30212
525 West Ottawa Street
Lansing, Michigan 48909-0212
(517) 373-1110

MINNESOTA

http://www.ag.state.mn.us
102 State Capitol
St. Paul, Minnesota 55155
(612) 296-6196

MISSISSIPPI

http://www.ago.state.ms.us
450 High Street
Jackson, Mississippi 39201
(601) 359-3692

MISSOURI

http://www.ago.state.mo.us
207 W. High Street
Supreme Court Building
Jefferson City, Missouri 65101
(573) 751-3321

MONTANA

http://www.doj.mt.gov
215 N. Sanders
P.O. Box 201401
Helena, Montana 59620-1401
(406) 444-2026

NEBRASKA

http://www.nol.org/home/ago
2115 State Capitol Building
Lincoln, Nebraska 68509
(402) 471-2682

NEVADA

http://www.state.nv.us/ag
100 North Carson Street
Carson City, Nevada 89701-4717
(702) 687-4170

NEW HAMPSHIRE

http://www.state.nh.us/nhdoj
33 Capitol Street
Concord, New Hampshire 03301
(603) 271-3658

NEW JERSEY

http://www.state.nj.us/lps
Dept. of Law and Public Safety
Office of Attorney General
Richard J. Hughes Justice Complex
CN 080
Trenton, New Jersey 08625
(609) 292-4925

NEW MEXICO

http://www.state.nm.us/
407 Galisteo Street, #260
Santa Fe, New Mexico 87501
(505) 827-6000

NEW YORK

http://www.oag.state.ny.us
N.Y. State Department of Law
The Capitol
Albany, New York 12224
(518) 474-7330

NORTH CAROLINA

http://www.jus.state.nc.us
2 E. Morgan Street
Raleigh, North Carolina 27601
(919) 733-3377

NORTH DAKOTA

http://www.state.nd.us/ndag
State Capitol
600 East Boulevard Avenue
Bismarck, North Dakota 58505-0040
(701) 328-2210

OHIO

http://www.ag.ohio.gov
Rhodes Tower
30 East Broad Street, 17th Floor
Columbus, Ohio 43215
(614) 466-4320

OKLAHOMA

http://www.oag.state.ok.us
2300 North Lincoln Boulevard
Suite 112
Oklahoma City, Oklahoma 73105
(405) 521-3921

OREGON

http://www.doj.state.or.us
1162 Court Street, NE
Salem, Oregon 97310
(503) 378-6002

PENNSYLVANIA

http://www.attorneygeneral.gov
Strawberry Square, 16th Floor
Harrisburg, Pennsylvania 17120
(717) 787-3391

RHODE ISLAND

http://www.riag.state.ri.us/
150 South Main Street
Providence, Rhode Island 02903
(401) 274-4400

SOUTH CAROLINA

http://www.scattorneygeneral.org
1000 Assembly Street
Columbia, South Carolina 29202
(803) 734-3970

SOUTH DAKOTA

http://www.state.sd.us/attorney/attor-
ney.html
500 East Capitol
Pierre, South Dakota 57501
(605) 773-3215

TENNESSEE

http://www.attorneygeneral.state.tn.us
500 Charlotte Avenue, Suite 114
Nashville, Tennessee 37243
(615) 741-6474

TEXAS

http://www.oag.state.tx.us
209 W. 14th Street
Austin, Texas 78701
(512) 463-2191

UTAH

http://www.state.ut.us/
236 State Capitol
Salt Lake City, Utah 84114
(801) 538-1326

VERMONT

http://www.state.vt.us/atg
109 State Street
Montpelier, Vermont 05609-1001
(802) 828-3171

VIRGINIA

http://www.oag.state.va.us
900 East Main Street
Richmond, Virginia 23219
(804) 786-2071

WASHINGTON

http://www.wa.gov/ago
1125 Washington Street S.E.
P.O. Box 40100
Olympia, Washington 98504-0100
(360) 753-6200

WEST VIRGINIA

http://www.state.wv.us/wvag
State Capitol, Building 1, Room E26
1900 Kanawha Boulevard East
Charleston, West Virginia
25305-0220

WISCONSIN

http://www.doj.state.wi.us
114 E. State Capitol
Madison, Wisconsin 53702
(608) 266-1221

WYOMING

http://www.state.wy.us/~ag
123 Capitol Building
Cheyenne, Wyoming 82002
(307) 777-7841

State Archives

The State Archives will have many resources if you need to go back many years to find your subject. Sometimes you will need old property records; professional licenses; manuscripts; newspapers; county records; photographs; maps; church and cemetery records; records of the Executive Branch (minutes, correspondence, reports, plans, registers, certificates, and ledgers documenting activities of the executive branch agencies); legislative records (bills, committee reports, journals, testimonies, petitions, messages, communications and minutes); Judiciary records (probate, divorce, criminal, civil, equity, law and admiralty case files, minute books and wills); Governor's records (correspondence, speeches, press releases, reports, and proclamations of the chief executive); and many other records that may assist you.

You will never know what records you will need to do a search, but look again at what the archives offer you with just the records from the Judiciary Records:

Probate will give names of many relatives from years back. You sometimes have to do a search from the past to the future instead of using the present. When finding a subject that has been missing many years, the most successful searches are completed by finding relatives that will lead you to your subject. The relatives are not hiding, but your subject may be hiding or had hid many years ago.

Divorce records give you much information, such as what property was given to whom. Then you can search the property addressees for your subject or relatives. This file will also give you the names of children, so if you know that your subject had a grandfather from the turn of the century, you may want to look up the divorce file of the grandfather if he had one, which you do not know but always check, so you can get the names of the grandfather's children and then you would go find them. One person leads you to the next. Follow the paper trail.

Criminal records are important because you may be looking for someone from many years ago that may have been incarcerated. If they had been arrested, then you would know from the state records what municipality or jurisdiction to order the complete arrest records from. The arrest records show much information, including the address of the subject at the time of arrest and the name of the next of kin. Remember to pull the arrest records of relatives, and not just the subject, because the more people you have in the mix, the easier the finding of your subject will be. All of the records I am discussing here are also excellent when you have to do a background check on someone. You may want to know more about a subject's past and the subject's relatives.

Civil records include so many different records of importance, such as name changes, corporations, lawsuits that were filed by your subject, mortgages, instruments of collateral, and more.

Equity, law and admiralty case files, and minute books are records that may be of use when you are looking for that small bit of information that cannot be found elsewhere. Your subject may have approached the Judiciary in court for special zoning changes, or your subject may have filed a suit against any number of shipping and export companies, or the subject may even have wanted to run for election and you want to see the records to see who the contributors were.

**Alabama Department
of Archives and History**
624 Washington Avenue
P.O. Box 300100
Montgomery, Alabama 36130
http://www.archives.state.al.us

**Alaska Division of Libraries,
Archives, and Museums**
141 Willoughby Avenue
Juneau, Alaska 99801
http://www.educ.state.ak.us/lam/-archives/home.html

**Arizona Department of Library,
Archives, and Public Records**
1700 West Washington
Room 442, State Capitol
Phoenix, Arizona 85007
http://www.dlapr.lib.az.us/archives/-index.html

**Arkansas History Commission
and State Archives**
One Capitol Mall
Little Rock, Arkansas 72201
http://www.state.ar.us/ahc

California State Archives
1020 "O" Street
Sacramento, California 95814
http://www.ss.ca.gov/archives/-archives.htm

Colorado State Archives
1313 Sherman Street, Room 1B-20
Denver, Colorado 80203
http://www.state.co.us/gov_dir/gss/-archives

**Connecticut State Library
History and Genealogy**
231 Capitol Avenue
Hartford, Connecticut 06106
http://www.cslib.org/archives.htm

Delaware Public Archives
Hall of Records
Dover, Delaware 19901
http://www.lib.de.us/archives

District of Columbia
Office of Public Records
1300 Naylor Court NW
Washington, DC 20001
http://www.washingtondc.gov/agencies

Florida State Archives
Bureau of Archives and
Records Management
Division of Library and
Information Services
500 South Bronough Street
Tallahassee, Florida 32399-09250
http://dlis.dos.state.fl.us/barm

**Georgia Department
of Archives and History**
330 Capitol Avenue SE
Atlanta, Georgia 30334
http://www.sos.state.ga.us/archives

**Department of Accounting
and General Services**
Kekauluohi Building
Iolani Palace Grounds
Honolulu, Hawaii 96813
http://kumu.icsd.hawaii.gov/dags/-
archives/welcome.html

Idaho State Historical Society
Library and Archives
450 North Fourth Street
Boise, Idaho 83702
http://www2.state.id.us/ishs/index.html

Illinois State Archives
Margaret Cross Norton Building
Capitol Complex
Springfield, Illinois 62756
http://www.sos.state.il.us/depts/archives/
arc_home.html

Indiana State Archives
117 State Library Building
140 North Senate Avenue
Indianapolis, Indiana 46204
http://www.ai.org/icpr/index.html

Iowa State Historical Society
600 East Locust
Des Moines, Iowa 50319
http://www.state.ia.us/

Kansas State Historical Society
6425 SW Sixth Avenue
Topeka, Kansas 66615
http://www.state.ks.us/history.html

Kentucky Archives Research Room
Kentucky Department
for Libraries and Archives
300 Coffee Tree Road
PO Box 537
Frankfort, Kentucky 40602
http://www.kdla.state.ky.us

Division of Archives and Records
3851 Essen Lane
Baton Rouge, Louisiana 70809
http://www.sec.state.la.us/arch-1.htm

Maine State Archives
State House Station #84
Augusta Maine 04333
http://www.state.me.us/sos/arc/

Maryland State Archives
350 Rowe Boulevard
Annapolis, Maryland 21401
http://www.mdarchives.state.md.us

Massachusetts Archives
Reference Supervisor
220 Morrissey Boulevard
Boston, Massachusetts 02125
http://www.magnet.state.ma.us/sec/arc/ar-
cidx.htm

State Archives of Michigan
Michigan Historical Center
717 West Allegan Street
Lansing, Michigan 48918
http://www.sos.state.mi.us/history/-
archive/archive.html

Minnesota Historical Society
345 Kellogg Boulevard West
St. Paul, Minnesota 55102
http://www.mnhs.org/preserve/records/-
index.html

**Mississippi Dept.
of Archives and History**
P.O. Box 571
Jackson, Mississippi 39205
http://www.mdah.state.ms.us

Missouri State Archives
State Information Center
P.O. Box 778
Jefferson City, Missouri 65102
http://mosl.sos.state.mo.us/rec-
man/arch.html

Montana Historical Society
225 North Roberts Street
Helena, Montana 59620
http://statedocs.msl.state.mt.us/default.-
html

Nebraska State Historical Society
1500 "R" Street
P.O. Box 82554
Lincoln, Nebraska 68501
http://www.nebraskahistory.org

**Nevada State Archives and
Records Management**
100 North Stewart Street
Carson City, Nevada 89710
http://www.state.nv.us/

**New Hampshire Division of Records
Management and Archives**
71 South Fruit Street
Concord, New Hampshire 03301
http://www.state.nh.us/state/archives.-
htm

**New Jersey Division of Archives
and Records Management**
185 West State Street, Level 2
New Jersey State Library Building
Trenton, New Jersey 08625
http://www.state.nj.us/state/darm/-
archives.html

**New Mexico State Records
Center and Archives**
404 Montezuma Street
Santa Fe, New Mexico 87503
http://www.state.nm.us/

New York State Archives
Cultural Education Center
Room 11D40
Albany, New York 12230
http://www.sara.nysed.gov

North Carolina State Archives
109 East Jones Street
Raleigh, North Carolina 27601
http://www.ah.dcr.state.nc.us/home/-
default.htm

North Dakota State Historical Society
North Dakota Heritage Center
612 East Boulevard Avenue
Bismarck, North Dakota 58505
http://www.state.nd.us/hist/sal.htm

Ohio Historical Society
Archives/Library Reference Questions
1982 Velma Avenue
Columbus, Ohio 43211
http://www.ohiohistory.org/resource/-
statearc/index.html

Oklahoma State Archives
200 Nebraska 18th Street
Oklahoma City, Oklahoma 73105
http://www.ok-history.mus.ok.us

Oregon State Archives
800 Summer Street Nebraska
Salem, Oregon 97310
http://arcweb.sos.state.or.us

Pennsylvania State Archives
Box 1026
Attn: ERA
Harrisburg, Pennsylvania 17108
http://www.state.pa.us/PA_Exec/Historical_Museum/DAM/ps

Rhode Island State Archives
Dept of Archives and History
337 Westminster Street
Providence, Rhode Island 02903
http://www.state.ri.us/pg1.htm

**South Carolina Department
of Archives and History**
8301 Parklane Road
Columbia, South Carolina 29223
http://www.state.sc.us/scdah/homepage.htm

South Dakota State Archives
900 Governors Drive
Pierre, South Dakota 57501
http://www.state.sd.us/deca/cultural/-archives.htm

Tennessee State Library and Archives
403 Seventh Avenue North
Nashville, Tennessee 37243
http://www.state.tn.us/sos/statelib/tsla-home.htm

Texas State Library and Archives
P.O. Box 12927
Austin, Texas 78711
http://www.tsl.state.tx.us/arc/index.html

Utah State Archives
P.O. Box 141021
Salt Lake City, Utah 84114
http://www.archives.state.ut.us

Vermont State Archives
109 State Street
Montpelier, Vermont 05609
http://vermont-archives.org

The Library of Virginia
Archives and Research Services
800 East Broad Street
Richmond, Virginia 23219
http://www.lva.lib.va.us/dlp

Washington State Archives
1120 Washington Street SE
P.O. Box 40238
Olympia, Washington 98504
http://www.cwu.edu/~archives

West Virginia State Archives
Archives and History Library
The Cultural Center
1900 Kanawha Blvd., East
Charleston, West Virginia 25305
http://www.wvculture.org/history

State Historical Society of Wisconsin
Archives Division
Reference Services
816 State Street
Madison, Wisconsin 53706
http://www.wisc.edu/shs-archives

Wyoming State Archives
Museums and Historical Department
Barrett Building
Cheyenne, Wyoming 82002
http://www.state.wy.us/

State Governors

If you have any problem that just cannot be resolved regarding records of any state then, please write to the Governor. The Governor will not, of course, personally see your letter, but here's what happens when a complaint is sent to the Governor's office. First, the letter is logged in. Then a letter is sent to you to acknowledge the receipt of your letter, and usually, the Governor thanks you for writing and tells you that he has forwarded your letter to the appropriate department for action. Then, a copy of your letter is sent to the appropriate department by the Governor's office with a routing slip that asks that a copy of the response be sent to both you and the Governor's office. The Governor's office always keeps a copy of the response so it can show that it is responsive to all.

I use the Governor's office when I need a record that is important and when I cannot wait for a response for a long period of time. Letters that the Governor's office sends to departments in the state government get priority and are handled by the special liaison that handles priority responses.

ALABAMA

http://www.governor.state.al.us
Governor's Office
State House
Montgomery, Alabama 36130

ALASKA

http://www.gov.state.ak.us
Governor's Office
State Capitol
P.O. Box 110001
Juneau, Alaska 99811-0001

ARIZONA

http://www.governor.state.az.us
Governor's Office
State House
Phoenix, Arizona 85007

ARKANSAS

http://www.state.ar.us/governor
Governor's Office
State Capitol
Little Rock, Arkansas 72201

CALIFORNIA

http://www.state.ca.us/s/governor
Governor's Office
State Capitol
First Floor
Sacramento, California 95814

COLORADO

http://www.state.co.us/gov_dir/governor_office.html
Governor's Office
State Capitol
Denver, Colorado 80203-1792

CONNECTICUT

http://www.state.ct.us/governor/
Governor's Office
State Capitol
210 State Capitol Avenue
Hartford, Connecticut 06106

DELAWARE

http://www.state.de.us/governor/index.htm
Governor's Office
Legislative Hall
Dover, Delaware 19901

FLORIDA

http://fcn.state.fl.us/eog
Governor's Office
State Capitol, PL05
Tallahassee, Florida 32399-0001

GEORGIA

http://www.ganet.org/governor
Governor's Office
State Capitol
Atlanta, Georgia 30334

HAWAII

http://gov.state.hi.us
Governor's Office
State Capitol
Honolulu, Hawaii 96813

IDAHO

http://www2.state.id.us/gov/govhmpg.htm
Governor's Office
State Capitol
Boise, Idaho 83720

ILLINOIS

http://www.state.il.us/gov
Governor's Office
State Capitol
Springfield, Illinois 62706

INDIANA

http://www.state.in.us/gov
Governor's Office
State Capitol
Indianapolis, Indiana 46204

IOWA

http://www.state.ia.us/government/-
governor
Governor's Office
State Capitol
Des Moines, Iowa 50319

KANSAS

http://www.ink.org/public/governor/-
main.html
Governor's Office
State Capitol
2nd Floor
Topeka, Kansas 66612-1590

KENTUCKY

http://www.state.ky.us/agencies/gov/-
govmenu6.htm
Governor's Office
State Capitol
700 Capitol Avenue
Frankfort, Kentucky 40601

LOUISIANA

http://www.gov.state.la.us
Governor's Office
P.O. Box 94004
Baton Rouge, Louisiana 70804-9004

MAINE

http://www.state.me.us/governor/gov-
home.htm
Governor's Office
State House, Station 1
Augusta, Maine 04333

MARYLAND

http://www.gov.state.md.us
Governor's Office
State House
Annapolis, Maryland 21401

MASSACHUSETTS

http://www.magnet.state.ma.us/gov
Governor's Office
State House, Room 360
Boston, Massachusetts 02133

MICHIGAN

http://www.migov.state.mi.us/migov.html
Governor's Office
P.O. Box 30013
Lansing, Michigan 48909

MINNESOTA

http://www.governor.state.mn.us
Governor's Office
130 State Capitol
St. Paul, Minnesota 55155

MISSISSIPPI

http://www.govoff.state.ms.us
Governor's Office
P.O. Box 139
Jackson, Mississippi 39205

MISSOURI

http://www.gov.state.mo.us/index.htm
Governor's Office
P.O. Box 720
Jefferson City, Missouri 65102

MONTANA

http://www.state.mt.us/governor/-
governor.htm
Governor's Office
State Capitol
Helena, Montana 59620

NEBRASKA

http://gov.nol.org
Governor's Office
State Capitol
Lincoln, Nebraska 68509

NEVADA

http://www.state.nv.us/gov/gov.htm
Governor's Office
State Capitol
Carson City, Nevada 89710

NEW HAMPSHIRE

http://www.state.nh.us/governor/index.html
Governor's Office
State House
Concord, New Hampshire 03301

NEW JERSEY

http://www.state.nj.us/governor/officeo.htm
Governor's Office
State House
CN 001
Trenton, New Jersey 08625

NEW MEXICO

http://www.governor.state.nm.us
Governor's Office
State Capitol
Santa Fe, New Mexico 87503

NEW YORK

http://www.state.ny.us/governor
Governor's Office
State Capitol
Albany, New York 12224

NORTH CAROLINA

http://www.governor.state.nc.us
Governor's Office
State Capitol
Raleigh, North Carolina 27603

NORTH DAKOTA

http://www.health.state.nd.us/gov
Governor's Office
State Capitol
600 E. Boulevard
Bismarck, North Dakota 58505-0001

OHIO

http://www.state.oh.us/gov
Governor's Office
77 South High Street
30th Floor
Columbus, Ohio 43366-0601

OKLAHOMA

http://www.state.ok.us/~governor
Governor's Office
State Capitol, Room 212
Oklahoma City, Oklahoma 73105

OREGON

http://www.governor.state.or.us/-governor.html
Governor's Office
Office of the Governor
State Capitol
Salem, Oregon 97310

PENNSYLVANIA

http://www.state.pa.us/PA_Exec/Governor/overview.html
Governor's Office
225 Main Capitol Building
Harrisburg, Pennsylvania 17120

RHODE ISLAND

http://www.governor.state.ri.us
Governor's Office
State House
Providence, Rhode Island 02903

SOUTH CAROLINA

http://www.state.sc.us/governor
Governor's Office
P.O. Box 11369
Columbia, South Carolina 29211

SOUTH DAKOTA

http://www.state.sd.us/governor/-governor.htm
Governor's Office
500 East Capitol
Pierre, South Dakota 57501

TENNESSEE

http://www.state.tn.us
Governor's Office
State Capitol
Nashville, Tennessee 37243-0001

TEXAS

http://www.governor.state.tx.us
Governor's Office
P.O. Box 12428, Capitol Station
Austin, Texas 78711

UTAH

http://www.governor.state.ut.us
Governor's Office
210 State Capitol
Salt Lake City, Utah 84114

VERMONT

http://www.cit.state.vt.us/governor/index.htm
Governor's Office
109 State Street
Montpelier, Vermont 05609

VIRGINIA

http://www.state.va.us/governor
Governor's Office
State Capitol
Richmond, Virginia 23219

WASHINGTON

http://www.governor.wa.gov
Governor's Office
Legislative Building
Olympia, Washington 98504

WEST VIRGINIA

http://www.state.wv.us/governor
Governor's Office
State Capitol
Charleston, West Virginia 25305

WISCONSIN

http://www.wisgov.state.wi.us
Governor's Office
State Capitol
P.O. Box 7863
Madison, Wisconsin 53707

WYOMING

Governor's Office
http://www.state.wy.us/governor/governor_home.html
State Capitol
Cheyenne, Wyoming 82002

Federal Records

Military Records

nder the Freedom of Information Act, you are permitted access to the following information about military personnel:

Full name
Rank
Gross salary
Past-duty assignments
Present-duty assignments
Office or duty telephone number
Awards and decorations
Attendance at military schools

The most important information from the above list is, of course, the present-duty assignment of your subject. If your subject has a close relative in the Armed Forces, you will want to order their records. This relative can turn out to be an excellent source and may give you the location of your subject.

Military Locator Services

The military will supply you with the current unit number and installation to which a person on active duty is assigned. If the person is retired, a letter will be forwarded to them.

ARMY

Active Duty
Army Locator
Fort Benjamin, Indiana 46249

Retired
Army Personnel Center
Attention: DARP—PAS
9700 Page Boulevard
Saint Louis, Missouri 63132

AIR FORCE

Active Duty
Air Force Locator Service
Air Force Military Personnel Center
Randolph Air Force Base,
Texas 78150

Retired
Retired Personnel Command
Air Force Military Personnel Center
Randolph Air Force Base,
Texas 78150

NAVY

Active Duty
Naval Personnel Command
Locator Service
NMC–21
Washington, DC 20307

Retired
Retired Personnel Command
Locator Service
4400 Dauphin Street
New Orleans, Louisiana 70149

MARINE CORPS

Active Duty
Marine Corps Locator Service
MMRD–10
Commandant of the Marine Corps
Washington, DC 20380

Retired
Marine Corps Retired
Locator Service
MMRD–06
Commandant of the Marine Corps
Washington, DC 20380

COAST GUARD

Active Duty	**Retired**
United States Coast Guard	United States Coast Guard
Locator Service	Retired Locator Service
Commandant–G-PIM	G–PS–5
2100 Second Street, Southwest	2100 Second Street, SW
Washington, DC 20593	Washington, DC 20593

The following addresses are to be used when you need to get someone's military records. Of course, provide as much identifying information about your subject as possible.

ARMY:
Chief, Information Access Section
HQ USAISC (ASQNS-OP-F)
Hoffman I, Room 1146
2461 Eisenhower Avenue
Alexandria, Virginia 22331-0301

AIR FORCE:
Secretary of the Air Force
Freedom of Information Manager
SAF/AADS (FOIA)
Pentagon, Room 4A1088C
Washington, DC 20330-1000

NAVY:
Director, OPNAV Services and Security Division
OP-09B30
Pentagon, Room 5E521
Washington, DC 20350-2000

MARINE CORPS:
Freedom of Information and Privacy Act
Office (Code MI-3)
Headquarters, U.S. Marine Corps, Room 4327
Washington, DC 20380-0001

COAST GUARD:
Freedom of Information Act
Commandant of the Coast Guard
2100 Second Street, Southwest
Washington, DC 20593-0201

Department of Veterans Affairs

http://www.acf.dhhs.gov/programs

The Department of Veterans Affairs will also forward a letter from you to a veteran. There is no charge for this service.

Department of Veterans Affairs
Veterans Benefits Administration
Administrative Support Staff (20A52)
810 Vermont Avenue, NW
Washington, DC 20420

Paternity and Child Support Locator Service

http://www.acf.dhhs.gov/

If you want to contact your subject because of a paternity or child support matter, then you may use the following address. This center will locate your subject and then guide you on what procedures to follow.

Armed Services Community and Family Support
Attention: TAPC–PDO–IP
200 Stovall Street
Alexandria, Virginia 22331

Civil Air Patrol Locator Service

http://www.capnhq.gov

Active Duty and Retired
Civil Air Patrol Locator Service
G–10
Maxwell Air Force Base, Alabama 36112

United States Civil Service

http://www.opm.gov

If your subject is a current or retired civil servant, then you will want to write to the Office of Personnel Management. They will give you the work site address of a current employer, or, if the subject is retired, forward a letter from you.

United States Office of Personnel Management
1900 East E Street
Washington, DC 20415

Railroad Retirement Board

http://www.rrb.gov

The Railroad Retirement Board administers the retirement and survivor benefit programs provided to the nation's railroad workers and their families. If your subject was a railroad worker and you believe that they may be collecting benefits, then write to the Board and request that they forward a letter to the subject from you.

Railroad Retirement Board
844 Rush Street
Chicago, Illinois 60611

United States Public Health Personnel

http://www.os.dhhs.gov/phs/corps/welcom1.html

You may write to the following address if your subject has ever been employed by the United States Public Health Service. They will forward a letter from you if the person is retired. If your subject is currently employed, you will be supplied with their grade and salary information, employment address, and date that employment started.

United States Public Health Service
Department of Health and Human Services
PHS/05G/DCP
5600 Fishers Lane
Parklawn Building, Room 4–35
Rockville, Maryland 20857

Peace Corps

http://www.peacecorps.gov

If you have reason to believe that your subject has served or is now serving in the Peace Corps, you will want to write requesting that a letter be forwarded to the subject at the last known address. Also request that you be supplied with the dates of service and duty locations of the subject.

If you are unable to secure any driving records, vehicle registrations, or other public record information regarding the subject, then this may indicate that they may have returned to a location of duty to reside. Look at this avenue closely if your subject does not respond to a forwarded letter.

Peace Corps
1990 K Street, NW
Washington, DC 20526

United States Soldiers' and Airmen's Home

http://www.va.gov

The United States Soldiers' and Airmen's Home is a fine source to contact if your subject is a person that has been missing for many years and was a member of the Armed Forces. Inquire by name, and the home will inform you if your subject now resides there.

This is a good source to use if you believe that the subject's father resides at the home. You may be able to receive information from the father that will lead to the location of your subject.

United States Soldiers' and Airmens' Home
3700 North Capitol Street, Northwest
Washington, DC 20317

National Aeronautics and Space Administration (NASA)

http://www.nasa.gov/

Over 85 percent of NASA's multibillion dollar budget goes to NASA's contractors. Procurement files maintained by its procurement office contain information about individual firms and their employees. NASA requires that contractors submit with the proposals their qualifications and resumés of the personnel who will be directly assigned to the project. The resumés should include each person's educational background, work experience, length of service with the firm, and work projects.

For the most recent address used for NASA, go to:
http://www.josephculligan.com.

Nuclear Regulatory Commission (NRC)

http://www.nrc.gov

NRC regulates commercial nuclear power reactors; nonpower research reactors; fuel-cycle facilities; medical, academic, and industrial uses of nuclear materials; and the transport, storage, and disposal of nuclear materials and waste. NRC also maintains applications and licenses of persons and companies that export nuclear material and equipment from the United States.

Securities and Exchange Commission (SEC)

http://www.sec.gov

SEC maintains public records of corporations with stock and securities sold to the public. These records include the following:

Financial statements
Identification of officers and directors
Identification of owners of more than 10 percent of a corporation's stock
A description of the registrant's properties and businesses

**A description of the significant provisions of the
    security to be offered for sale and its relationship
    to the registrant's other capital securities
Identification of events of interest to investors
Identification of accountants and attorneys
A history of the business**

SEC maintains files on individuals and firms that have been reported to it as having violated federal or state securities laws. The information contained in these files pertains to official actions taken against such persons and firms, including denials, refusals, suspensions, and revocations of registrations; injunctions, fraud orders, stop orders, cease-and-desist orders; and arrests, indictments, convictions, sentences, and other official actions.

The Securities and Exchange Commission Summary lists the changes in beneficial ownership by officers, directors, and principal stockholders of securities listed and registered on a national securities exchange or those relating to public utility companies and certain closed-end investment companies.

Copies of the documents maintained by SEC are available at its regional or branch offices in the following cities: Atlanta, Georgia; Miami, Florida; Boston, Massachusetts; Chicago, Illinois; Cleveland, Ohio; Detroit, Michigan; St. Louis, Missouri; Denver, Colorado; Salt Lake City, Utah; Fort Worth, Texas; Los Angeles, California; San Francisco, California; New York, New York; Seattle, Washington; Washington, DC; and Philadelphia, Pennsylvania.

Corporate filings include the following:

**Annual Report of Publicly Traded Company (Form
10-K)—excerpts or complete report via DIALOG or
Lexis databases, both of which are discussed in
Chapter 4**

**Quarterly Report of Publicly Traded Company
(Form 10–Q)—same as Form 10–K**

**Registration of Security (Form 8–A)—prospectus,
data relative to the issuer**

**Registration of Security by the Successor to (Form
8–B)—name of issuer, relationship to primary
registrant/issuer**

Federal Aviation Administration

http://www.faa.gov/

If your subject is a pilot or owns an aircraft, you may write to the Federal Aviation Administration. A search will be conducted by name. The subject's address, date of birth, pilot rating, and even the date of the last medical exam will be furnished to you if the subject has a pilot's license.

You may wish to order a list of any aircraft your subject may own. The request for a search can be conducted by your subject's name or by the name of the company he owns. If there is a listing of an aircraft, you will be given the address that the aircraft is registered to, the year and make of the aircraft, the name of pilots that will utilize the aircraft, and the name of an insurance carrier.

Once you have the registration number for an aircraft, the name of all the previous owners may be retrieved. These former owners may have a personal knowledge of the habits and personal details of the life of your subject. Order a copy of the bill of sale of the aircraft that your subject owns. This document will contain much information, including witnesses to the signing of the bill of sale and their addresses, the name of the financial institution that may have a lien on the aircraft, and the names and addresses of any other owners. The aforementioned sources may be able to direct you to the location of your subject if your subject cannot be located at the address listed on the registration.

Federal Aviation Administration
P.O. Box 25504
Oklahoma City, Oklahoma 73125

Interstate Commerce Commission

http://www.dot.gov

If your subject is in any form of the transportation business that crosses state lines, there will be records with important information on file. The Interstate Commerce Commission regulates moving companies, trucking firms, and many other entities that use the nation's interstate highway system.

Interstate Commerce Commission
12th Street and Constitution Avenue
Washington, DC 20423

Passport Records

http://travel.state.gov/passport_services.html

If you are searching for a subject who may have been a minor when taken and hidden by an adult years ago, you may want to explore passport records. If, for instance, you discover that the person who had absconded with the minor has died, but you do not have the whereabouts of the subject, write for the passport records of the deceased.

These records will contain the information that was on the passport application. This information will, of course, list much personal data about the deceased, including addresses, references, etc., that will, perhaps, give you new information that may lead to the location of your subject. Many times the person and address listed by the applicant to contact in case of emergency may be the person who now has possession of your subject.

Third-party requesters may request the release of documents in the custody of the Department of State, under provisions of the Freedom of Information Act (5 USC 552). Write to:

Department of State
Office of Freedom of Information (IM/IS/FPC)
2201 C Street, NW
Washington, DC 20520–1239

While on the subject of passports, you may need to obtain one if your search indicates that your subject is abroad. The following is a complete list of all United States Passport Agencies. You may also apply for a passport at many larger post offices and at certain state and federal courts. Also, you may visit the Website: http://travel.state.gov/get_forms.html.

Passport Agencies

http://travel.state.gov/agencieslist.html

Boston Passport Agency
Thomas P. O'Neill Federal Building
10 Causeway Street
Boston, Massachusetts 02222
*Recording: (617) 565–6998
**Public Inquiries: (617) 565-6990

Chicago Passport Agency
Kluczynski Federal Building
230 South Dearborn Street
Chicago, Illinois 60604
*Recording: (342) 353-5426
**Public Inquiries: (342) 353-7155

Honolulu Passport Agency
New Federal Building
300 Ala Moana Boulevard
Honolulu, Hawaii 96850
*Recording: (808) 541-1919
**Public Inquiries: (808) 541-1918

Houston Passport Agency
Concord Towers
1919 Smith Street
Houston, Texas 77002
*Recording: (713) 653-3159
**Public Inquiries: (713) 229-3600

Los Angeles Passport Agency
11000 Wilshire Boulevard
Los Angeles, California 90024
*Recording: (213) 209-7070
**Public Inquiries: (213) 209-7075

Miami Passport Agency
Federal Office Building
51 Southwest First Avenue
Miami, Florida 33130
*Recording: (305) 536-5395 (English)
(305) 536-4448 (Spanish)
**Public Inquiries: (305) 536-4681

New Orleans Passport Agency
Postal Services Building
Room T—12005
701 Loyola Avenue
New Orleans, Louisiana 70113
*Recording: (504) 589-6728
**Public Inquiries: (504) 589-6161

New York Passport Agency
Rockefeller Center
630 Fifth Avenue
New York, New York 10111
*Recording: (212) 541-77000
**Public Inquiries: (212) 541-7710

Philadelphia Passport Agency
Federal Building
600 Arch Street
Philadelphia, Pennsylvania 19106
*Recording: (215) 597-7482
**Public Inquiries: (215) 597-7480, 7481

San Francisco Passport Agency
525 Market Street
San Francisco, California 94105
*Recording: (415) 974-7972
**Public Inquiries: (415) 974-9941, 9948

Seattle Passport Agency
Federal Office Building
915 Second Avenue
Seattle, Washington 98174
*Recording: (206) 442-7941
**Public Inquiries: (206) 442-7945

Stamford Passport Agency
One Landmark Square
Street Level
Stamford, Connecticut 06901
*Recording: (203) 325-4401
**Public Inquiries: (203) 325-3538, 3539

United States Court of Military Appeals

http://jaglink.jag.af.mil

The United States Court of Military Appeals was created by Congress in 1950 and is composed of three civilian judges. Even though this court operates as part of the Department of Defense for administrative purposes, it is independent of any influence from the military. The court's function is to be an impartial final appeals board for members of the military who have been convicted of crimes.

You will want to order a photocopy of your subject's complete court file if they have ever availed themselves of this avenue of redress. The file will contain information you will need to start a current search for your subject. The date of birth, Social Security Number, grade and rank information, addresses, and the details of the court case will be part of the file.

United States Court of Military Appeals
450 E Street NW
Washington, DC 20442

United States Court of Veterans Appeals

http://www.armfor.uscourts.gov/

Your subject may be a veteran of the Armed Forces that had made an appeal to the United States Court of Veterans Appeals. Cases are filed, in some cases, decades after the veteran had been separated from the service.

Much information such as Social Security Number, date of birth, and home address will be in this public record. Spouse and dependent information will be included if applicable, and they may be easier to contact than the subject and can be of assistance in locating your subject.

United States Court of Veterans Appeals
625 Indiana Avenue
Washington, DC 20004

The United States Claims Court

http://www.fedcir.gov

The United States Claims Court may have been used by your subject to make a claim against the federal government. If you had heard that at one time your subject had filed suit, then you can write and order a photocopy of the court file. You will be able to learn such information as the Social Security Number, date of birth, home and business address, and the spouse information of the subject.

The amount of any award of damages will be listed. If the address of the subject contained in the file is no longer valid, then you will be able to use the other listed personal information to continue your search.

United States Claims Court
717 Madison Place, Northwest
Washington, DC 20005

United States Tax Court

http://ustaxcourt.gov

Congress created the United States Tax Court to provide a forum where a taxpayer may dispute a deficiency in taxes claimed by the Internal Revenue Service. The court allows only cases where the amount disputed is $10,000 or less.

Write to the tax court for a photocopy of the court file if you believe your subject may have had a case heard in this arena. The file will contain much information that will be of a personal nature, such as Social Security Number, home and business address, name of spouse, and nature of the tax dispute.

If you have reason to believe that a parent or close relative may have had a case in this court and you do not know where this person can be found at the present time, then you may order that person's file. The information supplied will enable you to contact the relative and query them on the whereabouts of your subject.

United States Tax Court
400 Second Street, Northwest
Washington, DC 20217

General Services Administration

http://gsa.gov

The General Services Administration's function is to evaluate and award contracts to firms so that they may supply products or services to branches of the federal government. If your subject is a business person and you have reason to believe that he may have conducted business with the federal government, then you will want to request photocopies of the files containing the contracts that have been or presently are in force.

The contracts will have the business, and, in many instances, home address, Social Security Number, personal references, business and bank references, former addresses, and other important information regarding the subject that will assist you in your search for the subject.

> **General Services Administration**
> **CAIR/Room 3016**
> **18th & F Street, Northwest**
> **Washington, DC 20405**

Many times I will need the telephone number and address of an agency of the Federal Government that I believe a subject may be employed by. I will want to check employment status with the least amount of delay. The following toll-free telephone numbers are of great assistance. The operators that staff those centers have access to every telephone number and address in the federal government, so even if the agency is obscure, this number will be able to satisfy your inquiry.

United States Post Office

http://www.usps.gov

The Postal Service will not provide you with a street address for a person who uses a Post Office Box (P.O. Box) for personal mail. But if your subject is conducting business using a P.O. Box for business purposes, the post office is required by law to furnish you with the street address. The street address may be of significant importance because this may actually be the residence of your subject. You may wish to check with the property appraiser's office to see who owns the property.

United States Government Depository Libraries

http://www.access.gpo.gov/su_docs/dpos/adpos003.html

Libraries that are considered complete and well-rounded are selected by the Superintendent of Documents to participate in the Depository Library

Program. These libraries will receive all federal government publications free of charge if they pledge to make available free access to their facilities for all library patrons.

The libraries selected to be United States Government Depository Libraries must maintain a high standard of responsiveness, inventory, and access. This is a quote from the Congressional edict that will clearly demonstrate that the government is serious about the accountability of the Depository Libraries:

> *"The Superintendent of Documents shall make firsthand investigation of conditions for which need is indicated and include the results of investigations in his annual report. When he ascertains that the number of books in a depository library is below ten thousand, other than Government publications, or it has ceased to be maintained so as to be* **accessible to the public,** *or that the Government publications which have been furnished the library have not been properly maintained, he shall delete the library from the list of depository libraries if the library fails to correct the unsatisfactory conditions within six months."*

I used these particular libraries because they provide a level of service and availability of different publications that I require for research. These libraries, for instance, have on hand crisscross directories. These directories can be accessed two ways:

1. The listings are by telephone number. Look for a telephone number in the numerical listing and, if the number is a published number, it will show the name and address of the person with that telephone number.

2. The listings are by address. You may look up a street address, and you will be shown the name of the occupant and the telephone number corresponding to the address. All of the information on the neighbors will, of course, also be in the sequence.

The library will have the books for the locale you are in, and, in many instances, the books for the surrounding cities will be available. The libraries also keep the previous issues of the criss-cross directories for several years. The importance of these publications is obvious. You may have retrieved a telephone number in your search but no address. Now you have the means to find the address. Or you may have an address, but no telephone number.

If the information operator is not of any assistance because your subject does not have the telephone number listed under his name, use the criss-cross directory. Retrieval of the telephone number at the subject's address is possible because the telephone listing is by address, not name. From these books, you now have the names, addresses, and telephone numbers of all the neighbors of your subject.

The library will have a publication called *Directory of United States Public and Private Companies.* You will want to review this reference if you believe your subject to be an owner of a business. The list of more than 107,000 business (of which 90 percent are privately held) includes the names of the principals in the business, address, regular and fax telephone numbers, financial information, and corporate structure information. Search for the company name you feel the subject may be using. Many persons will move to another state and use basically the same company name that they had used previously.

You may want to refer to the publication that is called the *Congressional Directory.* Not only does this book list the names, addresses, and telephone numbers of members of Congress, but it contains the names, addresses, and telephone numbers of every Freedom of Information officer in every agency of the federal government. You are permitted to ask if your subject is an employee of any department of government by just directing your inquiry to the appropriate Freedom of Information officer.

If your subject was or is a member of any union, trade organization, hobby group, or club, then you will be able to access the address and telephone number of the desired organization. Ask for the Gale Research edition of organizations, and you will have more than 47,000 entries to assist you in locating the correct information. The international edition lists more than 10,300 entries. Write to the above-noted sources and ask if your subject is a member, and, if so, what local chapter or unit he or she belongs to. This will give you a defined geographical location to start or continue your search in. This is an excellent technique to use, because just about everyone will belong to some type of organization. Even if your subject does not want to be found, they probably will still maintain a membership in a local group of the organization that they belonged to when they were in the mainstream.

Directory of Corporate Affiliations— Who Owns Whom?

This three-volume annual directory provides information on almost 150,000 public and private parent, subsidiary, and associate companies in the United States and overseas. Entries are arranged first by the parent's location, and then hierarchically by the company's organization. Criteria for inclusion is revenue in excess of $10 million or a work force in excess of 300 for U.S. companies, and revenue in excess of $50 million for non-U.S. firms. A two-volume master index provides access by company name, brand name, location, **personnel**, and standard industrial classification code.

Dun & Bradstreet's Million Dollar Directory

This three-volume Dun & Bradstreet directory contains information on over 20,000 public and 140,000 private utilities, transportation companies, banks, trust companies, mutual and stock insurance companies, wholesalers, and retailers. The type of information available includes annual sales, **corporate officers, locations, phone numbers**, type of business, and number of employees. To be included in the directory, a company must be a headquarters or a single location and have 250 or more employees, $25 million or more in sales, or a net worth of $500,000 or more. Company names are arranged alphabetically. A two-volume index is arranged by location and standard industrial classification code.

Financial Yellow Book

This directory lists over **41,000 top executives at leading financial institutions from chief executives to subject-area officers, and over 8,500 board members** and their affiliates. The directory has five indexes—on company, parent organization, geographical location, financial services rendered, and individual name.

Foreign Representatives in the U.S. Yellow Book

This directory has sections on foreign corporations, foreign-based financial institutions, foreign governments (embassies and consulates), intergovernmental organizations, non-U.S. media, and **personnel** who represent foreign corporations and government in the United States. **It includes officials' titles, addresses, and telephone and fax numbers.**

Moody's International Manual

This manual contains background and financial information on over 3,000 foreign firms. It is arranged by country, and gives economic and political information and statistics for each geographical area. It provides statistical information regarding foreign stock exchanges, consumer price indexes, money market rates, imports, and exports.

Moody's Investors Services

Moody's broad business sector manuals cover companies whose stock is traded in the New York and American stock exchanges, regional American stock exchanges, and in over-the-counter transactions. Each entry contains history and background; data on acquisitions, mergers, and subsidiaries; business and product descriptions; names and titles of officers and directors; number of stockholders and employees; location of plants and properties; the headquarters' phone number and address; and financial statements. Separate annual volumes with weekly supplements cover industries, transportation, utilities, and banking. Another series supplies detailed data on corporate and government bond sales and ratings.

Predicasts Funk and Scott Index, United States

Issued weekly and cumulated monthly, quarterly, and annually, this directory indexes articles on products, companies, and industries that appear in most business periodicals and newspapers. Funk and Scott also publishes the quarterly Index of Corporate Change, which lists recent business activities such as mergers and acquisitions. The indexes are available on CD-ROM.

Standard & Poor's Corporation Records

Originally provided to Standard & Poor subscribers, this directory is now available on CD-ROM. The records cover over 12,000 publically traded companies and 34,000 subsidiaries, affiliates, and privately held firms. Coverage consists of a company's brief history, financial statements, capital structure, lines of business, subsidiaries, and **officers and directors.** Information on 70,000 executives is also available.

Standard & Poor's Register of Corporations, Directors, and Executives

This three-volume annual directory lists about 56,000 public and private companies and the **names and titles of over 400,000 officials.** Company information similar to that provided by the Dun and Bradstreet and Moody directories, this register includes financial data, standard industrial classification code products and services, and number of employees. Indexing is by standard industrial classification code, geographical area, and subsidiaries/divisions/affiliates. The set is updated in April, July, and October.

American Medical Directory

Published by the American Medical Association, this source contains listings for the presidents and secretaries of all county medical associations. The directory also has **listings of doctors—by state and city, year of birth, medical school and year of graduation, year of license, residence and office addresses, specialties, and membership in associated medical organizations. A name index of all doctors is provided.**

In addition to the directories focusing on individuals that are listed in this section, several other directories cited in this chapter, under other sections, contain information about individuals. These other directories are the Associations Yellow Book; Directory of Corporate Affiliations—Who Owns Whom; Dun & Bradstreet's Million Dollar Directory; Law Firms Yellow Book; Martindale-Hubbell Law Directory; Moody's Bank and Finance Manual; National Directory of Law Enforcement Administrators, Prosecutors, Correctional Institutions, and Related Agencies; National Trade and Professional Associations in the United States; Standard & Poor's Corporation Records; Standard & Poor's Register of Corporations, Directors and Executives; and Thomson Bank Directory.

Congressional Directory

This directory is prepared by the Joint Committee on Printing and is the official directory of the Congress. It presents short bibliographies of each member of the Senate and the House—listed by states and districts, respectively. It includes such additional data as his or her committee memberships, terms of service, administrative assistant and/or secretary, and room and telephone numbers. The Congressional Directory also lists officials of the courts; the military establishments; and other federal departments and agencies, including the District of Columbia government, governors of states and territories, foreign diplomats; and members of the press, radio, and television galleries. The directory is available both in paper format and online. The database is updated irregularly as changes are provided by the Joint Committee on Printing.

Congressional Staff Directory

One of a series of directories produced by the Congressional Quarterly, this directory has an extensive section on Congressional staff biographies. Two lists—one of large-city mayors and the other of state governors—are also helpful, as are two indexes—key word/subject and individual/personal name. This source is updated every four months.

Congressional Yellow Book

This source has extensive lists of office staff for and party posts of each member of the Congress. Additionally, it is updated quarterly and has a three-part index by staff, organization, and subject. It also contains biographical information.

Corporate Yellow Book

This is a directory of the people who manage, direct, and shape the largest public and privately held companies in the United States. It enables subscribers to access corporate leaders, including board members who are taking increased responsibility for corporate decision making. The directory features (1) over 1,000 leading corporations and over 7,500 subsidiaries and divisions; (2) **names and titles of over 45,000 executives, including more than**

10,000 corporate board members and their outside affiliations; (3) over **18,700 direct-dial telephone numbers of executives;** (4) business descriptions and annual revenues; (5) addresses, telephone and fax numbers, and Internet addresses of corporate headquarters and domestic and foreign subsidiaries and divisions; and (6) Washington DC, government affairs offices, with addresses and telephone and fax numbers.

Defense Organization Service

From Carroll Publishing Company, this service provides coverage exclusively for the Department of Defense (DOD). Detailed charts describe the organization and list the **staff of the Office of the Secretary, the Joint Chiefs of Staff,** the unified commands, and the individual services. Indexes reference locations, acronyms, key words, personal names, and program elements. This source is updated monthly.

Federal Organization Service

This loose-leaf chart produced by Carroll Publishing Company provides **names, addresses, and telephone numbers for staff members in the White House, executive departments, independent agencies, quasi-governmental organizations, and Congressional support offices.** It has name and key word indexes and it is updated monthly. Due to its high cost and time-consuming maintenance, it is mostly available at selected federal government libraries.

Federal Regional Yellow Book

This yellow book describes federal regional offices located outside Washington, DC It contains over 3,000 regional directors and over 29,000 administrative staff of federal departments and agencies. It also has information on **administrators and professional staff** at federal laboratories, research centers, military installations, and service academies.

Federal Staff Directory

Another Congressional Quarterly tool, this item is similar to the Federal Yellow Book. One of its strong points is its "Quasi-Official, International and Non-Government Organizations" section that describes the mission and lists the **staff of almost 50 such organizations**. In addition, it contains over **2,600 biographies of key executives and senior staff** as well as entries for U.S. ambassadors to other countries and other countries' ambassadors to the United States. It is indexed by key word/subject and individual/personal name. It is updated semiannually.

Federal Yellow Book

This quarterly publication provides detailed listings of **the names, locations, and telephone numbers of more than 40,000 staff members in the White House, the executive departments, and the independent agencies.** Like its Congressional counterpart, it has subject, organization, and staff indexes. Over 4,000 fax numbers and e-mail addresses are also included.

Government Affairs Yellow Book

This yellow book lists over 18,000 government affairs professionals who lobby at both the state and federal levels. It details the issues the lobbyists contest, as well as the coalitions they form to advance their legislative agenda. Five indexes are included—on organization, subject, current legislative issues, geographical location, and individual name. Biographical data is included on each professional.

Judicial Yellow Book

This directory provides detailed biographical information for **state and federal judges and gives information on each judge's staff, including law clerks.** It features more than 2,000 judges in the federal court system, and more than 1,200 state judges of the highest appellate courts.

Municipal Yellow Book

This directory provides information on over **30,000 elected and appointed officials in U.S. cities, counties, and authorities, including name,**

address, and telephone and fax numbers. It contains sections on cities and counties, which feature complex hierarchies of municipal officials. This directory also has listings for local departments, agencies, subdivisions, and branches.

State Yellow Book

This directory provides information on who's who in the executive and legislative branches of the 50 state governments, as well as American Samoa, Guam, Puerto Rico, and the Virgin Islands. It has both a subject and **personnel index and includes information on government officials,** departments, agencies, and legislative committees. Informational profiles of all states and territories are also provided.

Who's Who Series

This biennial series of international, U.S., regional, and professional biographical sources contains information submitted by the individual at the request of the publisher. *Who's Who in America* contains entries for over **100,000 nationally prominent individuals,** and the regional and professional volumes cover many thousands more people who are renowned in a locality or an occupation. Each entry includes information about an **individual's family, schooling, profession, writings, and awards and about offices held** by the individual. Indexing is by location, profession, who retired, and who died. Non-U.S.-wide titles, while following the same format as U.S. entries, do not have indexes.

Associations Yellow Book

This is a directory of major trade and professional associations. Semi-annual editions of the Associations Yellow Book provide current information on executive turnovers, changes in staff and governing boards, mergers, and name changes. It features (1) **over 45,000 officers, executives, and staff;** with titles, affiliations, education, and telephone and fax numbers, at more than 1,175 associations with budgets over $1 million; (2) addresses and e-mail addresses and telephone and fax numbers of headquarters and branches, and Internet addresses for headquarters; (3) boards of directors, with outside affiliations; (4) committees and chairmen, Washington representatives, political action committees, and foundations; (5) publications, including editors; and (6) annual budget, tax status, number of employees, and number of members.

Encyclopedia of Associations

This four-volume annual directory describes more than 22,000 nonprofit associations in the United States and some foreign countries. Each entry includes the organization's name, address, telephone and fax numbers, purpose, recurring publications, and computer services. A two-volume set covering more than 15,000 international organizations is also available. Since the books are alphabetically arranged by subject, keyword, and name, it is important to use the name, keyword, geographical, or executive index. These resources are also available as a commercial computer database file or on CD-ROM.

National Trade and Professional Associations
(In the United States)

This annual directory lists about 7,500 active U.S. national trade and professional associations, labor unions, scientific societies, and technical organizations. Alphabetically arranged entries contain the name, location, telephone, and fax numbers, **executives' names,** history, recurring publication titles, budget amount, membership count, and annual meeting times. The directory has subject, geographical, budget, executive, acronym, and management firm indexes.

Directories of Banks and Financial Institutions
(Moody's Bank and Finance Manual)

This four-volume annual manual covers the field of finance represented by banks (including trust companies and savings and loan associations), federal government financial agencies, insurance companies, investment companies, unit investment trusts, and miscellaneous financial enterprises. Information is also given on real estate companies and real estate investment trusts. Material for the manual (history, subsidiaries, officers, directors, financials, policies, and property) comes from the institutions themselves, the stock exchanges, or SEC filings.

Moody's News Reports

These reports are weekly supplements to the annually published Moody's manuals, which provide information on more than 30,000 publicly traded companies worldwide, and 20,000 municipal and government entities. There are currently eight manuals and corresponding News Reports, grouped according to size of company, exchanges traded on, and nature of business. The objective of News Reports is to inform customers of announcements that may affect companies' financial condition, stability, and growth by providing reports on their financial, structural, operational, legal, capital, and market activities.

Thomson Bank Directory
(Replaces the Rand McNally Bankers Directory)

This semiannual directory in four volumes is a guide to all U.S. and non-U.S. banks. Entries include: the name, address, and telephone number of the bank; type of charter; funds processor; automated clearinghouse; holding company; asset rank; financial figures; balance sheets; **officers and directors;** branches; subsidiaries; and foreign offices.

Law Firm and Law Enforcement Directories
Law Firms Yellow Book

This directory has information on 715 of the largest corporate law firms in the United States. It focuses on the **4,500 administrators and 10,000 attorneys** in these firms, and it is indexed by specialties, law schools, management/administrative personnel, geography, and personnel. It is updated semiannually.

Martindale-Hubbell Law Directory

This 19-volume annual directory contains over 900,000 entries consisting of profiles of law firms, corporate law departments, state bar associations, and law schools; biographies of lawyers in private and corporate practice; and descriptions of legal service, supplier, and consultant firms in the United States and Canada. **Indexing is by individual**, firm, specialty, and geographic area. The 4-volume International Law Directory, which is part of the 19-volume work, has similar entries and indexes for non-U.S. and non-Canadian firms and individuals. It includes law digests for 140 countries and is available electronically on CD-ROM and LEXIS.

National Directory of Law Enforcement Administrators, Prosecutors, Correctional Institutions, and Related Agencies

This annual source lists the following information: **names, addresses, telephone numbers, and fax numbers of city chiefs of police, county sheriffs, district attorneys, state highway patrols, and federal law enforcement agencies.**

Lloyd's Directories about the Shipping Industry
(List of Ship Owners)

This list includes over **40,000 owners, managers, and managing agents** for vessels listed in the Register of Ships. It is published annually in August and includes postal addresses; telephone, telex, and telefax numbers; fleet lists; and a geographical index. Subscribers receive eight cumulative supplements with the list.

Register of International Ship-Owning Groups

This register is available in three volumes annually (April, August, and December). The register is indexed by ship and company name and lists 20,000 companies operating on ships of at least 1,000 gross tons or more; ownership of 30,000 ships; **registered owners**, grouped by ship management company; and subsidiaries and associate companies, identified together with owners' representatives.

Register of Offshore Units, Submersibles, and Underwater Systems

This register is published annually in October. It contains sections listing mobile drilling rigs, submersibles, underwater systems, work units (ships, barges, and platforms) used for a variety of offshore work, **owners**, and addresses of offshore support ships with their fleet lists.

Register of Ships

This register is published in three volumes annually in July, listing details of over 80,000 merchant ships. Cumulative monthly supplements are provided to update the volumes.

Shipping Index

This index is published every week with reports on current voyages, latest reported movements, and essential characteristics of approximately 22,000 merchant vessels worldwide. There are three sections in the index: (1) the World Fleet Details section, which lists 22,000 vessels engaged in oceangoing trade and records over 40,000 changes to their **ownership**, characteristics, latest positions, and casualty histories; (2) the Marketing Briefing section, which highlights major changes in the market, from launches and name changes to demolition sales; and (3) the Buyer's Guide, which lists products and services directly related to the world's marine market.

Voyage Record

This record details the recent voyage history of 22,000 vessels in commercial service by reporting movements collected continually by Lloyd's agents worldwide. It is a companion to the Shipping Index, which lists the historical movements of vessels.

Index Medicus

This monthly classified index of the world's biomedical literature (including research, clinical practice, administration, policy issues, and healthcare services) is produced by the National Library of Medicine. It covers publications in all principal languages, and includes periodical articles and other analytical material; as well as books, pamphlets, and theses. The January issue includes lists of the periodicals indexed and medical subject headings used. Quarterly and annual cumulations are provided, and electronic access via commercial databases and CD-ROM is also available.

News Media Yellow Book

Over 31,000 reporters, writers, editors, and producers at more than 2,900 national news media organizations are listed in this yellow book. It features 12 media categories—on newspapers, news services, and bureaus; television, radio, and cable stations and networks; publishers; independent journalists; and consumer, trade, and association magazines. This directory is fully updated on a quarterly basis.

Public Affairs Information Service

This subject index to the articles, books, documents, microfiche, pamphlets, and reports in the public affairs field is published monthly and cumulated annually. Each year, it includes selective indexing to more than 1,600 periodicals and 8,000 books from around the world. It contains factual and statistical information about political science, government, legislation, economics, and sociology. It is also available electronically via CD-ROMs and commercial databases.

Reader's Guide to Periodical Literature

This guide indexes articles by subject and author in over 225 popular magazines. It is published semimonthly and cumulates annually. Each entry includes the article's author, title, and pages, as well as the periodical's title, volume, and date. The presence of graphic material is also noted. This tool is also available electronically on a commercial database and on CD-ROM.

The New York Times Index

This source, published semimonthly and cumulated annually, includes an exact reference to the date, section, page, and column of *The New York*

Times edition in which articles will be found. It contains cross-references to names and related topics, and has a brief synopsis of articles. Electronic access to the index is available in many forms from many sources; searchable, full-text files in the NEXIS and Dow Jones databases; a searchable, full-text CD-ROM called *The New York Times* ONDISC; and a searchable, full-text Internet site known as THE NEW YORK TIMES ON THE WEB.

Similar resources exist for many large-city newspapers in the United States, including the *Wall Street Journal* and *The Washington Post*. Every newspaper in the United States and the world can be read by going to the resources page at my Website: **http://www.josephculligan.com/resources.html.**

Abstract and Title Companies

Abstract and title companies generally develop an overview of the property, examine the title for liens and other conditions, and prepare a commitment to insure. Information contained in supporting records may include **transfer of property, locations, mortgage amounts, and releases of mortgages.**

Small Business Administration (SBA)

SBA guarantees loans made by commercial lenders to eligible small businesses; makes loans to businesses and individuals following federally declared disasters; and licenses investment companies to provide venture capital to eligible small businesses. SBA also (1) connects small firms owned by socially and economically disadvantaged Americans with contracts set aside by other federal agencies, and (2) seeks to increase federal contract opportunities for small businesses in general. SBA-guaranteed loans are made by private-sector lenders, with SBA promising to reimburse a specified percentage of any amount lost by the lender. By law, the amount of SBA's guarantee under its most popular and least restricted lending program is limited to $750,000, and the loan maturity to 25 years.

SBA may be the best source of financial and other information about the small businesses **(and their principals)** to which it provides assistance; many of them are exempt from public disclosure laws because of their smallness. Records on businesses and individuals that have received SBA assistance are maintained by the division that administers the program involved.

The local SBA district office maintains most records. Contact the local office of SBA's Office of Inspector General, Investigations Division, for assistance in obtaining records and other information.

Jails and Prisons

One of the best, free-of-charge, and most overlooked research techniques are jails and prisons. When you absolutely cannot find someone, that person may be incarcerated. The following will assist you in checking whether or not your subject is in custody, and you may also use the contact numbers to start a background check on someone.

The Freedom of Information Act (5 USC 552) and the Privacy Act of 1974 (5 USC 552a) authorize the release of certain information about federal inmates to any member of the general public requesting it. This includes information such as name, age, and register number; as well as sentencing and confinement data (offense, date sentenced, institution of confinement, etc.). With a few exceptions, only inmates convicted of violating federal laws (laws of the United States) are sent to federal prisons. Individuals awaiting trial for violating federal laws are also held in federal prisons. The Federal Bureau of Prisons also houses a few state inmates. However, most inmates convicted of violating state or local laws are sent to state prisons or city or county jails.

How to Get Inmate Information: Write to the Freedom of Information Act (FOIA) office, 320 First St., NW, Washington, DC 20534. FOIA requests are processed within several weeks, and there is usually no charge for inmate location requests. However, please be aware that if you request additional information, you may be charged for research time.

Federal Inmates: For federal inmates released before 1982, please write to the Office of Communications and Archives, Federal Bureau of Prisons, 320 First St., NW, Washington, DC 20534. Attn: Historic Inmate Locator Request. Please include as much identifying information as possible, such as, name (including middle name or middle initial if known), aliases, date of birth, race, crime, approximate dates in prison, name of prison, etc. The more information you provide, the more quickly the request can be processed.

State Inmates: Most states have their own locator systems. Contact the Department of Corrections in your state for further information.

State Prison Websites

**Alabama Department
of Corrections**
(334) 240-9500
http://agencies.state.al.us/doc

Alaska Department of Corrections
(907) 269-7400
http://www.correct.state.ak.us/

Arizona Department of Corrections
(602) 542-5536
http://www.state.az.us/

**Arkansas Department
of Corrections**
(501) 247-6200
http://www.state.ar.us/doc

California Department of Corrections
(916) 445-7688
http://www.cdc.state.ca.us/

California Youth Authority
(916) 262-1480
http://www.cya.ca.gov/index.html

Colorado Department of Corrections
(719) 579-9580
http://www.doc.state.co.us/

**Connecticut Department
of Corrections**
(860) 566-4457
http://www.state.ct.us/doc/

Delaware Department of Corrections
(302) 739-5601
http://www.state.de.us/correct/

**District of Columbia
Department of Corrections**
(202) 673-7316
http://www.washingtondc.gov/agen-
cies/detail.asp?id=25

Florida Department of Corrections
(850) 488-5021
http://www.dc.state.fl.us/
Florida Department of Juvenile Justice
http://www.djj.state.fl.us/

Georgia Department of Corrections
(404) 656-4593
http://www.dcor.state.ga.us/

Georgia Department of Juvenile Justice
http://www.djj.state.ga.us/

Hawaii Department of Public Safety
(808) 587-1288
http://www.hawaii.gov/icsd/psd/psd.html

Idaho Department of Corrections
(208) 334-2318
http://www.corr.state.id.us/

Illinois Department of Corrections
(217) 522-2666
http://www.idoc.state.il.us/

Indiana Department of Corrections
(317) 232-5715
http://www.corrections.com/ICA
http://www.state.in.us/indcorrection/

Iowa Department of Corrections
(515) 281-4811
http://www.state.ia.us/corrections/doc/-
index.html

Kansas Department of Corrections
(913) 296-3310
http://www.ink.org/public/kdoc

**Kansas Regional
Juvenile Detention Center**
http://www.gardencity.net/fico/juvenile/

Kentucky Department of Corrections
(502) 564-4726
http://www.jus.state.ky.us/

Louisiana Department of Public Safety and Correctional Services
(504) 342-6741
http://www.cole.state.la.us/

Maine Department of Corrections
(207) 287-4360
http://janus.state.me.us/corrections

Maryland Department of Public Safety and Correctional Services
(410) 764-4003
http://www.dpscs.state.md.us/doc/

Massachusetts Executive Office of Public Safety
(617) 727-7775
http://www.magnet.state.ma.us/doc/

Michigan Department of Corrections
(517) 373-0720
http://www.state.mi.us/mdoc

Minnesota Department of Corrections
(612) 642-0200
http://www.corr.state.mn.us/

Mississippi Department of Corrections
(601) 359-5621
http://www.mdoc.state.ms.us/

Missouri Department of Corrections
(314) 751-2389
http://www.corrections.state.mo.us/

Montana Department of Corrections
(406) 444-3930
http://www.state.mt.us/cor/

Nebraska Department of Correctional Services
(402) 471-2654
http://www.corrections.state.ne.us/

Nevada Department of Prisons
(702) 887-3285
http://www.state.nv.us/inprog.htm

New Hampshire Department of Corrections
(603) 271-5600
http://www.state.nh.us/doc/

New Jersey Department of Corrections
(609) 292-9860
http://www.state.nj.us/corrections

New Mexico Department of Corrections
(505) 827-8709
http://www.state.nm.us/corrections/

New York Department of Correctional Services
(518) 457-8126
http://www.docs.state.ny.us/

North Carolina Department of Corrections
(919) 733-4926
http://www.doc.state.nc.us/

North Dakota Department of Corrections and Rehabilitation
(701) 328-6390
http://www.state.nd.us/docr/Directory.htm

Ohio Department of Rehabilitation and Corrections
(614) 752-1164
http://www.drc.ohio.gov/

Ohio Department of Youth Services
http://www.state.oh.us/dys

Oklahoma Department of Corrections
(405) 425-2500
http://www.doc.state.ok.us/

Oregon Department of Corrections
(503) 945-0920
http://www.doc.state.or.us/

**Pennsylvania Department
of Corrections**
(717) 975-4860
http://www.cor.state.pa.us/

**Rhode Island Department
of Corrections**
(401) 464-2611
http://www.doc.state.ri.us/

**South Carolina Department
of Corrections**
(803) 896-8555
http://www.state.sc.us/scdc/

**South Dakota Department
of Corrections**
(605) 773-3478
http://www.state.sd.us/corrections/adult.htm

**Tennessee Department
of Corrections**
(615) 741-2071
http://www.state.tn.us/correction

Texas Department of Criminal Justice
(409) 294-6231
http://www.tdcj.state.tx.us

Texas Youth Commission
http://www.tyc.state.tx.us/

Utah Department of Corrections
(801) 265-5500
http://www.cr.ex.state.ut.us/

**Vermont Department
of Corrections**
(802) 241-2442
http://www.doc.state.vt.us/

Virginia Department of Corrections
(804) 674-3000
http://www.cns.state.va.us/doc/

**Washington Department
of Corrections**
(360) 753-1573
http://www.wa.gov/doc/

**West Virginia Department
of Military Affairs and Public Safety**
(304) 558-2037
http://www.state.wv.us/wvdoc/htm

**Wisconsin Department
of Corrections**
(608) 266-4548
http://badger.state.wi.us/agencies/doc/

**Wyoming Department
of Corrections**
(307) 777-7405
http://doc.state.wy.us/corrections.html

I am reprinting the following government Websites (agency, organization, and bureau), because you may have an interest (perhaps on a personal note), in the statistics of crime in this country. The Office for Victims of Crime may also be of interest to you if you or someone you know was a victim of **your subject**. Some of the other links below include Websites of the Most Wanted because **your subject** may be listed.

America's Most Wanted
http://www.amw.com/

America's Most Wanted Criminals
http://cpcug.org/user/jlacombe/wanted.html

American Probation and Parole Association
http://www.appa-net.org/

Bureau of Justice Statistics
http://www.ojp.usdoj.gov/bjs

Corrections Connections—American Correctional Assn. and American Jail Assn.
http://www.corrections.com/index.html

Corrections Today—American Correctional Association's Magazine
http://www.corrections.com/aca/cortoday/index.html

Crime and Victims Statistics—US Bureau of Justice Statistics
http://www.ojp.usdoj.gov/bjs/

Crime Statistics by State
http://www.disastercenter.com/crime/

Crime Statistics Tutorial
http://crime.org/

FBI's 10 Most Wanted
http://www.fbi.gov/mostwanted.htm

FBI (Federal Bureau of Investigation)
http://www.fbi.gov/

Federal Judicial Center
http://www.fjc.gov/

Midwest Gang Investigators Association
http://www.mgia.org/

National Alliance of Gang Investigations
http://www.nagia.org/

National Archive of Criminal Justice Data
http://www.icpsr.umich.edu/nacjd

National Criminal Justice
http://www.sso.org/ncja

National Crime Statistics Link Guide
http://www.crime.org

National Institute of Corrections Information Center
http://www.nicic.org/

National Major Gang Task Force
http://www.nmgtf.org/

Office for Victims of Crime
http://www.ojp.usdoj.gov/ovc

Source Book of Criminal Justice Statistics (BJS)
http://www.albany.edu/sourcebook

US Alcohol, Tobacco and Firearms Most Wanted
http://www.atf.treas.gov/wanted/index.htm

US Bureau of Justice Statistics on Capital Punishment
http://www.ojp.usdoj.gov/bjs/cp.htm

US Department of Justice
http://www.usdoj.gov/

Victims National Criminal Justice Reference Service
http://www.ncjrs.org/

World's Most Wanted
http://mostwanted.com
http://www.mostwanted.org

Workers' Compensation Records

When a search does not reveal a driver's license, vehicle or boat registration, a license for one of the more than 100 professions that require licensing by the state, a military record, evidence that the subject has died, or any of the other facets of a normal paper trail, I then turn to the Workers' Compensation Bureau.

Persons who receive benefit from the Workers' Compensation Bureau are those who have suffered injuries during the performance of their jobs. Many cases require that the person not engage in any employment, that they restrict activity outside the home, and that they not perform routine functions such as driving an automobile. Thus, the reason for a lack of records.

Many states will provide a complete file which, of course, may yield information including addresses, previous employers, dependents, etc. It is important to remember that states may change their policies on releasing compensation information. Many states, including California, Florida, and New Jersey, consider Workers' Compensation files to be public records, whereas several states will not release information. Write and inquire about the current policy using the following list:

ALABAMA

http://www.dir.state.al.us/wc.htm
Workman's Compensation Division
Industrial Relation Building
649 Monroe St.
Montgomery, Alabama 36131
(334) 242-2868 or (800) 528-5166

ALASKA

http://www.labor.state.ak.us/wc/wcbrochr.htm
Workers' Compensation Division
P.O. Box 25512
Juneau, Alaska 99802
(907) 465-2790

ARIZONA

http://www.statefund.com/toc.htm
State Compensation Fund
3031 North Second Street, Suite 110
Phoenix, Arizona 85012
(602) 631-2900
Fax: (602) 631-2955

ARKANSAS

http://www.awcc.state.ar.us/ruleind.html
Workers' Compensation Commission
4th and Spring Streets
Little Rock, Arkansas 72203-0950
(501) 682-3930 or (800) 622-4472

CALIFORNIA

http://www.dir.ca.gov/
Commission on Health, Safety, and
Workers' Compensation
455 Golden Gate Avenue, 10th Floor
San Francisco, California 94102
(415) 703-4220

COLORADO

http://workerscomp.cdle.state.co.us
Division of Workers' Compensation
1515 Arapahoe
Denver, Colorado 80202-2117
(303) 575-8700 or (888) 390-7936

CONNECTICUT

http://wcc.state.ct.us
Workers' Compensation Commission
21 Oak Street
Hartford, Connecticut 06106
(860) 493-1500
Fax: (860) 247-1361

DELAWARE

http://www.state.de.us/
Industrial Accident Board
820 North French Street
Wilmington, Delaware 19801

DISTRICT OF COLUMBIA

http://www.washingtondc.gov/
Office of Workers' Compensation
P.O. Box 56098
Washington, DC 20011

FLORIDA

http://www.fdles.state.fl.us/wc/
Division of Workers' Compensation
2810 Sharer Road, Suite 27
Tallahassee, Florida 32312-2107
(850) 922-0426
Fax: (850) 414-1238

GEORGIA

http://www.ganet.org/sbwc
Board of Workers' Compensation
270 Peachtree Street NW
Atlanta, Georgia 30303-1299
(404) 656-2048

HAWAII

http://www.uhwo.hawaii.edu/clear/HRS
386-1.html
Disability Compensation Division
96-043 Ala Ike
Pearl City, Hawaii 96782-3366
(808) 454-4774
Fax: (808) 454-4776

IDAHO

http://www.state.id.us/
Idaho Industrial Commission
317 Main Street
Boise, Idaho 83720

ILLINOIS

http://www.state.il.us/agency/iic
Illinois Industrial Commission
100 West Randolph St. #8-200
Chicago, Illinois 60601
(312) 814-6611

INDIANA

http://www.state.in.us/wkcomp
Workers' Compensation
Industrial Board
402 W. Washington Street, Rm. W-196
Indianapolis, Indiana 46204
(317) 232-3809

IOWA

http://www.state.ia.us/
Industrial Commissioner's Office
1000 East Grand Street
Des Moines, Iowa 50319

KANSAS

http://www.hr.state.ks.us/wc/html/wc.htm
Workers' Compensation
Department of Human Resources
800 SW Jackson, Room 600
Topeka, Kansas 66612-1227
(785) 296-3441

KENTUCKY

http://www.state.ky.us/agencies/
Kentucky Labor Cabinet
1047 U.S. 127S, Suite 4
Frankfort, Kentucky 40601
(502) 573-3505

LOUISIANA

http://www.state.la.us/
Office of Workers' Compensation
224 Florida Blvd, Suite 100
Baton Rouge, Louisiana 70801
(225) 219-4378 or (800) 209-7175
Fax: (225) 219-4377

MAINE

http://www.state.me.us/
Workers' Compensation Commission
24 Stone Street
Augusta, Maine 04330
(207) 287-2308 or (800) 400-6854

MARYLAND

http://www.charm.net/~wcc
Workers' Compensation Commission
6 North Liberty Street
Baltimore, Maryland 21201-3785
(410) 767-0900 or (800) 492-0479
Fax: (410) 333-8122

MASSACHUSETTS

http://www.magnet.state.ma.us/wcac
Workers' Compensation Advisory Council
600 Washington Street
Boston, Massachusetts 02111
(617) 727-4900 x 378
Fax: (617) 727-7122

MICHIGAN

http://www.cis.state.mi.us/wkrcomp/
Workers' Compensation Appellate Commission
1375 S. Washington
Lansing, Michigan 48909-7968
(517) 334-9719
Fax: (517) 334-9750

MINNESOTA

http://www.doli.state.mn.us/workcomp.html
Minnesota Department
of Labor and Industry
443 Layafette Road N.
St. Paul, Minnesota 55155
(651) 297-4377 or (800) 342-5354

MISSISSIPPI

http://www.mwcc.state.ms.us
Workers' Compensation Commission
1428 Lakeland Drive
Jackson, Mississippi 39216
(601) 987-4294 or (800) 840-3550

MISSOURI

http://www.dolir.state.mo.us/wc
Division of Workers' Compensation
P.O. Box 58
Jefferson City, Missouri 65102-0058
(573) 751-4231
Fax: (573) 751-2012

MONTANA

http://www.state.mt.us/
Division of Workers' Compensation
5 South Last Chance Gulch
Helena, Montana 59604

NEBRASKA

http://www.state.ne.us/
Workers' Compensation Court
P.O. Box 98908
Lincoln, Nebraska 65809

NEVADA

http://www.state.nv.us/
Department of Industrial Relations
1390 South Curry Street
Carson City, Nevada 98710

NEW HAMPSHIRE

http://www.state.nh.us/
Workers' Compensation Board
19 Pillsbury Street
Concord, New Hampshire 03301

NEW JERSEY

http://www.state.nj.us/
Division of Workers' Compensation
State Office Building, Room 381
Trenton, New Jersey 08625

NEW MEXICO

http://www.state.nm.us/
Workers' Compensation Division
P.O. Box 27198
Albuquerque, New Mexico 87125

NEW YORK

http://www.ci.nyc.ny.us/
State Insurance Fund
199 Church Street
New York, New York 10007

NORTH CAROLINA

http://www.state.nc.us/
Industrial Commission
430 North Salisbury Street
Raleigh, North Carolina 27611

NORTH DAKOTA

http://www.state.nd.us/
Workers' Compensation Bureau
4007 North State Street
Bismarck, North Dakota 58501

OHIO

http://www.state.oh.us/
Bureau of Workers' Compensation
246 North High Street
Columbus, Ohio 43215

OKLAHOMA

http://www.state.ok.us/
Oklahoma Workers' Compensation Court
1915 North Stiles
Oklahoma City, Oklahoma 73105

OREGON

http://www.state.or.us/
Department of Insurance and Finance
Labor and Industries Building
Salem, Oregon 97310

PENNSYLVANIA

http://www.state.pa.us/
Bureau of Workers' Compensation
1171 South Cameron Street
Harrisburg, Pennsylvania 17104

PUERTO RICO

http://fortaleza.govpr.org/
State Insurance Fund
GPO Box 5038
San Juan, Puerto Rico 00936

RHODE ISLAND

http://www.state.ri.us/
Department of Workers' Compensation
610 Manton Avenue
Providence, Rhode Island 02909

SOUTH CAROLINA

http://www.state.sc.us/
Industrial Commission
1615 Marian Street
Columbia, South Carolina 29202

SOUTH DAKOTA

http://www.state.sd.us/
Department of Labor
700 Governors Drive
Pierre, South Dakota 57501

TENNESSEE

http://www.state.tn.us/
Workers' Compensation Division
501 Union Building
Nashville, Tennessee 37219

TEXAS

http://www.state.tx.us/
Industrial Accident Board
200 East Riverside Drive
Austin, Texas 78704

UTAH

http://www.state.tx.us/
Workers' Compensation Fund
P.O. Box 510250
Salt Lake City, Utah 84151

VERMONT

http://www.state.vt.us/
Department of Labor and Industry
120 State Street
Montpelier, Vermont 05602

VIRGINIA

http://www.state.va.us/
Industrial Commission
P.O. Box 1794
Richmond, Virginia 23220

WASHINGTON

http://access.wa.gov/
Department of Labor and Industries
General Administration Building
Olympia, Washington 98504

WEST VIRGINIA

http://www.state.wv.us/
Workers' Compensation Appeal Board
601 Morris Street
Charleston, West Virginia 25301

WISCONSIN

http://www.state.wi.us/
Workers' Compensation Bureau
P.O. Box 7901
Madison, Wisconsin 53707

WYOMING

http://www.state.wy.us
Workers' Compensation Division
122 West 25th Street
Cheyenne, Wyoming 82002

Workers' Compensation Division
21 Labor & Industries Building, Salem, OR 97310 FAX: (503) 378-6828

Oregon

DEPARTMENT OF
INSURANCE AND
FINANCE

February 25, 1993

RE: Claimant: Robert K. Pavella
     SSN: 242/23/8376

     DOB: 6/17/35

This is in response to your letter requesting information on the
above-captioned claimant.

Based on the information provided, the claimant identified in your letter has
not been found in our data system. Claims are submitted to the Department
only when they are disabling or a denial has been issued.

R. Sherwood

Rebecca A. Sherwood
Information Unit
Operations Section

This letter states that there is no claim, but please note that Workers'
Compensation Offices also will tell you if a claim has been denied. This is
important because your subject may have applied and been denied benefits,
but there will be a whole file waiting for you to review that they had submitted. Excluding medical information, you will be able to find home
addresses, employers' names, wives' and children's names, and much
more. Many times you may use the information gleaned for background
checks and not just finding someone.

It is important that you understand that Workers' Compensation Offices sometimes enter into "agreements" with people. So make sure when writing for information on your subject that you ask about "agreements" because your subject may not be getting any benefit checks now, but may have signed a deal with the state for a one-time lump sum payment. If this is the case, ask for details of the "agreement," such as the amount given to your subject, home addresses, employer's name, etc. This is an excellent way to see if your subject has any assets.

Corporations and UCC Filings

A person is listed in corporation records because he or she is an officer, director, or registered agent. Even clubs, organizations, teams, churches, and associations require incorporation many times; therefore, if your subject is involved in a club, you may find him or her in a search of corporate records.

Write to the corporation division, and most states will be able to provide a list of all persons with a particular name, the names of the corporations they are associated with, and the addresses of the corporations. Many times the home addresses will be listed for officers and directors in smaller corporations such as the ones noted above.

The corporation division will also conduct a search that will generate a list of all persons with a particular name who have a Uniform Commercial Code (UCC) transaction. The UCC, in most states, is a transaction that is intended to create a security interest in personal property or fixtures including goods, documents, instruments, general intangibles, chattel paper; and a contract that creates a security interest in a chattel trust, trust deed, equipment trust, conditional sale, trust receipt, and lease or consignment intended as security.

If your subject has, for example, ever lent money or equipment to someone who has opened a business or has borrowed money or equipment, then they would be listed in UCC transactions. When you isolate your subject on the UCC list, you will want to order a complete photocopy of the transaction. This will show the business and/or home address of the subject, the names of any witnesses, the name of the business, and the name of the other party to the transaction.

ALABAMA

http://www.sos.state.al.us
Office of the Secretary of State
Corporations Division
State of Alabama
P.O. Box 5616-R
Montgomery, Alabama 36103

ALASKA

http://www.state.ak.us/
Division of Corporations
State of Alaska
P.O. Box 110807-O
Juneau, Alaska 99811

AMERICAN SAMOA

Corporations
Territory of American Samoa
Moata Fona
Pago Pago, American Samoa 96799

ARIZONA

http://www.state.az.us/
Arizona Corporation Commission
Secretary of State
State of Arizona
1200 West Washington
Phoenix, Arizona 85005

ARKANSAS

http://www.state.ar.us/
Office of the Secretary of State
Corporation Department
State of Arkansas
State Capital
Little Rock, Arkansas 72201

CALIFORNIA

http://www.state.ca.us/
Office of the Secretary of State
Corporation Division
State of California
1230 J Street
Sacramento, California 95814

COLORADO

http://www.state.co.us/gov_dir/sos
Department of State
Corporation Section
1560 Broadway, Suite 200
Denver, Colorado 80202

CONNECTICUT

http://www.sots.state.ct.us/
Office of the Secretary of State
Corporations
30 Trinity Street
Hartford, Connecticut 06106

DELAWARE

http://www.state.de.us/
Secretary of State
Division of Corporations
State of Delaware
P.O. Box 793-B
Dover, Delaware 19903

DISTRICT OF COLUMBIA

Recorder of Deeds
Recorder of Deeds Building
6th and D Street, N.W.
Washington, DC 20001

FLORIDA

http://www.dos.state.fl.us/
Office of the Secretary of State
Division of Corporations
State of Florida
P.O. Box 6327-I
Tallahassee, Florida 32301

GEORGIA

http://www.sos.state.ga.us/
Office of the Secretary of State
Corporations
State of Georgia
#2 Martin Luther King Jr. Drive S.E.
Atlanta, Georgia 30034

GUAM

Corporations
Government of Guam
P.O. Box 2796-N
Agana, Guam 96910

HAWAII

http://www.state.hi.us/
Department of Regulatory Agencies
Corporations
State of Hawaii
1010 Richards Street
Honolulu, Hawaii 96813

IDAHO

http://www.idsos.state.id.us/
Office of the Secretary of State
Corporations
State of Idaho
Statehouse, Room 203
Boise, Idaho 83720

ILLINOIS

http://www.sos.state.il.us/
Office of the Secretary
Corporation Department
State of Illinois
Centennial Building, Room 328
Springfield, Illinois 62756

INDIANA

http://www.state.in.us/sos
Office of the Secretary of State
Corporation Division
State of Indiana
Statehouse, Room 155
Indianapolis, Indiana 46204

IOWA

http://www.sos.state.ia.us
Office of the Secretary of State
Corporation Division
East 14th & Walnut Streets
Des Moines, Iowa 50319

KANSAS

http://www.kssos.org
Office of the Secretary of State
Corporation Services
Statehouse, Room 200
Topeka, Kansas 66612

KENTUCKY

http://www.sos.state.ky.us
Office of the Secretary of State
Corporation Department
State of Kentucky
P.O. 718-B
Frankfort, Kentucky 40602

LOUISIANA

http://www.sec.state.la.us
Department of State
Corporation Division
State of Louisiana
P.O. Box 94125-A
Baton Rouge, Louisiana 70804

MAINE

http://www.state.me.us/sos/sos.htm
Secretary of State
Bureau of Corporations
State of Maine
Statehouse, Station 101
Augusta, Maine 04333

MARSHALL ISLANDS

Corporations
P.O. Box 100-R
Republic of the Marshall Islands
Mojuro, Marshall Islands 96960

MARYLAND

http://www.sos.state.md.us
Department of Assessments & Taxations
Corporations
State of Maryland
301 West Preston Street
Baltimore, Maryland 21201

MASSACHUSETTS

http://www.magnet.state.ma.us/sec
Secretary of the Commonwealth
Corporations Division
One Ashburton Place, Room 1713
Boston, Massachusetts, 02133

MICHIGAN

http://www.sos.state.mi.us
Department of Commerce
Corporation Division
State of Michigan
6546 Mercantile Drive
Lansing, Michigan 48909

MICRONESIA

Corporations
Department of Resources
& Development
FSM National Government
Kolonia, Ponape, E.C.I. 96941

MINNESOTA

http://www.sos.state.mn.us
Office of the Secretary of State
Corporation Division
State of Minnesota
State Office Building, Room 180
St. Paul, Minnesota 55155

MISSISSIPPI

http://www.sos.state.ms.us
Office of the Secretary of State
Corporations
State of Mississippi
P.O. Box 136
Jackson, Mississippi 39205

MISSOURI

http://mosl.sos.state.mo.us
Office of the Secretary of State
Corporations
State of Missouri
P.O. Box 1159
Jefferson City, Missouri 65101

MONTANA

http://www.state.mt.us/
Office of the Secretary of State
Corporations Bureau
State Capitol, Room 202
Helena, Montana 59620

NEBRASKA

http://www.state.ne.us/
Office of the Secretary of State
Corporation Department
State of Nebraska
301 Centennial Mall South
Lincoln, Nebraska 68509

NEVADA

http://sos.state.nv.us
Office of the Secretary of State
Corporation Department
State of Nevada
Capitol Complex
Carson City, Nevada 89710

NEW HAMPSHIRE

http://www.state.nh.us/
Office of the Secretary of State
Corporate Division
State of New Hampshire
Statehouse Annex, Room 204
Concord, New Hampshire 03301

NEW JERSEY

http://www.state.nj.us/state
Office of the Secretary of State
Corporations
State of New Jersey
Statehouse, CN 308
Trenton, New Jersey 08625

NEW MEXICO

http://web.state.nm.us/
Secretary of State
State Corporation Commission
State of New Mexico
State Office Building, Room 420
Santa Fe, New Mexico 87503

NEW YORK

http://www.state.ny.us/
Department of State
Division of Corporations
State of New York
162 Washington Avenue
Albany, New York 12231

NORTH CAROLINA

http://www.state.nc.us/
Office of the Secretary of State
Corporation Division
300 North Salisbury Street
Raleigh, North Carolina 27611

NORTH DAKOTA

http://www.state.nd.us/
Office of the Secretary of State
Division of Corporations
State of North Dakota
601 East Boulevard Avenue
Bismarck, North Dakota 58501

OHIO

http://www.state.oh.us/
Office of the Secretary of State
Corporations Department
State of Ohio
50 East Broad Street
Columbus, Ohio 43215

OKLAHOMA

http://www.state.ok.us/
Office of the Secretary of State
Corporation Department
State of Oklahoma
State Capitol Building, Room 101
Oklahoma City, Oklahoma 73105

OREGON

http://www.state.or.us/
Department of Commerce
Corporation Division
State of Oregon
158 12th Street, N.E.
Salem, Oregon 97310

PENNSYLVANIA

http://www.state.pa.us/
Office of the Secretary of State
Corporations Bureau
State of Pennsylvania
North Office Building, Room 308
Harrisburg, Pennsylvania 17120

PUERTO RICO

Corporation Division
Commonwealth of Puerto Rico
Fortaleza Street #50
San Juan, Puerto Rico 00904

RHODE ISLAND

http://www.state.ri.us/
Secretary of State
Corporation Division
State of Rhode Island
270 Westminister Mall
Providence, Rhode Island 02903

SOUTH CAROLINA

http://www.state.sc.us/
Office of the Secretary of State
Corporation Department
State of South Carolina
P.O. Box 11350
Columbia, South Carolina 29211

SOUTH DAKOTA

http://www.state.sd.us/
Office of the Secretary of State
Corporation Department
State of South Dakota
500 East Capitol
Pierre, South Dakota 57501

TENNESSEE

http://www.state.tn.us/
Office of the Secretary of State
Corporation Section
State of Tennessee
James K. Polk, Building, Room 500
Nashville, Tennessee 37219

TEXAS

http://www.sos.state.tx.us
Office of the Secretary of State
Corporations Section
State of Texas
P.O. Box 13193-K
Austin, Texas 78711

UTAH

http://www.state.ut.us/
Secretary of State
Corporations
State of Utah
160 East Third Street
Salt Lake City, Utah 84145

VERMONT

http://www.state.vt.us/
Office of the Secretary of State
Corporations
109 State Street, Pavilion Building
Montpelier, Vermont 05602

VIRGIN ISLANDS

Corporations
Territory of Virgin Islands
Charlette Amalie, St. Thomas
Virgin Islands 00801

VIRGINIA

http://www.soc.state.va.us
Secretary of State
State Corporation Commission
P.O. Box 1197
Richmond, Virginia 23209

WASHINGTON

http://access.wa.gov/
Office of the Secretary of State
Corporations
211 12th Street
Olympia, Washington 98504

WEST VIRGINIA

http://www.state.wv.us/
Office of the Secretary of State
Corporations
State Capitol Building
Charleston, West Virginia 25305

WISCONSIN

http://www.state.wi.us/
Office of the Secretary of State
Division of corporations
P.O. Box 7648-E
Madison, Wisconsin 53707

WYOMING

http://soswy.state.wy.us
Office of the Secretary of State
Corporation
110 Capitol Building
Cheyenne, Wyoming 82002

CANADA

ALBERTA

Department of Corporate Affairs
Corporate Registry
10365 97th Street
Edmonton, Alberta T5J 3W7

BRITISH COLUMBIA

Ministry of Corporate Affairs
940 Blanchard Street
Victoria, British Columbia V8W 3E6

MANITOBA

Department of Corporate Affairs
Corporations
10th Floor, Woodsworth Building
405 Broadway Avenue
Winnipeg, Manitoba R3C 3L6

NEW BRUNSWICK

Corporations
348 King Street, Lynch Bldg, 2nd Floor
P.O. Box 6000
Fredericton, New Brunswick E3B 5H1

NEWFOUNDLAND & LABRADOR

Department of Justice
Corporations
P.O. 4750
St. John's, Newfoundland A1C 5T7

NORTHWEST TERRITORIES

Department of Justice
and Public Services
Corporations
Yellowknife, Northwest Territories
X1A 2L9

NOVA SCOTIA

Department of the Attorney General
Corporations
1660 Hollis Street
Halifax, Nova Scotia B3J 2Y4

PRINCE EDWARD ISLAND

Department of Justice
Corporations
73 Rochford Street
Charlottetown,
Prince Edward Island C1A 7N8

ONTARIO

Department of Corporate Affairs
Corporations
555 Yonge Street
Toronto, Ontario M7A 2H6

QUEBEC

Bureau de L'Inspecteur General des
Institutions Financieres
800 Place d'Youville
Quebec, P.Q. G1R 4Y5

SASKATCHEWAN

Department Commercial Affairs
Corporations Branch
1871 Smith Street
Regina, Saskatchewan S4P 3V7

YUKON

Department of Corporate Affairs
Corporate Affairs
P.O. Box 2703-R
Whitehorse, Yukon Y1A 2C6

STATE OF ALABAMA

OFFICE OF THE SECRETARY OF STATE

BUSINESS DIVISION

BILLY JOE CAMP
SECRETARY OF STATE

February 25, 1993

P.O. BOX 5616
MONTGOMERY, AL 36103

Re: Robert K. Pavella

Dear Sir/Madam:

An examination of the foreign and domestic corporate records on file in this office discloses no record of a corporation(s) by the above name.

With kindest regards, I am

Sincerely,

Billy Joe Camp
Secretary of State

BJC:rj

CORPORATIONS	LANDS & TRADEMARKS	UNIFORM COMMERCIAL CODE
(205) 242-5324	(205) 242-5325	(205) 242-5231

This will be the typical response from most states. You will note that there was no mention of any charge for this search on Robert K. Pavella. When there is information on file about your subject, you will want to order the Articles of Incorporation, which will show the original officers; and the annual report, which shows current officers. When you receive the paperwork on the corporations of your subject, you will want to look closely for any amendments. Amendments are added after incorporation to change by-laws, but many times amendments will give power of attorney or full ownership to another person who is not mentioned in any other corporate papers.

The Abandoned Property Technique

If you are searching for a subject who disappeared abruptly years ago, then the abandoned property files will be a source for you to explore.

The state takes possession of the following if a person has disappeared for, in most states, at least seven years:

Bank accounts
State income tax refunds
Payroll checks
Overpayment of insurance premiums
Credit balance on credit cards
Utility refunds
Dividend checks
Annuity checks
Telephone deposit refunds
Safe deposit boxes

Each state maintains an alphabetical listing of all persons who have had property or monies held in escrow by the state. Write to any state where your subject may have lived or has conducted any business in.

If your subject is listed and is due any significant amount of property or monies, you can be assured that companies that find persons listed in the abandoned property lists are searching for your subject. These companies assess the person found, a percentage—usually 30 percent of the money that is held in escrow.

You may check periodically with the state that has your subject listed to see if a research company has located the subject, or you can request that the state check the refund file that indicates if a person had been due property or monies and were located. The address that the state sent the refund to is public information.

I have made available on Joseph Culligan's Resources CD links to all the offices that are listed in this chapter. Additionally, I have included links to other sites where refunds are made available such as: Housing and Urban Development Refunds for mortgage insurance obtained by a government loan, Pension Guarantee Benefit Fund Refunds on retirement accounts, the Swiss Bank Accounts site created for holocaust victims, Canadian Unclaimed Property, and refunds from the National Credit Union Administration.

ALABAMA

http://www.treasury.state.al.us/website/-ucpd/ucpd_frameset.html
Alabama Revenue Department
Unclaimed Property Section
P.O. Box 327350-E
Montgomery, Alabama 36132

ALASKA

http://www.revenue.state.ak.us/tax/
Alaska Department of Revenue
Unclaimed Property Section
Box 8A
Juneau, Alaska 99811

ARIZONA

http://www.revenue.state.az.us/uncl-prop.htm
Arizona Department of Revenue
Unclaimed Property Processing Unit
1600 West Monroe, Sixth Floor
Phoenix, Arizona 85007

ARKANSAS

http://www.state.ar.us/auditor/unclprop/
Auditor of State
Unclaimed Property Department
230 State Capitol
Little Rock, Arkansas 72201

CALIFORNIA

http://scoweb.sco.ca.gov/scoucp/inquiry/index.htm
Office of the State Controller
Division of Unclaimed Property
P.O. Box 942850-N
Sacramento, California 94250

COLORADO

http://www.treasurer.state.co.us/pay-back.html
Colorado State Treasury
Great Colorado Payback
1560 Broadway, Ste. 1225
Denver, Colorado 80202

CONNECTICUT

http://www.state.ct.us/ott/ucp.html
Office of the State Treasurer
Unclaimed Property Division
20 Trinity Street
Hartford, Connecticut 06160

DELAWARE

http://www.state.de.us/revenue/
Delaware State Escheator
P.O. Box 89311-J
Wilmington, Delaware 19899

DISTRICT OF COLUMBIA

http://www.washingtondc.gov/
Department of Finance and Revenue
Unclaimed Property Division
300 Indiana Avenue N.W.
Washington, DC 20002

FLORIDA

http://up.dbf.state.fl.us/
Office of the Comptroller
Division of Finance
Abandoned Property Section
The Capitol
Tallahassee, Florida 32399

GEORGIA

http://www.state.ga.us/dor/ptd/ucp/
Georgia Department of Revenue
Property Tax Division
Unclaimed Property Section
405 Trinity—Washington Building
Atlanta, Georgia 30334

HAWAII

http://www.state.hi.us/
Finance Division
Department of Budget and Finance
P.O. Box 150-O
Honolulu, Hawaii 96810

IDAHO

http://www2.state.id.us/tax/unclaimed_i
daho.htm
Unclaimed Property Section
State Tax Commission
P.O. Box 36-Y
Boise, Idaho 83722

ILLINOIS

http://www.cashdash.net/
State of Illinois
Department of Financial Institutions
Unclaimed Property Division
421 East Capitol Avenue
Springfield, Illinois 62706

INDIANA

http://www.state.in.us/serv/ag_ucp
Unclaimed Property Division
Office of the Attorney General
219 State House
Indianapolis, Indiana 46204

IOWA

http://www.treasurer.state.ia.us/
Unclaimed Property Division
State Treasurer's Office
Hoover State Office Building
Des Moines, Iowa 50319

KANSAS

http://www.treasurer.state.ks.us/upsearch
.htm
Division of Unclaimed Property
Office of State Treasurer
900 Jackson, Suite 201
Topeka, Kansas 66612

KENTUCKY

http://www.state.ky.us
Miscellaneous Excise Tax Section
Revenue Cabinet
The Capitol
Frankfort, Kentucky 40620

LOUISIANA

http://www.rev.state.la.us/Unclaimed.-
htm
Unclaimed Property Division
P.O. Box 91010-E
Baton Rouge, Louisiana 70821

MAINE

http://www.state.me.us/treasurer/prop-
erty.htm
Abandoned Property Division
Treasury Department
Station Number 39
Augusta, Maine 04333

MARYLAND

http://www.comp.state.md.us/unclaim.-
asp
Comptroller of the Treasurer
Unclaimed Property Division
301 West Preston Street
Baltimore, Maryland 21201

MASSACHUSETTS

http://www.magnet.state.ma.us/treas-
ury/abp.htm
Office of the Treasurer
Unclaimed Property Division
50 Franklin Street, Second Floor
Boston, Massachusetts 02110

MICHIGAN

http://www.mlive.com/news/miou.html
Escheats Division
Michigan Department of the Treasury
Lansing, Michigan 48922

MINNESOTA

http://www.commerce.state.mn.us/-
mainup.htm
Unclaimed Property Office
500 Metro Square Building
Saint Paul, Minnesota 55101

MISSISSIPPI

http://www.treasury.state.ms.us./claim.-
htm
State Treasury Department
Attention: Unclaimed Property
P.O. Box 138-D
Jackson, Mississippi 39205

MISSOURI

http://www.sto.state.mo.us/ucp/data-
base/search.htm
Unclaimed Property Department
P.O. Box 1272-R
Jefferson City, Missouri 65102

MONTANA

http://www.unclaimed.org/mainframe.asp
Department of Revenue
Abandoned Property Section
Mitchell Building
Helena, Montana 59620

NEBRASKA

http://www.state.ne.us
Office of the State Treasurer
Unclaimed Property Section
P.O. Box 94788
Capitol Building
Lincoln, Nebraska 68509

NEVADA

http://www.upd.state.nv.us/
Department of Commerce
Unclaimed Property Division
State Mail Room
Las Vegas, Nevada 89158

NEW HAMPSHIRE

http://www.state.nh.us/treasury/search.-
html
Abandoned Property Department
State House Annex
Room 121
Concord, New Hampshire 03301

NEW JERSEY

http://www.state.nj.us/treasury/taxa-
tion/unclaimsrch.htm
Department of the Treasury
Office of Financial Management
1 West State Street
Trenton, New Jersey 08625

NEW MEXICO

http://www.state.nm.us/
Unclaimed Property Unit
Taxation and Revenue Department
P.O. Box 630-V
Santa Fe, New Mexico 87509

NEW YORK

http://www.osc.state.ny.us/cgi-
bin/db2www/ouffrm.d2w/input
New York State Comptroller
Office of Unclaimed Funds
P.O. Box 7003
Albany, New York 12225

NORTH CAROLINA

http://www.treasurer.state.nc.us/escheats/
fresc000.htm
Treasurer
Escheat and Unclaimed Property
325 North Salisbury Street
Raleigh, North Carolina 27611

NORTH DAKOTA

http://www.land.state.nd.us/
Unclaimed Property Division
State Land Department
Sixth Floor, State Capitol
Bismarck, North Dakota 58505

OHIO

http://www.state.oh.us/
Ohio Department of Commerce
Division of Unclaimed Funds
77 South High Street
Columbus, Ohio 43266

OKLAHOMA

http://www.kocotv.com/5oys/fortune.html
Oklahoma Tax Commission
Business Tax Division
Unclaimed Property Section
2501 Lincoln Boulevard
Oklahoma City, Oklahoma 73194

OREGON

http://rogue.sscgis.state.or.us/dsl/search.-
cfm
Division of State Lands
Unclaimed Property Division
1600 State Street
Salem, Oregon 97310

PENNSYLVANIA

http://www.treasury.state.pa.us/Unclaimed-
PropertyInquiry.html
Department of Revenue
Abandoned and Unclaimed Property
Bureau of Administrative Services
2850 Turnpike Industrial Park
Middletown, Pennsylvania 17057

PUERTO RICO

www.prstar.net/default1aeng.htm
Secretary of the Treasury
Unclaimed Property Division
San Juan, Puerto Rico 00940

RHODE ISLAND

http://www.state.ri.us/treas/moneylst.htm
Office of General Treasurer
Unclaimed Property Division
P.O. Box 1435-S
Providence, Rhode Island 02901

SOUTH CAROLINA

http://www.state.sc.us/treas/uprop/search
.html
South Carolina Tax Division
P.O. Box 125-I
Columbia, South Carolina 29214

SOUTH DAKOTA

http://www.state.sd.us/state/executive/-
treasurer/prop.htm
Unclaimed Property Administrator
500 East Capitol
Pierre, South Dakota 57501

TENNESSEE

http://www.state.tn.us
Unclaimed Property Division
Andrew Jackson Building
11th Floor
Nashville, Tennessee 37219

TEXAS

http://www.window.state.tx.us/comp-
trol/unclprop/upsearch.html
Office of the State Treasurer
P.O. Box 12608-N
Capitol Station
Austin, Texas 78711

UTAH

http://www.treasurer.state.ut.us/
Utah State Treasurer
Unclaimed Property Division
219 State Capitol
Salt Lake City, Utah 84114

VERMONT

http://www.tre.state.vt.us/
Abandoned Property Division
Office of State Treasurer
133 State Street
Montpelier, Vermont 05602

VIRGINIA

http://www.trs.state.va.us/
Division of Unclaimed Property
P.O. Box 3-R-G
Richmond, Virginia 23207

WASHINGTON

http://dor.wa.gov/index.asp?//unclaim/-
index.htm
Unclaimed Property Section
Department of Revenue
P.O. Box 448-T
Olympia, Washington 98507

WEST VIRGINIA

http://www.wvtreasury.com/search_un-
claimed_property_databa.htm
Office of the Treasurer of State
Division of Unclaimed Property
The State Capitol, Room E-147
Charleston, West Virginia 25305

WISCONSIN

http://prd1.state.wi.us/servlet/trdUn-
claimProperty
Office of State Treasurer
Unclaimed Property Division
P.O. Box 2114-H
Madison, Wisconsin 53701

WYOMING

http://www.state.wy.us/~sot/text_unc_-
prop.html
Office of the State Treasurer
Unclaimed Property Division
State Capitol Building
Cheyenne, Wyoming 82002

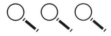

Bankruptcy Records

n 1999, 1,322,000 individuals filed for bankruptcy. If you have reason to believe that your subject has ever filed for bankruptcy or will file for bankruptcy, then this is an excellent source.

Bankruptcy records are public information. The petition file will contain the subject's Social Security Number, date of birth, current and former addresses, bank accounts, stock ownership, employment history (including a list of the salaries and fringe benefits earned for the past several years), and a list of all property, including vehicles and other important financial and personal information.

The Vehicle Identification Number (VIN) of each vehicle listed in the file will be shown. You may access the current address by writing to the appropriate motor vehicle department listed elsewhere in this manual.

Property that the subject will retain because it qualifies as exempt from the bankruptcy will be listed. This property may provide another lead in your search for the subject because the address of property will be listed.

Chapter 7 bankruptcy is commonly known as *liquidation bankruptcy,* and any person or business may file. *Chapter 11 bankruptcy* is a reorganization of debt. *Chapter 13 bankruptcy* is an adjustment of debts for a wage earner. This option is available to individuals with a regular income and who have fixed unsecured debts less than $100,000, and secured debts of less than $350,000.

Write to the bankruptcy court you feel that your subject may have filed in. If your subject does have a bankruptcy file, then review the file completely, and you will be provided with much information that will assist in your search.

Remember that a person's business bankruptcy is as important as their personal bankruptcy. The purpose of checking bankruptcy records is to find your subject. A business bankruptcy file contains all of the people and companies that your subject conducted business with. You can call, write, or visit any of these people or businesses, and you will be pleasantly surprised at the level of cooperation you will receive. These entities were forced to absorb monetary losses because of your subject, and they will in most instances be more than happy to provide you with information that will lead you to your subject.

ALABAMA

United States Bankruptcy Court
500 South 22nd Street
Birmingham, Alabama 35233
http://www.alnd.uscourts.gov

United States Bankruptcy Court
P.O. Box 1248-I
Montgomery, Alabama 36192
http://www.alnd.uscourts.gov

United States Bankruptcy Court
P.O. Box 2865-S
Mobile, Alabama 36652
http://www.als.uscourts.gov

ALASKA

United States Bankruptcy Court
222 West 7th Avenue
Anchorage, Alaska 99513
http://www.akd.uscourts.gov

ARIZONA

United States Bankruptcy Court
230 North 1st Avenue
Phoenix, Arizona 85025
http://www.azb.uscourts.gov

United States Bankruptcy Court
110 South Church
Tucson, Arizona 85702
http://www.azb.uscourts.gov

ARKANSAS

United States Bankruptcy Court
P.O.Box 2381-A
Little Rock, Arkansas 72203
http://www.arwd.uscourts.gov

CALIFORNIA

United States Bankruptcy Court
1130 O Street
Fresno, California 93721
http://www.caed.uscourts.gov

United States Bankruptcy Court
325 West F Street
San Diego, California 92101-6998
http://www.casb.uscourts.gov

United States Bankruptcy Court
235 Pine Street, 19th Floor
San Francisco, California 94104
http://www.canb.uscourts.gov

United States Bankruptcy Court
1130 12th Street, Suite C
Modesto, California 95354
http://www.caeb.uscourts.gov

COLORADO

United States Bankruptcy Court
721 19th Street
Denver, Colorado 80202-2508
http://www.co.uscourts.gov

CONNECTICUT

United States Bankruptcy Court
450 Main Street
Hartford, Connecticut 06103
http://www.ctb.uscourts.gov

DELAWARE

United States Bankruptcy Court
824 Market Street, 5th Floor
Wilmington, Delaware 19801
http://www.deb.uscourts.gov

DISTRICT OF COLUMBIA

United States Bankruptcy Court
333 Constitution Avenue, Northwest
Washington, DC 20001
http://www.dcd.uscourts.gov

FLORIDA

United States Bankruptcy Court
4921 Memorial Highway, #200
Tampa, Florida 33634
http://www.flmd.uscourts.gov

United States Bankruptcy Court
311 W. Monroe Street, #206
Jacksonville, Florida 32202
http://www.flmb.uscourts.gov

United States Bankruptcy Court
227 North Bronough Street
Tallahassee, Florida 32301
www.flnd.uscourts.gov

United States Bankruptcy Court
51 Southwest 1st Avenue, Room 1517
Miami, Florida 33130
http://www.flmd.uscourts.gov

United States Bankruptcy Court
299 East Broward Boulevard
Fort Lauderdale, Florida 33301
http://www.flmp.uscourts.gov

GEORGIA

United States Bankruptcy Court
P.O. Box 1957-W
433 Cherry Street
Macon, Georgia 31202
http://www.gamb.uscourts.gov

United States Bankruptcy Court
75 Spring Street
Atlanta, Georgia 30303
http://www.ganb.uscourts.gov

United States Bankruptcy Court
P.O. Box 8347-E
Savannah, Georgia 31412
www.ganb.uscourts.gov

HAWAII

United States Bankruptcy Court
P.O. Box 50121-S
1132 Bishop Street, Suite 250-L
Honolulu, Hawaii 96813
http://www.hib.uscourts.gov

IDAHO

United States Bankruptcy Court
P.O. Box 2600-O
550 W. Fort St. MSC 042
Boise, Idaho 83724
http://www.id.uscourts.gov

ILLINOIS

United States Bankruptcy Court
P.O. Box 2438-M
Springfield, Illinois 62705
http://www.ilcb.uscourts.gov

United States Bankruptcy Court
219 South Dearborn Street
Chicago, Illinois 60604
http://www.ilnb.uscourts.gov

United States Bankruptcy Court
P.O. Box 309
750 Missouri Avenue
East St. Louis, Illinois 62201
http://www.ilsb.uscourts.gov

INDIANA

United States Bankruptcy Court
204 South Main Street
South Bend, Indiana 46601
http://www.innd.uscourts.gov

United States Bankruptcy Court
610 Connecticut Street
Gary, Indiana 46402
http://www.innb.uscourts.gov

United States Bankruptcy Court
46 East Ohio Street
Indianapolis, Indiana 46204
http://www.insd.uscourts.gov

IOWA

United States Bankruptcy Court
425 Second St. SE
Cedar Rapids, Iowa 52407
http://www.ianb.uscourts.gov

KANSAS

United States Bankruptcy Court
401 North Market Street
Wichita, Kansas 67202
http://www.ksb.uscourts.gov

KENTUCKY

United States Bankruptcy Court
P.O. Box 1111-E
100 East Vine St. #200
Lexington, Kentucky 40507
http://www.kyeb.uscourts.gov

United States Bankruptcy Court
601 West Broadway
Louisville, Kentucky 40202
http://www.kywd.uscourts.gov

LOUISIANA

United States Bankruptcy Court
500 Camp Street
New Orleans, Louisiana 70130
http://www.laed.uscourts.gov

United States Bankruptcy Court
500 Fannin Street
Shreveport, Louisiana 71109
http://www.lawb.uscourts.gov

United States Bankruptcy Court
412 North 4th Street
Baton Rouge, Louisiana 70802
http://www.laed.uscourts.gov

MAINE

United States Bankruptcy Court
537 Congress St.
Portland, Maine 04101
http://www.meb.uscourts.gov

MARYLAND

United States Bankruptcy Court
101 West Lombard Street
Baltimore, Maryland 21201
http://www.mdd.uscourts.gov

MASSACHUSETTS

United States Bankruptcy Court
1101 Thomas O'Neill Federal Building
Boston, Massachusetts 02222-1074
http://www.mab.uscourts.gov

MICHIGAN

United States Bankruptcy Court
211 W. Fort Street
Detroit, Michigan 48226
http://www.mieb.uscourts.gov

United States Bankruptcy Court
110 Michigan Street. NW
Grand Rapids, Michigan 49503
http://www.miwd.uscourts.gov

MINNESOTA

United States Bankruptcy Court
316 North Robert Street
Saint Paul, Minnesota 55101
http://www.mnb.uscourts.gov

United States Bankruptcy Court
300 South 4th Street
Minneapolis, Minnesota 55415
http://www.mnb.uscourts.gov

MISSISSIPPI

United States Bankruptcy Court
301 W. Commerce St.
Aberdeen, Mississippi 39730
http://www.msnb.uscourts.gov

United States Bankruptcy Court
245 East Capitol Street, Suite 316
Jackson, Mississippi 39201
http://www.mssd.uscourts.gov

United States Bankruptcy Court
725 Washington Loop
Biloxi, Mississippi 39530
http://www.msnd.uscourts.gov

MISSOURI

United States Bankruptcy Court
211 N. Broadway
St. Louis, Missouri 63102-2734
http://www.moed.uscourts.gov

United States Bankruptcy Court
400 E. 9th St., Room 1800
Kansas City, Missouri 64106
http://www.moept.uscourts.gov

MONTANA

United States Bankruptcy Court
400 N. Main St.
Butte, Montana 59701
http://www.mtb.uscourts.gov

NEBRASKA

United States Bankruptcy Court
215 N. 17th St., Room 8400
Omaha, Nebraska 68102
http://www.ned.uscourts.gov

United States Bankruptcy Court
460 Federal Building
100 Centennial Mall
Lincoln, Nebraska 68508
http://ned.uscourts.gov

NEVADA

United States Bankruptcy Court
300 Las Vegas Boulevard, Room 3210
Las Vegas, Nevada 89101
http://www.nvb.uscourts.gov

United States Bankruptcy Court
300 Booth Street, Room 1109
Reno, Nevada 89509
http://nvb.uscourts.gov

NEW HAMPSHIRE

United States Bankruptcy Court
55 Pleasant Street, Room 110
Concord, New Hampshire 03301-3941
http://www.nhd.uscourts.gov

NEW JERSEY

United States Bankruptcy Court
401 Market Street, 2nd Floor
Camden, New Jersey 08101
http://www.njb.uscourts.gov

United States Bankruptcy Court
402 E. State Street
Trenton, New Jersey 08608
http://www.njb.uscourts.gov

United States Bankruptcy Court
50 Walnut Street
Newark, New Jersey 07102
http://www.njb.uscourts.gov

NEW MEXICO

United States Bankruptcy Court
421 Gold Avenue SW, Room 314
Albuquerque, New Mexico 87103
http://www.nmcourt.fed.us/bkdocs

NEW YORK

United States Bankruptcy Court
225 Cadman Plaza East
Brooklyn, New York 11201
http://www.nyed.uscourts.gov

United States Bankruptcy Court
1 Bowling Green
New York, New York 10004
http://www.nysb.uscourts.gov

United States Bankruptcy Court
445 Broadway, Room 222
Albany, New York 12207-2924
www.nynd.uscourts.gov

United States Bankruptcy Court
300 Pearl St., Suite 250
Buffalo, New York 14202-2501
www.nywb.uscourts.gov

United States Bankruptcy Court
100 State Street
Rochester, New York 14614
http://www.nywb.uscourts.gov

NORTH CAROLINA

United States Bankruptcy Court
1760 Parkwood Blvd
Wilson, North Carolina 27894-2807
http://www.nceb.uscourts.gov

United States Bankruptcy Court
300 Fayetteville Street Mall
P.O. Box 144-B
Raleigh, North Carolina 27602-1441
http://www.ncmb.uscourts.gov

United States Bankruptcy Court
P.O. Box 26100-O
101 S. Edgeworth St.
Greensboro, North Carolina 27401
http://www.ncmb.uscourts.gov

United States Bankruptcy Court
100 Otis Street
Asheville, North Carolina 28801
http://www.ncwd.uscourts.gov

NORTH DAKOTA

United States Bankruptcy Court
P.O. Box 1110-O
655 First Avenue N
Fargo, North Dakota 58107
http://www.ndb.uscourts.gov

OHIO

United States Bankruptcy Court
1716 Spielbusch Avenue
Toledo, Ohio 43624
http://www.ohnb.uscourts.gov

United States Bankruptcy Court
127 Public Square
Cleveland, Ohio 44114-1309
http://www.ohnb.uscourts.gov

United States Bankruptcy Court
2 South Main Street
Akron, Ohio 44308
http://www.ohnb.uscourts.gov

United States Bankruptcy Court
125 Market Street
Youngstown, Ohio 44501
http://www.ohnb.uscourts.gov

United States Bankruptcy Court
201 Cleveland Avenue SW
Canton, Ohio 44702
http://www.ohnb.uscourts.gov

OKLAHOMA

United States Bankruptcy Court
224 S. Boulder Avenue
Tulsa, Oklahoma 74103
http://www.oknb.uscourts.gov

United States Bankruptcy Court
111 W. 4th Street, Room 229
Okmulgee, Oklahoma 74447
http://www.okeb.uscourts.gov

United States Bankruptcy Court
201 Dean McGee Avenue
Oklahoma City, Oklahoma 73102
http://oknb.uscourts.gov

OREGON

United States Bankruptcy Court
P.O. Box 1335-U
Eugene, Oregon 97440
http://www.ord.uscourts.gov/

United States Bankruptcy Court
1001 Southwest Fifth Avenue
Portland, Oregon 97204
http://www.ord.uscourts.gov

PENNSYLVANIA

United States Bankruptcy Court
600 Grant Street
Pittsburgh, Pennsylvania 15219
http://www.pawb.uscourts.gov

United States Bankruptcy Court
197 South Main Street
Wilkes Barre, Pennsylvania 18701
http://www.pamd.uscourts.gov

United States Bankruptcy Court
601 Market Street, Room 2609
Philadelphia, Pennsylvania 19106-1797
http://www.paed.uscourts.gov

RHODE ISLAND

United States Bankruptcy Court
380 Westminster Mall
Providence, Rhode Island 02903
http://www.rib.uscourts.gov

SOUTH CAROLINA

United States Bankruptcy Court
P.O. Box 1448-S
1100 Laurel Street
Columbia, South Carolina 29202
http://www.scb.uscourts.gov

SOUTH DAKOTA

United States Bankruptcy Court
400 S. Phillips Avenue, Room 117
Sioux Falls, South Dakota 57117
http://www.sdb.uscourts.gov

TENNESSEE

United States Bankruptcy Court
800 Market Street, Suite 330
Knoxville, Tennessee 37902
http://www.tneb.uscourts.gov

United States Bankruptcy Court
701 Broadway, P.O. Box 24890-J
Nashville, Tennessee 37202
http://www.tnmb.uscourts.gov

TEXAS

United States Bankruptcy Court
200 East Ferguson Street
Tyler, Texas 75702
http://www.txeb.uscourts.gov

United States Bankruptcy Court
1100 Commerce Street, Room 12A24
Dallas, Texas 75242-1496
http://www.txnb.uscourts.gov

United States Bankruptcy Court
501 West 10th Street
Fort Worth, Texas 76102-3643
http://www.txnb.uscourts.gov

United States Bankruptcy Court
1205 Texas Avenue
Lubbock, Texas 79401-4002
http://www.txnb.uscourts.gov

United States Bankruptcy Court
P.O. Box 15960-O
Amarillo, Texas 79105-0960
http://www.txeb.uscourts.com

United States Bankruptcy Court
515 Rusk Avenue
Houston, Texas 77002
http://www.txnd.uscourts.gov

United States Bankruptcy Court
P.O. Box 1439-E
San Antonio, Texas 78295
http://www.txeb.uscourts.com

UTAH

United States Bankruptcy Court
350 South Main Street
Salt Lake City, Utah 84101
http://www.state.ut.us/government.htm

VERMONT

United States Bankruptcy Court
P.O. Box 6648-P
Rutland, Vermont 05702
http://www.state.vt.us/

VIRGINIA

United States Bankruptcy Court
200 South Washington Street
Alexandria, Virginia 22314
http://www.vaeb.uscourts.gov

United States Bankruptcy Court
1100 E. Main St., Suite 310
Richmond, Virginia 23219-3515
http://www.vaeb.uscourts.gov

United States Bankruptcy Court
600 Granby Street, 4th Floor
Norfolk, Virginia 23510
http://www.vaeb.uscourts.gov

United States Bankruptcy Court
101 25th Street, Room 106
Newport News, Virginia 23607
http://vaeb.uscourts.com

United States Bankruptcy Court
210 Church Avenue SW, Room 200
Roanoke, Virginia 24011
http://www.vawb.uscourts.gov

WASHINGTON

United States Bankruptcy Court
904 W. Riverside, Suite 304
P.O. Box 2164-I
Spokane, Washington 99201
http://www.waeb.uscourts.gov

United States Bankruptcy Court
1200 Sixth Avenue, Room 315
Seattle, Washington 98101
http://www.wawb.uscourts.gov

WEST VIRGINIA

United States Bankruptcy Court
324 Main Street,
Clarkesburg, West Virginia 26302
http://www.wvnb.uscourts.gov

United States Bankruptcy Court
12th and Chapline Streets
Wheeling, West Virginia 26003
http://www.wvnb.uscourts.gov

WISCONSIN

United States Bankruptcy Court
517 East Wisconsin Avenue
Milwaukee, Wisconsin 53202
http://www.wieb.uscourts.gov

United States Bankruptcy Court
P.O. Box 548
Madison, Wisconsin 53701
http://www.wieb.uscourts.gov

WYOMING

United States Bankruptcy Court
2120 Capitol Avenue
Cheyenne, Wyoming 82001
http://www.wyb.uscourts.gov

John L. Cawler
Name
59 Huser Lane Apt. 23
Street
Nanuet, New York 10954
City, State, Zip
914-675-7723
Telephone

☐ Attorney for Debtor(s)   (If applicable) Attorney's
☒ Debtor in Pro Se   State Bar I.D. No.

RECORDED

MAR 20 1993

CLERK OF CIRCUIT

UNITED STATES BANKRUPTCY COURT
Northeast DISTRICT OF New York

In re _____
[Set forth here all names including married, maiden, and trade names used by debtor within last 6 years.]

John L. Cawler   Debtor
Cawler Liquor Store
Cawler Food and Gas Station
Barbara Cawler
Barbara Cawler's Secretarial Service
Social Security No(s). 078-90-0061 and all
Employer's Tax Identification Nos.[If any]_____

Case No. 93-827361-9

Chapter Chapter 13

NOTICE OF AVAILABLE CHAPTERS BY THE CLERK OF THE COURT

1. Section 342(b) of 11 U.S. Code ("The Bankruptcy Code") states:
   "Prior to the commencement of a case under this title by an individual whose debts are primarily consumer debts, the clerk shall give written notice to such individual that indicates each chapter of this title under which such individual may proceed."

2. If your debts are primarily consumer ones (as opposed to business debts) and they do not exceed $100,000.00 unsecured or $350,000.00 secured (11 U.S.C. § 109(e)), you are eligible to file under Chapter 13 and to use future income to pay all or a portion of your existing debts.

3. You are also eligible to file under Chapter 11 ($500.00 filing fees) for debt reorganization.

4. You are not eligible to file under Chapter 9.

5. You are eligible to file under Chapter 7 ("straight bankruptcy"), whereby debts are eliminated and your non-exempt assets are liquidated by the trustee for the benefit of your creditors.

6. You may be eligible to file under Chapter 12.

7. All general filing eligibility is subject to 11 U.S.C. §§ 109, 727(a)(8) and (9), and 707(b). Consult your attorney.

Robert T. Vernon, Jr.
Clerk of the Court

I HAVE READ THE ABOVE "NOTICE OF AVAILABLE CHAPTERS".

Signature of Debtor

Signature of Joint Debtor

You will be able to find your subject in the bankruptcy files by name only. When you find the first application to the bankruptcy court, you will note that you now have the case number. Pull the entire file using this number. The subject's Social Security Number is listed, along with other important information, including the address, home telephone number, spouse's name, etc.

Child Support Enforcement

Many readers of this book will be able to use the government to conduct a search without charge. If an individual has a child support order against a subject, with minimum information (the subject's name and Social Security Number), the Federal Parent Locator Service can search for a current address in the records of the Department of Defense, the National Personnel Records Center, the Social Security Administration, and the Veterans' Administration.

The Federal Parent Locator Service is a service operated by the Office of Child Support Enforcement within the purview of the United States Department of Health and Human Services to assist the individual states in locating persons for the purpose of obtaining child support payments. This agency is also used in cases of parental kidnapping related to custody and visitation cases.

The first step in seeking the location of a subject that has an obligation to pay child support is to contact your state's Child Support Enforcement office. They will first use the State Parent Locator Service. This service, which is free of charge, will check the records of other state agencies such as motor vehicle registration, unemployment insurance, state income tax, and correctional facilities. If the subject has moved to another state, the above noted Federal Parent Support Service will be contacted.

The Internal Revenue Service, in conjunction with State and Federal Child Enforcement agencies, will disclose information from the tax return of the subject to the child support office, which will be of assistance in finding the subject and determining the subject's financial condition.

STATE CHILD SUPPORT ENFORCEMENT OFFICES

http://www.acf.dhhs.gov/programs/cse/extinf.htm#exta

ALABAMA

http://www.dhr.state.al.us/csed/
Department of Human Resources
Child Support Enforcement
50 Ripley Street
Montgomery, Alabama 36130-1801
(334) 242-9300
FAX: (334) 242-0606

ALASKA

http://www.csed.state.ak.us/
Child Support Enforcement Division
550 West 7th Avenue, Suite 310
Anchorage, Alaska 99501-6699
(907) 269-6900 or (800) 478-33000
FAX: (907) 269-6650

ARIZONA

http://www.de.state.az.us/links/dcse/
index.html
Division of Child Support Enforcement
P.O. Box 40458
Phoenix, Arizona 85067
(602) 252-4045 or (800) 882-4151
FAX: (602) 248-3126

ARKANSAS

http://www.state.ar.us/dfa/childsupport/
index.html
Office of Child Support Enforcement
P.O. Box 8133
Little Rock, Arkansas 72203
Street Address: 712 West Third Street
Little Rock, Arkansas 72201
(501) 682-8398 or (800) 264-2445
FAX: (501) 682-6002

CALIFORNIA

http://www.childsup.cahwnet.gov/-
Default.htm
Office of Child Support
Department of Child Support Services
(DCSS)
P.O. Box 944245
Sacramento, California 94244-2450
(916) 654-1532 or (800) 777-2515
FAX: (916) 657-3791

COLORADO

http://www.childsupport.state.co.us
Department of Human Services
Colorado Child Support Enforcement
1200 Federal Boulevard
Denver, Colorado 80204-3221
(720) 944-3666
FAX: (720) 944-3096

CONNECTICUT

http://www.dss.state.ct.us/svcs/csupp.htm
Department of Social Services
Bureau of Child Support Enforcement
25 Sigourney Street
Hartford, Connecticut 06106-5033
(860) 424-5251 or (800) 228-5437
FAX: (860) 951-2996

DELAWARE

http://www.state.de.us/dhss/irm/dcse/
dcsehome.htm
Division of Child Support Enforcement
Delaware Health and Social Services
1901 North Dupont Hwy.
Biggs Bldg.
New Castle, Delaware 19720
(302) 577-4863, 577-4800
FAX: (302) 577-4783

DISTRICT OF COLUMBIA

http://www.csed.dcgov.org
Office of Paternity and
Child Support Enforcement
Department of Human Services
800 9th Street, S.W, 2nd Floor
Washington, DC 20024-2485
(202) 645-7500

FLORIDA

http://sun6.dms.state.fl.us/dor/childsupport
Child Support Enforcement Program
Department of Revenue
2410 Allen Road
Tallahassee, Florida 32312
(800) 622-5437
FAX: (850) 413-9011

GEORGIA

http://www.div.dhr.state.ga.us/dfcs_cse/
Child Support Enforcement
2812 Spring Road, Suite 150
Atlanta, Georgia 30339
(770) 434-4901
FAX: (770) 434-2551

GUAM

Department of Law
Child Support Enforcement Office
238 Archbishop F.C. Flores, 7th Floor
Agana, Guam 96910
(671) 475-3360

HAWAII

http://kumu.icsd.hawaii.gov/csea/csea.htm
Child Support Enforcement Agency
Department of Attorney General
601 Kamokila Boulevard, Suite 251
Kapolei, Hawaii 96707
(808) 587-4250 or (888) 317-9081
FAX: (808) 692-7001

IDAHO

http://www2.state.id.us/dhw/hwgd_-
www/contentlist.html#child
Bureau of Child Support Services
Department of Health and Welfare
1720 Westgate Drive
Boise, Idaho 83704
(208) 334-0750
FAX: (208) 334-0759

ILLINOIS

http://www.state.il.us/dpa/html/cs_pro-
grams.htm
Child Support Enforcement Division
Illinois Department of Public Aid
32 West Randolph Street
Room 900
Chicago, Illinois 60601-3405
(800) 447-4278 or (800) 374-3346
FAX: (312) 793-1961

INDIANA

http://www.state.in.us/fssa/HTML/PRO-
GRAMS/DFCSupport.html
Child Support Office
129 East Market St., Suite 100
Indianapolis, Indiana 46204
(317) 327-1800
FAX: (317) 327-1801

IOWA

http://www.dhs.state.ia.us/HomePages/D-
HS/csrunit.htm
Bureau of Collections
Department of Human Services
Hoover Building, 5th Floor
Des Moines, Iowa 50319
(515) 281-5580 or (888) 229-9223
FAX: (515) 281-8854

KANSAS

http://www.state.ks.us/
Child Support Enforcement Program
Department of Social
& Rehabilitation Services
415 S.W. Eighth St.
Topeka, Kansas 66603
(785) 296-3237
FAX: (785) 296-5206

KENTUCKY

http://www.law.state.ky.us/childsup-
port/Default.htm
Division of Child Support Enforcement
P.O. Box 1040
Frankfurt, Kentucky 40602-1040
(502) 564-5390 or (800) 248-1163
FAX: (502) 564-4035

LOUISIANA

http://www.dss.state.la.us/
Support Enforcement Services
530 Lakeland Avenue
Baton Rouge, Louisiana 70804
(225) 342-4780
FAX: (225) 342-7397

MAINE

http://www.state.me.us/dhs/main/bfi.htm
Bureau of Family Independence
Department of Human Services
11 State House Station—Whitten Road
Augusta, Maine 04333
(207) 287-2826
FAX: (207) 287-5096

MARYLAND

http://www.dhr.state.md.us/csea/index.htm
Child Support Enforcement
Administration
Department of Human Resources
311 West Saratoga Street
Baltimore, Maryland 21201
(800) 332-6347 or (800) 234-1528
FAX: (410) 333-8992

MASSACHUSETTS

http://www.state.ma.us/cse/cse.htm
Child Support Enforcement Division
Department of Revenue
51 Sleeper Street
Boston, Massachusetts 02205-9492
(617) 626-2300 or (800) 332-2733
FAX: (617) 626-2330

MICHIGAN

Michigan Family Independence
1200 6th St.
Detroit, Michigan 48226
(313) 256-1028
FAX: (313) 256-1095

MINNESOTA

http://www.dhs.state.mn.us/ecs/Pro-
gram/csed.htm
Office of Child Support Enforcement
Department of Human Services
444 Lafayette Road
St. Paul, Minnesota 55155-3846
(651) 282-5272
FAX: (612) 297-4450

MISSISSIPPI

http://www.mdhs.state.ms.us/cse.html
Division of Child Support Enforcement
Department of Human Services
939 N. President
Jackson, Mississippi 39202
(601) 359-4861
FAX: (601) 359-4415

MISSOURI

http://www.dss.state.mo.us/cse/cse.htm
Department of Social Services
Division of Child Support Enforcement
P.O. Box 2320
Jefferson City, Missouri 65102-2320
(573) 751-4301
FAX: (573) 751-8450

MONTANA

http://www.state.mt.us/
Child Support Enforcement Division
Department of Public Health and
Human Services
P.O. Box 202943
Helena, Montana 59620
(406) 442-7278

NEBRASKA

http://www.hhs.state.ne.us/cse/cseindex.htm
Child Support Enforcement Office
Department of Health
and Human Services
P.O. Box 94728
Lincoln, Nebraska 68509-4728
(402) 479-5555 or (800) 831-4573
FAX: (402) 479-5543

NEVADA

http://www.state.nv.us/ag/agpub/chld-supp.htm
Child Support Enforcement Program
Nevada State Welfare Division
2527 North Carson Street
Carson City, Nevada 89706-0113
(775) 687-4744
FAX: (775) 684-8026

NEW HAMPSHIRE

http://www.dhhs.state.nh.us
Office of Child Support
Division of Human Services
Health and Human Services Building
129 Pleasant St.
Concord, New Hampshire 03301-3857
(603) 271-4427
FAX: (603) 271-4787

NEW JERSEY

http://www.njchildsupport.org
Division of Family Development
Bureau of Child Support
and Paternity Programs
Quakersbridge Plaza, Bldg 6
P.O. Box 716
Trenton, New Jersey 08625-0716
(609) 588-2915 or (877) 655-4371
FAX: (609) 588-2064

NEW MEXICO

http://www.state.nm.us/
Child Support Enforcement Bureau
Department of Human Services
P.O. Box 25109
Santa Fe, New Mexico 87504
Street Address: 2025 S. Pacheco
Santa Fe, New Mexico 87504
(505) 476-7040
FAX: (505) 827-7285

NEW YORK

http://www.dfa.state.ny.us/csms
Division of Child Support Enforcement
NY State Office of
Temporary Assistance
40 N. Pearl Street
Albany, New York 12243
(518) 474-9081
FAX: (518) 486-3127

NORTH CAROLINA

http://www.dhhs.state.nc.us/dss/cse/cse_-mission.htm
Child Support Enforcement Office
Department of Human Resources
Courthouse, Suite 819
Raleigh, North Carolina 27602
(919) 856-6630 or (800) 992-9457
FAX: (919) 856-5714

NORTH DAKOTA

http://discovernd.com/government/agencies.html
Department of Human Services
Child Support Enforcement Agency
P.O. Box 7190
Bismarck, North Dakota 58507-7190
(701) 328-3582
FAX: (701) 328-6575

OHIO

http://www.state.oh.us/odhs/ocs
Office of Family Assistance and Child
Support Enforcement
Department of Human Services
899 East Broad Street—4th Floor
Columbus, Ohio 43205-1190
(614) 644-9000 or (800) 686-1568
FAX: (614) 644-6674

OKLAHOMA

http://www.okdhs.org/ichildsupport
Child Support Enforcement Division
Department of Human Services
P.O. Box 53552
Oklahoma City, Oklahoma 73152
Street Address: 2409 N. Kelley Avenue
Annex Building
Oklahoma City, Oklahoma 73111
(405) 522-5871
FAX: (405) 522-2753

OREGON

http://www.afs.hr.state.or.us/rss/childsupp.html
Recovery Services Section
Adult and Family Services Division
Department of Human Resources
500 Summer Street N.E., 2nd Floor
Salem, Oregon 97310-1013
(503) 945-5601
FAX: (503) 373-7032

PENNSYLVANIA

http://www.pachildsupport.com
Bureau of Child Support Enforcement
Department of Public Welfare
Office of Income Maintenance
Health & Welfare Building, Room 432
Harrisburg, Pennsylvania 17105-2675
(717) 787-1894
FAX: (717) 787-6765

PUERTO RICO

Child Support Enforcement
Department of Social Services
P.O. Box 3349
San Juan, Puerto Rico 00902-3349
Street Address: Majagua Street, Bldg 2
Wing 4, 2nd Floor
Rio Pedras, Puerto Rico 00903-9938
(787) 767-1500
FAX: (787) 282-7411

RHODE ISLAND

http://www.state.ri.us/
Child Support Enforcement
Division of Administration
Division of Taxation
77 Dorrance Street
Providence, Rhode Island 02903
(401) 222-2847
FAX: (401) 277-6674

SOUTH CAROLINA

http://www.state.sc.us/dss/csed
Department of Social Services
Child Support Enforcement Division
P.O. Box 1469
Columbia, South Carolina 29202-1469
(800) 768-5858

SOUTH DAKOTA

http://www.state.sd.us/
Office of Child Support Enforcement
Department of Social Services
700 Governor's Drive, Suite 84
Pierre, South Dakota 57501-2291
(605) 773-3641
FAX: (605) 773-7295

TENNESSEE

http://www.state.tn.us/humanserv
Child Support Services
Department of Human Services
Citizens Plaza Building–12th Floor
400 Deadrick Street
Nashville, Tennessee 37248-7400
(615) 313-4880
FAX: (615) 532-2791

TEXAS

http://www.oag.state.tx.us
Office of the Attorney General
Child Support Division
P.O. Box 12017-K
Austin, Texas 78711-2017
(512) 460-6000
FAX: (512) 479-6478

UTAH

http://www.ors.state.ut.us
Bureau of Child Support Services
Department of Human Services
515 E. 100 South
Salt Lake City, Utah 84145-0011
(801) 536-8500 or (800) 662-8525 /
(800) 257-9156
Fax: (801) 536-8509

VERMONT

http://www.ocs.state.vt.us
Office of Child Support
103 South Main Street
Waterbury, Vermont 05671-1901
(802) 479-4204 or (800) 786-3214
FAX: (802) 479-4225

VIRGIN ISLANDS

Paternity and Child Support Division
Department of Justice
GERS Building, 2nd Floor
48B-50C Krondprans Gade
St. Thomas, Virgin Islands 00802
(809) 775-3070
FAX: (809) 774-3808

VIRGINIA

http://www.dss.state.va.us/division/-
childsupp
Division of Child Support Enforcement
Department of Social Services
730 East Broad Street
Richmond, Virginia 23219
(800) 468-8894, FAX: (804) 692-1405

WASHINGTON

http://www.wa.gov
Division of Child Support
Department of Social Health Services
P.O. Box 9162
Olympia, Washington 98504-9162
Street Address: 712 Pear St. S.E.
Olympia, Washington 98504
(800) 737-0617 or (800) 442-5437
FAX: (360) 586-3274

WEST VIRGINIA

http://www.wvdhhr.org/bcse
Bureau of Child Support Enforcement
Department of Health &
Human Resources
350 Capitol Street, Room 147
Charleston, West Virginia 25301-3703
(800) 249-3778

WISCONSIN

http://www.dwd.state.wi.us/bcs/
Bureau of Child Support
Division of Economic Support
P.O. Box 7935-E
Madison, Wisconsin 53707-7935
Street Address: 1 West Wilson Street,
Room 382
Madison, Wisconsin 53707
(608) 266-9909, FAX: (608) 267-2824

WYOMING

http://dfsweb.state.wy.us/
Child Support Enforcement Program
Department of Family Services
2300 Capital Avenue
Hathaway Building, room 361
Cheyenne, Wyoming 82002-0170
(307) 777-6948, FAX: (307) 777-3693

REGIONAL OFFICES
OF CHILD SUPPORT ENFORCEMENT

REGION I

Connecticut, Maine, Massachusetts, New Hampshire, Rhode Island, Vermont
OCSE Program Manager
Administration for Children and Families
John F. Kennedy Federal Building
Room 2000
Boston, Massachusetts 02203
(617) 565-2478

REGION II

New York, New Jersey, Puerto Rico, Virgin Islands
OCSE Program Manager
Administration for Children and Families
Federal Building, Room 4114
26 Federal Plaza
New York, New York 10278
(212) 341-0900
FAX: (212) 264-4881

REGION III

Delaware, Maryland, Pennsylvania, Virginia, West Virginia,
District of Columbia
OCSE Program Manager
Administration for Children and Families
150 South Independence Mall West, Suite 864
Philadelphia, Pennsylvania 19106-3499
(215) 861-4054

REGION IV

Alabama, Florida, Georgia, Kentucky, Mississippi, North Carolina,
South Carolina, Tennessee
OCSE Program Manager
Administration for Children and Families
Atlanta Federal Center
61 Forsyth Street S.W., Suite 4M60
Atlanta, Georgia 30303-8909
(404) 562-2900
FAX: (404) 562-2981

REGION V

Illinois, Indiana, Michigan, Minnesota, Ohio, Wisconsin
OCSE Program Manager
Administration for Children and Families
233 N. Michigan Avenue, Suite 400
Chicago, Illinois 60601-5519
(312) 353-4237
FAX: (312) 886-5373

REGION VI

Arkansas, Louisiana, New Mexico, Oklahoma, Texas
OCSE Program Manager
Administration for Children and Families
1301 Young Street, Room 914 (ACF-3)
Dallas, Texas 75202
(214) 767-3749

REGION VII

Iowa, Kansas, Missouri, Nebraska
OCSE Program Manager
Administration for Children and Families
601 East 12th Street, Room 276
Federal Building, Suite 276
Kansas City, Missouri 64106
(816) 426-3584
FAX: (816) 426-2888

REGION VIII

Colorado, Montana, North Dakota, South Dakota, Utah, Wyoming
OCSE Program Manager
Administration for Children and Families
Federal Office Building
1961 Stout Street, Room 325
Denver, Colorado 80294-3538
(303) 844-3100

REGION IX

Arizona, California, Hawaii, Nevada, Guam
OCSE Program Manager
Administration for Children and Families
50 United Nations Plaza, Room 450
San Francisco, California 94012
(415) 437-8400
FAX: (415) 437-8444

REGION X

Alaska, Idaho, Oregon, Washington
OCSE Program Manager
Administration for Children and Families
2201 Sixth Avenue
Seattle, Washington 98121
(206) 615-2547
FAX: (206) 615-2574

The Main Objective

The main objective of the Child Support Enforcement Program is to make sure that child support payments are made regularly and in the correct amount. While many *noncustodial parents* are involved in their children's lives and are willing to pay child support, lapses of payment do occur. When they do, a family's budget can be quickly and seriously threatened, and the anxiety the *custodial parent* feels can easily disrupt the family's life.

For this reason, Congress decided that immediate wage withholding should be included in all child support orders. (States must also apply withholding to sources of income other than wages.) For child support orders issued or modified through state Child Support Enforcement (CSE) Programs, immediate wage withholding began November 1, 1990. Immediate wage withholding began January 1, 1994, for all initial orders that are not established through the CSE Program. The law allows for an exception to immediate wage withholding if the court (or administrative process) finds good cause, or if both parents agree to an alternative arrangement. In these cases, an arrearage equal to one month's payment will trigger withholding.

If the noncustodial parent has a regular job, wage withholding for child support can be treated like other forms of payroll deduction—income tax, social security, union dues, or any other required payment.

If payments are skipped or stop entirely, especially if the noncustodial parent is self-employed, works for cash or commissions, changes employment, or moves frequently, the CSE office will try to enforce the support order through other means.

Subject to due process safeguards, states have laws which allow them to use enforcement techniques such as state and federal income tax offset, liens on real or personal property owned by the debtor, orders to withhold and deliver property that may satisfy the debt, or a seizure and sale of property with the proceeds from the sale applied to the support debt. These methods can be used by the CSE office without directly involving the courts.

The success you have in obtaining regular, adequate, and full child support payments depends to a great extent on how well you can make the Child Support Enforcement system work for you. At the same time, it is important to remember that not all the solutions to your child support problems are within your control. The legal rights and welfare of all parties must be carefully guarded, and sometimes laws that protect the rights of one parent seem unfair to the other.

Knowledge is power. The more you know about child support enforcement procedures where you and the noncustodial parent live, the better you will be able to exercise your rights and responsibilities under the law, and the more successful you will be in obtaining the support that rightfully belongs to your children. As you proceed with your enforcement case, it is a good idea to keep a written account of the actions taken and the outcomes of those actions. Do not hesitate to ask questions and make suggestions to your enforcement caseworker. If you are not satisfied with the actions taken on your behalf, you have recourse to go to the head of the local CSE office as well as to the director of the State Child Support Enforcement agency. Keep in mind that it is always best to communicate the problem in writing. Either parent can request a review, and adjustment, if appropriate, of a child support obligation every 36 months, or sooner if there has been a substantial change in circumstances such as reduced income of the obligated parent. Check with your CSE office to see if your child support obligation is in line with state guidelines and ask how to request a review.

If your case does not meet the state's standards for review, either because the order has been reviewed within three years or the change in income is smaller than would merit an adjustment under state standards, you may still be able to petition the courts for a hearing. In this case, it may be helpful to have the services of an attorney. Your local legal aid society may be able to provide low-cost counsel to parents who cannot afford a private attorney. Also, a number of states have information about how to handle your case *pro se* (a legal term for representing yourself) to have the courts determine if your support obligation should be changed. Contact your local CSE office or the court.

If child support enforcement becomes an issue, it is necessary to have a legal order for child support spelling out the amount of the obligation and how it is to be paid. Data from the United States Census Bureau show that, of the more than 11 million families with a parent living elsewhere, only 56 percent have legally binding support orders.

Establishing a support order depends on how much success you and your caseworker or lawyer have in several critical areas, such as locating the non-custodial parent if necessary, identifying what he or she can pay, and determining the financial needs of the child.

States are required to have child support guidelines available to all people who set child support amounts. Most state guidelines consider the needs of the child, other dependents, and the ability of the parents to pay. States must use the guidelines unless they can be shown to be inappropriate in a particular case.

States today have arrangements for establishing the support order by an administrative procedure or other expedited legal procedure. The hearing may be conducted by a master or a referee of the court, or by an administrative hearings officer. An agreement made between the parents, based on the appropriate child support guidelines, and approved by this kind of agency, generally has the same effect as one established in court. It is legally binding to the parties concerned.

The agreements that the parents make should provide for the child's present and future well-being. It may be useful to discuss these issues together if you can, or with a mediator or family counselor. You may call your Child Support Enforcement (CSE) office to find out about your state's guidelines.

To establish the paternity of a child, to obtain an order for support, and in most cases, to enforce that order, the CSE agency must know where the other parent lives or works. When a legal claim is made by one person against another, the *defendant* must be given notice of the legal action taken and the steps necessary to protect his or her rights. To notify the noncustodial parent in advance—either by certified mail or in person—Child Support Enforcement officials need a correct address. If you do not have the address, the CSE office can try to find it. The most important information that you can provide to the child support office is the noncustodial parent's Social Security Number (SSN).

The Personal Responsibility and Work Opportunity Reconciliation Act of 1996 (PRWORA) has given us an important new tool for locating parents who owe child support. It requires state and national directories of newly hired employees. Employers will be required to report their employees within 20 days of their hiring to a State Directory of New Hires. The State Directory will report the information to a National Directory of New Hires provided by the Federal Office of Child Support Enforcement.

State CSE Agencies, with due process and security safeguards, have access to information from the following state and local government offices:

Vital Statistics
State Tax Files
Real and Titled Personal Property Records
Occupational and Professional Licenses
and Business Information
Employment Security Agency
Public Assistance Agency
Motor Vehicle Departments
Law Enforcement Departments
Records of private entities, such as public utilities and cable
television companies (names and addresses of individuals
and their employers as they appear in customer records)
Information held by financial institutions, including asset
and liability data

A father can acknowledge paternity by signing a written admission or voluntary acknowledgment of paternity. All states have programs under which birthing hospitals give unmarried parents of a newborn the opportunity to acknowledge the father's paternity of the child. States must also help parents acknowledge paternity up until the child's 18th birthday through vital records offices or other entities designated by the state. Parents are not required to apply for child support enforcement services when acknowledging paternity.

Under the Personal Responsibility and Work Opportunity Act of 1996 (PRWORA), an acknowledgment of paternity becomes a finding of paternity unless the man who signed the acknowledgment denies that he is the father within 60 days. If it becomes necessary to seek child support, a finding of paternity creates the basis for a child support order. A support order against the father cannot be established for a child who is born to unmarried parents until paternity has been established.

It is important to establish paternity as early as possible. While CSE offices must try to establish paternity for any child up to the child's 18th birthday, it is best to do it as soon after the child's birth as possible. If the man will not acknowledge that he is the father, the CSE agency can order *genetic testing*. These tests are simple to take and highly accurate.

The Native American Child Support Program in the Federal Office of the Child Support Enforcement Program has been consulting with the Tribes and Native American organizations to ensure that Native American children receive the child support to which they are entitled. New provisions in the

Personal Responsibility and Work Opportunities Reconciliation Act (PRWORA) provide more options to achieve this goal.

American Indian Tribes or tribal organizations will be eligible to apply for grants to operate full or partial child support enforcement programs. The projects must meet child support enforcement criteria that will be issued through regulations in mid-1998. Formal consultation is planned for the proposed rules.

Native American reservations are governed by tribal laws that may differ from those of the states, just as laws differ from state to state. The differences, and the various types of state and tribal court systems, sometimes make it difficult to enforce child support orders or to locate absent parents on reservations.

Some states and tribes have entered into cooperative agreements to facilitate obtaining child support for Native American children, and it is expected that more tribes and states will enter into cooperative agreements and work together to carry out their child support responsibilities.

In the interim, tribal and state child support staffs will continue to pursue all available means to assist Native American children to receive support. What works best, and which barriers are encountered, will be shared. This will assist tribes to decide how best to meet child support enforcement requirements, through tribal programs and cooperative agreements with states.

Child Support and the Military

My purpose for including this information on child support and the military is to assist anyone, male or female, who is owed support. What could be more important than my telling people how to find someone in the military, establish paternity, and provide children the money they are due? People who owe child support have certain exemptions and restrictions insofar as being contacted civilians. I will identify and discuss tools used successfully to cope with some of the most common difficulties in child support enforcement cases involving military personnel.

Some persons find working through military channels and observing military protocols to be challenging and/or frustrating. To help minimize such difficulties I include helpful hints, practice tips, and also I include acronyms and jargon.

There are at least three helpful hints for dealing with the military on civil matters such as child support enforcement. First, ask for help; do not insist on it. Invoking your civilian authority and making demands will often meet with resistance. Respect is significant in all military matters. If you show respect for both military personnel and their mission, they will generally show you and your mission the same level of respect.

Second, be prepared to recognize that there are some valid limitations on the military's abilities to respond to your request. To illustrate, some military information, such as ship schedules and dates or locations of military exercises, is routinely classified and cannot be revealed. National security does require some secrecy. Nonetheless, there are well-established ways that you can ask for and expect to receive the military's help in communicating with any member of any active unit.

Third, use the military command structure to your advantage. Contact the service member first. Then, if necessary, contact the service member's commander or the commander's representative. If you still do not get an acceptable response, then contact the commander's superior and make sure you highlight all your previous attempts to use other points of contact. You will frequently find superiors who will push to resolve personal matters such as child support before they interfere with military duties.

Locating Military Personnel

Locating active duty members of the Armed Services can sometimes be difficult. This difficulty is intensified if you cannot provide the member's Social Security Number. Always strive to use the military service member's full name and Social Security Number in any written or telephonic contact with the military.

As a starting point in locating military personnel, begin with the most convenient resource—the Armed Services recruiting office. Recruiters may be able to provide the member's duty station, particularly if he or she enlisted locally within the last year or so. The recruiter's cooperation with your location efforts can usually be encouraged as a matter of good public relations.

Military personnel can often be located directly by telephone. Military installations have a central locator office for assigned personnel. Once you discover the member's duty station, you can use this service by calling the installation locator (the number is available through the installation's information operator) and giving the member's name and Social Security Number. You will get his/her military unit address, which will enable you to correspond both with the member (using registered or certified mail and return receipt service) and with the member's commanding officer(s).

Most large bases have legal assistance offices. These offices are authorized to assist spouses and legitimate children (and in some cases, even children born out of wedlock) obtain a member's military address.

Military personnel usually leave a copy of their reassignment orders at their old unit when they depart. To help yourself avoid delays in locating military personnel, whenever you have occasion to write or talk with a commander, specifically ask to be advised of the member's next duty station if he or she has moved.

In all cases, you can obtain the work address of an active duty military member from the World Wide Military Locator Services (WWML). The current addresses of these services and a sample location inquiry are noted later in this chapter. The WWML can provide the member's work address. You can then contact either the U.S. Post Office or the postal officer at the nearest military installation for assistance in determining the actual geographic location of the active duty member's APO or FPO work address.

There is no charge for WWML location information. You will need to provide the member's full name and Social Security Number. Be advised that military records may run up to 60 to 90 days behind reassignments, most of which tend to occur during the summer. (Avoid making requests from May through October.) Military addresses often look like alphabet soup to civilians. Whenever you use a military address in correspondence with the military, you want to make double sure you have all the right abbreviations in all the right places.

Obtaining the home addresses of military personnel can pose special problems due to the Privacy Act, 5 U.S.C. § 552a. However, it may be possible to obtain this information via the Freedom of Information Act, 5, U.S.C. § 552. You can request home address information from the installation personnel officer where the member is assigned.

Avoid seeking a member's home address from the military unless it is absolutely necessary. Military personnel may be away from their homes for months at a time, but they are rarely away from their military addresses for more than two weeks. So use the military address, and remember to always try to put the military's command structure to work for you whenever possible.

Finally, the Federal Parent Locator Service (FPLS), operated by OCSE (Office of Child Support Enforcement), may also be a source for location information. Please note that individuals may not make direct requests to the FPLS for information, and it is best that you contact your local child support enforcement agency. They are responsive. I have been writing about child support enforcement for many years in my books, and I have gotten a 100 percent positive response rate from my readers regarding their dealings with the personnel from child support enforcement agencies. After using normal procedures to locate noncustodial parents, the FPLS can be used to obtain home addresses for most members of the Armed Services. (Unit addresses will be released for certain categories of service members, i.e., those stationed overseas). This locator service is DOD-wide.

Service of Process and Obtaining Evidence from Military Personnel

The basis for legal jurisdiction over military personnel in routine child support enforcement matters (domicile or state long-arm status) is the same as for civilians. Under general principles of law, military personnel usually retain the domicile they held when they enlisted. Thus, in most cases you can proceed against a member of the Armed Forces just in the same way as you would against any other person located out-of-state. Jurisdiction under long-arm statutes usually works best.

Service of process on military installations in the U.S. and on ships in U.S. waters is governed under federal regulations. See Army, 32 C.F.R. Part 516.1(e) and Navy and Marine Corps, 32 C.F.R. Part 720.20.

The easiest method for service of process is by the U.S. mail, if your state law permits. Check with your local bar association office or court to see if service of process via the U.S. mail is allowed. If so, then a certified or registered letter sent to the absent parent's military address is an option. This applies to any U.S. military facility located in the continental U.S. or overseas. Both APO and FPO military addresses overseas are in the U.S. mail, and all normal U.S. postal procedures apply.

Be advised that military authorities have no responsibility for serving process (and may violate federal law if they do). But, upon request, they can give the member the opportunity to voluntarily accept service. You can send documents to a unit commander and request that they be served on the member. The member will be given the chance to talk to a legal assistance attorney before deciding whether to accept the documents.

The military's legal assistance attorneys may be unfamiliar with your state laws. In a letter to the commander or to the member, be sure to mention the adverse effects that can result from delays in your state (e.g., the possibility of a retroactive support order and the resulting arrearage when a support order is finally issued). This may help to reduce delays.

Service of process can sometimes be achieved by the appropriate state official (e.g., the sheriff) serving the area where the member is stationed. Military officials will often cooperate to make the member available for service of process. This procedure may not work, however, when the documents to be served are issued by a court outside the county or state where the installation is located.

For service of process overseas, be advised that each country tends to have unique procedures to follow and forms for foreign applicants to use when initiating requests for services. Both the required documentation and the most appropriate method of serving process may vary from nation to nation and/or over time. In general, the term "letters rogatory" refers to a request for judicial assistance from a court in one country to a court in another country. Letters rogatory can be used to request service of process, assistance in obtaining evidence, or enforcement of judgments.

For service of process in overseas locations, the easiest method may again be by the U.S. mail, if your state law permits, and if the law where process is to be served permits. Military postal clerks will sometimes neglect to send the return receipt back to you. If you do not receive a return receipt after a reasonable time: (1) prepare a second set of documents and place them in an envelope addressed to the member, with the return receipt affixed and postage paid; (2) put this envelope inside a larger envelope, and address the outside envelope to the military postal officer for the APO or FPO where the member is located; and (3) include a note on your unsuccessful effort to get a return receipt and ask that proper postal procedures be followed to deliver the enclosed letter and to send you the receipt.

If service of process by the U.S. mail is not permitted in your state or is not permitted by the law where the process is to be served, then you may be able to use The Hague Convention on Service Abroad of Judicial and Extrajudicial Documents. See TIAS 6638, 20 UST 361, 15 Nov 65. The text of the Convention is in Martindale-Hubbell Law Directory, Vol. VIII, and the appendix to the Federal Rules of Civil Procedure 4 in West's U.S. Code Annotated (U.S.C.A.).

There are 35 members of the Hague Service Convention, each with a central authority designated to receive requests for service of process, to serve process, and to certify that service was or was not made. The U.S. Department of State, Office of Overseas Citizens Services at **(202) 647-5225** has compiled a general circular on the Hague Service Convention. Among other things, this circular provides the name and address of each signatory nation's Central Authority and includes a comprehensive guide for filling out the required forms.

For service of process originating in the U.S., the plaintiff's attorney fills out a request on Form USM 94, Request For Service Abroad of Judicial or Extrajudicial Documents, which is available from any U.S. Marshall's Office, and mails it with other required documents to the foreign nation's Central Authority requesting their assistance in making the necessary arrangements.

If the foreign country involved in your case is not a signatory of the Hague Service Convention, then they may be signatories of the Interamerican Convention on Letters Rogatory. The Interamerican Convention designates a nation's Central Authority and the required forms to be used for service of process in Mexico, Central and South America, and Spain. See the U.S. Department of State publication by the Office of the Legal Advisor called Treaties in Force for the text of the Interamerican Convention on Letters Rogatory.

For assistance and information on service of process in nonsignatory nations of the Hague Service Convention or the Interamerican Convention on Letters Rogatory, you can consult with the U.S. Office of Citizens' Consular Services at **(202) 647-3444.**

For some countries, the required documents will have to be translated. If so, a high school or university may be able to help in this regard.

In some cases, you may be able to transfer the case to a foreign UIFSA office. For example, you can use the German federal attorney's office if your state has an agreement with Germany. Most, but not all, states have such an agreement in place.

For military personnel aboard ships outside U.S. waters, service of process is also best handled through the U.S. mail, if your state law permits. You can request the commander's help in arranging voluntary service of process. As a last resort, you can arrange for service through foreign nation authorities when member's ship reaches port. Remember, however, that ports and dates of arrival or departure may not be available for security reasons.

Obtaining evidence from military personnel stationed overseas is complicated. Complications arise, in part, because members stationed overseas are subject to the host nation's laws on most civil (and on some criminal) matters. Always coordinate your efforts with the other nation's UIFSA agency (if one exists).

You can also use The Hague Convention on the Taking of Evidence Abroad in Civil or Commercial Matters, see TIAS 7444, 23 UST 2555,

March 18, 1970. The text is reprinted at 28 U.S.C.A. § 1781. The Convention has been signed by almost all nations where U.S. forces are stationed. The Convention provides for working with and through the U.S. Secretary of State's Office and the other nation's Foreign Ministry to send a "letter rogatory" to authorities where the member is stationed, asking the foreign court to order the member to produce the evidence. A sample form making such a request can be found at 28 U.S.C.A. § 1781. It may be possible to obtain court orders for blood samples in this way; contact laboratories can often make the necessary arrangements.

Establishing Paternity

Paternity establishment is essentially a civilian matter. As a rule, the military explicitly prefers not to become directly involved in civil matters such as paternity establishment.

If you have contacted the member without securing cooperation, then contact the member's commander, who has very limited powers in such matters. The commander's roles are: (1) to advise the member of the paternity claim and to refer him to counsel; (2) to assist those members who wish to acknowledge paternity; and (3) to respond to the complainant. Be advised that the commander has no authority to order a blood sample or to even enforce compliance with a court order to submit a blood sample. Voluntary blood samples drawn by military health officials are possible, but no set policy exists and the degree of cooperation may vary from location to location.

Make sure you state clearly in the letter to the commander what you intend to do if the member refuses to cooperate with genetic testing. Options begin with writing the commander's boss detailing your prior unsuccessful attempts to resolve the matter. Other options include pointing out that— if paternity is established—the child support not paid during the interim will accrue with interest and will not stop until the child reaches the age of majority; this debt, under recent changes in the law, is not likely to be discharged or reduced by a court and that this enormous obligation will be waiting for the member whenever he leaves military service to return to civilian life. You may need to be persistent. Show them you will not be easily discouraged.

A closely related issue involves health care for children born out of wedlock to military personnel. Children born out of wedlock to military personnel are entitled to military health care and insurance (TRICARE) if the child is acknowledged and supported by the member or if there is a judicial decree of paternity. A military I.D. card is required to prove eligibility. If the member will not cooperate in getting a military I.D. card for the child, his or her commander can coordinate issuance of an I.D. card.

Determining the Support Obligation

Military regulations specify that military duty will not be used as a basis for avoiding family support obligations, but setting the level of support is a civilian matter. Army, Navy, Marine, and Coast Guard directives do specify an amount of support, but these figures are to be used only when there is no agreement between the parties and no court order. Ignore the complexities of military compensation (as discussed further below), and set the support obligation based on basic military pay. Go to my Website **www.josephculligan.com** for the link that shows you how much someone makes in the military. All the pay grades are shown.

Military pay consists of basic pay and may also include a Basic Allowance for Housing (BAH), a Basic Allowance for Subsistence or Separate Rations (BAS or Sep Rats), and/or special skill pay (e.g., flight pay) and bonuses (e.g., for reenlistment).

BAH is a new pay designation. As of January 1, 1998, service members receive BAH in place of the old Basic Allowance for Quarters (BAQ) and Variable Housing Allowance (VHA). The BAH received by the service member reflects the old BAQ amount combined with the VHA rate for the locale.

Determining the BAQ amounts is still important. Under the Army's regulations, the BAQ will be the support obligation imposed absent a court order or an agreement. A separate table identifies the amount of compensation that reflects the BAQ with dependents rate and the differential (the amount reflecting the difference between what service members with dependents draw and what those without dependents draw). The table is called BAH Table II and Differential.

Be advised that there is no set "military allotment" for family support. The amount of BAH varies due to family status, but members with families get only about $100 to $150 more per month than single members living off post or base. Note the amount of BAH is not intended by the Armed Forces or Congress to constitute full support for families. Use your state's guidelines to set the amount of the obligation.

Military regulations provide that members who do receive increased BAH because they have dependents can be disciplined and past BAH payments can be recouped, if the member fails to use the full amount of BAH received as a result of having dependents to support family members. These provisions in the military regulations may provide caseworkers with some leverage when negotiating with a nonsupporting member whom they suspect may be drawing "BAH with dependents."

In general, all pay and allowances may be considered in setting the support obligation. It may also be appropriate under state law/guidelines to consider other factors. For example, all members receive BAS/Sep Rats, or they live in government accommodations and eat in the mess hall for free. This "in kind" compensation may justify an upward adjustment of cash income in setting the support obligation. Thus, the BAH and BAS/Sep Rats amount should be constructively added to the member's pay, as the reasonable value of the "in kind" income, even if (s) he is not receiving these.

BAH and BAS/Sep Rats are not taxable. If state guidelines are based on gross pay, it may be appropriate to adjust military pay upward. The amount of the adjustment would be the marginal tax rate on the member's nontaxable income. A member can be entitled to a limited BAH payment based solely on paternity of a child born out of wedlock, and generally all the BAH money received solely as a result of having this child must be used to support the child.

These tax-free components of total military pay show that an income tax return may not provide the best picture of total military pay. To determine the member's income, you should get copies of monthly pay statements called Leave and Earning Statements (LES). Insist on seeing total gross income as well as other data. To illustrate, you should carefully review allotment deductions as they can be easily manipulated (e.g., an allotment can be part of an automatic savings plan). A Freedom of Information Act request for copies of LES statements may be honored.

Additional information is also available from the LES. The LES shows how much leave the member has accrued, and this may help determine whether a delay in court proceedings is really needed. The LES shows what state the member claims as domicile for income tax purposes and thus may help to establish legal jurisdiction. It will show whether or not the member is receiving BAH and BAS/Sep Rats and how many dependents are being claimed for income tax purposes.

You may find using military regulations to establish a support obligation results in uneven enforcement, especially regarding payment of arrearages. State guidelines usually require more support, but in some cases (e.g., children born out of wedlock), the regulations call for more money than most guidelines. Always seek a judicial or administrative child support order at the earliest opportunity.

Collecting Support from Military Personnel

Collecting child support from military personnel is generally governed by military regulations. See Army, 32 C.F. R. Part 584, Army Regulations 608-99, 1 Nov 94; Navy/Marine Corps, 32 C.F. R. Part 733; and Air Force, 32 C.F. R. Part 818.

These regulations require military personnel to pay child support in accordance with support agreements and court orders. In the absence of a court order or support agreement, Army and Marine regulations criminalize failure to pay support at a level generally equivalent to a member's authorized "Basic Allowance for Housing (BAH)." All other services have established guidelines in the regulations for use by the commander where there is no court order or support agreement.

Under military regulations, one solution is a voluntary allotment. Please note, however, a voluntary allotment is completely under the member's control and can be started, stopped, or amended at will. A voluntary allotment is a convenience that the government provides military personnel to help them meet their obligations.

Be advised that without some sort of allotment, child support enforcement is largely outside of a commander's discretion. Commanders cannot direct that a member's pay be diverted to family members, even if a court order exists; a commander can only punish a member for failure to comply. Obtaining a court or administrative court is critically important. With a court order, a family can receive child support withheld involuntarily from military personnel through use of garnishments, involuntary allotments, and/or wage assignments.

For use of Garnishments, see 42 U.S.C. §§ 659-662; 5 C.F.R. Part 581. The allowable bases for garnishments include enforcement of periodic family support obligations (including costs and attorney fees if state law defines these items as components of *support*).

Pay subject to garnishment generally includes: (1) federal civilian employee pay and retirement annuities; (2) military active duty pay (basic pay and certain bonuses, but not BAH and BAS/Sep Rats); (3) military retired pay; (4) military reserve pay; and (5) any other "remuneration for employment."

The amount subject to garnishment is the lower of state or federal ceilings. The federal ceiling is 50 to 60 percent of net pay, depending on the family situation and length of time in arrears; arrears in excess of 12 weeks adds another five percent.

Procedures require obtaining a garnishment order from a state court (naming the employing federal agency as garnishee) and serving the order, with a copy of the underlying support order, on the employing agency by registered or certified mail; include member's name, status (i.e., active duty, civilian, retiree) and the member's Social Security Number.

The member's defenses against garnishment include garnishment for impermissible purpose; garnisher's noncompliance with 5 C.F.R. Part 581; subsequent litigation enjoining the garnishment; and possibly an appeal of the underlying support order, depending on the state's laws.

For the use of Involuntary or Mandatory Allotments, see 42 U.S.C. § 665; 32 C.F.R. Part 54. Involuntary allotments are essentially wage withholding actions enforceable against active duty military pay (basic pay, plus bonuses, plus BAH and BAS in some cases).

Involuntary allotments are almost always superior to garnishment actions. Involuntary allotments tend to be easier to obtain, longer lasting, and more lucrative in terms of meeting support obligations.

The prerequisites for involuntary allotments begin with a court or administrative order establishing a child support (or spousal and child support) obligation and an arrearage in an amount equal to or greater than two months support under the order.

The procedure for establishing involuntary allotments begins with a "Notice" from any court or any State CSE agent to the military requesting initiation of an involuntary allotment. The Notice can simply be a letter. No prior notice to the obligor is necessary. The Notice is sent by registered or certified mail to the same officials as for garnishments.

The Notice should include the member's full name and Social Security Number; a statement that there are arrearages equal to or greater than two months' child support; a copy of the underlying order certified by the Clerk of the Court (or by the head of the administrative agency if it is an administrative order); the date the allotment should stop; and a statement certifying the writer is an "authorized person" or a State CSE agent.

The involuntary allotment will only be for the amount of the monthly support obligation. If arrearages are sought, they must be requested and there must be a court or administrative order which specifically requires the payment of accrued arrearages. There are limitations on the amount of involuntary allotments, which are the same as the limits for garnishment (50 to 60 percent, plus five percent if 12 or more weeks is in arrears).

The member's defenses against involuntary allotments require that the defendant establish by affidavit and evidence that the underlying child support order has been vacated or modified or that the amount alleged to be in arrears is erroneous.

Be advised that administrative wage assignment withholding notices that are based on a conditional court order and an arrearage sometimes are not honored by military pay offices; they may insist on a subsequent order issued by a court. When sending an administrative withholding order, include a copy of the applicable statute to show that it constitutes valid "process" under State Law. Military pay offices almost always honor automatic wage withholding orders (i.e., those that take effect whether or not there is an arrearage).

Send state wage assignment withholding orders to the same office as garnishment orders. Compensation subject to withholding includes basic pay and bonuses, but not BAH or BAS/Sep Rations. The amount of compensation withheld is limited to 50 to 60 percent plus five percent if 12 or more weeks is in arrears.

The Uniformed Services Former Spouses' Protection Act (see 10 U.S.C. § 1408; 32 C.R.F. Part 63) essentially authorizes wage withholding against military retired pay for child support and/or spousal support obligations created by a final decree of divorce or legal separation (but not a paternity decree).

No arrearage is necessary to trigger the withholding; the former spouse can initiate a direct payment simply by written request to the appropriate finance center. The right to receive direct payment is personal to the former spouse and cannot be assigned to a CSE agency, although a request for payment through such an agency may be honored.

The primary alternatives to using this Act to collect child support from retired pay are garnishments and state wage withholding orders.

The Soldiers' and Sailors' Civil Relief Act

The Soldiers' and Sailors' Civil Relief Act (SSCRA) is a necessary protective device for U.S. soldiers and sailors during a time of conflict or training. See 50 U.S.C. App. 500-548, 560-593 1990, Supp. 1993. The SSCRA is not intended to be used as a shelter from facing legal and family responsibilities, although that sometimes appears to be the case. In any event, there is little or no likelihood of abolishing SSCRA in the near future. You should learn how to work with the SSCRA when it is necessary. SSCRA provisions apply only to judicial proceedings.

If administrative proceedings are not possible in your state, there are four key SSCRA provisions that are important to observe when enforcing child support. One, the SSCRA permits stays of civil court proceedings whenever military service prevents a plaintiff or defendant in military service from asserting or protecting a right. Members' requests for a stay of proceedings under SSCRA must be granted unless the members' military service does not materially affect their ability to defend themselves.

Note that DOD has recently revised its regulations in this area. DOD directive 1327.5 section 6.25 now specifically provides: "When a service member requests leave on the basis of need to attend hearings to determine paternity or to determine an obligation to provide child support, leave shall be granted, unless (a) member is serving in or with a unit deployed in a contingency operation, or (b) exigencies of military service require a denial of such request. The leave shall be charged as ordinary leave."

Note also that some courts might not consider presence of service member necessary to the proceeding; thus, no stay will be granted. To illustrate, as general rule, temporary modifications of child support do not materially affect rights of the military defendant, as they are interlocutory and subject to modification. The facts of each case will determine whether the trial court abused discretion in refusing a stay request.

Whenever a service member requests a stay, inquire about the reasons for the delay. If the service member is requesting a stay because he or she does not have sufficient accrued leave and/or the available resources to travel, then it may be possible to conduct a telephone conference instead.

Two, the SSCRA provides that the maximum duration of a stay of proceedings is the member's period of military service, plus three months after discharge. Following this period, the defendant must appear in court.

Three, the SSCRA affords service members relief against default judgment by providing potential means to have the judgment reopened. If there is default of any appearance by the defendant, before the plaintiff can obtain a default judgment, the plaintiff must submit an affidavit stating whether the defendant is or is not in the military service or that the plaintiff does not know whether defendant is in the military service. A judgment obtained without the affidavit is voidable (not void) upon defendant's showing that presentation of the defense was prejudiced by defendant's military service.

The court then must appoint an attorney if the defendant is in the service and does not have an attorney present in court or if the plaintiff does not know whether the defendant is in the service. The responsibility of the court-appointed attorney is to ascertain whether the defendant is in the military and, if so, typically to request a stay of proceedings on the defendant's behalf.

Members may request to reopen a default judgment if there has been no appearance, the service member has a meritorious or legal defense, and military service adversely affected the member's ability to defend. The application to reopen must be to same court that rendered the judgment. The SSCRA does not empower a district court to collaterally review, vacate, or impede decisions of a state court.

Four, the SSCRA provides that any judgment or garnishment may be stayed or vacated unless military service does not materially affect the member's ability to comply. Service members can, for example, request modification of child support or alimony. Courts may grant prospective relief as well. Members can initiate a proceeding to determine the extent of their support obligations because of changes in circumstances when they entered active duty.

Neither Federal law nor military regulations provide military personnel with any permanent protections from U.S. or foreign courts proceedings to establish paternity and child support obligations.

The Soldiers' and Sailors' Civil Relief Act does provide for temporary stays of proceedings and for re-opening judgments under certain circumstances. However, in all other important respects, child support cases involving military personnel can be handled the same way as civilian cases.

Addresses for Worldwide Locator Services
(For Members' Military Address)

ARMY ACTIVE DUTY

Army Worldwide Locator
USAER 8899 E. 56th Street
Indianapolis, Indiana 46249-5301
(703) 325-3732

NAVY

Navy Personnel Command
(Pers 312)
5720 Integrity Drive
Millington, Tennessee 38055-3120
(901) 874-3388

COAST GUARD

Commander (MPC-53)
U.S. Coast Guard
2100 2nd St. SW
Washington, DC 20593
(202) 267-1340

ARMY RESERVE—RETIRED

Commander
ARPERCEN
9700 Page Blvd.
St. Louis, Missouri 63132
(314) 538-3777

AIR FORCE

Headquarters
AFMPCC/RMIQL
550 C St. West, Suite 50
Randolph AFB, Texas 78150
(210) 652-5774 / 5775 / 6377

MARINE CORPS

Headquarters, U.S.M.C.
Code MMSB-10
2008 Elliot Rd., Rm 201
Quantico, Virginia 22134
(703) 784-3942

ARMY—RETIRED

U.S. Army Community and Family Support Center
Retired & Veterans Affairs Division
ATTN: DACF-IS-RV
Alexandria, Virginia 22331-0522

Addresses for
Service of Garnishment and Other Orders

(For Members of the Army, Air Force, Navy, and Marine Corps)

Defense Finance and Accounting Service
Cleveland Center
Garnishment Operations Directorate
Code L
P.O. Box 998002
Cleveland, Ohio 44199-8002
(216) 522-5301

(For Coast Guard Personnel)

Commanding Officer (LGL)
U.S. Coast Guard Pay
and Personnel Center
Federal Building
444 S.E. Quincy Street
Topeka, Kansas 66683-3591
(913) 295-2984

Additional Sources of
Assistance in Enforcing Support
(Obligations and Facilitating Service of Legal Process)

ARMY

Ft. Myer Military Community
Attn: ANJA-Legal Services
204 Lee Avenue
Ft. Myer, Virginia 22211-1199
(703) 696-0761

NAVY

Bureau of Naval Personnel
Office of Legal Counsel
(Pers 06)
2 Navy Annex
Washington, DC 20370-5006
(703) 325-7928

MARINE CORPS

Paralegal Specialist
Headquarters, U.S. Marine Corp (JAR)
2 Navy Annex
Washington, DC 20380
(703) 614-3880

AIR FORCE

AFLSA/JACA
1420 Air Force Pentagon
Washington, DC 20330-1420
(703) 697-0413

COAST GUARD

United States Coast Guard
G-PC (USCG)
Room 4100E, CGHQ
Department of Transportation
Washington, DC 20590
(202) 267-2799

The agency points of contact listed above are designated officials responsible for facilitating the service of legal process on members of the Uniformed Services. They may also provide useful assistance in resolving problems created by a nonresponsive chain of command. Tips for using these agencies:

1. Write to the member's commander first.

2. Provide the member's name and Social Security Number.

3. Give specific facts on periods of nonsupport or other problems. Note your previous efforts to resolve the issues, and state how the results were unsatisfactory.

4. State clearly the relief you see. These agencies will ensure the command is aware of the problem and that the member is counseled regarding support obligations.

Glossary of Child Support Enforcement Terms

administrative procedure. Method by which support orders are made and enforced by an executive agency rather than by courts and judges.

Aid to Families with Dependent Children (AFDC). Assistance payments made on behalf of children who don't have the financial support of one of their parents by reason of death, disability, or continued absence from the home; known in many States as ADC (Aid to Dependent Children).

arrearage. Unpaid child support for past periods owed by a parent who is obligated to pay.

assignment of support rights. A person receiving public assistance agrees to turn over to the state any right to child support, including arrearages, paid by the obligated parent in exchange for receipt of a cash assistance grant and other benefits.

complaint. Written document filed in court in which the person initiating the action names the persons, allegations, and relief sought.

consent agreement. Voluntary written admission of paternity or responsibility for support.

custodial parent. Person with legal custody and with whom the child lives; may be parent, other relative, or someone else.

custody order. Legal determination that establishes with whom a child shall live.

default. Failure of a defendant to appear, or file an answer or response in a civil case, after having been served with a summons and complaint.

default judgment. Decision made by the court when the defendant fails to respond.

defendant. Person against whom a civil or criminal proceeding is begun.

electronic funds transfer. Transfer of money from one bank account to another or to a CSE Agency.

enforcement. Obtaining payment of a child support or medical support obligation.

Federal Income Tax Offset Program. A program under the Federal Office of Child Support Enforcement that makes available to state CSE agencies a route for securing the tax refund of parents who have been certified as owning substantial amounts of child support.

Federal Parent Locator Service (FPLS). A service operated by the Federal Office of Child Support Enforcement to help the states locate parents in order to obtain child support payments; also used in cases of parental kidnapping related to custody and visitation determinations; FPLS obtains addresses and employer information from Federal agencies.

Federally Assisted Foster Care. A program funded in part by the Federal Government, under which a child is raised in a household by someone other than his or her own parent.

finding. A formal determination by a court, or an administrative process that has legal standing.

full faith and credit. A doctrine under which a state must honor an order or judgment entered in another state.

garnishment. A legal proceeding under which part of a person's wages and/or assets is withheld for payment of a debt.

genetic testing. Analysis of inherited factors (usually by blood or tissue test) of mother, child, and alleged father that can help to prove or disprove that a particular man fathered a particular child.

guidelines. A standard method for setting child support obligations based on the income of the parent(s) and other factors as determined by state law.

immediate wage withholding. Automatic deductions from income which start as soon as the agreement for support is established (see wage withholding).

jurisdiction. Legal authority that a court has over particular persons, certain types of cases, and in a defined geographical area.

legal father. A man who is recognized by law as the male parent.

lien. A claim upon property to prevent sale or transfer until a debt is satisfied.

long arm statute. A law that permits one state to claim personal jurisdiction over someone who lives in another state.

Medicaid Program. Federally funded medical support for low-income families.

medical support. Legal provision for payment of medical and dental bills.

noncustodial parent. Parent who does not have primary custody of a child.

obligation. Amount of money to be paid as support by the responsible parent and the manner by which it is to be paid.

offset. Amount of money taken from a parent's state or federal income tax refund to satisfy a child support debt.

order. Direction of a magistrate, judge, or properly empowered administrative officer.

paternity judgment. Legal determination of fatherhood.

plaintiff. Person who brings an action, complaint or suit in a civil case.

presumption of paternity. A rule of law under which evidence of a man's paternity (e.g., voluntary acknowledgment or genetic test results) creates a presumption that the man is the father of a child. A rebuttable presumption can be overcome by evidence that the man is not the father, but it shifts the burden of proof to the father to disprove paternity.

probability of paternity. The probability that the alleged father is the biological father of the child as indicated by genetic test results.

public assistance. Money granted from the State or Federal Aid to Families with Dependent Children Program to a person or family for living expenses; eligibility based on need.

State Parent Locator Service (SPLS). A service operated by the State Child Support Enforcement Agencies to locate noncustodial parents to establish paternity, and establish and enforce child support obligations.

statute of limitations. The period during which someone can be held liable for an action or a debt. Statutes of limitations for collecting child support vary from state to state.

stay. An order by a court which suspends all or some of the proceedings in a case.

TANF. Temporary Assistance to Needy Families; time-limited assistance payments to poor families. The program provides parents with job preparation, work and support services to help them become self-sufficient.

Uniform Interstate Family Support Act (UIFSA), and Uniform Reciprocal Enforcement of Support Act (URESA). Laws enacted at the state level which provide mechanisms for establishing and enforcing support obligations when the noncustodial parent lives in one state and the custodial parent and children live in another.

visitation. The right of a noncustodial parent to visit or spend time with his or her children.

voluntary acknowledgment of paternity. An acknowledgement by a man, or both parents, that the man is the father of the child, usually provided in writing on an affidavit or form.

wage withholding. Procedure by which automatic deductions are made from wage or income to pay some debt such as child support; may be voluntary or involuntary.

Foreign Diplomatic Representatives and Foreign Consular Offices in the United States

I use the following list of Foreign Diplomatic Representatives and Foreign Consular offices with great success. When I discover that the missing person may be in a particular country, I request assistance from the embassy closest to my location. They are ready to assist and can cut through much red tape.

Write, and explain in detail what your objective is and give as much information as possible regarding the vital statistics of your subject. Give the reason why you believe your subject may be in a particular country, i.e., employment, extended vacation, or simply to hide from others. There are updated links to every embassy in the United States and worldwide on Joseph Culligan's Resources CD.

AFGHANISTAN

2341 Wyoming Avenue
Washington, DC 20008
Phone: (202) 234-3770
Fax: (202) 328-3516

ALBANIA

2100 S Street NW
Washington, DC 20008
Phone: (202) 223-4942
Fax: (202) 628-7342

ALGERIA

2118 Kalorama Road
Washington, DC 20008
Phone: (202) 265-2800
Fax: (202) 667-2174
http://www.algeria-us.org/

ANGOLA

1615 M Street NW Suite 900
Washington, DC 20036
Phone: (202) 785-1156
Fax: (202) 785-1258
http://www.angola.org/

ANTIGUA AND BARBUDA

3216 New Mexico Avenue NW
Washington, DC 20016
Phone: (202) 362-5122
Fax: (202) 362-5225

ARGENTINA

1600 New Hampshire Avenue
Washington, DC 20009
Phone: (202) 238-6400
Fax: (202) 332-3171
http://www.embassyofargentina-usa.org/

ARMENIA

2225 R Street
Washington, DC 20008
Phone: (202) 319-1976
Fax: (202) 319-2982
http://www.armeniaemb.org/

AUSTRALIA

1601 Massachusetts Avenue
Washington, DC 20036
Phone: (202) 797-3000
Fax: (202) 797-3168
http://www.austemb.org/

AUSTRIA

3524 International Court NW
Washington, DC 20008
Phone: (202) 895-6700
Fax: (202) 895-6750

AZERBAIJAN

927 15th Street NW Suite 700
Washington, DC 20035
Phone: (202) 842-0001
Fax: (202) 842-0004
http://www.azembassy.com/

THE COMMONWEALTH OF THE BAHAMAS

2220 Massachusetts Avenue NW
Washington, DC 20008
Phone: (202) 319-2660
Fax: (202) 319-2668

STATE OF BAHRAIN

3502 International Drive
Washington, DC 20008
Phone: (202) 342-0741
Fax: (202) 362-2192
http://www.bahrainembassy.org/

PEOPLE'S REPUBLIC OF BANGLADESH

2201 Wisconsin Avenue NW, Suite 300
Washington, DC 20007
Phone: (202) 342-8372
Fax: (202) 333-4971
http://members.aol.com/banglaemb/-
index.html

BARBADOS

2144 Wyoming Avenue
Washington, DC 20008
Phone: (202) 939-9200
Fax: (202) 332-7467

BELARUS

1619 New Hampshire Avenue NW
Washington, DC 20009
Phone: (202) 986-1604
Fax: (202) 986-1805

BELGIUM

3330 Garfield Street
Washington, DC 20008
Phone: (202) 333-6900
Fax: (202) 333-3079
http://www.diplobel.org/usa/default.htm

BELIZE

2535 Massachusetts Avenue NW
Washington, DC 20008
Phone: (202) 332-9636
Fax: (202) 332-6888

PEOPLE'S REPUBLIC OF BENIN

2737 Cathedral Avenue NW
Washington, DC 20008
Phone: (202) 232-6656
Fax: (202) 265-1996

BHUTAN

2 United Nations Plaza 27th Floor
New York, New York 10017
Phone: (212) 826-1919
Fax: (212) 826-2998

BOLIVIA

3014 Massachusetts Avenue
Washington, DC 20008
Phone: (202) 483-4410
Fax: (202) 328-3712

BOSNIA AND HERZEGOVINA

2109 E Street NW
Washington, DC 20037
Phone: (202) 337-1500
Fax: (202) 337-1502
http://www.bosnianembassy.org/

REPUBLIC OF BOTSWANA

1531-3 New Hampshire Avenue NW
Washington, DC 20036
Phone: (202) 244-4990
Fax: (202) 244-4164

BRAZIL

3006 Massachusetts Avenue
Washington, DC 20008
Phone: (202) 238-2700
Fax: (202) 238-2827
http://www.brasilemb.org/

STATE OF BRUNEI

Watergate, Suite 300
2600 Virginia Avenue
Washington, DC 20037
Phone: (202) 342-0159
Fax: (202) 342-0158

PEOPLE'S REPUBLIC OF BULGARIA

1612 22nd Street NW
Washington, DC 20008
Phone: (202) 387-7969
Fax: (202) 234-7973
http://www.bulgaria-embassy.org

BURKINA FASO

2340 Massachusetts Avenue
Washington, DC 20008
Phone: (202) 332-5577
Fax: (202) 667-1882
http://www.burkinaembassy-usa.org/

BURMA (see MYANMAR)

BURUNDI

2233 Wisconsin Avenue, Suite 212
Washington, DC 20007
Phone: (202) 342-2574
Fax: (202) 342-2578
REPUBLIC OF THE CAMEROON
2349 Massachusetts Avenue NW
Washington, DC 20008
Phone: (202) 265-8790
Fax: (202) 387-3826

CAMBODIA

4500 16th Street NW
Washington, DC 20011
Phone: (202) 726-7742
Fax: (202) 726-8381

CANADA

501 Pennsylvania Avenue
Washington, DC 20001
Phone: (202) 682-1740
Fax: (202) 682-7726
http://www.canadianembassy.org/splash/

CAPE VERDE

3415 Massachusetts Avenue NW
Washington, DC 20007
Phone: (202) 965-6820
Fax: (202) 965-1207
http://www.capeverdeusembassy.org/

CENTRAL AFRICAN REPUBLIC

1618 22nd Street
Washington, DC 20008
Phone: (202) 483-7800
Fax: (202) 332-9893

CEYLON (see Sri Lanka)

CHAD

2002 R Street
Washington, DC 20009
Phone: (202) 462-4009
Fax: (202) 265-1937
http://www.chadembassy.org

CHILI

1732 Massachusetts Avenue NW
Washington, DC 20036
Phone: (202) 785-1746
Fax: (202) 887-5579

CHINA

2300 Connecticut Avenue NW
Washington, DC 20008
Phone: (202) 328-2500
Fax: (202) 588-0032
http://www.china-embassy.org/

COLUMBIA

2118 Leroy Place
Washington DC 20008
Phone: (202) 387-8338
Fax: (202) 232-8643
http://www.colombiaemb.org/

COMOROS

336 East 45th Street 2nd Floor
New York, New York 10017
Phone: (212) 972-8010

CONGO (Formerly Zaire)

1800 New Hampshire Avenue NW
Washington, DC 20009
Phone: (202) 234-7690
Fax: (202) 237-0748

COSTA RICA

2114 S Street NW
Washington, DC 20008
Phone: (202) 234-2945
Fax: (202) 265-4795
http://www.costarica.com/embassy/

COTE D'IVOIRE (Ivory Coast)

2424 Massachusetts Avenue NW
Washington, DC 20008
Phone: (202) 797-0300

CROATIA
2343 Massachusetts Avenue NW
Washington, DC 20008
Phone: (202) 588-5899
Fax: (202) 588-8936
http://www.croatiaemb.org/

CUBA
2630 and 2639 16th Street NW
Washington, DC 20009
Phone: (202) 797-8518

REPUBLIC OF CYPRUS
2211 R Street NW
Washington, DC 20008
Phone: (202) 462-5772
Fax: (202) 483-6710

CZECH REPUBLIC
3900 Spring of Freedom Street NW
Washington, DC 20008
Phone: (202) 274-9100
Fax: (202) 966-8540
http://www.czech.cz/washington/

DENMARK
3200 Whitehaven Street NW
Washington, DC 20008
Phone: (202) 234-4300
Fax: (202) 328-1470
http://www.denmarkemb.org/

DJIBOUTI
1156 15th Street NW Suite 515
Washington, DC 20005
Phone: (202) 331-0270

DOMINICAN REPUBLIC
1715 22nd Street NW
Washington, DC 20008
Phone: (202) 332-6280
Fax: (202) 265-8057
http://www.domrep.org/

ECUADOR
2535 15th Street NW
Washington, DC 20009
Phone: (202) 234-7200
http://www.ecuador.org/

EGYPT
3521 International Court NW
Washington, DC 20008
Phone: (202) 966-6342

EL SALVADOR
2308 California Street NW
Washington, DC 20008
Phone: (202) 265-9671
http://www.elsalvador.org
EQUATORIAL GUINEA
1721 I Street NW, Suite 400
Washington, DC 20006

ERITREA
1708 New Hampshire Avenue NW
Washington, DC 20009
Phone: (202) 319-1991
Fax: (202) 319-1304

ESTONIA
2131 Massachusetts Avenue NW
Washington, DC 20008
Phone: (202) 588-0101
Fax: (202) 588-0108
http://www.estemb.org/

ETHIOPIA
3506 International Drive NW
Washington, DC 20008
Phone: (202) 364-1200
Fax: (202) 686-9951
http://www.ethiopianembassy.org/

FIJI
2233 Wisconsin Avenue NW, Suite 240
Washington, DC 20007
Phone: (202) 337-8320
Fax: (202) 337-1996

FINLAND

3301 Massachusetts Avenue, NW
Washington, DC 20008
Phone: (202) 298-5800
Fax: (202) 298-6030
http://www.finland.org/

FRANCE

4101 Reservoir Road, NW
Washington, DC 20007
Phone: (202) 944-6000
Fax: (202) 944-6072
http://www.info-france-usa.org/

GABON

2034 20th Street NW, Suite 200
Washington, DC 20009
Phone: (202) 797-1000
Fax: (202) 332-0668

THE GAMBIA

1155 15th Street NW, Suite 1000
Washington, DC 20005
Phone: (202) 785-1399
http://www.gambia.com/index.html

GEORGIA

1511 K Street NW Suite 400
Washington, DC 20005
Phone: (202) 393-5959
Fax: (202) 393-4537
http://www.steele.com/embgeorgia/

GERMANY

4645 Reservoir Road NW
Washington, DC 20007
Phone: (202) 298-4000
Fax: (202) 298-4249 or 333-2653
http://www.germany-info.org/

GHANA

3512 International Drive NW
Washington, DC 20008
Phone: (202) 686-4520
http://www.ghana-embassy.org/

GREECE

2221 Massachusetts Avenue NW
Washington, DC 20008
Phone: (202) 939-5800
Fax: (202) 939-5824
http://www.greekembassy.org/

GRENADA

1701 New Hampshire Avenue NW
Washington, DC 20009
Phone: (202) 265-2561

GUATEMALA

2220 R Street NW
Washington, DC 20008
Phone: (202) 745-4952
Fax: (202) 745-1908
http://www.mdngt.org/agremilusa/embas
sy.html

GUINEA

2112 Leroy Place NW
Washington, DC 20008
Phone: (202) 483-9420

GUINEA BISSAU

918 16th Street NW
Washington, DC 20006

GUYANA

2490 Tracy Place NW
Washington, DC 20008
Phone: (202) 265-6900
Fax: (202) 232-1297
http://www.wam.umd.edu/~swi/embassy
.htm

HAITI

2311 Massachusetts Avenue NW
Washington, DC 20008
Phone: (202) 332-4090
Fax: (202) 745-7215
http://www.haiti.org/

HONDURAS

3007 Tilden Street NW
Washington, DC 20008
Phone: (202) 966-7702

HUNGARY

3910 Shoemaker Street, NW
Washington, DC 20008
Phone: (202) 362-6730
Fax: (202) 686-6412
http://www.hungaryemb.org/

ICELAND

1156 15th Street NW, Suite 1200
Washington, DC 20005
Phone: (202) 265-6653
Fax: (202) 265-6656
http://www.iceland.org/

INDIA

2107 Massachusetts Avenue NW
Washington, DC 20008
Phone: (202) 939-7000
Fax: (202) 265-4351
http://www.indianembassy.org/

INDONESIA

2020 Massachusetts Avenue NW
Washington, DC 20036
Phone: (202) 775-5200
http://kbri.org/

IRAN

2209 Wisconsin Avenue (NW)
Washington, DC 20007
Phone: (202) 965-4990
Fax: (202) 965-1073
http://www.daftar.org/default_eng.htm

IRAQ

1801 P Street NW
Washington, DC 20036
Phone: (202) 483-7500
Fax: (202) 462-5066

IRELAND

2234 Massachusetts Avenue NW
Washington, DC 20008
Phone: (202) 462-3939
Fax: (202) 232-5993
http://www.irelandemb.org/

ISRAEL

3514 International Drive NW
Washington, DC 20008
Phone: (202) 364-5500
Fax: (202) 364-5423
http://www.israelemb.org/

ITALY

1601 Fuller Street NW
Washington, DC 20009
Phone: (202) 328-5500
Fax: (202) 462-3605
http://www.italyemb.org/

JAMAICA

1520 New Hampshire Avenue NW
Washington, DC 20036
Phone: (202) 452-0660
Fax: (202) 452-0081
http://www.caribbean-
online.com/jamaica/embassy/washdc/

JAPAN

2520 Massachusetts Avenue NW
Washington, DC 20008
Phone: (202) 238-6700
Fax: (202) 328-2187
www.embjapan.org/

JORDAN

3504 International Drive NW
Washington, DC 20008
Phone: (202) 966-2664
Fax: (202) 966-3110
http://www.jordanembassyus.org/

KAZAKHSTAN

1401 16th Street NW
Washington, DC 20036
Phone: (202) 232-5488

KENYA

2249 R Street NW
Washington, DC 20008
Phone: (202) 387-6101
Fax: (202) 462-3829
http://www.kenyaembassy.com

KOREA

2450 Massachusetts Avenue NW
Washington, DC 20008
Phone: (202) 939-5600
Fax: (202) 797-0595
http://www.mofat.go.kr/en_usa.htm

KUWAIT

2940 Tilden Street NW
Washington, DC 20008
Phone: (202) 966-0702

KYRGYZ

1732 Wisconsin Avenue NW
Washington, DC 20007
Phone: (202) 338-5141
Fax: (202) 338-5139
http://www.kyrgyzstan.org/

LAOS

2222 S Street NW
Washington, DC 20008
Phone: (202) 332-6416
Fax: (202) 332-4923
http://www.laoembassy.com/

LATVIA

4325 17th Street NW
Washington, DC 20011
Phone: (202) 726-8213
Fax: (202) 726-6785
http://www.latvia-usa.org/

LEBANON

2560 28th Street NW
Washington, DC 20008
Phone: (202) 939-6300
Fax: (202) 939-6324

LESOTHO

2511 Massachusetts Avenue NW
Washington, DC 20008
Phone: (202) 797-5533

LIBERIA

5201 16th Street NW
Washington, DC 20011
Phone: (202) 723-0437
Fax: (202) 723-0436
http://www.liberiaemb.org/

LITHUANIA

2622 16th Street NW
Washington, DC 20009
Phone: (202) 234-5860
Fax: (202) 328-0466
http://www.ltembassyus.org/

LUXEMBOURG

2200 Massachusetts Avenue NW
Washington, DC 20008
Phone: (202) 265-4171

MACEDONIA

3050 K Street NW, Suite 210
Washington, DC 20007
Phone: (202) 337-3063
Fax: (202) 337-3093

MADAGASCAR

2374 Massachusetts Avenue
Washington, DC 20008
Phone: (202) 265-5525
http://www.embassy.org/madagascar/

MALAWI

2408 Massachusetts Avenue NW
Washington, DC 20008
Phone: (202) 797-1007

MALAYSIA

2401 Massachusetts Avenue NW
Washington, DC 20008
Phone: (202) 328-2700

MALI

2130 R Street NW
Washington, DC 20008
Phone: (202) 332-2249
Fax: (202) 332-6603
http://www.maliembassy-usa.org

MALTA

2017 Connecticut Avenue NW
Washington, DC 20008
Phone: (202) 462-3611

MARSHALL ISLANDS

2433 Massachusetts Avenue NW
Washington, DC 20008
Phone: (202) 234-5414
Fax: (202) 232-3236
http://www.rmiembassyus.org/usemb.html

MAURITANIA

2129 Leroy Place NW
Washington, DC 20008
Phone: (202) 232-5700
Fax: (202) 232-5701

MAURITIUS

4301 Connecticut Avenue NW,
Suite 441
Washington, DC 20008
Phone: (202) 244-1491
Fax: (202) 966-0983

MEXICO

1911 Pennsylvania Avenue NW
Washington, DC 20006
Phone: (202) 728-1600
http://www.embassyofmexico.org/eng-
lish/main2.htm

MICRONESIA

1725 N Street NW
Washington, DC 20036
Phone: (202) 223-4383

MOLDOVA

2101 S Street NW
Washington, DC 20008
Phone: (202) 667-1130
Fax: (202) 667-1204
http://www.moldova.org/

MONGOLIA

2833 M Street NW
Washington, DC 20007
Phone: (202) 333-7117
Fax: (202) 298-9227
http://members.aol.com/monemb

MOROCCO

1601 21st Street NW
Washington, DC 20009
Phone: (202) 462-7979

MOZAMBIQUE

1990 M Street NW, Suite 570
Washington, DC 20036
Phone: (202) 293-7146
Fax: (202) 835-0245
http://www.embamoc-usa.org/

MYANMAR (formerly Burma)

2300 S Street
Washington, DC 20008
Phone: (202) 332-9044

NAMIBIA

1605 New Hampshire Avenue NW
Washington, DC 20009
Phone: (202) 986-0540

NEPAL

2131 Leroy Place NW
Washington DC, 20008
Phone: (202) 667-4550

NETHERLANDS

4200 Linnean Avenue NW
Washington, DC 20008
Phone: (202) 244-5300
Fax: (202) 362-3430
http://www.netherlands-embassy.org/

NEW ZEALAND

37 Observatory Circle
Washington, DC 20008
Phone: (202) 328-4800
Fax: (202) 667-5227
http://www.nzemb.org/

NICARAGUA

1627 New Hampshire Avenue NW
Washington, DC 20009
Phone: (202) 939-6570
Fax: (202) 939-6542

NIGER

2204 R Street NW
Washington, DC 20008
Phone: (202) 483-4224

NIGERIA

1333 16th Street NW
Washington, DC 20036
Phone: (202) 986-8400
Fax: (202) 775-1385

NORWAY

2720 34th Street NW
Washington, DC 20008
Phone: (202) 333-6000
http://www.norway.org/

OMAN

2535 Belmont Rd NW
Washington, DC 20008
Phone: (202) 387-1980

PAKISTAN

2315 Massachusetts Avenue NW
Washington, DC 20008
Phone: (202) 939-6200
http://www.pakistan-embassy.com/

PANAMA

2862 McGill Terrace NW
Washington, DC 20008
Phone: (202) 483-1407

PAPUA NEW GUINEA

1779 Massachusetts Avenue NW,
Suite 805
Washington, DC 20036
Phone: (202) 745-3680
Fax: (202) 745-3679
http://www.pngembassy.org

PARAGUAY

2400 Massachusetts Avenue NW
Washington, DC 20008
Phone: (202) 483-6960

PERU

1700 Massachusetts Avenue NW
Washington, DC 20036
Phone: (202) 833-9860 to 9869
Fax: (202) 659-8124
http://www.peruemb.org

PHILIPPINES

1600 Massachusetts Avenue NW
Washington, DC 20036
Phone: (202) 467-9300
Fax: (202) 467-9417
http://us.sequel.net/rpinus

POLAND

2640 16th Street NW
Washington, DC 20009
Phone: (202) 234-3800
Fax: (202) 328-6271
http://www.polishworld.com/polemb/

PORTUGAL

2125 Kalorama Road NW
Washington, DC 20008
Phone: (202) 328-8610
Fax: (202) 462-3726
http://www.portugalemb.org/

QATAR

4200 Wisconsin Avenue NW, Suite 200
Washington, DC 20016
Phone: (202) 274-1600
Fax: (202) 237-0061

ROMANIA

1607 23rd Street
Washington, DC 20008
Phone: (202) 232-4747
http://www.roembus.org

RUSSIA

2650 Wisconsin Avenue NW
Washington, DC 20007
Phone: (202) 298-5700
Fax: (202) 298-5749
http://www.russianembassy.org

RWANDA

1714 New Hampshire Avenue NW
Washington, DC 20009
Phone: (202) 232-2882
Fax: (202) 232-4544
http://www.rwandemb.org/

SAINT KITTS AND NEVIS

3216 New Mexico Avenue NW
Washington, DC 20016
Phone: (202) 686-2636
Fax: (202) 686-5740
http://www.stkittsnevis.org/

SAINT LUCIA

3216 New Mexico Avenue NW
Washington, DC 20016
Phone: (202) 364-6792
Fax: (202) 364-6723

SAINT VINCENT and the GRENADINES

3216 New Mexico Avenue NW
Washington, DC 20016
Phone: (202) 364-6730
Fax: (202) 364-6736

SAUDI ARABIA

601 New Hampshire Avenue NW
Washington, DC 20037
Phone: (202) 337-4076
Fax: (202) 337-4134
http://www.saudiembassy.net/

SENEGAL

2112 Wyoming Avenue
Washington, DC 20008
Phone: (202) 234-0540

SEYCHELLES

800 Second Avenue, Suite 400
New York, New York 10017
Phone: (212) 687-9766

SIERRA LEONE

1701 19th Street
Washington, DC 20009
Phone: (202) 939-9261

SINGAPORE

3501 International Place NW
Washington, DC 20008
Phone: (202) 537-3100
Fax: (202) 537-0876
http://www.gov.sg/mfa/washington

SLOVAK REPUBLIC

2201 Wisconsin Avenue NW, Suite 250
Washington, DC 20007
Phone: (202) 965-5160
Fax: (202) 965-5166
http://www.slovakemb.com/

SLOVENIA

1525 New Hampshire Avenue NW
Washington, DC 20036
Phone: (202) 667-5363
Fax: (202) 667-4563
http://www.embassy.org/slovenia/

SOUTH AFRICA

3051 Massachusetts Avenue NW
Washington, DC 20008
Phone: (202) 232-4400
Fax: (202) 265-1607
http://www.southafrica.net/

SPAIN

2375 Pennsylvania Avenue NW
Washington, DC 20037
Phone: (202) 452-0100
Fax: (202) 833-5670
http://www.spainemb.org/information/

SRI LANKA

2148 Wyoming Avenue NW
Washington, DC 20008
Phone: (202) 483-4025
Fax: (202) 232-7181
http://www.slembassy.org/

SUDAN

2210 Massachusetts Avenue NW
Washington, DC 20008
Phone: (202) 338-8565
Fax: (202) 667-2406
http://www.sudanembassyus.org/

SURINAME

4301 Connecticut Avenue NW,
Suite 460
Washington, DC 20008
Phone: (202) 244-7488
Fax: (202) 244-5878

SWAZILAND

3400 International Drive NW
Washington, DC 20008
Phone: (202) 362-6683
Fax: (202) 244-8059

SWEDEN

1501 M Street NW
Washington, DC 20005
Phone: (202) 467-2600
Fax: (202) 467-2656
http://www.swedenemb.org/

SWITZERLAND

2900 Cathedral Avenue NW
Washington, DC 20008
Phone: (202) 745-7900
Fax: (202) 387-2564
http://www.swissemb.org/

SYRIA

2215 Wyoming Avenue NW
Washington, DC 20008
Phone: (202) 232-6313
Fax: (202) 234-9548

TAIWAN

4201 Wisconsin Avenue NW
Washington, DC 20016
Phone: (202) 895-1800
Fax: (202) 966-0825

TANZANIA

2139 R Street NW
Washington, DC 20008
Phone: (202) 939-6125
Fax: (202) 797-7408

THAILAND

1024 Wisconsin Avenue NW, Suite 401
Washington, DC 20007
Phone: (202) 944-3600
Fax: (202) 944-3611
http://www.thaiembdc.org/

TOGO

2208 Massachusetts Avenue NW
Washington, DC 20008
Phone: (202) 234-4212
Fax: (202) 232-3190

TONGA

Tonga High Commission
36 Molyneux St.
London, England W1H 6AB
Phone 0171-724-5828
Fax 0171-723-9074

TRINIDAD AND TOBAGO

1708 Massachusetts Avenue NW
Washington, DC 20036
Phone: (202) 467-6490
Fax: (202) 785-3130

TUNISIA

1515 Massachusetts Avenue NW
Washington, DC 20005
Phone: (202) 862-1850

TURKEY

1714 Massachusetts Avenue NW
Washington, DC 20036
Phone: (202) 659-8200
Fax: (202) 659-0744
http://www.turkey.org/turkey/

TURKMENISTAN

2207 Massachusetts Avenue NW
Washington, Dc 20008
Phone: (202) 588-1500
Fax: (202) 588-0697
http://www.turkmenistanembassy.org/

UGANDA

5911 16th Street NW
Washington, DC 20011
Phone: (202) 726-7100
Fax: (202) 726-1727
http://www.ugandaweb.com/ugaembassy

UKRAINE

3350 M Street NW
Washington, DC 20007
Phone: (202) 333-7507
Fax: (202) 333-7510
http://www.ukremb.com

UNITED ARAB EMIRATES

1255 22nd Street NW, Suite 700
Washington, DC 20037
Phone: (202) 955-7999

UNITED KINGDOM

3100 Massachusetts Avenue NW
Washington, DC 20008
Phone: (202) 588-6500
Fax: (202) 588-7870
http://www.britainusa.com

URUGUAY

2715 M Street 3rd Floor
Washington, DC 20007
Phone: (202) 331-1313
Fax: (212) 331-8142
http://www.embassy.org/uruguay/

UZBEKISTAN

1746 Massachusetts Avenue NW
Washington, DC 20036
Phone: (202) 887-5300
Fax: (202) 293-6804
http://www.uzbekistan.org/

VATICAN (Holy See)

3339 Massachusetts Avenue NW
Washington, DC 20008

VENEZUELA

1099 30th Street NW
Washington, DC 20007
Phone: (202) 342-2214
Fax: (202) 342-6820

VIETNAM

1233 20th Street NW, Suite 400
Washington, DC 20037
Phone: (202) 861-0737
Fax: (202) 861-0917
http://www.vietnamembassy-usa.org/

WESTERN SAMOA

800 Second Avenue Suite 400D
New York, New York 10017
Phone: (212) 599-6197

YEMEN

2600 Virginia Avenue NW, Suite 705
Washington, DC 20037
Phone: (202) 965-4760
Fax: (202) 337-2017
http://www.yemenembassy.org/

YUGOSLAVIA

2410 California Street NW
Washington, DC 20008
Phone: (202) 462-6566

ZAMBIA

2419 Massachusetts Avenue NW
Washington, DC 20008
Phone: (202) 265-9717

ZIMBABWE

1608 New Hampshire Avenue NW
Washington, DC 20009
Phone: (202) 332-7100

The National Archives

The National Archives preserves and makes available for reference and research the well-known valuable records of the U.S. government. These records include well-known documents, such as the Declaration of Independence and the Constitution, as well as 3 billion textual documents, 2 million cartographic items, 5 million still photographs, 9 million aerial photographs, 91 million feet of motion picture film, and 122,000 video and sound recordings. The National Archives also makes available for research a select number of collections donated to the federal government for that purpose.

Known formally as the National Archives and Records Administration (NARA), the agency operates 14 records centers, 11 field branches, and 8 Presidential libraries in 15 states.

Genealogical Records in the National Archives

The National Archives has custody of millions of records relating to persons who have had dealings with the federal government. These records are deposited in the National Archives facilities in the Washington, DC area and in the 11 National Archives Regional Archives. These records may contain full information about a person or give little information beyond a name.

The original records may be freely consulted in the National Archives facility that has custody of them. In addition, many of the most heavily used records have been microfilmed, with copies available for research use at more than one facility. Photocopies of most of the records can be supplied for a moderate fee per page. If you are unable to come to the National Archives, you may hire someone to do research for you. Many researchers who work for a fee advertise in genealogical periodicals, which are usually available in public libraries.

Records About Indians

Within the National Archives, there are many records relating to Indians who maintained their tribal affiliation. The original records of the headquarters of the Bureau of Indian Affairs are in the National Archives in Washington, DC. These records often contain information about specific tribal members. Original records created by the various field offices and Indian schools are among the holdings of the regional archives.

They include the following:

Lists of Indian tribes including Cherokee, Chickasaw, Choctaw, and Creek. Each entry on these lists usually contains **the name of the head of the family,** the number of persons in the family by age and sex, and a description of property owned before removal (including the location of real property).

Annuity Payrolls, showing the **name, age, and sex** of each person who received payment.

Annual Census Rolls. These records (available on microfilm) normally show for each person in a family the **Indian or English name** (or both names); **and age, sex,** and relationship to the head of the family and sometimes to another enrolled Indian. The records occasionally include supplementary information, such as names of persons who died or were born during the year.

Land Records

Land records in the National Archives include bounty-land-warrant files, donation land entry files, homestead application files, and private land claim files. The donation land entry files and homestead application files show, in addition to the name of the applicant, the location of the land and the date it was acquired, residence or post office address, **age or date and place of birth, marital status,** and, if applicable, the given **name of spouse,** or size of family. If any applicant for homestead land was of foreign birth, the application file contains evidence of naturalization or of intention to become a citizen. Supporting documents show the immigrant's country of birth and sometimes the date and port of arrival. Genealogical information in records relating to private land claims varies from the mention of the claimant's name and location of the land to such additional information as the claimant's place of residence when the claim was made and the **names of relatives,** both living and dead.

Naturalization Records

Naturalization records generally show, for each person who petitioned for naturalization, **name, age, date of birth, nationality**, and whether citizenship was granted. The 11 regional archives hold original records of naturalizations filed in most of the federal courts located in their regions.

The Immigration and Naturalization Service (INS), Washington, DC 20536, has duplicate records of all naturalizations that occurred after September 26, 1906. When records relating to citizenship granted after that date are not available in the National Archives, inquiries should be sent to the INS on a form that can be obtained from any of the service's district offices. Local postmasters will give the address of the nearest INS district office.

Passenger Lists

The National Archives contain customs passenger lists and immigration passenger lists of ships arriving from abroad at many Atlantic, Pacific, and Gulf Coast ports. There are also arrival records for immigration via Canada.

A customs passenger list normally contains the following information for each passenger: **name, age, sex, and occupation;** the country of embarkation; and the country of destination. For one who died in passage, the date and circumstances of death are given. Immigration passenger lists vary in informational content but usually show the place of birth and last place of residence in addition to the information found in the customs passenger lists. Some of the immigration passenger lists include the **name and address of a relative** in the country from which the passenger came.

Microfilm copies of available passenger lists earlier than 1955 can be used in the National Archives in Washington, DC. Some microfilm copies of lists are also available in the regional archives.

Passport Applications

The National Archives in Washington, DC has passport applications and related papers. The name of the person who applied for a passport and the place and approximate date of application should be supplied. Requests for information from passport records should be addressed to the Passport Office, Department of State, Washington, DC 20520.

Personnel Records

There are records in the National Archives in Washington, DC relating to civilian employees of the federal government whose service ended before 1940. These records may contain information about the **date and place of birth of an employee.** The National Archives staff will search for records about employees if given the full name and address of the employing agency and the approximate dates of employment. The personnel records for most civilian employees whose service terminated after 1940 are in Civilian Personnel Records, 11 Winnebago Street, St. Louis, Missouri 63118.

A veteran's claim will show his **place and date of birth, place of residence after service, and a summary of military service.** A dependent's claim normally includes the **dependent's age and residence,** relationship to the veteran, and information about the veteran's death. A widow's application usually includes her **maiden name, the date of her marriage to the veteran, and the names of their children.**

When a claim file is found, documents that normally contain information of a personal nature about the veteran and his family will be selected and photocopied. The inquirer is notified of costs, and copies are sent after payment is received. The selected documents furnished generally contain the basic information in the pension file, as the remaining documents rarely contain any additional genealogical data. If an inquirer wishes to have photocopies of all the reproducible papers in the claim file, they can be furnished for a moderate cost per page.

The National Archives has applications or abstracts of applications of seamen on U.S. vessels for "protection certificate," or certificates of U.S. citizenship. Such applications are usually supported by evidence of the **date and place of birth and of the citizenship** of the seaman.

Requests for information about army officers separated after 1916 and army enlisted personnel separated after 1912 should be made on Standard Form 180, Request Pertaining to Military Records, and sent to Military Personnel Records, 9700 Page Boulevard, St. Louis, Missouri 63132.

Records of commissioned officers in the U.S. Marine Corps usually show each officer's name and rank and the date of appointment or of acceptance of a commission. They may also give **age** and information about residence. Service records for enlisted marines usually show **name, age, and the date, place, and term of enlistment**.

The National Archives staff will make a limited search in its naval and marine service records in response to letters of inquiry. If a request concerns a navy or marine officer or enlisted person, his name and the name of the war in which he served or the dates of service should be given.

The U.S. Coast Guard was created on January 28, 1915, which consolidated the former Revenue Cutter and Lifesaving Services of the Department of the Treasury. The Bureau of Lighthouses of the Department of Commerce became a part of the Coast Guard on July 1, 1939. Revenue-Cutter Service vessels were manned by military personnel.

The inspectors of the Lifesaving Service were also military personnel, but the superintendents, keepers, and other employees at the lifesaving stations were civilian employees. The inspectors and engineers of the lighthouse district were officers detailed from the Navy and Army. All other employees of the Lighthouse Service were civilians. Personnel and card records, for civilians formerly employed by the Revenue-Cutter Service, Lifesaving Service and Lighthouse Service are on file at the National Personnel Records Center (Civilian Personnel Records).

Civilian employment records are subject to Office of Personnel Management regulations governing the release of information from federal employees' personnel records under the term of the Freedom of Information Act of 1967 (5 USC 522). Information furnished is limited to **names, position, titles, grades, salaries, and duty stations.** Inquiries, with as much identification as possible, should be submitted to Civilian Personnel Records, 111 Winnebago Street, St. Louis, Missouri 63118.

Births and Marriages at Foreign Service Posts

The National Archives has records of births and marriages of U.S. citizens abroad registered at Foreign Service posts. Birth and marriage records extend through 1941, and reports of deaths extend through 1949. Requests for information should be addressed to the Department of State, Washington, DC 20520. Requests for information about earlier registrations should be addressed to the Civil Reference Branch (NNRC), National Archives, Washington, DC 20408.

How to Search in an Orderly Fashion

For records accessioned by the National Archives, the concept of moving from the smallest to the largest citation element (from the record item to the repository) is recommended. Citations may differ because internal record group arrangement is based on the organizational structures of the bureaus, departments, and agencies that created the records; some agencies were organized in more complex structures than others. Citations to records should reflect the hierarchical arrangement of the records as closely as possible.

The citations elements to be used (going from the smallest element to the largest) are as follows:

RECORD: At the National Archives, a record is piece of information or an item in any physical form (e.g., paper, photographic or motion picture film, audio tape, computer tape, etc.) that gives information created or received by a government agency in carrying out its duties and functions. Example: a letter in a pension application file.

FILE UNIT: A file unit holds the records concerning a transaction, person, case, date, or subject. Example: a pension application file based on the military service of one veteran. A pension file often contains record items of various types in addition to the actual application, or claim, such as supporting depositions, affidavits, correspondence, etc.

SERIES: A series consists of file units that deal with a particular subject, function, or activity and that are related by arrangement, source, use, physical form, or action taken. Example: within pension application files for widows and dependents of sailors, pension applications that were not approved constitute one series while pension applications that were approved constitute another series.

SUBGROUP: A subgroup contains two or more series that are related by subject, activity, and source. Example: the two previously mentioned series for approved and unapproved pension applications based on sailors military service (plus other series of pension applications based on military service in the U.S. Army and the Marine Corps for roughly the same time period) form the subgroup of Pension Files.

RECORD GROUP: Subgroups are combined into record groups according to the origin of the subgroup material. Most often, a record group exists for the records of a bureau or other administrative body of an executive department, or for an independent government agency that is equivalent to a bureau in size. Example: the subgroup Pension Files plus other subgroups constitute Records of the Veterans Administration.

REPOSITORY: The repository is the institution in which the cited record is kept. Give the name of the institution and the city in which it is located. National Archives repositories in Washington, DC; Suitland, Maryland; Alexandria, Virginia; and other locations in the Washington, DC area should be cited as "National Archives—Washington, DC." Regional archives should be cited as "National Archives—[name of region]."

REGIONAL ARCHIVES

http://www.nara.gov

For each of the following, address inquiries to: Director, National Archives—[name of region].

NEW ENGLAND REGION

Connecticut, Maine, Massachusetts, New Hampshire, Rhode Island, and Vermont

380 Trapelo Road
Waltham, Massachusetts 02452-6399
Telephone: (781) 647-8104
Fax: (781) 647-8088
e-mail: archives@waltham.nara.gov

NORTHEAST REGION

New Jersey, New York, Puerto Rico, and the Virgin Islands

201 Varick Street
New York, New York 10014-4811
Telephone: (212) 337-1300
Fax: (212) 337-1306
e-mail: archives@newyork.nara.gov

MID ATLANTIC REGION

Delaware, Maryland, Pennsylvania, Virginia, and West Virginia

900 Market Street, Room 1350
Philadelphia, Pennsylvania 19107-4292
Telephone: (215) 597-3000
Fax: (215) 597-2303
e-mail: archives@philarch.nara.gov

SOUTHEAST REGION

Alabama, Georgia, Florida, Kentucky, Mississippi, North Carolina, South Carolina, and Tennessee.

1557 St. Joseph Avenue
East Point, Georgia 30344-2593
Telephone: (404) 763-7474
Fax: (404) 763-7059
e-mail: center@atlanta.nara.gov

GREAT LAKES REGION

Illinois, Indiana, Michigan, Minnesota, Ohio, and Wisconsin

7358 South Pulaski Road
Chicago, Illinois 60629-5898
Telephone: (773) 581-7816
Fax: (312) 886-7883
e-mail: archives@chicago.nara.gov

CENTRAL PLAINS REGION

Iowa, Kansas, Missouri, and Nebraska

2312 East Bannister Road
Kansas City, Missouri 64131-3011
Telephone: (816) 926-6272
Fax: (816) 926-6982
e-mail: archives@kansascity.nara.gov

SOUTHWEST REGION

Arkansas, Louisiana, New Mexico, Oklahoma, and Texas

501 West Felix Street, Bldg. 1
Fort Worth, Texas 76115-3405
Telephone: (817) 334-5525
Fax: (817) 334-5621
e-mail: archives@ftworth.nara.gov

ROCKY MOUNTAIN REGION

Colorado, Montana, North Dakota, South Dakota, Utah, and Wyoming

Building 48, Denver Federal Center
West 6th Avenue and Kipling Street
Denver, Colorado 80225
Telephone: (303) 236-0804
Fax: (303) 236-9297
e-mail: archives@denver.nara.gov

PACIFIC SOUTHWEST REGION

Arizona; the southern California counties of Imperial, Inyo, Kern, Los Angeles, Orange, Riverside, San Bernardino, San Diego, San Luis Obispo, Santa Barbara, and Ventura; and Nevada's Clark County

24000 Avila Road (building address)
P.O. Box 6719 (mailing address)
Laguna Niguel, California 92677-6719
Telephone: (949) 360-2641
Fax: (949) 360-2624
e-mail: archives@laguna.nara.gov

PACIFIC SIERRA REGION

Hawaii, Nevada except Clark County, Northern California, the Pacific Trust Territories and American Samoa

1000 Commodore Drive
San Bruno, California 94066-2350
Telephone: (650) 876-9009
Fax: (650) 876-9233
e-mail: archives@sanbruno.nara.gov

PACIFIC NORTHWEST REGION

Idaho, Oregon, and Washington

6125 Sand Point Way N.E.
Seattle, Washington 98115-7999
Telephone: (206) 526-6501
Fax: (206) 526-6575
e-mail: archives@seattle.nara.gov

PACIFIC ALASKA REGION

Alaska

654 West Third Avenue
Anchorage, Alaska 99501-2145
Telephone: (907) 271-2443
Fax: (907) 271-2442
e-mail: archives@alaska.nara.gov

National Cemetery System

The National Cemetery System is a source that is not used to its full potential by finders of missing persons. The National Cemetery System was created by President Lincoln in 1862, and 12 cemeteries were established. In 1933, an Executive Order authorized the transfer of national cemeteries from the War Department (now Department of the Army) to the National Park Service, Department of the Interior. In June 1973, the national cemeteries were transferred from the Department of the Interior to the Veterans Administration. Within the Veterans Administration, the National Cemetery System is the responsibility of the Department of Memorial Affairs.

You can request a search to be conducted for your subject, but I use the National Cemetery System to find dependents of the subject. If your subject was in the armed forces, the reserves, or a member of the public health service, they may have dependents who are buried in one of the National Cemeteries. The guidelines for the burial of a dependent are as follows:

A. The eligible spouse of an active duty member or veteran.

B. The minor children of an eligible active duty member or veteran. For purpose of burial in a national cemetery, a minor child is a person who is unmarried and

(1) Who is under the age of 21 years;

(2) Who, after attaining the age of 21 years and until completion of education or training (but not after attaining the age of 23

years), is pursuing a course of instruction at an educational institution.

C. Unmarried adult children of an eligible active duty member or veteran if they become permanently incapable of self-support because of a physical or mental disability incurred before attaining the age of 21 years.

If your inquiry indicates that your subject, who may be on active status but is more likely a veteran for our purposes here, has a family member buried, you want to write and ask for the records of interment. This will yield information about your subject including date of birth, Social Security Number, and addresses. A current address is usually available from these records.

You may go to Joseph Culligan's Resource CD for the link titled "Cemeteries." This will bring you to many different cemetery links that cover local and state cemeteries. The following is a list of all cemeteries in the National Cemetery System. You may also visit: http://www.cem.va.gov/.

ALABAMA

Fort Mitchell National Cemetery
P.O. Box 2517
Phoenix City, Alabama 36867

Mobile National Cemetery
1202 Virginia Street
Mobile, Alabama 36604

ALASKA

Fort Richardson National Cemetery
P.O. Box 5-498
Fort Richardson, Alaska 99505

Sitka National Cemetery
P.O. Box 1065
Sitka, Alaska 99835

ARIZONA

Prescott National Cemetery
500 Highway 89N
Prescott, Arizona 86301

National Memorial Cemetery
23029 North Cave Creek Road
Phoenix, Arizona 85024

ARKANSAS

Fayetteville National Cemetery
700 Government Avenue
Fayetteville, Arkansas 72701

Fort Smith National Cemetery
522 Garland Avenue and South 6th Street
Fort Smith, Arkansas 72901

Little Rock National Cemetery
2523 Confederate Boulevard
Little Rock, Arkansas 72206

CALIFORNIA

Fort Rosecrans National Cemetery
P.O. Box 6237
San Diego, California 92106

Golden Gate National Cemetery
1300 Sneath Lane
San Bruno, California 94066

Los Angeles National Cemetery
950 South Sepulveda Boulevard
Los Angeles, California 90049

Riverside National Cemetery
22495 Van Buren Boulevard
Riverside, California 92508

San Francisco National Cemetery
P.O. Box 29012
San Francisco, California 94129

COLORADO

Fort Logan National Cemetery
3698 South Sheridan Boulevard
Denver, Colorado 80235

Fort Lyon National Cemetery
Virginia Medical Center
Fort Lyon, Colorado 81038

FLORIDA

Barrancas National Cemetery
Naval Air Station
Pensacola, Florida 32508

Bay Pines National Cemetery
P.O. Box 477
Bay Pines, Florida 33504

Florida National Cemetery
P.O. Box 337
Bushnell, Florida 33513

St. Augustine National Cemetery
104 Marine Street
St. Augustine, Florida 32084

GEORGIA

Marietta National Cemetery
500 Washington Avenue
Marietta, Georgia 30060

HAWAII

**National Memorial Cemetery
of the Pacific**
2177 Puowaina Drive
Honolulu, Hawaii 96813

ILLINOIS

Alton National Cemetery
600 Pearl Street
Alton, Illinois 62003

Camp Butler National Cemetery
R.R. #1
Springfield, Illinois 62707

Danville National Cemetery
1900 East Main Street
Danville, Illinois 61832

Mound City National Cemetery
Junction—Highway 37 & 51
Mound City, Illinois 62963

Quincy National Cemetery
36th and Maine Street
Quincy, Illinois 62301

Rock Island National Cemetery
Rock Island Arsenal
Rock Island, Illinois 61299

INDIANA

Crown Hill National Cemetery
700 West 38th Street
Indianapolis, Indiana 46208

Marion National Cemetery
VA Medical Center
Marion, Indiana 46952

New Albany National Cemetery
1943 Ekin Avenue
New Albany, Indiana 47150

IOWA

Keokuk National Cemetery
1701 J Street
Keokuk, Iowa 52632

KANSAS

**Fort Leavenworth
National Cemetery**
Fort Leavenworth, Kansas 66027

Fort Scott National Cemetery
P.O. Box 917
Fort Scott, Kansas 66701

Leavenworth National Cemeteries
P.O. Box 1649
Leavenworth, Kansas 66048

KENTUCKY

Camp Nelson National Cemetery
6980 Danville Road
Nicholasville, Kentucky 40356

Cave Hill National Cemetery
701 Baxter Avenue
Louisville, Kentucky 40204

Danville National Cemetery
377 North First Street
Danville, Kentucky 40442

Lebanon National Cemetery
R.R. #1, Box 616
Lebanon, Kentucky 40033

Lexington National Cemetery
833 West Main Street
Lexington, Kentucky 40508

Mill Springs National Cemetery
Rural Route #2, P.O. Box 172
Nancy, Kentucky 42544

Zachary Taylor National Cemetery
4701 Brownsboro Road
Louisville, Kentucky 40207

LOUISIANA

Alexandria National Cemetery
209 Shamrock Avenue
Pineville, Louisiana 71360

Baton Rouge National Cemetery
220 North 19th Street
Baton Rouge, Louisiana 70806

Port Hudson National Cemetery
Route No. 1, Box 185
Zachary, Louisiana 70791

MAINE

Togus National Cemetery
VA Medical and
Regional Office Center
Togus, Maine 04330

MARYLAND

Annapolis National Cemetery
800 West Street
Annapolis, Maryland 21401

Baltimore National Cemetery
5501 Frederick Avenue
Baltimore, Maryland 21228

Loudon Park National Cemetery
3445 Frederick Avenue
Baltimore, Maryland 21229

MASSACHUSETTS

Massachusetts National Cemetery
P.O. Box 100
Bourne, Massachusetts 02532

MICHIGAN

Fort Custer National Cemetery
15501 Dickman Road
Augusta, Michigan 49012

MINNESOTA

Fort Snelling National Cemetery
7601 34th Avenue, South
Minneapolis, Minnesota 55450

MISSISSIPPI

Biloxi National Cemetery
P.O. Box 4968
Biloxi, Mississippi 39535

Corinth National Cemetery
1551 Horton Street
Corinth, Mississippi 38834

Natchez National Cemetery
61 Cemetery Road
Natchez, Mississippi 39102

MISSOURI

Jefferson Barracks
National Cemetery
101 Memorial Drive
St. Louis, Missouri 63125

Jefferson City National Cemetery
1024 East McCarty Street
Jefferson City, Missouri 65101

Springfield National Cemetery
1702 East Seminole Street
Springfield, Missouri 65804

NEBRASKA

Fort McPherson National Cemetery
HCO 1, Box 67
Maxwell, Nebraska 69151

NEW JERSEY

Beverly National Cemetery
RD #1, Bridge Boro Road
Beverly, New Jersey 08010

Finn's Point National Cemetery
R.F.D. No. 3, Fort Mott Road,
Box 542
Salem, New Jersey 08079

NEW MEXICO

Fort Bayard National Cemetery
P.O. Box 189
Bayard, New Mexico 88036

Santa Fe National Cemetery
P.O. Box 88
Santa Fe, New Mexico 87501

NEW YORK

Bath National Cemetery
VA Medical Center
Bath, New York 14810

Calverton National Cemetery
210 Princeton Boulevard
Calverton, New York 11933

Cypress Hills National Cemetery
625 Jamaica Avenue
Brooklyn, New York 11208

Long Island National Cemetery
P.O. Box 250
Farmingdale, New York 11735

Woodlawn National Cemetery
1825 Davis Street
Elmira, New York 14901

NORTH CAROLINA

New Bern National Cemetery
1711 National Avenue
New Bern, North Carolina 28560

Raleigh National Cemetery
501 Rock Quarry Road
Raleigh, North Carolina 27610

Salisbury National Cemetery
202 Government Road
Salisbury, North Carolina 28144

Wilmington National Cemetery
2011 Market Street
Wilmington, North Carolina 28403

OHIO

Dayton National Cemetery
VA Medical Center
4100 West Third Street
Dayton, Ohio 45428

OKLAHOMA

Fort Gibson National Cemetery
R.R. #2, P.O. Box 47
Fort Gibson, Oklahoma 74434

OREGON

Eagle Point National Cemetery
2763 Riley Road
Eagle Point, Oregon 97524

Roseburg National Cemetery
VA Medical Center
Roseburg, Oregon 97470

Williamette National Cemetery
11800 S.E. Mt. Scott Blvd
Portland, Oregon 97266

PENNSYLVANIA

Indiantown Gap National Cemetery
P.O. Box 187
Annville, Pennsylvania 17003

Philadelphia National Cemetery
Haines Street and Limekiln Pike
Philadelphia, Pennsylvania 19138

PUERTO RICO

Puerto Rico National Cemetery
P.O. Box 1298
Bayamon, Puerto Rico 00621

SOUTH CAROLINA

Beaufort National Cemetery
1601 Boundary Street
Beaufort, South Carolina 29902

Florence National Cemetery
803 East National Cemetery Road
Florence, South Carolina 29501

SOUTH DAKOTA

Black Hills National Cemetery
P.O. Box 640
Sturgis, South Dakota 57785

Fort Meade National Cemetery
VA Medical Center
Fort Meade, South Dakota 57785

Hot Springs National Cemetery
VA Medical Center
Hot Springs, South Dakota 57747

TENNESSEE

Chattanooga National Cemetery
1200 Bailey Avenue
Chattanooga, Tennessee 37404

Knoxville National Cemetery
939 Tyson Street, N.W.
Knoxville, Tennessee 37917

Memphis National Cemetery
3568 Townes Avenue
Memphis, Tennessee 38122

Mountain Home National Cemetery
P.O. Box 8
Mountain Home, Tennessee 37684

Nashville National Cemetery
1420 Gallatin Road, South
Madison, Tennessee 37115

TEXAS

Fort Bliss National Cemetery
P.O. Box 6342
Fort Bliss, Texas 79906

Fort Sam Houston National Cemetery
1520 Harry Wurzbach Road
San Antonio, Texas 78209

Houston National Cemetery
10410 Veterans Memorial Drive
Houston, Texas 77038

Kerrville National Cemetery
VA Medical Center
3600 Memorial Boulevard
Kerrville, Texas 78028

San Antonio National Cemetery
517 Paso Hondo Street
San Antonio, Texas 78202

VIRGINIA

Alexandria National Cemetery
1450 Wilkes Street
Alexandria, Virginia 22314

Balls Bluff National Cemetery
P.O. Box 200
Leesburg, Virginia 22075

City Point National Cemetery
10th Avenue and Davis Street
Hopewell, Virginia 23860

Cold Harbor National Cemetery
Route 156 North
Mechanicsville, Virginia 23111

Culpeper National Cemetery
305 U.S. Avenue
Culpeper, Virginia 22701

Danville National Cemetery
721 Lee Street
Danville, Virginia 24541

Fort Harrison National Cemetery
8620 Varina Road
Richmond, Virginia 23231

Glendale National Cemetery
9301 Willis Church Road
Richmond, Virginia 23231

Hampton National Cemetery
Cemetery Road at Marshall Avenue
Hampton, Virginia 23669

Hampton National Cemetery
VA Medical Center
Hampton, Virginia 23669

Quantico National Cemetery
P.O. Box 10
Triangle, Virginia 22172

Richmond National Cemetery
1701 Williamsburg Road
Richmond, Virginia 23231

Seven Pines National Cemetery
400 East Williamsburg Road
Sandson, Virginia 23150

Staunton National Cemetery
901 Richmond Avenue
Staunton, Virginia 24401

Winchester National Cemetery
401 National Avenue
Winchester, Virginia 22601

WEST VIRGINIA

Grafton National Cemetery
431 Walnut Street
Grafton, West Virginia 26354

West Virginia National Cemetery
Route 2, Box 127
Pruntytown, West Virginia 26354

WISCONSIN

Wood National Cemetery
P.O. Box 500
VA Medical Center
Milwaukee, Wisconsin 53295

Bar Associations

The following list of Bar Associations will be of assistance because you will retrieve records such as divorce, foreclosures, and other legal instruments that have an attorney's name on them. Many of the records will be decades old. You can contact the Bar Association and they will give you the current address and phone number of the attorney. Explain to the attorney what you are doing and who you are seeking. He or she may be able to provide information heretofore unknown to you.

ALABAMA

http://www.alabar.org
Alabama State Bar
P.O. Box 671
Montgomery, Alabama 36101
(205) 269-1515

ALASKA

http://www.alaskabar.org
Alaska Bar Association
P.O. Box 279
Anchorage, Alaska 99510
(907) 272-7496

ARIZONA

http://www.azbar.org
State Bar of Arizona
234 North Central
Phoenix, Arizona 85004
(602) 252-4804

ARKANSAS

http://www.arkbar.com/
Arkansas Bar Association
400 West Markham
Little Rock, Arkansas 72201
(501) 375-4605

CALIFORNIA

http://www.calbar.org
State Bar of California
555 Franklin Street
San Francisco, California 94102
(415) 561-8200

COLORADO

http://www.cobar.org/
Colorado Bar Association
250 West 14th Street
Denver, Colorado 80204
(303) 629-6873

CONNECTICUT

http://www.ctbar.org
Connecticut Bar Association
15 Lewis Street
Hartford, Connecticut 06103
(203) 249-9141

DELAWARE

http://www.dsba.org
Delaware State Bar Association
820 North French Street
Wilmington, Delaware 19801
(302) 658-5278

DISTRICT OF COLUMBIA

http://www.dcbar.org
The District of Columbia Bar
1426 H Street NW
Washington, DC 20005
(202) 638-1500

FLORIDA

http://www.flabar.org/
The Florida Bar Association
650 Apalachee Parkway
Tallahassee, Florida 32301
(904) 561-5600

GEORGIA

http://www.gabar.org/
State Bar of Georgia
84 Peachtree Street
Atlanta, Georgia 30303
(404) 522-6255

HAWAII

http://www.hsba.org/
Hawaii State Bar
820 Mililani
Honolulu, Hawaii 96813
(808) 537-1868

IDAHO

http://www.state.id.us/isb
Idaho State Bar
P.O. Box 895
Boise, Idaho 83701
(208) 342-8958

ILLINOIS

http://www.illinoisbar.org
Illinois Bar Center
424 South 2nd Street
Springfield, Illinois 62701
(217) 525-1760

INDIANA

http://www.ai.org/isba
Indiana State Bar Association
230 Eat Ohio Street
Indianapolis, Indiana 42604
(317) 639-5465

IOWA

http://www.iowabar.org
Iowa State Bar Association
1101 Fleming Building
Des Moines, Iowa 50309
(515) 243-3179

KANSAS

http://www.ksbar.org
Kansas Bar Association
P.O. Box 1037
Topeka, Kansas 66601
(913) 234-5696

KENTUCKY

http://www.kybar.org
Kentucky Bar Association
West Main at Kentucky River
Frankfort, Kentucky 40601
(502) 564-3795

LOUISIANA

http://www.lsba.org
Louisiana State Bar Association
210 O'Keefe Avenue
New Orleans, Louisiana 70112
(504) 566-1600

MAINE

http://www.mainebar.org
Maine State Bar Association
P.O. Box 788
August, Maine 04330
(207) 622-7523

MARYLAND

http://www.msba.org/
Maryland State Bar Association
207 East Redwood Street
Baltimore, Maryland 21202
(301) 685-7878

MASSACHUSETTS

http://www.massbar.org/
Massachusetts Bar Association
One Center Plaza
Boston, Massachusetts 02108
(617) 523-4529

MICHIGAN

http://www.michbar.org/
State Bar of Michigan
306 Townsend Street
Lansing, Michigan 48933
(517) 372-9030

MINNESOTA

http://www.mnbar.org
Minnesota State Bar Association
430 Marquette Avenue
Minneapolis, Minnesota 55402
(612) 335-1183

MISSISSIPPI

http://www.msbar.org/
Mississippi State Bar
P.O. Box 2168
Jackson, Mississippi 39205
(601) 948-4471

MISSOURI

http://www.mobar.org/
The Missouri Bar
P.O. Box 119
Jefferson City, Missouri 65102
(314) 635-4128

MONTANA

http://www.montanabar.org/
State Bar of Montana
P.O. Box 4669
Helena, Montana 59604
(406) 442-7660

NEBRASKA

http://www.nebar.com
Nebraska State Bar Association
206 South 13th Street
Lincoln, Nebraska 65808
(402) 475-7091

NEVADA

http://www.nvbar.org/
State Bar of Nevada
834 Willow Street
Reno, Nevada 89501
(702) 329-4100

NEW HAMPSHIRE

http://www.nhbar.org/
New Hampshire Bar Association
18 Centre Street
Concord, New Hampshire 03301
(603) 224-6942

NEW JERSEY

http://www.cjnj.org/html/the_nj_-
bartender.html
New Jersey State Bar Association
172 West State Street
Trenton, New Jersey 08608
(609) 394-1101

NEW MEXICO

http://www.nmbar.org/
State Bar of New Mexico
P.O. Box 25883
Albuquerque, New Mexico 87125
(505) 842-6132

NEW YORK

http://www.nysba.org
New York State Bar Association
One Elk Street
Albany, New York 12207
(518) 463-3200

NORTH CAROLINA

http://www.barlinc.org
North Carolina State Bar
P.O. Box 25908
Raleigh, North Carolina 27611
(919) 828-4620

NORTH DAKOTA

http://www.sdbar.org/
State Bar Association of North Dakota
P.O. Box 2136
Bismarck, North Dakota 58502
(701) 255-1404

OHIO

http://www.ohiobar.org/
Ohio State Bar Association
33 West 11th Avenue
Columbus, Ohio 42301
(614) 421-2121

OKLAHOMA

http://www.okbar.org/publicinfo/admissions/
Oklahoma Bar Association
P.O. Box 53036
Oklahoma City, Oklahoma 73152
(405) 524-2365

OREGON

http://www.osbar.org/
Oregon State Bar
1776 S.W. Madison
Portland, Oregon 97205
(503) 224-4280

PENNSYLVANIA

http://www.pabar.org/
Pennsylvania Bar Association
P.O. Box 186
Harrisburg, Pennsylvania 17108
(717) 238-6715

PUERTO RICO

http://home.microjuris.com/federalbar/
Bar Association of Puerto Rico
Box 1900
San Juan, Puerto Rico 00903
(809) 721-3358

RHODE ISLAND

http://www.ribar.com/
Rhode Island Bar Association
1804 Industrial Bank Building
Providence, Rhode Island 02903
(401) 421-5740

SOUTH CAROLINA

http://www.scbar.org/
South Carolina Bar Association
P.O. Box 11039
Columbia, South Carolina 29211
(803) 799-6653

SOUTH DAKOTA

http://www.sdbar.org/
State Bar of South Dakota
222 East Capitol
Pierre, South Dakota 57501
(605) 224-7554

TENNESSEE

http://www.tba.org/
Tennessee Bar Association
3622 West End Avenue
Nashville, Tennessee 37205
(615) 383-7421

TEXAS

http://www.texasbar.com/start.htm
State Bar of Texas
P.O. Box 12487
Austin, Texas 78711
(512) 475-4200

UTAH

http://www.utahbar.org/
Utah State Bar
425 East First South
Salt Lake City, Utah 84111
(801) 531-9077

VERMONT

http://www.vtbar.org/
Vermont Bar Association
P.O. Box 100
Montpelier, Vermont 05602
(802) 223-2020

VIRGINIA

http://www.vba.org/
Virginia State Bar
700 East Main Street
Richmond, Virginia 23219
(804) 786-2061

WASHINGTON

http://www.wsba.org/
Washington State Bar Association
505 Madison
Seattle, Washington 98104
(206) 622-6054

WEST VIRGINIA

http://www.wvbar.org/
West Virginia State Bar
2006 Kanawha Boulevard
Charleston, West Virginia 25311
(304) 346-8414

WISCONSIN

http://www.wisbar.org/
State Bar of Wisconsin
P.O. Box 7158
Madison, Wisconsin 53707
(608) 257-3838

WYOMING

http://www.wyomingbar.org/
Wyoming State Bar
P.O. Box 109
Cheyenne, Wyoming 82003
(307) 632-9061

The Internet

In the late 1960s, during the "cold war," nuclear war was foremost in our minds because of the military power of Russia. There was not an open and meaningful dialogue between the two superpowers. I, like many of my readers, remember when we had bomb shelters built in our homes. The threat of nuclear war was very real, even to the point of having "air raid" drills at school where we would go into the halls, put our hands behind our heads, and lean against the wall. China had developed nuclear weapons but at that point did not have the capability to deliver bombs to their designated targets worldwide. The United States was the superpower that decided to seriously explore an alternative method of communication should a nuclear holocaust impair or destroy surface or satellite communication.

An America that suffered the calamity of massive destruction would need a network of communications linked from city to city, county to county, state to state. The solution proposed by many was to make the current system of communication that was being used destruction-proof, by burying cable and lines, by making more use of satellites, and by building smaller phases and parts of the current communication network. The solution was not the preceding, because the destructive capacity of nuclear war makes no system of communication impregnable to the impact of nuclear blast and the subsequent fallout.

Another question that had been asked and could not be answered was that if a network of communication could be created, then who would be in control? From what place would the command operate from? If there were essential parts of the system destroyed, including the demise of the person in command, then how would there be a leader to be custodian of the communication network?

The Department of Defense had an agency called the Defense Advanced Research Projects Agency (DARPA), and the researchers developed many proposals. One idea that kept coming to the surface was a system of communications that would have no central command or authority. The intention was not to usurp the authority of the President of the United States, but rather to ensure continuity.

Another proposal was that no matter what network was to be in place as a "doomsday" backup, it was to be operable in the worst of all possible scenarios—that being total destruction of ground links in communication. An important part of the network would be that all parts of the new communications system would work both independently of each other and dependent with each other—sort of a centralized, yet decentralized, system.

And much to their credit, the founders of this new network thought of an important consideration and sought to resolve it at the outset. If one part of this system was destroyed, the other parts would pick up and deliver the instructions. That is why today when we send e-mail to someone, the message is sent along a different route each time. You can call it the path of least resistance. Whatever avenue is open at the second you send your e-mail is the way it travels. If the system would be able to work independently, then if someone sent a message over this system, it would go to many computers and the message could be retrieved by any computer going to any other computer because the message would be everywhere. If destruction has arrived, then instructions to rebuild would need to be sent over the new network. Instructions for the health and welfare of the public would be delivered by this system. Instructions from the Defense Department would be sent so a military infrastructure could be maintained. Timely news reports could be sent to allow the mass populace to know what was happening. So as you can see, information in the form of instructions was of paramount importance. The vehicle would be messages. You can see now where we are going with this—e-mail.

In 1968, UCLA, at the request and funding of the United States Department of Defense, started a small network of four computers to see if a decentralized, yet connected, communication network could work. Four computers transferred data on dedicated high-speed transmission lines. In 1971, UCLA and its sister institutions of higher learning expanded the network to eight computers, and the next year the system was expanded even more, to 37 computers online.

The mid 1970s saw a continued rapid expansion of the communication network that was started by UCLA. A decentralized system where anyone could go online, yet be connected to other computers in the network, offered possibilities heretofore not thought of by anyone.

In 1983, the Defense Department took away its funding from UCLA. The military made its own network, for security reasons, and named it MIL-NET, which of course, stands for *military network*. The same year, the Department of Defense invited the National Science Foundation to assist in the administration and coordination of the many computers that were coming online.

The many computers that were coming online daily created a need for further identification of the computers. Six basic categories were created, and they were: gov, mil, edu, com, org, and net. The network that UCLA started became known as the Internet.

I will explain the basics of the Internet because it is important that we are reminded of how incredible this recent communications tool is. What is more amazing is that there is not one central owner or controlling authority of the Internet! It is a coalition of millions of computers that speak the same computer language with the common goal of exchanging information and commerce.

The Internet is a computer network that has one master terminal that acts, sort of, like a Grand Central Station. Messages from all computers asking to be routed to a specific location come into it, and then the messages are dispatched to their proper location.

When you send a request to go to a site from your computer, you usually see a name, such as IBM.COM. (This is explained more, later in this chapter.) That address is really a string of numbers underneath. Those numbers are then sent to the master computer, the numbers are read, and it then gets funneled to IBM.COM.

This is accomplished because the Internet has its own language called Hypertext Transfer Protocol, or HTTP. The Web uses hypertext as its way of exchanging information. Hypertext is a string of words and numbers that links computers and documents to each other—hence, the name links that you are so familiar with.

Hypertext is created by making a language that is called Hypertext Markup Language, or HTML. Within the lines of information of HTML, tags or small lines of data are placed. These little bits of additional information are actually the instructions to the computer to produce on your monitor features such as font size, graphics, colors, sounds, and other multimedia effects. A single hypertext string sometimes has many, many links to other information and documents.

We even have different names for some types of hypertext. Java is a popular type of tag used extensively. When you go to a Website and you see a banner with a moving or jumping image, or you see a banner scrolling information, then that is Java. Java got its name because a group of young, industrious people got together to try to make a fancier hypertext. They wanted a hypertext that was not just text or still pictures. It was an arduous task, but they were successful and created a very different type of hypertext. They did not know what to call their creation, and all around their work area they saw strewn about paper cups that had contained coffee. They though that Java would be an appropriate and different name. Remember, odd names are more the norm instead of the exception on the Internet. All one has to do is look to Amazon or Yahoo to see creative and odd names.

FTP, which is the abbreviation for File Transfer Protocol, is the actual method by which files are transferred between computers. FTP allows the smooth and uninterrupted transference of text, books, articles, software, games, graphics, images, sounds, multimedia, video images, still photographs, spreadsheets, and much more.

Electronic mail, or e-mail, is the means by which computer users contact each other in an instant—worldwide and free of charge. E-mail brings forth what the Internet does best, which is allowing people to communicate. That was the basis of the Web. Do not ever put anything in e-mail communication that you do not want a third party to see. E-mail does not afford you the confidence, security, and sanctity that using a credit card on a secure server gives you. Your Internet Service Provider (ISP) has access to all your e-mail. That is just one example of who can see your e-mail. Sending attachments on e-mail allows you to send pictures, even in color, to your designated recipient. The process of sending accompaniments in e-mail is referred to as sending MIME attachments. MIME stands for Multimedia Internet Mail Extension.

Groups and forums are, basically, a worldwide electronic bulletin board where millions of computer users exchange information on every possible subject. One of the joys of the Internet and e-mail is the ability of everyone to participate in forums and groups that are of interest to them. Whether it is a favorite hobby, sport, educational interest, or something personal, there are people who want to communicate with you. There are no locks on the doors, and chat groups are open 24 hours a day.

The major difference between groups and forums and e-mail is the fact that group and forum messages are stored on central computers and are not a one-on-one e-mail communication. It is a group e- mail endeavor. You can even use a search engine using keywords, phrases, or someone's name to see if it has been mentioned in a group or forum session, because search engines sweep and catalog the contents of groups and forums. A great feature of groups and forums is that you can reply to one person, or you can reply to all members, by just a keystroke.

Still another fine feature in groups and forums is instant messaging. That means participants around the world can "talk" to each other by typing in real time and having their thoughts and ideas visible to many other people immediately. This allows for the exchanging of ideas from people worldwide instantly, which was heretofore not available in any medium.

The Internet, or Web, is made of files most commonly called pages, or home pages. Home pages can be visited by typing in the URL. URL stands for Uniform Resource Locator. The URL is the specific Internet address of the home page that is stored on an Internet Service Provider's computer that is connected to the Internet. Every file on the Internet has a unique URL. URLs are translated into numeric addresses using the Internet Domain Name System (DNS). Since numeric strings are difficult to remember, alphanumeric addresses are used.

For example, this is a URL for my home page:

http://www.josephculligan.com

Here is what the Uniform Resource Locator consists of:

The Protocol is: **http**
Host computer name: **www**
Domain name: **josephculligan**
Top level domain: **com**

The top-level domains (TLDs) that are common:

com	commercial enterprise
edu	educational institution
gov	U.S. government
mil	U.S. military
net	network access provider
org	nonprofit organizations

You need a software program called a Web browser to access the Internet Web. There are two types of browsers. The first is graphical: Sound, text, images, graphics, audio, and video are received through a graphical software program such as Netscape Navigator and Internet Explorer. Navigation is done by pointing and clicking a mouse on highlighted words and graphics. The second web browser is text: Lynx is a browser that allows you to visit the Internet in text form only. Navigating is done by highlighting emphasized words on the monitor with the arrow up-and-down keys. Then you key the forward arrow (or Enter) key to follow the link.

Web browsers come with several plug-ins that will allow you to use multimedia functions. There are many multimedia programs and real-time communication programs available today. You can even listen to radio stations anywhere in the world. I have provided links to thousands of radio stations on my Website.

You can even watch video with the sound that is not staccato and jumpy as it was a few short years ago. The video and sound is just about as smooth as you will see on your television at home. You can access sites of the news networks and watch the same video that was shown on the nightly television news. One advantage of watching the video on your monitor is that your computer can download the video. You do not need a video tape, and if the story is of sufficient interest, you can send the video via the Internet to your friends or business associates. The biggest obstacle until recently has been the slow download times when trying to save videos. Technology has now expanded multimedia capability by creating streaming data. Streaming data allows audio or video files to be played as they are downloading into your computer. You may also download or just watch real-time events such as press conferences, speeches, news events, concerts, and much more.

As readers of my books know, I have always provided sources that were current, reliable, and accessible. With the creation of a CD-Rom, I am now creating a source that will continue in the tradition of my books. It is important that when conducting an investigation, you go to sources that will provide you with a road map that will lead you to other sources. Below is a list of more than 100 categories on the aforementioned CD-Rom. These categories have more than 85,000 links contained within them:

Accessories and Equipment

Action Groups—International

Adoption-Related

Alliances—International

Archives by State

Arts and Show Business, The

Auctions—Federal Government

Automobiles

Banks—International

Bar Associations

Biotechnology—International

Books and Book Information

Business, Finance, and Stocks

Canadian Government

Canadian Parks and Others

Cemeteries

Census and Statistics—
   International

China Information

Cities on the Web

Colleges, Schools, and
Universities

Commerce—International

Communications—International

Congress—House Committees

Congress—House and Senate
   Members

Congress—Senate Committees

Conservation and Wildlife

Conservation Groups—
   International

Courts—State

Crime Statistics

Education—International

Embassies—Worldwide

Employment

Environmental Protection Agency

Executive Branch

Family Assistance—International

Federal Agencies and Departments

Federal Courts

Federal Law Enforcement
Agencies

Foreign Governments

Forensic Law and Science

Freedom—International

Genealogy

Geology—International

Heads of State—International

Health

Health Care—International

Health Departments—by State

Hospitals—America

Hospitals—Worldwide

Industry—International

International Business and Social

International Development

International Laws

International Organizations—
   Rights

Japan Information

Languages—International

Languages—Translations

Law

Law Enforcement

Law Firms on the Net

Law Schools

Library of Congress Gateways

Libraries of Law Schools

Look-ups and Directories

Magazines

Maps

Missing and the Wanted

Missing Persons

National Parks

National Science Foundation

Newspapers of Africa, Asia, North America, and Worldwide

Online Dictionaries

People—International

Private Detective Websites of Interest

Radio Stations

Regional Resources

Resources You Need

Resources—International

Scholarships

Science Groups–International

Search Engines and Portals

Secretaries of State

Sex Offenders

Sports

State Libraries

State Parks

State Websites

Unclaimed Property

United States Bankruptcy Courts

Various Government Related Information

Vital Records and Information

Water—International Resources

Weather

Weather by Countries

Weather by Forecast Centers

Weather by University

The following is a description of each of the foregoing sites. In these 85,000 links, you will be able to have every link needed to conduct your search and more. I have included links that I use on major investigations.

Accessories and Equipment: This will lead you to many vendors that sell equipment you may need if you go into the investigative business.

Action Groups—International: I use these links to find people world-wide who have gotten lost in church groups, missions, fringe groups, and organizations throughout the world where a person can become anonymous.

Adoption-Related: This is a comprehensive list of links involving adoptions that cover everything from bulletin boards, adoption registries, newspapers on microfilm, and much more that will give you ideas and leads that you may never have known existed.

Alliances—International: This category provides organizations and alliances that will give you much-needed assistance in difficult-to-locate cases. International Brotherhood of Electrical Workers, International Brotherhood of Magicians, International Brotherhood of Teamsters, and many other worldwide alliances are excellent sources you will now have access to.

Archives by State: Remember, more and more states will be going online with their archives division, and I will have new links added as they come online. Archives are an excellent avenue to find a subject that has been missing for a long period of time. Check with archives when you want to find out about a relative of a subject so you can contact some other relatives that will lead you to your quarry.

Arts and Show Business: I have these online links in this category so that I may do research on some subjects that are in show business. Many of my subjects have relocated to California or New York. They are not actors, but are involved in the business, such as grips, best boys, electricians, set designers, and other behind-the-scenes personnel.

Auctions—Federal Government: I sometimes have to search for subjects who buy at auctions. At this site, I can find out dates, times, and locations of auctions so that I may have a surveillance done when the event occurs.

Automobiles: I need links to major automobile companies so that I may ask about trade-in policies regarding leased vehicles. Many subjects lease vehicles because they hide under the automobile company's name when a license tag check is done by a private investigator. I need to know when a lease may expire so I can be alerted as to when to commence a surveillance.

Banks—International: I sometimes need the locations of banks in foreign countries because I need to do a surveillance of my subject. What I do is make a matrix of the bank locations in the foreign city and then see where they are in relation to the work site or residence of my subject.

Bar Associations: In this book, I have a chapter on Bar Associations. This site enhances that chapter by giving you the address on the Internet of all Bar Associations. Of course, this category is constantly being updated.

Biotechnology—International: Subjects sometimes get lost as workers in zoos or the conservation and forest industry worldwide. These links are a great help in searching.

Books and Book Information: It is important that you be able to locate any book on any subject without delay when you are in the middle of a search. The reasons you may need a particular book are varied, but you may need to become familiar with certain professions or hobbies of subjects so that you know what your subjects are thinking.

Business, Finance, and Stocks: So many subjects that are missing may have invested in stocks or may have had some association with brokers. This category gives many sources so that you may pursue this avenue of investigation.

Canadian Government: Many subjects go to Canada, and this category will give you many links to various government departments in the Canadian Government.

Canadian Parks and Others: Links to many of the parks and forests throughout Canada where your subject may be hiding.

Cemeteries: In this book, I discuss the value of cemeteries in assisting in the search for a subject. The foreign cemeteries are adding sites increasingly.

Census and Statistics—International: You can use the census in many countries to do background research on the family of your subject, which may lead you to the present whereabouts of the individual.

China Information: The links in this category are of great help if your subject is Chinese. The China Cities links is particularly useful because it goes into detail about everything in each major city—including telephone numbers.

Cities on the Web: This category provides links to cities that include the many varied departments of each municipality. Some sites have the all-important voter's registration department, which you know is a valuable resource. Cities are being added constantly.

Colleges, Schools, and Universities: In this book, I discuss how alumni information may be of use. Now, in this category, there are over 3,000 institutions of higher learning online.

Commerce—International: Worldwide stamp collectors, insurance company personnel, freighter employees, and hundreds of other occupations are in this category. Look at this section even if you do not need it now. It will show you just how many organizations, alliances, associations, and other entities are available to explore so that you may find your subject.

Communications—International: You will need to contact an international communications entity on occasion if your subject is involved in the field of radio, newspaper, magazine, television, or any other facet of communications.

Congress—House Committees: You can contact various committees in the House of Representatives to get more information about something that you are trying to become an expert in so you can figure out what your subject is thinking.

Congress—House and Senate Members: If you are being blocked by a department in the federal government for a public record you need, then contact your representative online immediately.

Congress—Senate Committees: There are many committees that may assist you, including the committee on Indian Affairs, if you think your subject is hiding on Native American property.

Conservation and Wildlife: Subjects interested in birds, wildlife, and the environment may belong to organizations. This site lists many sources and more are being added on a regular basis.

Conservation Groups—International: Your subject may be anywhere in the world engaging in some form of environmental conservation, and you now have access to research this avenue online.

Courts—State: This category is expanding on an accelerated basis. You will be able to check many civil indexes online, or, if they do not provide this service, you can ask online what the current fees are to order records by hard copy.

Crime Statistics: If your subject has a proclivity toward a certain type of crime, then you may want to check certain locales to see if they are aggressive in stopping that particular crime, or if they let it proliferate.

Education—International: Whether your subject is a student or is employed in any way with education, then this category gives many links that may assist you.

Embassies—U.S. and Worldwide: You may need assistance from a U.S. Embassy. The countries listed in the category that have U.S. Embassies will cover any country your subject may be in.

Employment: This is a site you may want to use yourself to obtain employment in any field, including government. It is also an excellent source to use as a starting point to find out where your subject is working.

Environmental Protection Agency (EPA): Your subject may have had some dealings with the EPA. Also, there are a surprising number of businesses that fall under the jurisdiction of the EPA, and if your subject was ever cited or fined, then there will be much information on record for you to review. One link that I use routinely is the Contract and Grants link.

Executive Branch: The Railroad Retirement Board, the Pension Benefit Guaranty Corporation, Department of Veterans Affairs, and many other links will assist you in finding your subject. You can get information online with the National Cemetery System, which, as you know from the cemetery system chapter of this book, is an excellent source.

Family Assistance—International: If your subject left and went abroad with the children, this is an excellent site to use. The many links will bring you many family and children assistance organizations in every country of the world. In parental kidnapping, your subject may have needed to check the children into clinics or had gotten them some programs involving home tutoring and education, since registering children is extremely difficult in foreign countries.

Federal Agencies and Departments: You will need to find specific agencies and departments of the federal government where your subject may have done business. Remember, all contracts and business dealings with the federal government is public information. There is much information in the section on Contracts and Applications—your subject will have left a wealth of information for you, such as home address, Social Security Number, banking information, and more.

Federal Courts: If your subject has had an appeal in federal court, or a bankruptcy, then this site will help you. More and more links are being created by the federal courts system every day. This book has shown you the value of bankruptcy records, and this site will assist you greatly in your research.

Federal Law Enforcement Agencies: Among the Law Enforcement links on this site, you will find the Office of Child Support Enforcement. I explain the details of how you can use this department in Chapter 11 of this book.

Foreign Governments: The convenience of having the following countries online is of great importance in searching for a subject in a foreign land. These sites will give you everything you need regarding local public records, policies, contact people in government that may assist you in your search, and much more. More countries are coming online constantly:

Albania, Algeria, Andorra, Angola, Antigua, Argentina, Armenia, Aruba, Australia, Austria, Azerbaijan, Bahamas, Bahrain, Bangladesh, Barbados, Barbuda, Belarus, Belgium, Belize, Benin, Bermuda, Bolivia, Bosnia, Botswana, Brazil, Brunei, Bulgaria, Burkina, Cambodia, Cameroon, Canada, Chechnya, Chili, China, Colombia, Costa Rica, Croatia, Cuba, Czech Republic, Denmark, Djibouti, Dominican Republic, Ecuador, Egypt, El Salvador, Eritrea, Estonia, Ethiopia, Fiji, Finland,

16-14   YOU CAN FIND ANYBODY!

France, Gabon, Gambia, Georgia, Germany, Ghana, Greece,
Greenland, Guatemala, Guyana, Haiti, Honduras, Hong Kong,
Hungary, Iceland, India, Indonesia, Iran, Iraq, Ireland, Israel,
Italy, Jamaica, Japan, Jordan, Kazakhstan, Kenya, Kuwait,
Kyrgyzstan, Latvia, Lebanon, Lesotho, Liberia, Libya,
Liechtenstein, Lithuania, Luxembourg, Macau, Macedonia,
Madagascar, Malaysia, Maldives, Mali, Malta, Marshall Islands,
Mauritania, Mauritius, Mexico, Micronesia, Moldova, Monaco,
Mongolia, Morocco, Mozambique, Myanmar, Nambia, Nepal,
Netherlands, New Zealand, Niue, Norway, Oman, Pakistan,
Palestine, Panama, Paraguay, Peru, Philippines, Poland, Portugal,
Romania, Russia, Rwanda, St. Kitts, San Marino, Saudi Arabia,
Senegal, Sierra Leone, Singapore, Slovakia, Slovenia, Solomon
Islands, South Africa, South Korea, Spain, Sri Lanka, Sudan,
Swaziland, Sweden, Switzerland, Syria, Taiwan, Tanzania,
Thailand, Togo, Tonga, Trinidad, Turkey, Turkmenistan, Uganda,
Ukraine, United Arab Emirates, United Kingdom, Uruguay,
Uzbekistan, Vatican, Venezuela, Vietnam, Western Samoa,
Yemen, Yugoslavia, Zambia, Zimbabwe.

Forensic Law and Science: This site is comprehensive and will give you so many tools to find people that range from profiling to Forensic Psychology.

Genealogy: This site has many links that will give you background on your subject. There is much useful information if you are trying to research an adoption case.

Geology—International: If your subject has ever been the type of person to be involved in Greenpeace and other related organizations, then this site offers many links to assist you.

Heads of States of the World: This site provides links to a great number of Heads of State worldwide that can be used as a conduit to other departments in government. If you are having trouble getting records you need from a foreign government, then e-mail a Head of State. Of course, the leader will not see your e-mail, but the staff of Heads of State are always more than happy to resolve routine problems so that their government looks responsive.

Health: You may want to use the wide assortment of links on this site to contact various foreign health practitioners regarding what quarantines are in place or have expired. If you are aware of what country your subject may be in, then you will want to know if any ailment that your subject has or had, affected his or her mobility in leaving the country.

Healthcare—International: The many societies and health organizations listed on this site will give you a complete list to work from if you need to find a physician that your subject may have visited in a foreign country. Your subject may have asthma or a colostomy or some type of rare disease. In fact, there are groups such as the Cocaine Anonymous World Service Office where people meet and talk about their problems. Remember, your subject may need a support group for a particular problem, and this site has a complete list that will help you in your search.

Health Departments—by State: These departments are another great way, besides the state bureau of archives in each state, to find birth certificates. More state health departments are going online regularly.

Hospitals—America: Your subject may be hospitalized, and this link will give you the e-mail address of many hospitals so you may inquire online as to whether your subject is a patient.

Hospital—Worldwide: This site will save you time and expense because you will be able to contact hospitals worldwide to see if your subject is hospitalized.

Industry—International: If your subject is in any number of different businesses such as the footwear industry, civil engineering, vinyl manufacturing, or many other different and unusual occupations in Europe, then this site may yield information for you.

International Development: This site covers many worldwide organizations to help you find your subject. These organizations, such as timber, oil, construction, etc., assist in the development of countries. Remember, if your subject has gone abroad and did not take sufficient cash or other negotiable instruments—he or she would need to find work or would be engaged in running a business.

International Laws: This site is very important because you will be able to research what the extradition policies are of each country so you will know if your subject can be extradited. If a country does not have an extradition treaty, then your subject may have gotten lazy and will be easy to find.

International Organizations—Rights: Sites like the International Bar Association (I explain in Chapter 16 of this book how valuable the Bar Association can be), the International Red Cross, the Peace Corps, and others will assist you in finding your subject. Remember, many of these sites have hundreds of links in them.

Japan Information: Since Japan mirrors the lifestyle of the United States, many subjects flee to this country. The links on this site cover every facet of Japanese living.

Languages—International: Much of the research you will do may involve a foreign language. The links on this page will assist you in finding entities that will help you with the language barrier.

Languages—Translations: There will be many occasions when you will need something translated quickly. The many links on this site offer translation of every language.

Law: This site has links that include sentencing and parole laws so you will know when a subject you are waiting to have released will, in fact, be released. Links to business, finance, economic, and consumer protection laws are included so you can see what laws were violated by your subject.

Law Enforcement: You can check many various law enforcement agencies to see if your subject has an arrest record. Of course, that is important because your subject may still be on probation and needs to report to a parole officer. That will give you a location to find your missing subject once a week or a month.

Law Firms on the Net: This site has extensive links to law firms online. You may need to retain a law firm to serve a subpoena on your subject once you find them if the subject owes you money.

Law Schools: Law schools are listed because you want to check the Alumni Association of a law school to find your subject even if they did not graduate. Also, you may use the Alumni Association to find an old girlfriend of the subject.

Library of Congress Gateways: Libraries keep telephone books going back many years. Having many libraries on the Internet will allow you to query a library as to what old telephone books they keep in storage. You are well aware what value old telephone books are in searching for people. Always look for relatives of your subject, too.

Libraries of Law Schools: These many libraries are open to the public. You may want to look up certain public record laws before ordering a record on your subject.

Lookups and Directories: You will need to use online telephone directories in your searches. Also, reverse directories are available where you key in the address and get back the telephone number. There is a wide selection of sites that offer telephone directories online.

Magazines: You may want to read some of your subject's favorite magazines online so that you may be aware of special events and conventions where your subject may attend.

Maps: Once you find your subject, you may want to go online and have a map printed for you by many of the links contained in this site. You can key in your address and the newly discovered address of the subject and print it out.

Missing and the Wanted: This site will bring you to many links that will assist you if you are looking for persons who owe child support, are wanted for serious assaults, are wanted for financial and other crimes. Please revisit this site every few weeks, because if your subject had been posted on one of these sites and now he is not, that would mean he is incarcerated somewhere. Find out what jurisdiction had put out the wanted alert on him, and contact them, because they will know where he is jailed.

Missing Persons: This site has many different telephone sources where you can check for a telephone anyplace in the world. The reverse telephone directory is also of much value, because you can key in an address, and the name of the subscriber will be returned.

National Parks: You may find that your subject just cannot be located at a permanent address. Fugitives and other skips will take up residence at national parks, living in recreation vehicles or tents. These online links will let you see what accommodations each national park offers.

National Science Foundation: If your subject has anything to do with computers or technology, then you will want to visit the links on this site. From associations to schools to societies, this site may help you find out what your subject is involved with at the present.

Newspapers of Africa, Asia, North America, and Worldwide: If you know that a subject is on a particular continent, then I use the online newspaper of that locale. Reading the paper that your subject reads may give you leads that you may not have ever thought of. Maybe there are conventions posted or some news-related item that will require participation by your subject.

Online Dictionaries: This site is very useful when you read the newspapers of a locale or need to translate words in a public record from a foreign land. Every language that you will need assistance with is listed here.

People—International: Your subject may be found by reviewing the many varied organizations such as World Association of Community Radio Broadcasters, Girl Guides and Girl Scouts, Women Entrepreneurs, International Society of Women Airline Pilots.

Private Detective Websites of Interest: You will find many links that may help you in your search, including sources private investigators use, lists of companies that sell information to assist in finding people, inmate locator online sites where you can see if someone has been or is incarcerated, and much more.

Regional Resources: This site has many sources such as online links to search for marriages, property ownership, corporations, professional licenses, court cases, civil indexes, business filings, statewide tax rolls, UCC searches, incarcerations, official county records, campaign finance records, and many other type of records.

Resources You Need: This site has many links to private investigators, search engines, the census, and much more.

Resources—International: Associations that may assist you in finding your subject include organizations for musicians, librarians, teachers, television personnel, law enforcement, journalists, and hundreds of other fields that your subject may be employed in.

Search Engines and Portals: This site offers a wide selection of search engines. Try several search engines when doing a search so that you can be assured that you have every possibility for your search returned.

Secretaries of State: You will be able to go online with the Secretaries of State in the United States to get up-to-the-minute information as to whether your subject has incorporated a business or taken a loan out and created a Uniform Commercial Code (UCC) loan.

Sex Offenders: You want to check to see if your subject has any arrest for sex offenses. Many sites even include a picture of the offender.

Sports: Your subject may be a member of sports clubs, or you may want to check the schedules of your subject's favorite sport to see if they show up at a game. There are many interesting links on this site.

State Libraries: The state libraries are a great source to find old telephone books statewide. This method of search has yielded excellent results over the years.

State Parks: The reasons for using the online sites to the state parks is the same as I gave for the national parks previously. Remember, your subject may be on the run, and there is no more economical way to live than in the state or national parks of the United States.

State Websites: It is important to be able to access all departments of state government when searching for people. State government sites contain information on corporations, property appraisals, government officials, and more. Professional licenses such as real estate, doctors, nurses, pest exterminators, attorneys, and more than 90 other occupations will give you much assistance in finding your subject.

Unclaimed Property: I discussed the value of using abandoned property when searching for someone previously in this book. Some other online links are Housing and Urban Development Refunds for mortgage insurance obtained by a government loan, Pension Guarantee Benefit Fund Refunds on retirement accounts, Swiss Bank Accounts Site created for holocaust victims, Canadian Unclaimed Property, and the National Credit Union Administration System.

United States Bankruptcy Courts: In the bankruptcy chapter of this book, you will find the explanation of why bankruptcy courts are of value when you are trying to find someone. Remember, these records are public information, and you can visit any bankruptcy court and they will assist you in reviewing a file.

Various Government Related Information: Many varied government links are contained on this page, including the Railroad Retirement Board, the Federal Information Center, American Law Sources Online (which gives online access to all courts in the United States), and more.

Internet Glossary

ACL. ACL is an acronym for *Access Control List.* Not all users of the Internet are permitted to go on every site. There are many reasons this is so, including the need of government sites to keep information restricted, business sites that provide internal support for projects for their employees only, sites that have a fee attached, etc. Some sites allow visitors to go on to certain pages but restrict other pages. In Internet nomenclature, you will hear someone say that a site is ACL.

Address Resolution. Address resolution is what happens when you type a domain name into your computer to visit a site. The Internet does not recognize names, only numbers. So when your name is accepted by the computer, all the letters of the domain name are converted into numbers.

Anonymous FTP. Anonymous FTP is the method on the Internet where you can get documents, files, text, and other information from another Website without having to get a user ID and password. The word *anonymous* may sound a bit strong, but it only refers to your request not being read for any preconditions. All publically accessible sites have the anonymous FTP program incorporated into their site.

Applet. A Java program that is made part of a HTML page. Applets are different from whole Java applications in that they do not permit access to certain resources on the local computer that includes files and serial devices (modems and printers). Applets are not allowed to communicate with other computers. Applets can only make an Internet connection with the Internet-connected computers from which the applet was sent.

Archie. This is one of the original software programs that is used to find files stored on anonymous FTP sites. With the Archie program, it is necessary to have the specific name or string of the FTP sites. The name *Archie* is derived from the word *archive.*

ARPANET. ARPANET is an acronym for *Advanced Research Projects Agency Network.* This is the original Internet that was invented in 1968 by the United States Department of Defense. The idea behind this project was to see if an international computer network would be able to survive a nuclear war or some act-of-God calamity.

ASCII. ASCII is an acronym for American Standard Code for Information Interchange. ASCII is the name given to the standardized code numbers used by computers to represent all the upper- and lower-case Latin letters, punctuation, and numbers. At the present time there are 128 standard ASCII codes, each of which can be represented by a seven-digit binary number: 0000000 through 1111111.

Asynchronous Connection. This is the connection that a modem makes over a telephone line.

Backbone. The common name given to the high-speed series of connections that is the basis for the major pathway within any network but particularly the Internet. This term is a carryover from the early days of the Internet when the developers at the United States Department of Defense were required to invent words and names because this technology had never existed before.

Bandwidth. The volume that is measured in the telephone lines that carry Internet connections is shown in bits-per-second. Two pages of text would be approximately 31,000 bits. A 56K modem, with a good solid connection without interference, can allow about 15,000 bits in one second to pass through a telephone line.

Baud. Baud is simply the name given to how many bits can travel through a line. It is commonly called the *baud rate*. Baud rate is really one quarter of the number it indicates. For example, a 28,800 bit-per-second modem actually runs at 7,200 baud, but it moves 4 bits per baud (4 x 7,200 = 28,800 bits per second). Baud is so named because of its inventor, J.M. Baudot.

BBS. BBS stands for *Bulletin Board System*. The BBS is just one of the best things the Internet has provided the mass populace—namely, communication. A BBS is a computerized group and forum meeting place that permits users to interact by having discussions, conversations, and to make announcements without being connected to the computer at the same time. A BBS can be as small as a home computer with one telephone line or as vast as BBS systems supported by nationwide Internet service providers.

Binhex. Binhex, a combination of the words, *BINary and HEXadecimalA*. It is the way the Internet converts non-text files (non-ASCII) into ASCII. The Internet cannot support non-ACSII files, especially when using e-mail.

Bit. Bit is a combination of the words, *Binary and digIT*. A bit is a single-digit number in base-2, or in other words, either a 1 or a zero. This is the smallest unit of data used in Internet communications.

Bitnet. Bitnet is a combination of the words, *Because It's Time NETwork*. Users of the Internet can send e-mail to users of Bitnet, but the two systems are distinctly separate entities. This is another example of newly created words because the Internet was uncharted territory.

BPS. Bps is a combination of the words, *Bits Per Second*. It is the speed data is measured on the Internet. Like a speedometer, a 28.8 modem can move at 28,800 bits per second.

Broadband. The transmission method that supports many kind of frequencies. It carries the many different signals by dividing the total capacity into multiple, independent bandwidth channels where each channel operates on a certain range of frequencies. The invention of broadband was necessary since without it there would be hundreds of lines going into your home to make your computer workable.

Browser. Software that is used to look at various kinds of Internet resources. Many companies now sell browsers, but, in most instances, your Internet Service Provider (ISP) will provide you with a browser that will be compatible with the Internet and will be free of charge.

BTW. BTW is an acronym for *By The Way*. It has been acceptable in common language usage in Internet communication, particularly in e-mails and discussion groups where time is of value.

BYTE. Byte is a set of bits that are considered a single character. Bytes consist of 8 bits. In certain advanced systems, a byte may be made of more than 8 bits, but never more than 16 bits.

CD-ROM. Compact Disk-Read Only Memory. It is an optical disk that can be read but does not have the capabilities for recording or being written.

CD-R or Compact Disk-Recordable. This is the name for computer peripheral disk drives that permit its user to record onto a blank compact disk.

CGI. CGI is an acronym for *Common Gateway Interface.* It is rules that show how a Web server communicates with a different piece of software on the same machine.

Client. This is the most commonly used name to describe the program used to communicate to, and obtain data from, server software programs on another computer. The Client Program was created to interact with one or more kinds of Server Programs. In other words, the Server is the big computer you are connected to, and the Client is your computer.

Configuration. This is the term that refers to the way your computer is set up. Your computer may have many different hardware parts that interact with the software side of the computer, and the total package is called the configuration. In other words, it's how your computer is set up.

Cookie. This unique term is the Internet's way of leaving a footprint. It means a piece of data sent by a Web Server to a Web Browser that the Browser software saves. It then returns to the Server any future requests for a site that the browser had visited previously. Cookies retain information that includes login and registration data, user preferences, passwords, and other information that usually stays the same over a period of time. Cookies are a great time.

Cyberspace. *Cyberspace* has become the most commonly used word to describe the presence of the Internet. Cyberspace has spawned the use of words such as *cyberjunk, cybermail, cyberpunk, cyberpet,* and just about anything else that requires a preface to describe Internet use.

Dial-Up Connection. This term describes the connection you most likely have at your home, connecting your computer to the host computer of your Internet Service provider. Many businesses now have a dedicated line that is a telephone line always connected to the Internet so that they have instant access.

Digerati. Digerati is used to describe any place, person, or thing that is considered to be in the loop or inside on the Internet. It is being used more and more because of the proliferation of articles and pieces on Internet people and what they know.

DNS. DNS is an acronym for *Domain Name Server.* DNS is the database of Internet names and addresses that translates the names to an address the computers can read, which is number-based.

Document. In the world of the Internet, the word *document* means any file of text or group of hyperlinks that are transferred from a host computer to a person's computer.

Download. This is the term that means to ask another computer for information and have it go to your computer to have it either print out on your printer or be added to your hard drive.

DSL. DSL is an acronym for *Digital Subscriber Line,* and describes the way data is transmitted over telephone lines. A regular DSL circuit has more speed than a regular telephone connection. DSL is being utilized more as communities provide the service, and it is becoming less costly than standard lines.

Domain Names. Domain names are becoming the identity of people and companies on the Internet. As mentioned before in this chapter, the domain name is the easy way for all of us to remember an Internet address, but it actually is converted into numbers sent out over the Internet. Of course, a domain name can only be assigned to one entity, so to make more combinations, endings for Domain names were created—such as *com, net, org, mil, edu,* and more than 250 others.

EDI. EDI is a combination of the words, *Electronic Data Interchange.* EDI systems permit linked computers to communicate with each other to conduct business, such as billing and ordering.

E-mail. E-mail is a combination of the words, *Electronic Mail.* Messages that can include attachments such as sound, pictures, and video are sent to individuals or forum and groups. E-mail's popularity continues to soar because it is instant communication, it is free of charge, and there is proof that it was sent.

Encryption. This is the term that means the method that is used to keep communication secure so only the recipient gets the data. Encryption is used when you use your credit card on the Internet. The signal is scrambled from your computer to the merchant's computer so no other person in between transmission and reception of the information can look at it.

FDDI. FDDI is an acronym for *Fiber Distributed Data Interface.* It represents the speed for transmitting information on optical fiber cables. The rate, which is approximately 100,000,000 bits-per-second, is exclusively for use on fiber optic.

Fire wall. The *fire wall* term has come to represent a security feature on sites. It attempts to make a site impregnable to attack by using both hardware and software to separate the site into two or more distinct entities. Fire walls were first designed to keep financial and banking sites safe from purloining.

FTP. FTP is an acronym for *File Transfer Protocol.* It is the standard by which files move between Internet sites. FTP is the method used to login to another Internet site so files can be retrieved or sent.

GIF. GIF is an acronym for *Graphic Interchange Format.* This is the term used to describe the formatting of image files, including those that are for images containing large areas of the same density of color. GIF are popular because the files are smaller than if they were stored in JPEG format. The limitation of GIF files is that they do not store photographic images as well as JPEG.

Gigabyte. Gigabyte simply means 1,000 megabytes. For technical purposes, the exact number of bits in a megabyte is 1,024.

Gopher. Gopher was the most widely used process for people to access files over the Internet until hypertext proved to be superior insofar as speed and accuracy is concerned. Gopher requires both the receiver of a file and the sender to have the same Gopher program. Gopher programs are still used in older systems but are not being replaced.

Header. This is the part of an e-mail that contains source and destination addresses, date, time, and the title of the message. It is always at the top of an e-mail message, and in some communications, it is in the body of the text.

Hierarchical Routing. The large networks that are on the Internet could not move information as quickly if they had to do it from one central location. That is why networks are broken down into, in most instances, three levels that are responsible for routing information on their own. The Internet's three levels are backbone, mid-level, and stub networks. The backbones rout information between mid-level sites. The mid-level sites rout information to the stub networks. Stub networks are the very basis of all networks—they rout information internally. Or in reverse, when you send information from your computer, it first appears on the stub network. The information is processed so it gets an identifier to know what address on the Internet it needs to go to. Then, the stub network sends the data to the mid-level network. At the mid-level network, the data is looked at again to verify information. Then, it gets routed to the backbone network, where the information goes to its final destination.

Hit. The term *hit* is used by many people to describe the amount of visitors a site receives. A hit means that a visitor could have had one short visit. However, the number of hits is suspect because a Web page that contains three graphics would generate four hits (one for the page itself, and one for each of the graphics). As you can see, figures for Websites become inflated, especially for sites that have many graphics on each page.

Home Page. The home page is the base or master page where a domain name or URL is located. From this home page, other pages can branch off without getting a new domain name. Extensions are put at the end of the URL, which then direct the home page to go to another internal page. Many Internet Service Providers that you may use to access the Internet will allow you to set up a free Web page.

HTML. HTML is a combination of the words, *Hypertext Markup Language.* It is the code that makes the language used to create hypertext documents. Groups of special codes within the HTML, called *tags*, are the vehicles that create multimedia effects, such as colors, sounds, video, etc.

HTTP. HTTP is a combination of the words, *Hypertext Transfer Protocol.* It is the way hypertext files move across the Internet. This is a server/client structure where the system requires a HTTP client program on one end, and a HTTP server program on the other end. HTTP is the most widely used program for transference of files because it is the simplest to construct.

Hypertext. Hypertext is text that has codes or tags that make links to other documents. Words, phrases, and numbers in a document can be chosen by a requester, which causes another document to be retrieved and displayed.

Internet. The Internet is the largest of all connected computer systems in the world. It consists of three hierarchy or tiered levels. Each level supports the other, and they are interconnected for the seamless flow of information. The largest of the three networks is the backbone, then the mid-level, and finally the stub network, which is where your request for information from the Internet is first entered.

Intranet. The internal system or network within a company or group of computers that exchange information with each other but do not connect to the Internet. The software in the computers is basically the same software as used to connect to the Internet.

ISP. ISP is an acronym for *Internet Service Provider*. This is the entity that will be your gateway to the World Wide Web. Your ISP also provides you with many useful extras, such as chat rooms, weather, news, entertainment, information, and much more.

Java. Java is programming language that is specifically designed for writing programs that can be downloaded to your computer through the Internet. Java programs or scripts are safe insofar as viruses being attached to them.

JPEG. JPEG is an acronym for *Joint Photographic Experts Group.* JPEG is the most commonly used image file, especially for photographic images, because the JPEG internal system allows for clear pictures.

Kilobyte. For general purposes, a kilobyte is 1,000 bytes. But for technical and commercial purposes, a kilobyte is exactly 1,024 bytes.

LAN. LAN is an acronym for *Local Area Network.* A local computer network is limited to the immediate area, such as in an office or building. It is an Intranet system and does not have access to the Internet.

Login. Login (as a verb) is when you *log in* to a system. Login (as a noun) is when you refer to your password or user ID as your login. The word *login*, as you can readily see, is the two words, *log* and *in*. With many Internet words that you are seeing, perhaps for the first time, the Internet has its own language.

Mail List. A system that allows people to send e-mail to one address where their message is reproduced and sent to many other subscribers of the mail list. This is the method where many, many people can join a discussion forum or group at one time.

Megabyte. The word *megabyte,* in everyday Internet usage, means 1,000 kilobytes, which is 100 bits. But for the technical definition, a megabyte is 1,024 kilobytes.

MIME. MIME is an acronym for *Multipurpose Internet Mail Extension.* This is the way of attaching non-text files to standard Internet mail messages. Non-text files include graphics, spreadsheets, formatted word-processor documents, sound files, and other multimedia functions brought to you by MIME.

Mirror. This simply is a description of Internet sites that mirror Websites, or FTP sites. These mirror sites maintain exact copies of material originated at another location, so as to provide more widespread access to the resource.

Modem. Modem is a combination of the words, MOdular and DEModulator. It is a device that you attached to your computer and to your telephone line. It permits your computer to talk to other computers through the telephone wires.

Mosaic. Mosaic was the first Internet browser that was available for the Macintosh and Windows. Even though there are many systems that surpass Mosaic insofar as reliability, speed, and clarity, there are many people who still use it to travel the Internet.

Netiquette. Netiquette is simply etiquette on the Internet. Netiquette is evolving. In time, people learn the kind of conduct that is expected of them.

Netizen. Netizen comes from the word *citizen,* and refers to a user as a member or citizen of the Internet. Netizen is the Internet's way of reinforcing the idea that there are responsibilities when traveling and using the Internet.

Octet. An octet consists of eight bits. In some large commercial systems, this term is used rather than the traditional word *byte*, because some bytes are not exactly eight bits. Commercial systems need to have exactly consistent numbers, so *octet* is their guarantee that something is eight bits, which is true for an octet.

Portal. A portal is an avenue or way that people can get to other places on the Internet. So when you see a site that advertises itself as a portal, then what they are telling you is that they will funnel you into many other links, which will then bring even further links.

Server. This term refers to software or a network that will bring you onto the Internet. Your Internet Service Provider (ISP) is an example of a server. When you go online, your ISP uses its computer to get you online, it gets you your e-mail, or sends e-mail you wish to have go to someone.

Spam. Spam is the inappropriate and unauthorized attempt to send the same message to a large number of people who didn't ask for it. The major Internet Service Providers now contact senders of spam and inform them that if they continue to send unwanted advertisements and messages, then their access to the Internet will be stopped.

T-1. T-1 is a line connection that can carry data at 1,544,000 bits-per-second. At its maximum capacity, a T-1 line can send a megabyte in less than 10 seconds. Even though that is fast, it still is not fast enough for full-screen, full-motion video in which at least 10,000,000 bits-per-second is required. T-1 is the fastest speed used so that networks are able to connect to the Internet.

T-3. T-3 is a line connection that can move data at 44,736,000 bits-per-second. This amount of transmission is sufficient for most multimedia uses on the Internet.

TCP/IP. TCP/IP is a combination of the words *Transmission Control Protocol/Internet Protocol.* This is the protocol that shapes what you see on the Internet. This type of language is now considered the universal language of access to any kind of network including the Internet.

URL. URL is an acronym for *Uniform Resource Locator.* This is the standard way to give any address on the Internet. *Domain Names* is a term that is also used. **http://www.josephculligan.com** is a URL, and is also a Domain Name.

Accessing Government Forms

I have mentioned for years how important it is to check applications of a subject so you can find information that is not available elsewhere. Let us take a look at what an application for a firearm permit filed through the Department of Alcohol, Tobacco, and Firearms (ATF) will yield. The applicant must give their full name, former and current addresses for ten years, former and current employment, Social Security Number, date of birth, the names of three references, name of next of kin, home and business telephone numbers (whether they are unlisted or not), and much more. I have included the following links so that you can go online and see what different applications are out there.

If your subject had been employed in the radio or television business, then you may want to pull up a blank form to see what information the subject was required to give. If you find a need for the data, then you can order a copy of the application that they submitted when they were a disk jockey or radio announcer. There are literally thousands of jobs that require applications that are subject to public inspections. In my chapter on state records, you will recall the many occupations I listed that require licensing, and all the applications for those jobs are open for review by the public.

The importance of applications and forms that people fill out is underestimated. In the aforementioned description of what is on the ATF application for a firearm permit, you can see that the information forms the basis of a background check. So, if you ever need to do a very complete background on a prospective mate, or possible business associates, or even someone you are going to lend money to, then it is worth the time and effort to figure out what type of licenses they have and ask the government for copies of the applications. Of course, forms and applications are excellent sources of information for finding someone because even though they may have filled out an application years ago, you can get information such as the names of relatives, the Social Security Number, the date of birth, and much more.

I am including many government Websites in the following pages, but also some for your personal use that will provide you with legal forms and applications at no charge. If you own land, rent out an apartment, or have filed a lawsuit against someone, the following sites will provide you with the proper paperwork, and much of it will be free of charge.

Government Applications, Documents, and Legal Forms—Online

All About Forms
http://www.allaboutforms.com

I am glad that this site is listed first because they give so much. Here is a quote from their Website. It says it all: *Free Legal Forms! Why pay for generic legal forms when you can get them for free? At All About Forms, we want to help you with your legal needs. We offer this service for free for thanking you for making our site successful.*

Bureau of Alcohol, Tobacco, and Firearms Forms
http://www.atf.treas.gov/

Your subject may have had to apply for a certain type of firearm permit through this agency. If so, then the application is public record. This application yields much information and is an excellent source for getting background information on someone, such as schooling, previous addresses, relatives, employment, and criminal record—no matter how minor and much more. If you are doing a background check on someone, then see if they have an application on file with the ATF.

Copyright Forms
http://www.loc.gov/copyright

If your subject had ever received a copyright, then the application is on file and is public information. But what most people do not realize is that if your subject had applied for a copyright and did not receive it, then the information is still on file and subject to public scrutiny. The copyright applications ask many questions that your subject may never let anyone else know. You can be also assured that the address the subject gave on the various forms and applications to the copyright office are correct and true. There isn't anyone who risks losing a copyright by giving incorrect information.

Corporate and Securities Forms
http://www.jefren.com/DOWNLOAD.HTML

Documents include Employees Stock Deferral Plan and Directors Stock Deferral Plan, Equity Based Long Term Incentive Plan, Indemnification Agreement, Liquidating Trust Agreement, Non-Employee Directors Deferred Compensation Plan, Restricted Stock Award Plan, Stock Appreciation Rights Plan, Standby Equity Agreement, Stock Option Plan, Stock Option

Plan for Non-Employee Directors, Subordinated Debenture, Voting Trust Agreement and Voting Trust, and Warrant documents.

Federal Communications Commission Forms
http://www.fcc.gov/forms/

If your subject was ever a radio disc jockey or a broadcaster of any type, then their application and subsequent renewal are public record and available from the FCC. This site will give you the latest address to write to for information.

FEMA Forms
http://www.fema.gov/library/lib04.htm

Flood hazard, hurricane, and many other natural disasters are what FEMA responds to. Your subject may have filled out an application for aid from this government entity. There are many parts of the country that consistently have weather-related problems, so if your subject is in one of those areas, then see if they applied for assistance in the form of a loan or grant. This is an excellent way to find people who lived an anonymous life in a trailer, but then were caught up in a weather-related storm.

General Business Forms
http://www.lectlaw.com/formb.htm

Applications and forms include bulk sale, stock purchase, contracts, corporate, joint venture, partnership, employment, consulting, indemnity, promissory notes, and other paperwork business uses.

General Forms and Model Documents
http://www.courttv.com/legalhelp/business/forms/

Documents include arbitration, copyright, distributorships, e-mail policy, employee handbook, sexual harassment policies, corporate minutes, software development, and confidentiality agreements.

General Legal Documents
http://www.tiac.net/users/nmayhews/legal.htm

Documents and forms include promissory notes, notice of default, demand for payment, notice of delinquent account, installment agreement, credit application, security agreement, subordination agreements, leases, termination of tenancy, assignments, bills of sale, contracts, bulk sale, employment, corporate minutes, and other business documents.

Immigration and Naturalization Forms
http://www.ins.usdoj.gov/graphics/

Some of the applications and forms that people fill out are restricted. The status of availability, as with all public records, changes constantly. As you see elsewhere in the section, I list many different applications and forms. This is to give you some idea of what type of form your subject may have filled out if they would have had an occasion to do so. You can view the complete form online. Some applications and forms may be of more interest to you than others because of the situation that your subject may have been in when they had filled out the particular form giving information. In general, the following includes immigration, naturalization, employment, and asylum forms:

G-28	Notice of Entry of Appearance as Attorney or Representative
G-639	Freedom of Information/Privacy Act Request
G-731	Inquiry about Status of 1-551 Alien Registration Card
G-942	Application Survey (for INS Employment)
I-9	Employment Eligibility Verification
I-90	Application to Replace Permanent Resident Card $110
I-129F	Petition for Alien Fiancé(e)
I-129S	Nonimmigrant Petition Based on Blanket L Petition
I-129W	Petition for Non-immigrant Worker Filing Fee Exemption
I-130	Petition for Alien Relative
I-131	Application for Travel Document
I-193	Application for Waiver of Passport

Health and Human Services Forms
http://directory.psc.gov/

If your subject has ever done business with the Department of Health and Human Services, then there will be much information for you. The department conducts other business with 32 other federal agencies, independent establishments, and government corporations.

Law Practice Forms
http://www.lectlaw.com/forma.htm

Documents include checklists, demand letters, fee agreements, litigation practice forms, affidavit, declarations, applications, answers, complaints, and many more litigation-type documents.

Legaldocs
http://www.legaldocs.com/~usalaw/misc-s.htm

Applications, documents, and forms, including last will and testament, living wills, durable powers of attorney, promissory note, request for credit report, request to correct credit report, child-care authorization, automobile insurance claim, homeowner's insurance claim, and hunting lease.

Office of Personnel Management
Federal Employees Retirement Program
http://www.opm.gov/retire/

This is such an important site because if your subject ever worked for the federal government (as 11,400,000 living people have done, as over 27 million deceased people have done, and as 5,300,000 current employees are doing), then they would be listed in one of the links on the OPM site. There are so many applications your subject may have filled out or programs that your subject may have used and that, of course, creates a paper trail. This site is also excellent for personal reasons also because if you or any of your family members have worked for the federal government or are now employed, then you will want to take a look at the links I have included below for your review. You will be convinced that you should also visit their Website.

Access America for Seniors
Accessibility of Documents on OPM Website
Addressing and Resolving Poor Performance
Addressing Sexual Orientation Discrimination
Addressing Mental Health
Administrative Law Judges
Adobe Acrobat PDF Files, Reading
Adoption Benefits Guide for Federal Employees
Advanced Learning Technology
Adverse Actions
Advocacy for Families

Agency Benefits Officers
Aggregate Limitation on Pay
Alternative Dispute Resolution
Alternative Instructional Methods
Alternative Work Schedules
Appeals, Position Classification, and Job Grading
Application Forms for Federal Employment
Appointed Positions
Appointments
Authorities for Career and Career-Conditional Appointments
Automation
Awards
Base Pay
Benefits
Benefits Administration Letters
Benefits Center Demo
Boards of Contract Appeals, Member Pay
Bone Marrow or Organ Donor Leave
Buyouts
Career and Career-Conditional Appointing Authorities
Career Transition
Career Transition Regulations
Census 2000 Jobs Center for Executive Leadership
Center for Partnership and Labor Management Relations
Central Personnel Data File
Charitable Contributions
Children
Child/Elder Care Fair
Child Care Guide
Child Care Resources Handbook
Citizenship, Requirements for Employment
Civil Service Retirement System
CSRS and FERS Handbook for Personnel and Payroll Offices
Claims for Compensation and Leave, Decisions on
Classification Appeals
Classifiers Handbook
Code of Federal Regulations
Comparison of Flexible and Compressed Work Schedules
Compensation

Compensation Administration
Compensation and Leave, Decisions on Claims for
Compensation Policy Memoranda
Compressed Work Schedules
Computing Retirement Benefits (CSRS)
Confidential Positions in the Federal Government
Cost of Living Allowances (COLA)
Death, Reporting Federal Employee
Delegated Examining Units Handbook
Delegation of Authority
Demonstration Projects
Dealing with Workplace Violence
Development of Training
Directory of E-mail Addresses
Discrimination, Addressing Sexual Orientation
Document Accessibility
Downsizing
Downsizing Statistics
Early Retirement Programs
Eastern Management Development Center
Electronic Forms
Electronic Reading Room
Emergency Guidance Memos
Employee Assistance Programs
Employee Health Services
Employee Relations
Employment and Trends
Employment Information
Employment in More Than One Federal Job
Employment of Military Retirees
Employment of Non-Citizens
Employment Service Center Network
Excepted Appointments in the Federal Government
Excepted Service
Executive Schedule Positions in the Federal Government
Executive Schedule Salary Tables
Executive Seminars
Executive Training F
Fact Book, Federal Civilian Workforce Statistics

Fair Labor Standards Act and Federal Employees
Family and Medical Leave
Family-Friendly Workplace Advocacy Office
Family Leave Policies
Federal Activities Report Act (FAIR)
Federal Classification Systems
Federal Appointments
Federal Benefits
Federal Civilian Employment Reporting Instructions, SF 113–A
Federal Employee's Group Life Insurance Program (FEGLI)
FEGLI Home Page
Federal Employee's Group Life Insurance Program: A Handbook for
    Employees, Annuitants, Compensationers, and Employing Offices
Federal Employees Health Benefits
Federal Employees Retirement System
FEHB, Federal Employees Health Benefits, 2000
Federal Executive Associations
Federal Executive Boards
Federal Employees Group Life Insurance
Federal Employees Health Benefits
Federal Holidays
Federal Human Resources Forum
Federal HRM for the 21st Century, Strategic Plan
Federal Labor Relations Authority Negotiability Determinations
Federal Medical Evidence of Record Program
Federal Positions Outside the Competitive Service
Federal Register Documents
Federal Salary Tables
Federal Wage System Job Grading
Fee For Service Health Plans
Financial Management Letters
Flexible Work Schedules
Flexifinder
Flexibilities, Personnel
FLSA and Federal Employees
Freedom of Information Act (FOIA)
Freedom of Information Act Index
Frequently Asked Questions
Furlough

Garnishment
General Schedule Leader Grade Evaluation Guide
General Schedule Pay Tables
General Schedule Supervisory Guide
Glossary of Federal Sector Labor-Management Relations Terms
Government Information Locator Service Records
Government Performance and Results Act
GPRA Resources for Federal Agencies
Guidelines for Settlement of Federal Personnel Actions
Guide to Adoption Benefits for Federal Employees
Guide to Personnel Data Standards
Guide to Personnel Recordkeeping
Guide to Processing Personnel Actions
Handbook of Occupational Groups and Families
Handbook on Alternative Work Schedules (AWS)
Hatch Act
Hazardous Duty Pay
Health Insurance
High Impact Performance Goals
Hiring Federal Retirees
Hispanic Employment Initiative
Holidays, Federal Gov
Human Resource Development Services
Human Resource Flexibilities in the Federal Government
Human Resource Management Accountability
    System Development Guide
Human Resource Forum
Human Resource Solutions on a Reimbursable Basis
Human Resource Technology Council
Hours of Work for Travel
Incentives
Information Technology Professionals, Recruiting and Retaining
Inspector General
Interagency Advisory Group
Interagency Agreements for Training Services
Intergovernmental Personnel Act Mobility Program
International Organizations, Details, and Transfers To
Information for Veterans
Insurance

Job Classification
Job Evaluation
Job Grading Appeals
Job Grading Standards
Job Related Injury or Illness, Restoration After
Labor Management Relations Advisories
Lawyers, Employment of
Law Enforcement Officers Pay Tables
Leader Grade Evaluation Guide
Leave
Leave Bank
Leave Transfer
Leave Without Pay
Life Insurance
Life Insurance Program (FEGLI)
Locality Pay Tables
Lump Sum Payments for Annual Leave
Managed Care Health Plans
Management Development
Management Development Centers
Management Intern Program
Medicare and FEHB
Merit System
Merged Records Personnel Folder
Merit Systems Oversight and Effectiveness
Military Leave
National Partnership for Reinventing Government
Nature of Action Codes
New Developments in Employee and Labor Relations
Non-appropriated Fund Retirement Program
Non-career Positions in the Federal Government
Non-career Senior Executive Service positions
Non-Citizens, Employment of
Non-foreign Area Cost-of-Living Allowances
Notices of Staffing Variations
Occupational Standards
Occupations of Federal White-Collar and Blue-Collar Workers
Official Duty Station Determinations for Pay Purposes
Office of Personnel Management Strategic Plan

Office of the Special Counsel
Official Personnel Folders
Open Season for Health Insurance
Operating Manual, The Guide to Processing Personnel Actions
Operating Manual, SF-113 Summary Data Reporting System
Organizational Assessment Survey
Outstanding Scholar Program
Pay
Pay Structure of the Federal Civil Service
Personnel Flexibilities
People with Disabilities
People with Disabilities in the Federal Government:
    An Employment Guide
Physical Fitness Programs
Policy Positions in the Federal Government
Political Appointments
Poor Performance
Poor Performance Study
Position Classification Appeals
Position Classification Standards
Positions in the Federal Government
Premium Pay Limitation
Presidential Appointments
President's Quality Award Program
Press Releases
Privacy Act Information
Processing Personnel Actions
Procurement (OPM)
Prohibited Personnel Practices
Recruiting and Retaining Information Technology Professionals
Recruiting and Retaining Women in the Federal Government
Retirement and Insurance
Qualification Requirements for Employment
Qualification Standards
Operating Manual: Qualification Standards for General
    Schedule Positions
Quality Award Program
Quality Management
Reading Room, Electronic

Reasonable Accommodation
Recordkeeping
Recruitment
Recruitment Bonuses
Recruitment Incentives
Reduction in Force
Re-employment After Uniformed Service
References for HR Specialists
Reimbursable Services
Reinstatement Eligibility
Reinvention Initiatives
Religious Observances, Work Schedules
Relocation Bonuses
Relocation Incentives
Reporting Instructions, Standard Forms 113–A and 113–G
Restoration of Annual Leave
Restoration Rights After Job Related Injury or Illness
Retention
Retention Allowances
Retention Incentives
Retirement S
Salaries and Wages
Senior Level and Scientific Positions, Pay
Senior Foreign Service positions in the Federal Government
Service Credit; Credit for Military Service
Services Online
Settlement of Federal Personnel Actions, Guidelines for
Sexual Orientation Discrimination, Addressing
Shepherdstown Management Development Center
Sick Leave
Significant Cases in Federal Employee and Labor Relations Newsletter
Size of the Federal Workforce
Smoking Cessation
Smoking Cessation Model Program
Social Security
Special Counsel, Office of the
Standards, Classification
Strategic Human Resources Management
Statistical Information on the Federal Workforce

Students
Student Educational Employment Program
Supervisory Guide, General Schedule
Summer Employment
Survivor Annuitants
Teachers, Overseas Employment of
Team Leader Grade Evaluation Guide, General Schedule
Technology Council, Human Resources
Telecommuting
Testimony and Speeches by OPM Officials
Thrift Savings Plan
Time Schedule for Reporting Data on SF 113–A and SF 113–G
Title–5 Exempt Agencies, Special Study of
Training
Training and Management Assistance
Training Policy Handbook
Transfer Between Federal Agencies
Traumatic Incidents
Travel and Hours of Work
Turnover, Employment, and Trends
Unscheduled Leave Policy
US Code Links
USACareers
USAJobs
Veterans
Veterans Employment Opportunities Act of 1998
Veteran's Preference
VetGuide
VetsInfo Guide
Voluntary Separation Incentives
Voluntary Separation Incentives Guide
Voluntary Early Retirement
Volunteer Activities
Volunteer Activities, Report to the President
Wage Schedules
Welfare-to-Work Hiring Statistics
Welfare-to-Work Plan for OPM
Western Management Development Center, Denver, Colorado
White Collar Position Classification Standards

Women in the Federal Government:
    A Guide to Recruiting and Retaining
Work and Family
Workers Compensation, Special Study of
Workforce Information
Workforce Statistics, Employment, and Trends
Work Leader Grade Evaluation Guide, General Schedule
Work Schedules
Work Schedules, Religious Observances
Worker Trainee Program
Workforce Development
Workforce Statistics
Work-Year Civilian Employment Reporting Instructions
Work Years and Personnel Costs

Passport Application Forms
http://travel.state.gov/get_forms.html

In the previous chapter on federal records, I go into detail on the use of passport records, which you may want to review. The United States Department of State has created a comprehensive site that will facilitate any research you may need to do.

Patent Forms
http://www.uspto.gov/web/forms/#patent

Forms include Declaration for Utility or Design Patent Application, Information Disclosure Statement by Applicant, Assignment of Application, Petition for Extension of Time, Re-issue Application Declarations, Petition for Revival of an Application for Patent Abandoned Unintentionally, Request for Access of Abandoned Application, and many more from the US Patent and Trademark Office (PTO).

Savings Bond Forms
http://www.publicdebt.treas.gov/sav/savforms.htm

This site will give you everything online that took months to get in the mail years ago. There are links to Market Regulation and forms for loss, reissuance, and redemption of bonds and other financial instruments from the United States Department of the Treasury.

Small Business Administration (SBA) Forms
http://www.sba.gov/library/pubsroom.html

This site has all the legal forms regarding the SBA, a current listing of all the changes in any regulations, and many forms that you may download or print as is. If your subject has ever had a loan with the Small Business Administration, then you will be able to retrieve an incredible amount of financial data, both business and personal:

Application for Business Loan
Schedule of Collateral
Lender's Application for Guaranty or Participation
SBA Application for Business Loan—Up to $150,000
Application for Small Business Loan (Short Form—
    $50,000 and Under)
Participating Security Opinion of Counsel
Debenture Opinion of Counsel
Application for Export Working Capital Guarantee
Overview of 1998 Changes to SBA
Transaction Report on Loan Serviced by Lender
Application For Small Business Size Determination
Statement of Personal History and Qualification of Management
Amendments to License Application
Listing Collateral Documents
Assurance of Compliance for Nondiscrimination
Statement of Policy of Equal Employment Opportunity
Personal Eligibility Statement
Program Application—Sole Proprietorship
Business Plan SBA Statement on Representatives and Fees
Small Business Development Center Counseling Record
Secondary Participation Guaranty Agreement
Lender's Transcript of Account
U.S. Small Business Administration's Applicant Survey
Financing Eligibility Statement
FOIA—Freedom of Information Requests Online Submission

Securities Act of 1933 Forms
http://www.law.uc.edu/CCL/33forms/

So many cases I have investigated (when searching for someone or doing background checks on a person or persons or tracing money) brought me to the area where a financial instrument of securities was involved. You can now retrieve so much online. I am including some of what is on the site because you will need to become familiar with what is asked and by whom and for what reason and at what time and at what place if you are to do a complete and comprehensive investigation. Forms include those prescribed for use under the Securities Act of 1933, including general forms and forms for registration statements.

Forms for Registration Statements

Form SB–1: Optional Form for the Registration of Securities to Be Sold to the Public by Certain Small Business Issuers

Form SB–2: Optional Form for the Registration of Securities to Be Sold to the Public by Small Business Issuers

Form S–1: Registration Statement Under the Securities Act of 1933

Form S–2: For Registration Under the Securities Act of 1933 of Securities of Certain Issuers

Form S–3: For Registration Under the Securities Act of 1933 of Securities of Certain Issuers Offered Pursuant to Certain Types of Transactions

Form S–4: For the Registration of Securities Issued in Business Combination Transactions

Form S–6: For Unit Investment Trusts Registered on Form N-8B-2

Form S–8: For Registration Under the Securities Act of 1933 of Securities to Be Offered to Employees Pursuant to Employee Benefit Plans

Form S–11: For Registration Under the Securities Act of 1933 of Securities of Certain Real Estate Companies

Form S–20: For Standardized Options

Pay particular attention to the following registrations involving foreign issuers, because in many cases the foreign issuer is your subject, or a representative of your subject.

Forms for the Use of Foreign Issuers:

Form F–1:   Registration Statement Under the Securities Act of 1933 for Securities of Certain Foreign Private Issuers

Form F–2:   For Registration Under the Securities Act of 1933 for Securities of Certain Foreign Private Issuers

Form F–3:   For Registration Under the Securities Act of 1933 of Securities of Certain Foreign Private Issuers Pursuant to Certain Types of Transactions

Form F–4:   For Registration of Securities of Foreign Private Issuers Issued in Certain Business Combination Transactions

Form F–6:   For Registration Under the Securities Act of 1933 of Depository Shares Evidenced by American Depository Receipts

Form F–7:   For Registration Under the Securities Act of 1933 of Securities of Certain Canadian Issuers Offered for Cash Upon the Exercise of Rights Granted to Existing Security Holders

Form F–8:   For Registration Under the Securities Act of 1933 of Securities of Certain Canadian Issuers to Be Issued in Exchange Offers or a Business Combination

Form F–9:   For Registration Under the Securities Act of 1933 of Certain Investment Grade Debt or Investment Grade Preferred Securities of Certain Canadian Issuers

Form F–10:   For Registration Under the Securities Act of 1933 of Securities of Certain Canadian Issuers

Form F–80:   For Registration Under the Securities Act of 1933 of Securities of Certain Canadian Issuers to Be Issued in Exchange Offers or a Business Combination

Make sure that when reading the following, you keep in mind that the investment companies could be a shell corporation your subject is using to hide assets.

Forms for the Use of Investment Companies:

Form N–1:   For Open-End Management Investment Companies Registered on Form N–8A

Form N–1A: Registration Statement of Open-End Management Investment Companies

Form N–2:   For Closed-End Management Investment Companies Registered on Form N–8A

Form N–3:   Registration Statement for Separate Accounts Organized as Management Investment Companies

Form N–4:   Registration Statement for Separate Accounts Organized as Unit Investment Trusts

Form N–5:   Form for Registration of Small Business Investment Company Under the Securities Act of 1933 and the Investment Company Act of 1940

Form N–14:   For the Registration of Securities Issued in Business Combination Transactions by Investment Companies and Business Development Companies

Form ET: Transmittal Form for Electronic Format Documents on Magnetic Tape or Diskette to Be Filed on the EDGAR System

Form ID: Uniform Application for Access Codes to File on EDGAR

Form SE: Form for Submission of Paper Format Exhibits by Electronic Filers

Form TH: Notification of Reliance on Temporary Hardship Exemption

Forms Pertaining to Exemptions:

Form 1–A: Offering Statement Under Regulation A

Form 2–A: Report Pursuant to Rule 257 of Regulation A

Form 144:   For Notice of Proposed Sale of Securities Pursuant to Rule 144

Form 1–E: Notification Under Regulation E

Form 2–E: Report of Sales Pursuant to Rule 609 of Regulation E

Form 1–F: Notification Under Regulation F

Form D: Notice of Sales of Securities Under Regulation D and Section 4 (6) of the Securities Act of 1933

Forms for Tender Offer Statements

Form C–B: Form for Tender Offer Statements for private Foreign Issuers

The following may apply to your subject because they could have formed a small business to have money change hands.

Form SB–1:   Optional form for the Registration of Securities to Be Sold to the Public by Certain Small Business Issuers

This is what the form looks like that your subject may use to conceal monies:

US Securities and Exchange Commission
Washington, DC 20549

Form SB-1
Registration statement under the
Securities Act of 1933
(Amendment No. . . . . .)

. . . .
(Name of small business issuer in its charter)

. . . .
(Address and telephone number of principal executive offices)

. . . .
(Address and principal place of business or
intended principal place of business)

. . . .
(Complete name, Social Security Number, and date of birth of all
principals, including residence addresses and telephone numbers)

. . . .
(Name, address, and telephone number of agent for service)

As you can see from the above application, there is much information that the executives and principals will have to supply. This information is an excellent source to find people who were involved with your subject, in business, or personally.

Read the following definition of a "small business" person. You will see that small, as you know the definition, is different when you are dealing in securities.

(a) A "small business issuer," defined in Rule 405 of the Securities Act of 1933 (the "Securities Act") may use this form to register up to $10,000,000 of securities to be sold for cash, if they have not registered more than $10,000,000 in securities offerings in any continuous 12-month period, including the transaction being registered. In calculating the $10,000,000 ceiling, issuers should include all offerings that were registered under the Securities Act, other than any amounts registered on Form S–8.

(b) A small business issuer may use this form until it:
(1) registers more than $10 million under the Securities Act in any continuous 12-month period (other than securities registered on Form S–8),
(2) elects to file on a non-transitional disclosure document (other than the proxy statement disclosure in Schedule 14A), or
(3) no longer meets the definition of small business issuer.

Non-transitional disclosure documents include:
(1) Securities Act registration statement forms other than Forms SB–1, S–3 (if the issuer incorporates by reference transitional Exchange Act reports), S–8 and S–4 (if the issuer relies upon the transitional disclosure format in that form);
(2) Exchange Act periodic reporting Forms 10–K and 10–Q;
(3) Exchange Act registration statement Form 10; and
(4) reports or registration statements on Forms 10-KSB, 10-QSB or 10-SB which do not use the transitional disclosure document format. A reporting company may not return to the transitional disclosure forms.

If the small business issuer is not a reporting company, it should file the registration statement in the regional office responsible for the region or district that is closest to its principal place of business, or the Washington, DC office. However, no filings may be made in the Southeast Regional Office; issuers with principal places of business in the region or district subject to its jurisdiction may file in the Atlanta District Office. While every effort is made to process filings where initially made, the Commission may reassign a filing to a different office for processing.

Read the following pertaining to Canada. Many subjects go to Canada, so do not assume that your subject is doing something exotic, such as going to the Cayman Islands or to Switzerland.

G. Canadian Issuer—Consent of Service

Canadian issuers eligible to use this form should file as an exhibit to this registration statement a written irrevocable consent and power of attorney on Form F-X.

Part I. Narrative Information Required in Prospectus
Alternative 1
Corporate issuers may elect to furnish the information required by Model A of Form 1-A, as well as the following information.

Item 1. Inside Front and Outside Back Cover Pages of Prospectus. Furnish the information required by Item 502 of Regulation S-B.

As you can see from item 2 and listed in number 1–13, there is much information that is required to be supplied by applicants

Item 2. Significant Parties
List the full names and business and residential addresses, as applicable, for the following persons:

(1) the issuer's directors
(2) the issuer's officers
(3) the issuer's general partners
(4) record owners of 5 percent or more of any class of the issuer's equity securities
(5) beneficial owners of 5 percent or more of any class of the issuer's equity securities
(6) promoters of the issuer
(7) affiliates of the issuer
(8) counsel to the issuer with respect to the proposed offering
(9) each underwriter with respect to the proposed offering
(10) the underwriter's directors
(11) the underwriter's officers
(12) the underwriter's general partners; and
(13) counsel to the underwriter

Item 3. Relationship with Issuer of Experts Named in Registration Statement. Furnish the information required by Item 509 of Regulation S-B, if applicable.

See if your subject's signature matches up with one of the principals.

Instructions for signatures:

(1) Who must sign: the small business issuer, its principal executive officer or officers, its principal financial officer, its controller or principal accounting officer, and at least the majority of the board of directors or persons performing similar functions. If the issuer is a limited partnership, then the general partner and a majority of its board of directors, if a corporation.

(2) Beneath each signature, type or print the name of each signatory. Any person who occupies more than one of the specified positions shall indicate each capacity in which he or she signs the registration statement. See Rule 402 of Regulation C concerning manual signatures, and Item 601 of Regulation S-B concerning signatures by powers of attorney.

Social Security Forms
http://www.ssa.gov/on-line/forms.html

Forms include:

— Application for Employer Identification Number (SS-4)
— Application for Social Security card
— Claimant's statement and Request for earnings and benefit estimate
— IRS Form W-4V (Voluntary Withholding Request)
— Form 6559
— A Continuation Sheet for Form 6559
— Transmitter Report and Summary of Magnetic Media
— Application for a Social Security card
— Foreign Service (ss-5fs)
— Authorizations for a Source to Release Information to SSA (SSA-827)
— Application for Special Benefits for World War II Veterans (SSA-2000)
— Appointment of Representative (SSA-1696)
— Claimant's Medications (HA-4632)

— Claimant's Recent Medical Treatment (HA-4631)
— Claimant's Statement when Requesting a Hearing (HA-4486)

There is also information available on this site to compute your own benefits, how to apply for Social Security Retirement benefits, a searchable database for the most frequently asked questions, and even a study of the most popular given names from 1880 to 1999 from the Office of the Chief Actuary.

Tax Forms and Publications (Federal)
http://www.irs.ustreas.gov/plain/forms_pubs/

This site, hosted by the Internal Revenue Service, supplies you with the following:

— Forms
— Instructions
— Publications
— Notices
— Prior year forms from 1992 to the present
— Tips on how to file an extension
— An area where there are answers to frequently asked questions
— A comment line
— Tax statistics
— Tax information for your business
— A list of all electronic services provided by the Internal Revenue Service
— IRS Newsstand (recent articles)
— A form to contact the IRS directly and even the Commissioner of the IRS
— Information on the modernization of the IRS
— An explanation on the Electronic Freedom of Information ACT (E-FOIA) Reading Room, which is something you should get familiar with if you are doing investigations
— A Special Taxpayer Alerts Program where they will tell you of any new changes in tax forms and law
— The budget of the Internal Revenue Service so you can see how money is spent in the collection effort of tax administration, and much more.

The Tax Calendar for small businesses contains helpful hints, general tax information, a listing of the most common tax filing dates, and more— all in one comprehensive publication. You can download the calendar in black and white. For a copy in color, call: (800) 829-3676, and ask for Publication 1518, catalog number 12350Z.

Tax Forms (State)
http://www.taxweb.com/forms/state_intforms.html

This site has links to the tax departments of all 50 states. In addition, there are links to many other tax-related sites, including tax code, tax regulations, tax manuals, and more.

Trademark Forms
http://www.uspto.gov/web/forms/#TM

The following forms are included:
— Trademark/Servicemark Applications
— Collective Membership Mark Application
— Certification Mark Application
— Application for Renewal of Registration of a Mark
— Declaration of Incontestability of a Mark
— Opposition to the Registration
— Patent Application Bibliographic Data Entry Format
— Request for Continued Examination (RCE)
— Transmittal Form (PTO/SB/30)
— Business Related Transactions Patent Related Forms
— Trademark Related Forms
— Patent Cooperation Treaty Related Forms
— Patent and Trademark Copy Sales Forms
— Patent Cooperation Treaty (PCT) Forms

Vandema—AAA Real Estate Related Forms
http://www.vandema.com/Legalfram.htm

This site has links to forms, agreements, and applications that are used in the real estate industry today. The links are updated so they have the most current and latest documents for your use.

Veteran's Administration Forms
http://www.va.gov/forms/

This site has forms and applications from the VA that include:

— Loan Applications

— Burial Forms

— Claim for Benefits Forms

— Education Forms

— Military Records

— Appeals Forms

If your subject has ever had any benefits paid from the Veterans Administration, then this would be an excellent place to start your research. Here is information from the site on getting someone's military records.

Standard Form 180—Request Pertaining to Military Records. With access to a printer and the Adobe Acrobat Reader software available below, you may download and print a copy of the Standard Form 180. The front and back of the form are separate files that must be downloaded separately. **NOTE:** Please download both sides of the form, as the back of the form contains important mailing addresses and instructions. The Standard Form 180 is formatted for legal size paper (8-1/2" x 14"). Please print that way if your printer can accommodate. If your printer can only print on letter size paper (8-1/2" x 11"), select "shrink to fit" when the Adobe Acrobat Reader "Print" dialog box appears. You may even click a box to download the latest version of the FREE Adobe Acrobat software.

If you do not have access to a printer, or are unable to download the SF 180, you may still submit a request for military records. Here are three options:

1. Contact the National Archives and Records Administration's Fax-on-Demand System. The Fax-on- Demand system makes brochures, informational sheets, and other documents available to federal agencies and the members of the public who have access to fax machines. The SF 180 is available as document number 2255. You must call the system from a fax machine (using the handset) in order to receive documents. Voice instructions will guide you. There is no charge for this service except for any long-distance telephone charges you may incur. The phone number to access the fax-on-demand system is: (301) 713-6905.

2. Call the NPRC (MPR) telephone information lines. Callers can leave the name and address to which they want the SF 180 sent.

3. Send your request as a letter. Requests must contain enough information to identify the record among the more than 70 million on file at NPRC (MPR). Certain basic information is needed to locate military service records. This information includes the following:

    — Veteran's complete name used while in service
    — Service number or Social Security Number
    — Branch of service
    — Dates of service

Date and place of birth may also be helpful, especially if the service number is not known. If the request pertains to a record that may have been involved in the 1973 fire at NPRC(MPR), also include place of discharge, last unit of assignment, and place of entry into the service, if known. Federal Law [5 USC 552a(b)] requires that all requests for records and information be submitted in writing. Each request must be signed and dated. The SF 180 may be photocopied as needed. Please submit a separate request (either SF 180 or letter) for each individual whose records are being requested.

Hackers

There are so many stories in the news where the actions of hackers are made to sound like they are full of adventure and daring. The federal government has now been finding, and very aggressively prosecuting, hackers who break into government computers and sell the information. I am including the law so you can see how serious the government is about protecting the sanctity of computer files. Do things legally on the Internet because there are enough resources out there so that there is no need to do otherwise.

§1030. Fraud and related activity in connection with computers

(a) Whoever—

(1) having knowingly accessed a computer without authorization or exceeding authorized access, and by means of such conduct having obtained information that has been determined by the United States Government pursuant to an Executive order or statute to require protection against unauthorized disclosure for reasons of national defense or foreign relations, or

any restricted data, as defined in paragraph y. of section 11 of the Atomic Energy Act of 1954, with reason to believe that such information so obtained could be used to the injury of the United States, or to the advantage of any foreign nation willfully communicates, delivers, transmits, or causes to be communicated, delivered, or communicated, delivered, or transmitted the same to any person not entitled to receive it, or willfully retains the same and fails to deliver it to the officer or employee of the United States entitled to receive it;

(2) intentionally accesses a computer without authorization or exceeds authorized access, and thereby obtains

(A) information contained in a financial record of a financial institution, or of a card issuer as defined in section 1602 (n) of title 15, or contained in a file of a consumer reporting agency on a consumer, as such terms are defined in the Fair Credit Reporting Act (15 U.S.C. 1681 et seq.);

(B) information from any department or agency of the United States; or

(C) information from any protected computer if the conduct involved an interstate or foreign communication;

(3) intentionally, without authorization to access any nonpublic computer of a department or agency of the United States, accesses such a computer of that department or agency that is exclusively for the use of the Government of the United States or, in the case of a computer not exclusively for such use is used by or for the Government of the United States and such conduct affects that use by or for the Government of the United States;

(4) knowingly and with intent to defraud, accesses a protected computer without authorization, or exceeds authorized access, and by means of such conduct furthers the intended fraud and obtains anything of value, unless the object of the fraud and the thing obtained consists only of the use of the computer and the value of such use is not more than $5,000 in any one-year period;

(5)

(A) knowingly causes the transmission of a program, information, code, or command, and as a result of such conduct, intentionally causes damage without authorization, to a protected computer;

(B) intentionally accesses a protected computer without authorization, and as a result of such conduct, recklessly causes damage; or

(C) intentionally accesses a protected computer without authorization, and as a result of such conduct, causes damage;

(6) knowingly and with intent to defraud traffics (as defined in section 1029) in any password or similar information through which a computer may be accessed without authorization, if

    (A) such trafficking affects interstate or foreign commerce; or

    (B) such computer is used by or for the government of the United States;

(7) with intent to extort from any person, firm, association, educational institution, financial institution, government entity, or other legal entity, any money or other thing of value, transmits in interstate or foreign commerce any communication containing any threat to cause damage to a protected computer;

shall be punished as provided in subsection (c) of this section.

(b) Whoever attempts to commit an offense under subsection (a) of this section shall be punished as provided in subsection (c) of this section.

(c) The punishment for an offense under subsection (a) or (b) of this section is,

    (1)

    (A) a fine under this title or imprisonment for not more than ten years, or both, in the case of an offense under subsection (a) (1) of this section, which does not occur after a conviction for another offense under this section, or an attempt to commit an offense punishable under this subparagraph; and

    (B) a fine under this title or imprisonment for not more than twenty years, or both, in the case of an offense under subsection (a) (1) of this section which occurs after a conviction for another offense under this section, or an attempt to commit an offense punishable under this subparagraph; and

    (2)

    (A) a fine under this title or imprisonment for not more than one year, or both, in the case of an offense under subsection (a) (2), (a) (3), (a) (5) or (a) (6) of this section which does not occur after a conviction for another offense under this section, or an attempt to commit an offense punishable under this subparagraph; and

    (B) a fine under this title or imprisonment for not more than 5 years, or both, in the case of an offense under subsection (a) (2) if

        (i) the offense was committed for purpose of commercial advantage or private financial gain.

(ii) the offense was committed in furtherance of any criminal or tortious act in violation of the Constitution or laws of the United States or of any State; or

(iii) the value of the information obtained exceeds $5,000.00;

(C) a fine under this title or imprisonment for not more than ten years, or both, in the case of an offense under subsection (a) (2), (a) (3) or (a) (6) of this section which occurs after a conviction for another offense under this section, or an attempt to commit an offense punishable under this subparagraph; and

(3)

(A) a fine under this title or imprisonment for not more than five years, or both, in the case of an offense under subsection (a) (4), (a) (5) (A), (a) (5) (B), or (a) (7) of this section which does not occur after a conviction for another offense under this section, or an attempt to commit an offense punishable under this subparagraph; and

(B) a fine under this title or imprisonment for not more than ten years, or both, in the case of an offense under subsection (a) (4), (a) (5) (A), (a) (5) (B), (a) (5) (C), or (a) (7) of this section which occurs after a conviction for another offense under this section, or an attempt to commit an offense punishable under this subparagraph; and

(d) The United States Secret Service shall, in addition to any other agency having such authority, have the authority to investigate offenses under subsections (a) (2) (A), (a) (2) (B), (a) (3), (a) (4), (a) (5), and (a) (6) of this section. Such authority of the United States Secret Service shall be exercised in accordance with an agreement which shall be entered into by the Secretary of the Treasury and the Attorney General.

(e) As used in this section:

(1) the term "computer" means an electronic, magnetic, optical, electrochemical, or other high speed data processing device performing logical, arithmetic, or storage functions, and includes any data storage facility or communications facility directly related to or operating in conjunction with such device, but such term does not include an automated typewriter or typesetter, a portable hand held calculator, or other similar device;

(2) the term "protected computer" means a computer:

(A) exclusively for the use of a financial institution or the United States Government or, in the case of a computer not exclusively for such use, used by or for a financial institution or the United States government and the conduct constituting the offense affects that use by or for the financial institution or the government; or

(B) which is used in interstate or foreign commerce of communications;

(3) the term "State" includes the District of Columbia, the Commonwealth of Puerto Rico, and any other commonwealth, possession or territory of the United States;

(4) the term "financial institution" means:

(A) an institution with deposits insured by the Federal Deposit Insurance Corporation;

(B) the Federal Reserve or a member of the Federal Reserve including any Federal Reserve Bank;

(C) a credit union with accounts insured by the National Credit Union Administration;

(D) a member of the Federal home loan bank system and any home loan bank;

(E) any institution of the Farm Credit System under the Farm Credit Act of 1971;

(F) a broker-dealer registered with the Securities and Exchange Commission pursuant to section 15 of the Securities Exchange Act of 1934;

(G) the Securities Investor Protection Corporation;

(H) a branch or agency of a foreign bank (as such terms are defined in paragraphs (1) and (3) of section 1(b) of the International Banking Act of 1978); and

(I) an organization operating under section 25 or section 25(a) of the Federal Reserve Act

(5) the term "financial record" means information derived from any record held by a financial institution pertaining to a customer's relationship with the financial institution;

(6) the term "exceeds authorized access" means to access a computer with authorization and to use such access to obtain or alter information in the computer that the accessor is not entitled so to obtain or alter;

(7) the term "department of the United States" means the legislative or judicial branch of the Government, or one of the executive departments enumerated in section 101 of title 5; and

(8) the term 'damage' means any impairment to the integrity or availability of data, a program, a system, or information, that—

(A) causes loss aggregating at least $5,000 in value during any one-year period to one or more individuals;

(B) modifies or impairs, or potentially modifies or impairs, the medical examination, diagnosis, treatment, or care of one or more individuals;

(C) causes physical injury to any person; or

(D) threatens public health or safety; and

(9) the term 'government entity' includes the Government of the United States, any State or political subdivision of the United States, any foreign country, and any state, province, municipality, or other political subdivision of a foreign country.

(f) This section does not prohibit any lawfully authorized investigative, protective, or intelligence activity of a law enforcement agency of the United States, a State, or a political subdivision of a State, or of an intelligence agency of the United States.

(g) Any person who suffers damage or loss by reason of a violation of the section may maintain a civil action against the violator to obtain compensatory damages and injunctive relief or other equitable relief. Damages for violations involving damage as defined in subsection (e) (8) (A) are limited to economic damages. No action may be brought under this subsection unless such action is begun within 2 years of the date of the act complained of or the date of the discovery of the damage.

(h) The Attorney General and the Secretary of the Treasury shall report to the Congress annually, during the first 3 years following the date of the enactment of this subsection, concerning investigations and prosecutions under section 1030 (a) (5) of title 18, United States Code.

Commonly Used Abbreviations

You may be new to the Internet, so I am including some commonly used abbreviations. You will, no doubt, be corresponding with businesses and persons via e-mail who may be pressed for time and they will use the following:

2U2 = To You, Too

AAMOF = As a Matter of Fact

AFAIK = As Far As I Know

AFAIC = As Far As I'm Concerned

AFAICT = As Far As I Can Tell

AFK = Away From Keyboard

ASAP = As Soon As Possible

BAK = Back At Keyboard

BBL = Be Back Later

BITMT = But In The Meantime

BOT = Back On Topic

BRB = Be Right Back

BTW = By The Way

C4N = Ciao For Now

CRS = Can't Remember "Stuff"

CU = See You

CUL(8R) = See You Later

CWOT =Complete Waste of Time

CYA = See Ya

DITYID = Did I Tell You I'm Distressed?

DIY = Do It Yourself

EOD = End Of Discussion

EZ = Easy

F2F = Face To Face

FAQ = Frequently Asked Questions

FBOW = For Better Or Worse

FOAF = Friend Of A Friend

FOCL = Falling Off Chair Laughing

FWIW = For What It's Worth

FYA = For Your Amusement

FYI = For Your Information

/ga = Go Ahead

GAL = Get A Life

GBTW = Get Back To Work

GFC = Going For Coffee

GFETE = Grinning From Ear To Ear

GMTA = Great Minds Think Alike

GRandD = Grinning, Running and Ducking

GTG = Got To Go

GTGTTBR = Got To Go To The Bathroom

GTRM = Going To Real Mail

HAND = Have A Nice Day

HHOK = Ha Ha Only Kidding

HTH = Hope This Helps

IAC = In Any Case

IAE = In Any Event

IC = I See

IDGI = I Don't Get It

IMCO = In My Considered Opinion

IMHO = In My Humble Opinion

IMNSHO = In My Not So Humble Opinion

IMO = In My Opinion

IMPE = In My Previous/Personal Experience

IMVHO = In My Very Humble Opinion

IOTTMCO = Intuitively Obvious To The Most Casual Observer

IOW = In Other Words

IRL = In Real Life

ISP = Internet Service Provider

IYKWIM = If You Know What I Mean

JIC = Just In Case

J/K = Just Kidding

KISS = Keep It Simple Stupid

L8TR = Later

LD = Later Dude

LOL = Laughing Out Loud

LTNS = Long Time No See

MorF = Male or Female, or person who asks that question

MTCW = My Two Cents Worth

NRN = No Reply Necessary

ONNA = Oh No, Not Again!

OTOH = On The Other Hand

OTTOMH = Off The Top Of My Head

OIC = Oh I See

OTF = On The Floor

OLL = Online Love

PCMCIA =People Can't Memorize Computer Industry Acronyms

PLS = Please

PU = That stinks!

REHI = Hello Again (Re-Hi!)

ROFL = Rolling On Floor Laughing

ROTF = Rolling On The Floor

ROTFL = Rolling On The Floor Laughing

RSN = Real Soon Now

RTDox = Read The Documentation/Directions

RTFM = Read The Frickin' Manual

RUOK = Are You OK?

SNAFU = Situation Normal; All Fouled Up

SO = Significant Other

SOL = Smiling Out Loud (or You're Out of Luck)

TANSTAAFL = There Ain't No Such Thing As A Free Lunch

TAFN = That's All For Now

TEOTWAWKI = The End Of The World As We Know It

THX = Thanks

TIA = Thanks in Advance

TLK2UL8R = Talk to you later

TMK = To My Knowledge

TOS = Terms Of Service

TPTB = The Powers That Be

TSWC = Tell Someone Who Cares

TTBOMK = To The Best Of My Knowledge

TTFN = Ta-Ta For Now

TTYL(8R) = Talk To You Later

TWIMC = To Whom It May Concern

Txs = Thanks

URL = Web Page Address

w/b = Welcome Back

w/o = Without

WRT = With Regard To

WTG = Way To Go

WU? = What's Up?

WWW = World Wide Web

WYSIWYG = What You See Is What You Get

Y2K = Year 2000

YGIAGAM = Your Guess Is As Good As Mine

YGWYPF = You Get What You Pay For

YMMV = Your Mileage May Vary

ZZZ = Sleeping

Smileys

The following symbols are what is known on the Internet as *smileys*. If a smiley does not look correct, then you may want to tilt your head to the left to view them properly. :) Please remember that most smileys come in two forms—with a nose and without.

0:) or 0:-) = Angel

:ll or :-ll = Angry

:@ or :-@ = Angry or screaming

>:-(= Angry, annoyed

I-l = Asleep

;)= or ;-)= = Big grin

:1 or :-1 = Bland face

:o or :-o = Bored

:c or :-c = Bummed out

:'(o or :'-(= Crying/sad

:> or :-> = Devilish grin

:6 or :-6 = Eating something sour

}) or }-) = Evil

:] or :-] = Friendly

:(or :-(= Frowning

:/ or :-/ = Frustrated

8) or 8-) = Glasses

:D or :-D = Grinning

{ } = Hug

:*) or :-*) = Kiss

:x or :-x = Kissing

:))) or :-))) = Laughing or double chin

:,) or :,-) = Laughing tears

:$ or :-$ = Mouth wired shut

:X or :-X = Mute

:1 or :-1 = Not talking

:Y or :-Y = Quiet aside

:[or :-[= Real downer

:< or :-< = Sad

:> or :-> = Sarcastic

B) or B-) = Shades

=:0 or =:-) = Shocked

:Z or :-Z = Sleeping

:) or :-) = Smiling

:O or :-O = Surprised

:() or :-() = Talking

:P or :-P = Tongue out

:and or :-and = Tongue-tied

l) or l-) = Trekkie

:^(= Unhappy, looking away

;) or ;-) = Winking

:} or :-} = Wry Smile

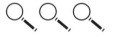

Appendix

he following addresses are county mailing addresses in the United States that you will need. Chapter 2 showed the myriad of public records that can be accessed from the County Hall of Records. You may also want to use these addresses to make inquiries as to what arrest record information is on file for your subject. Address your inquiries to the "Chief Administrative Judge."

ALABAMA

http://www.archives.state.al.us/referenc/vital.html

Autauga County
4th and Court Streets
Prattville, Alabama 36067

Baldwin County
County Courthouse
P.O. Box 459-J
Bay Minnette, Alabama 36507

Barbour County
County Courthouse
P.O. Box 758-O
Eufaula, Alabama 36027-0758

Bibb County
Courthouse Square
Centerville, Alabama 35042

Blount County
County Courthouse
P.O. Box 549
Oneonta, Alabama 35121

Bullock County
County Courthouse
P.O. Box 71-E
Union Springs, Alabama 36089

Butler County
County Courthouse
P.O. Box 756-Y
Greenville, Alabama 36037

Calhoun County
County Courthouse
1702 Noble St. Suite 102
Anniston, Alabama 36201

Chambers County
County Courthouse
Lafayette, Alabama 36862

Cherokee County
Courthouse on Main St.
Centre, Alabama 35960

Chilton County
County Courthouse
P.O. Box 270-E
Clanton, Alabama 35045

Choctaw County
County Courthouse
117 South Mulberry St.
Butler, Alabama 36904

Clarke County
County Courthouse
117 Court St.
Grove Hill, Alabama 36451

Clay County
County Courthouse
P.O. Box 1120
Ashland, Alabama 36251

Cleburne County
406 Vickery St.
Heflin, Alabama 36264

Coffee County
County Courthouse
P.O. Box 1256
Enterprise, Alabama 36331

Colbert County
County Courthouse
201 N. Main St.
Tuscumbia, Alabama 35647

Conecuh County
County Courthouse
P.O. Box 149
Evergreen, Alabama 36410

Coosa County
County Courthouse
P.O. Box 218
Rockford, Alabama 35136

Covington County
County Courthouse
P.O. Box 789
Andalusia, Alabama 36240

Crenshaw County
County Courthouse
P.O. Box 328
Luverne, Alabama 36049

Cullman County
County Courthouse
P.O. Box 237
Cullman, Alabama 35055

Dale County
County Courthouse
P.O. Box 580
Ozark, Alabama 36361

Dallas County
County Courthouse
P.O. Box 997
Selma, Alabama 36702

Dekalb County
County Courthouse
301 S. Grand Ave.
Fort Payne, Alabama 35967

Elmore County
County Courthouse
P.O. Box 280
Wetumpka, Alabama 36092

Escambia County
County Courthouse
P.O. Box 557
Brewton, Alabama 36427

Etowah County
County Courthouse
800 Forrest Ave.
Gadsden, Alabama 35902

Fayette County
County Courthouse
P.O. Box 509
Fayette, Alabama 35555

Franklin County
County Courthouse
410 N. Jackson St.
Russellville, Alabama
35653

Geneva County
County Courthouse
P.O. Box 430
Geneva, Alabama 36340

Greene County
County Courthouse
P.O. Box 790
Eutaw, Alabama 35462

Hale County
1001 Main St.
Greensboro, Alabama
36744

Henry County
County Courthouse
101 West Court Square St.
Abbeville, Alabama 36310

Houston County
County Courthouse
P.O. Box 6406
Dothan, Alabama 36302

Jackson County
County Courthouse
P.O. Box 128
Scottsboro, Alabama 35768

Jefferson County
County Courthouse
716 N. 21st St.
Birmingham, Alabama
35263

Lamar County
County Courthouse
P.O. Box 338
Vernon, Alabama 35592

Lauderdale County
County Courthouse
P.O. Box 1059
Florence, Alabama 35631

Lawrence County
County Courthouse
14330 Court St.
Moulton, Alabama 35650

Lee County
County Courthouse
215 South 9th St.
Opelika, Alabama
36803-2266

Limestone County
County Courthouse
310 West Washington St.
Athens, Alabama 35611

Lowndes County
County Courthouse
P.O. Box 5
Hayneville, Alabama 36040

Macon County
County Courthouse
210 N. Elm St.
Tuskegee, Alabama 36083

Madison County
100 Courthouse Square SE
Huntsville, Alabama 35801

Marengo County
101 East Coats Ave.
Linden, Alabama 36748

Marion County
County Courthouse
P.O. Box 1687
Hamilton, Alabama 35570

Marshall County
County Courthouse
425 Gunter Ave.
Guntersville, Alabama
35976

Mobile County
County Courthouse
109 Government St.
Mobile, Alabama 36602

Monroe County
County Courthouse
South Mount Plaza Ave.
Monroeville, Alabama
36461

Montgomery County
County Courthouse
P.O. Box 223
Montgomery, Alabama
36140

Morgan County
County Courthouse
302 Lee St. NE
Decatur, Alabama 35601

Perry County
County Courthouse
P.O. Box 478
Marion, Alabama 36756

Pickens County
County Courthouse
P.O. Box 370
Carrollton, Alabama 35447

Pike County
County Courthouse
120 West Church St.
Troy, Alabama 36081

Randolph County
County Courthouse
P.O. Box 249
Wedowee, Alabama 36278

Russell County
County Courthouse
P.O. Box 700
Phoenix City, Alabama
36868

Shelby County
County Courthouse
P.O. Box 825
Columbiana, Alabama
35051

St Clair County
County Courthouse
P.O. Box 220
Ashville, Alabama 35953

Sumter County
County Courthouse
Franklin St.
Livingston, Alabama 35470

Talladega County
County Courthouse
P.O. Box 755
Talladega, Alabama 35160

Tallapoosa County
County Courthouse
125 N. Broadnax St.
Dadeville, Alabama 36853

Tuscaloosa County
County Courthouse
714 Greensboro Ave.
Tuscaloosa, Alabama
35401

Walker County
County Courthouse
P.O. Box 502
Jasper, Alabama 35502

Washington County
County Courthouse
P.O. Box 549
Chatom, Alabama 36518

Wilcox County
County Courthouse
P.O. Box 668
Camden, Alabama 36726

Winston County
County Courthouse
P.O. Box 27
Double Springs, Alabama
35553

ALASKA

http://www.hss.state.ak.us/d
ph/bvs/bvs_home.htm

Aleutians East Borough
P.O. Box 349
Sandpoint, Alaska 99661

Anchorage Borough
P.O. Box 196650
Anchorage, Alaska 99519

Bristol Bay Borough
P.O. Box 189
Naknek, Alaska 99633

Denali Borough
P.O. Box 480
Healy, Alaska 99743

Fairbanks North Star Borough
809 Pioneer Rd.
Fairbanks, Alaska 99701

Haines Borough
P.O. Box 1209
Haines, Alaska 99827

Juneau Borough
155 S. Seward St.
Juneau, Alaska 99801

Kenai Peninsula Borough
144 N. Binkley St.
Soldolna, Alaska 99669

Ketchikan Borough
344 Front St.
Ketchikan, Alaska 99901

Kodiak Borough
710 Mill Bay Rd.
Kodiak, Alaska 99615

Matanuska-Susitna Borough
350 E. Dahlia Ave.
Palmer, Alaska 99645

North Slope Borough
P.O. Box 69
Barrow, Alaska 99723

Northwest Arctic Borough
P.O. Box 1110
Kotzebue, Alaska 99752

Silka Borough
100 Lincoln St.
Sitka, Alaska 99835

Yakutat Borough
P.O. Box 160
Yakutat, Alaska 99689

ARIZONA

http://www.state.az.us/

Apache County
P.O. Box 365
St. Johns, Arizona 85936

Cochise County
P.O. Box CK
Bisbee, Arizona 85603

Coconino County
100 E. Birch Ave.
Flagstaff, Arizona 86001

Gila County
1400 E. Ash St.
Globe, Arizona 85501

Graham County
800 W. Main St.
Safford, Arizona 85546

Greenlee County
Webster St.
Clifton, Arizona 85533

La Paz County
1713 S. Kola Ave.
Parker, Arizona 85344

Maricopa County
201 W. Jefferson St.
Phoenix, Arizona 85003

Mohave County
401 E. Spring St.
Kingman, Arizona 86401

Navajo County
P.O. Box 668
Holbrook, Arizona 86025

Pima County
150 West Congress St.
Tucson, Arizona 85701

Pinal County
P.O. Box 827
Florence, Arizona 85232

Santa Cruz County
P.O. Box 1265
Nogales, Arizona 85628

Yavapai County
Clerk of Superior Court
Prescott, Arizona 86301

Yuma County
198 S. Main St.
Yuma, Arizona 85364

ARKANSAS

http://www.state.ar.us

Arkansas County Clerk
P.O. Box 719
Stuttgart, Arkansas
72160-0719

Ashley County Clerk
215 E. Jefferson Ave.
Hamburg, Arkansas 71646

Baxter County Clerk
County Courthouse
Mountain Home, Arkansas
72653-4065

Benton County Clerk
P.O. Box 699
Bentonville, Arkansas
72712-0699

Boone County Clerk
100 N. Main, Suite 201
Harrison, Arkansas 72601

Bradley County Clerk
County Courthouse
Warren, Arkansas 71671

Calhoun County Clerk
P.O. Box 626
Hampton, Arkansas
71744-0626

Carroll County Clerk
210 West Church St.
Berryville, Arkansas
72616-4233

Chicot County Clerk
County Courthouse
Lake Village, Arkansas
71653

Clark County Clerk
County Courthouse Square
Arkadelphia, Arkansas
71923

Clay County Clerk
P.O. Box 306
Piggott, Arkansas 72454

Cleburne County Clerk
301 W. Main St.
Heber Springs, Arkansas
72543

Cleveland County Clerk
Main and Magnolia Streets
Rison, Arkansas 71665

Columbia County Clerk
1 Court Square
Magnolia, Arkansas 71753

Conway County Clerk
117 S. Moose St.,
Rm. 203
Morrilton, Arkansas
72110-3427

Craighead County Clerk
511 Union St.
Jonesboro, Arkansas
72401-2849

Crawford County Clerk
3rd and Main Streets
Van Buren, Arkansas
72946-5765

Crittenden County Clerk
County Courthouse
Marion, Arkansas 72364

Cross County Clerk
705 E. Union St.
Wynne, Arkansas
72396-3039

Dallas County Clerk
206 3rd St. W.
Fordyce, Arkansas 71742

Desha County Clerk
P.O. Box 188
Arkansas City, Arkansas
71630-0188

Drew County Clerk
210 S. Main St.
Monticello, Arkansas
71655

Faulkner County Clerk
801 Locust St
Conway, Arkansas 72032

Franklin County Clerk
Courthouse
Ozark, Arkansas 72949

Fulton County Clerk
P.O. Box 278
Salem, Arkansas
72576-0278

Garland County Clerk
501 Ouachita Ave.
Hot Springs, Arkansas
71901-5154

Grant County Clerk
Main and Center Streets
Sheridan, Arkansas 72150

Greene County Clerk
320 W. Court, Rm. 102
Paragould, Arkansas 72450

Hempstead County Clerk
P.O. Box 1420
Hope, Arkansas 71801

**Hot Springs County
Clerk**
3rd and Locust St.
Malvern, Arkansas 72104

Howard County Clerk
421 N. Main St.
Nashville, Arkansas
71852-2008

**Independence County
Clerk**
192 E. Main St.
Batesville, Arkansas
72501-3135

Izard County Clerk
P.O. Box 95
Melbourne, Arkansas
72556

Jackson County Clerk
P.O. Box 641
Newport, Arkansas
72112-0641

Jefferson County Clerk
P.O. Box 6317
Pine Bluff, Arkansas
71611-6317

Johnson County Clerk
P.O. Box 57
Clarksville, Arkansas
72830

Lafayette County Clerk
#2 Courthouse Square
Lewisville, Arkansas 71845

Lawrence County Clerk
315 W. Main St., Rm. 1
Walnut Ridge, Arkansas
72476-0553

Lee County Clerk
15 E. Chestnut St.
Marianna, Arkansas
72360-2302

Lincoln County Clerk
Drew and Wiley Streets
Star City, Arkansas 71667

Little River County Clerk
351 N. 2nd St.
Ashdown, Arkansas 71822

Logan County Clerk
Broadway St.
Booneville, Arkansas
72927

Lonoke County Clerk
P.O. Box 431
Lonoke, Arkansas 72086

Madison County Clerk
P.O. Box 37
Huntsville, Arkansas
72740-0037

Marion County Clerk
Courthouse Square
Yellville, Arkansas 72687

Miller County Clerk
400 Laurel St.
Texarkana, Arkansas 75502

Mississippi County Clerk
Walnut and 2nd Streets
Blytheville, Arkansas
72315

Monroe County Clerk
123 Madison St.
Clarendon, Arkansas
72029-2742

**Montgomery County
Clerk**
P.O. Box 717
Mount Ida, Arkansas 71957

Nevada County Clerk
County Courthouse
Prescott, Arkansas 71857

Newton County Clerk
P.O. Box 410
Jasper, Arkansas 72641

Ouachita County Clerk
145 Jefferson St.
Camden, Arkansas 71701

Perry County Clerk
P.O. Box 358
Perryville, Arkansas
72126-0358

Phillips County Clerk
626 Cherry St.
Helena, Arkansas 72342

Pike County Clerk
Washington St.
Murfreesboro, Arkansas
71958

Poinsett County Clerk
Courthouse Square
Harrisburg, Arkansas
72432

Polk County Clerk
507 Church Ave.
Mena, Arkansas 71953

Pope County Clerk
100 W. Main St.
Russellville, Arkansas
72801

Prairie County Clerk
P.O. Box 278
Des Arc, Arkansas 72040-
0278

Pulaski County Clerk
405 W. Markham St.
Little Rock, Arkansas
72201-1407

Randolph County Clerk
201 Marr St
Pocahontas, Arkansas
72455-3322

Saline County Clerk
200 N. Main St.
Benton, Arkansas 72015

Scott County Clerk
P.O. Box 1578
Waldron, Arkansas
72958-1578

Searcy County Clerk
P.O. Box 297
Marshall, Arkansas 72650

Sebastian County Clerk
6th and Rogers
Fort Smith, Arkansas
72901

Sevier County Clerk
115 N. 3rd St.
De Queen, Arkansas 71832

Sharp County Clerk
County Courthouse
Ash Flat, Arkansas 72513

St. Francis County Clerk
313 S. Izard St.
Forrest City, Arkansas
72335-3856

Stone County Clerk
P.O. Box 120
Mountain View, Arkansas
72560

Union County Clerk
101 N. Washington Ave.
El Dorado, Arkansas 71730

Van Buren County Clerk
Rt.6, Box 254-9
Clinton, Arkansas 72031

**Washington
County Clerk**
280 N. College St.,
Suite 300
Fayetteville, Arkansas
72701-5309

White County Clerk
300 N. Spruce St.
Searcy, Arkansas
72143-7720

Woodruff County Clerk
500 N. 3rd St.
Augusta, Arkansas
72006-2056

Yell County Clerk
P.O. Box 219
Danville, Arkansas 72833

CALIFORNIA

http://www.state.ca.us/

Alameda County
1106 Madison St., 1st Fl
Oakland, California 94607

Alpine County
99 Water St.
Markleeville, California
96120

Amador County
500 Argonaut Lane
Jackson, California 95642

Butte County
25 County Center Dr.
Oroville, California
95965-3316

Calaveras County
Government Center
San Andreas, California
95249

Colusa County
546 Jay St.
Colusa, California
95932-2491

Contra Costa County
730 Las Juntas
Martinez, California
94553-1233

Del Norte County
450 H St.
Crescent City, California
95531-4021

El Dorado County
360 Fair Lane
Placerville, California
95667

Fresno County
220 Tulare St., Rm. 303
Frenso, California 93721

Glenn County
526 W. Sycamore St.
Willows, California 95988

Humboldt County
714 4th St.
Eureka, California 95501

Imperial County
940 Main St., Rm. #206
El Centro, California 92243

Inyo County
168 N. Edwards St.
Independence, California
93526

Kern County
1655 Chester Ave.
Bakersfield, California
93301

Kings County
1400 W. Lacey Blvd.
Hanford, California
93230-5905

Lake County
255 N. Forbes St.
Lakeport, California
95453-4731

Lassen County
220 S. Lassen St., Suite 5
Susanville, California
96130

Los Angeles County
Los Angeles Registrar-
Recorder/County Clerk
P.O. Box 53120
Los Angeles, California
90053-0120

Madera County
209 W. Yosemite Ave.
Madera, California
93637-3534

Marin County
3501 Civic Center Dr.,
Rm. 234
San Rafael, California
94903

Mariposa County
P.O. Box 35
Mariposa, California 95338

Mendocino County
501 Low Gap Rd., Rm. 1020
Ukiah, California 95482

Merced County
2222 M St.
Merced, California
95340-3729

Modoc County
200 Court St.
Alturas, California
96101-4026

Mono County
P.O. Box 537
Bridgeport, California
93517-0537

Monterey County
240 Church St., Rm. 305
Salinas, California 93902

Napa County
900 Coombs St., Rm. 116
Napa, California 94559

Nevada County
950 Maidu Ave.
Nevada City, California
95959-2504

Orange County
12 Civic Center Plaza,
Rm. 106
Santa Ana, California
92701

Placer County
2954 Richardson Dr.
Auburn, California 95603

Plumas County
520 Main St. Rm. 102
Quincy, California
95971-9366

Riverside County
2724 Gateway Dr.
Riverside, California 92502

Sacramento County
600 8th St., Rm. 108
Sacramento, California
95814

San Benito County
440 5th St., Rm. 206
Hollister, California
95023-3843

San Bernardino County
222 W. Hospitality Lane.
San Bernardino, California
92415

San Diego County
1600 Pacific Highway,
Rm. 260
San Diego, California
92112-4147

San Francisco County
Birth and Death Records:
San Francisco Dept of
Public Health
101 Grove St. Rm. 105
San Francisco, California
94102

Marriage Records:
San Francisco
County Recorder
875 Stevenson St., Rm. 100
San Francisco, California
94103

San Joaquin County
24 S. Hunter #304
Stockton, California 95201

San Luis Obispo County
1144 Monterey St., Suite A
San Luis Obispo,
California 93408

San Mateo County
401 Marshall St., 6th Fl.
Redwood City, California
94063-1636

Santa Barbara County
1100 Anacapa St.
Santa Barbara, California
93101-2000

Santa Clara County
Birth, Death,
Marriage Records:
Santa Clara
County Recorder
70 West Hedding St.
San Jose, California 95112

Divorce Records:
Santa Clara County
Superior Court
191 N. 1st St.
San Jose, California
53113-1001

Santa Cruz County
701 Ocean St., Rm. 230
Santa Cruz, California
95060

Shasta County
1500 Court St.
Redding, California
96001-1662

Sierra County
P.O. Box D
Downieville, California
95936-0398

Siskiyou County
P.O. Box 338
Yreka, California
96097-9910

Solano County
701 Texas St.
Fairfield, California 94533

Sonoma County
585 Fiscal Dr.
Santa Rosa, California
95403

Stanislaus County
P.O. Box 1098
Modesto, California
95353–1098

Sutter County
433 2nd St.
Yuba City, California
95991-5524

Tehama County
P.O. Box 250
Red Bluff, California
96080-0250

Trinity County
P.O. Box 1258
Weaverville, California
96093-1258

Tulare County
Tulare County Civic
Center, Rm. 203
Visalia, California 93291

Tuolumne County
2 S. Green St.
Sonora, California
95370-4617

Ventura County
800 S. Victoria Ave.
Ventura, California
93009-1260

Yolo County
625 Court St., Rm. 105
Woodland, California
95695

Yuba County
935 14th St.
Marysville, California
95901

COLORADO

http://www.state.co.us/

Adams County
450 S. 4th Ave.
Brighton, Colorado 80601

Alamosa County
P.O. Box 178
Alamosa, Colorado 81101

Arapahoe County
5334 Prince St.
Littleton, Colorado
80120-1136

Archuleta County
P.O. Box 148
Pagosa Springs, Colorado
81147-0148

Baca County
741 Main St.
Springfield, Colorado
81073-0116

Bent County
P.O. Box 350
Las Animas, Colorado
81054-0350

Boulder County
3450 Broadway
Boulder, Colorado 80304

Chaffee County
P.O. Box 699
Salida, Colorado
81201-0699

Cheyenne County
P.O. Box 67
Cheyenne Wells, Colorado
80810-0067

Clear Creek County
P.O. Box 2000
Georgetown, Colorado
80444-2000

Conejos County
P.O. Box 157
Conejos, Colorado
81129-0157

Costilla County
P.O. Box 100
San Luis, Colorado 81152

Crowley County
6th and Main St.
Ordway, Colorado 81063

Custer County
205 S. 6th St.
Westcliffe, Colorado 81252

Delta County
501 Palmer St.
Delta, Colorado
81416-1725

Denver County
Clerk and
Recorder's Office
1437 Bannock St., Rm. 281
Denver, Colorado 80202

Dolores County
4th and Main St.
Dove Creek, Colorado
81324-0164

Douglas County
301 Wilcox St.
Castle Rock, Colorado
80104-2440

Eagle County
P.O. Box 537
Eagle, Colorado
81631-0850

El Paso County
Vital Statistics Section
301 S. Union Blvd.
Colorado Springs,
Colorado 80910
(719) 520-7475

Elbert County
751 Ute Ave.
Kiowa, Colorado
80117-9315

Fremont County
615 Macon Ave.
Cannon City, Colorado
81212

Garfield County
109 8th St.
Glenwood Springs,
Colorado 81601-3362

Gilpin County
P.O. Box 366
Central City, Colorado
80427-0366

Grand County
308 Byers Ave.
Hot Sulphur Springs,
Colorado 80451

Gunnison County
200 E. Virginia Ave.
Gunnison, Colorado
81230-2248

Hinsdale County
P.O. Box 403
Lake City, Colorado 81235

Huerfano County
400 Main St., Rm. 201
Walsenburg, Colorado
81089-2034

Jackson County
P.O. Box 337
Walden, Colorado
80480-0337

Jefferson County
260 S. Kipling St.
Lakewood, Colorado 80226

Kiowa County
1305 Golf St.
Eads, Colorado
81036-0037

Kit Carson County
P.O. Box 248
Burlington, Colorado
80807-0248

La Plata County
1060 E. 2nd Ave.
Durango, Colorado
81301-5157

Lake County
P.O. Box 964
Leadville, Colorado 80461

Larimer County
1525 Blue Spruce Dr.
Fort Collins, Colorado
80524-2004

Las Animas County
1st and Maple St.
Trinidad, Colorado 81082

Lincoln County
718 3rd Ave.
Hugo, Colorado 80821

Logan County
315 Main St.
Sterling, Colorado 80751

Mesa County
515 Patterson Rd.
Grand Junction, Colorado
81506

Mineral County
P.O. Box 70
Creede, Colorado
81130-0070

Moffat County
221 W. Victory Way
Craig, Colorado
81625-2732

Montezuma County
109 W. Main St.
Cortez, Colorado
81321-3154

Montrose County
P.O. Box 1289
Montrose, Colorado
81402-1289

Morgan County
231 Ensign St.
Fort Morgan, Colorado
80701-0596

Otero County
P.O. Box 511
LaJunta, Colorado
81050-0511

Ouray County
541 4th St.
Ouray, Colorado
81427-0615

Park County
501 Main St.
Fairplay, Colorado
80440-0220

Phillips County
221 S. Interocean Ave.
Holyoke, Colorado
80734-1534

Pitkin County
530 E. Main St.
Aspen, Colorado 81611

Prowers County
301 S. Main St.
Lamar, Colorado
81052-1046

Pueblo County
211 W. 10th St.
Pueblo, Colorado
81003-2905

Rio Blanco County
P.O. Box 1150
Meeker, Colorado 81641

Rio Grande County
P.O. Box 160
Del Norte, Colorado
81132-0160

Routt County
P.O. Box 773598
Steamboat Springs,
Colorado 80477

Saguache County
P.O. Box 356
Saguache, Colorado
81149-0356

San Juan County
P.O. Box 466
Silverton, Colorado 81433

San Miguel County
305 W. Colorado
Telluride, Colorado 81435

Sedgwick County
P.O. Box 3
Julesburg, Colorado
80737-0003

Summitt County
208 E. Lincoln St.
Breckenridge, Colorado
80424

Teller County
P.O. Box 959
Cripple Creek, Colorado
80813-0959

Washington County
150 Ash Ave.
Akron, Colorado
80720-1510

Weld County
915 10th St.
Greeley, Colorado
80631-3811

Yuma County
Third and Ash
Wray, Colorado 80758

CONNECTICUT
http://www.state.ct.us/

Fairfield County Clerk
1061 Main St.
Bridgeport, Connecticut
06601-4222

Hartford County Clerk
95 Washington St.
Hartford, Connecticut
06106-4406

Litchfield County Clerk
20 West St.
Litchfield, Connecticut
06759

Middlesex County Clerk
1 Court St.
Middletown, Connecticut
06457-3442

New Haven County Clerk
235 Church St.
New Haven, Connecticut
06510-0998

**New London
County Clerk**
181 State St.
New London, Connecticut
06320

Tolland County Clerk
69 Brooklyn St.
Vernon Rockville,
Connecticut 06066-3643

Windham County Clerk
Courthouse
Putnam, Connecticut 06260

DELAWARE
http://www.state.de.us/

Kent County Clerk
414 Federal St.
Dover, Delaware
19901-3615

New Castle County Clerk
800 N. French St.
Wilmington, Delaware
19801-3590

Sussex County Clerk
P.O. Box 743
Georgetown, Delaware
19947

FLORIDA
http://www.state.fl.us/

Alachua County Clerk
21 E. University Ave.
Gainesville, Florida
32602-3028

Baker County Clerk
55 N. 3rd St.
MacClenny, Florida
32063-2101

Bay County Clerk
300 E. 4th St.
Panama City, Florida
32402-2269

Bradford County Clerk
P.O. Box B
Starke, Florida 32091-1286

Brevard County Clerk
700 S. Park Ave.
Titusville, Florida 32781

Broward County Clerk
2421 S.W. 6th Ave.
Ft. Lauderdale, Florida
33315

Calhoun County Clerk
425 E. Central Ave.
Blountstown, Florida
32424-2242

Charlotte County Clerk
514 E. Grace St.
Punta Gorda, Florida 33950

Citrus County Clerk
110 N. Apopka Ave.
Inverness, Florida 33450

Clay County Clerk
P.O. Box 698
Green Cove Springs,
Florida 32043-0698
(904) 284-6300

Collier County Clerk
3301 Tamiami Trail
Naples, Florida
33962-4902

Columbia County Clerk
35 N. Herndaz St.
Lake City, Florida 32055

Dade County Clerk
1350 NW 14th St.
Miami, Florida 33125

De Soto County Clerk
P.O. Box 591
Arcadia, Florida 34265

Dixie County Clerk
P.O. Box 1206
Cross City, Florida 32628

Duval County Clerk
515 W. 6th St.
Jacksonville, Florida
32206-4397

Escambia County Clerk
223 S. Palafox Pl.
Pensacola, Florida
32501-5845

Flagler County Clerk
200 E. Moody Blvd
Bunnell, Florida
32110-0787

Franklin County Clerk
33 Market St., Suite 203
Apalachicola, Florida
32320

Gadsden County Clerk
10 E. Jefferson St.
Quincy, Florida
32351-0231

Gilchrist County
112 S. Main St.
Trenton, Florida
32693-0037

Glades County Clerk
P.O. Box 10
Moore Haven, Florida
33471-0010

Gulf County Clerk
1000 5th St.
Port St. Joe, Florida
32456-1648

Hamilton County Clerk
P.O. Box 789
Jasper, Florida 32052

Hardee County Clerk
412 W. Orange St.
Wauchula, Florida
33873-2831

Hendry County Clerk
P.O. Box 1760
La Belle, Florida
33935-1760

Hernando County Clerk
20 N. Main St.
Brooksville, Florida 34601

Highlands County Clerk
430 S. Commerce Ave.
Attn: Recording Dept.
Sebring, Florida
33870-3701

**Hillsborough
County Clerk**
1105 E. Kennedy Blvd,
Rm. 276
Tampa, Florida 33602

Holmes County Clerk
201 N. Oklahoma St.
Bonifay, Florida
32425-2243

**Indian River
County Clerk**
1840 25th St.
Vero Beach, Florida
32960-3365

Jackson County Clerk
P.O. Box 510
Marianna, Florida
32446-0510

Jefferson County Clerk
P.O. Box 547
Monticello, Florida 32344

Lafayette County Clerk
P.O. Box 88
Mayo, Florida 32066-0088

Lake County Clerk
315 W. Main St.
Tavares, Florida
32778-3813

Lee County Clerk
2115 2nd St.
Fort Myers, Florida
33902-2469

Leon County Clerk
301 S. Monroe St.
Tallahassee, Florida 32301

Levy County Clerk
P.O. Box 610
Bronson, Florida
32621-0610

Liberty County Clerk
P.O. Box 399
Bristol, Florida 32321-0399

Madison County Clerk
P.O. Box 237
Madison, Florida
32340-0237

Manatee County Clerk
410 East 6th Ave.
Bradenton, Florida
34208-1928

Marion County Clerk
Department of Vital
Records
1801 S. E. 32nd Ave.
Ocala, Florida 34471

Martin County Clerk
Health Department
620 S. Dixie Highway
Stuart, Florida 34994

Monroe County Clerk
500 Whitehead St.
Key West, Florida
33040-6547

Nassau County Clerk
P.O. Box 456
Fernandina Beach, Florida
32034-0456

**Okaloosa County Public
Health Unit**
221 Hospital Dr. NE
Ft. Walton Beach, Florida
32548

**Okeechobee
County Clerk**
304 NW 2nd St.
Okeechobee, Florida 34972

Orange County Clerk
832 W. Central Blvd.,
Rm. 200
Orlando, Florida 32805

Osceola County Clerk
12 S. Vernon Ave.
Kissimmee, Florida
32741-5188

Palm Beach County Clerk
Vital Statistics Department
705 N. Olive Ave.
West Palm Beach, Florida
33402

Pasco County Clerk
38053 E. Live Oak Ave.
Dade City, Florida 33525

**Pinellas County Health
Department**
Vital Statistics
300 31st St. N., Suite 100
St. Petersburg, Florida
33713

Polk County Clerk
255 N. Broadway Ave.
Bartow, Florida 33830

Putnam County Clerk
P.O. Box 758
Palatka, Florida
32078-0758

Santa Rosa County Clerk
801 Caroline St. SE
Milton, Florida 32570-4978

Sarasota County Clerk
2000 Main St.
Sarasota, Florida 34237

Seminole County Clerk
300 N. Park Ave.
Sanford, Florida
32771-1244

St. Johns County P.H.U.
180 Marine St.
St. Augustine, Florida
32084

St. Lucie County Clerk
221 South Indian River Dr.
Ft. Pierce, Florida 34950

Sumter County Clerk
209 N. Florida St.
Bushnell, Florida
33513-9308

Suwannee County Clerk
200 South Ohio Ave.
Live Oak, Florida 32060

Taylor County Clerk
P.O. Box 620
Perry, Florida 32347-0620

Union County Clerk
55 W. Main St.
Lake Butler, Florida
32054-1637

Volusia County Clerk
120 W. Indiana Ave.
De Land, Florida
32720-4210

Wakulla County Clerk
P.O. Box 337
Crawfordville, Florida
32327-0337

Walton County Clerk
P.O. Box 1260
De Funiak Springs, Florida
32434-1260

**Washington
County Clerk**
203 W. Cypress Ave.
Chipley, Florida
32428-1821

GEORGIA

http://www.state.ga.us/

Appling County Clerk
100 N. Oak St.
Baxley, Georgia 31513

Atkinson County Clerk
P.O. Box 855
Pearson, Georgia 31642

Bacon County Clerk
502 W. 12th St.
Alma, Georgia 31510

Baker County Clerk
P.O. Box 548
Newton, Georgia 31770

Baldwin County Clerk
201 W. Hancock St.
Milledgeville, Georgia
31061

Banks County Clerk
P.O. Box 130
Homer, Georgia 30547

Barrow County Clerk
310 S. Broad St., Suite 321
Winder, Georgia 30680

Bartow County Clerk
135 W. Cherokee Ave.,
Suite 251
Cartersville, Georgia 30120

Ben Hill County Clerk
401 E. Central Ave.
Fitzgerald, Georgia 31750

Berrien County Clerk
105 E. Washington Ave.
Nashville, Georgia
31639-0446

Bibb County Clerk
Attn: Vital Records
171 Emery Hwy
Macon, Georgia 31217

Bleckley County Clerk
306 2nd St. SE
Cochran, Georgia
31014-1622

Brantley County Clerk
P.O. Box 398
Nahunta, Georgia 31553

Brooks County Clerk
P.O. Box 665
Quitman, Georgia
31643-0665

Bryan County Clerk
401 S. College St.
Pembroke, Georgia 31321

Bullock County Clerk
1 W. Altman St.
Statesboro, Georgia 30458

Burke County Clerk
6th and Liberty St.
Waynesboro, Georgia
30830-0062

Butts County Clerk
P.O. Box 320
Jackson, Georgia 30233

Calhoun County Clerk
Courthouse Square
Morgan, Georgia 31766

Camden County Clerk
P.O. Box 99
Woodbine, Georgia 31569

Candler County Clerk
705 N. Lewis St.
Metter, Georgia 30439

Carroll County Clerk
311 Newnan St.
Carrollton, Georgia
30117-1620

Catoosa County Clerk
Health Dept-Vital Records
182 Tiger Trail
Ringgold, Georgia
30736-1712

Charlton County Clerk
100 3rd St.
Folkston, Georgia
31537-3706

Chatham County Clerk
P.O. Box 31416
Savannah, Georgia 31406

**Chattahoochee
County Clerk**
P.O. Box 299
Cusseta, Georgia 31805

Chattooga County Clerk
P.O. Box 211
Summerville, Georgia
30747

Cherokee County Clerk
90 North St.
Canton, Georgia
30114-2725

Clarke County Clerk
325 E. Washington St.
Athens, Georgia
30601-2776

Clay County Clerk
P.O. Box 550
Ft. Gaines, Georgia
31751-0550

Clayton County Clerk
112 Smith St.
Jonesboro, Georgia 30236

Clinch County Clerk
100 Court Square
Homerville, Georgia
31634-1415

Cobb County Clerk
1650 County
Services Pkwy.
Marietta, Georgia 30008

Coffee County Clerk
County Courthouse
Douglas, Georgia 31533

Colquitt County Clerk
P.O. Box 886
Moultrie, Georgia 31776

Columbia County Clerk
P.O. Box 58
Appling, Georgia 30802

Cook County Clerk
212 N. Hutchinson Ave.
Adel, Georgia 31620

Coweta County Clerk
P.O. Box 945
Newnan, Georgia
30264-0945

Crawford County Clerk
P.O. Box 420
Knoxville, Georgia
31050-0420

Crisp County Clerk
210 7th St. South
Cordele, Georgia 31015

Dade County Clerk
P.O. Box 417
Trenton, Georgia
30752-0417

Dawson County Clerk
P.O. Box 192
Dawsonville, Georgia
30534

Decatur County Clerk
P.O. Box 234
Bainbridge, Georgia 31717

Dekalb County Clerk
445 Winn Way-Box 987
Decatur, Georgia 30031

Dodge County Clerk
P.O. Box 818
Eastman, Georgia
31023-0818

Dooly County Clerk
P.O. Box 322
Vienna, Georgia
31092-0322

Dougherty County Clerk
225 Pine Ave.
Albany, Georgia
31701-2561

Douglas County Clerk
6754 Broad St.
Douglasville, Georgia
30134-1711

Early County Clerk
105 Courthouse Square
Blakely, Georgia
31723-0525

Echols County Clerk
P.O. Box 118
Statenville, Georgia 31648

Effingham County Clerk
901 N. Pine St.
Springfield, Georgia
31329-0307

Elbert County Clerk
Elbert County Courthouse
14 N. Oliver St.
Elberton, Georgia 30635

Emanuel County Clerk
101 S. Main St.
Swainsboro, Georgia 30401

Evans County Clerk
3 Freeman St.
Claxton, Georgia 30417

Fannin County Clerk
P.O. Box 245
Blue Ridge, Georgia 30513

Fayette County Clerk
145 Johnson Ave.
Fayetteville, Georgia 30214

Floyd County Clerk
315 W. 10th St.
Rome, Georgia 30161-2678

Forsyth County Clerk
P.O. Box 128
Cumming, Georgia
30130-0128

Franklin County Clerk
Courthouse Square
Carnesville, Georgia 30521

Fulton County Clerk
99 Butler St. SE, 2nd Fl.
Atlanta, Georgia 30303

Gilmer County Clerk
1 Westside Square
Ellijay, Georgia
30540-1071

Glascock County Clerk
P.O. Box 231
Gibson, Georgia 30810

Glynn County Clerk
701 G St.
Brunswick, Georgia 31520

Gordon County Clerk
100 S. Wall St. Annex 1
Calhoun, Georgia 30701

Grady County Clerk
250 N. Broad St.
Cairo, Georgia 31728-4101

Greene County Clerk
113-C N. Main St.
Greensboro, Georgia 30642

Gwinnett County Clerk
75 Langley Dr.
Lawrenceville, Georgia
30245

Habersham County Clerk
P.O. Box 227
Clarkesville, Georgia
30523-0227

Hall County Clerk
116 Spring St. East
Gainesville, Georgia 30501

Hancock County Clerk
Courthouse Square–
Drawer G
Sparta, Georgia 31087

Haralson County Clerk
P.O. Box 488
Buchanan, Georgia
30113-0488

Harris County Clerk
P.O. Box 528
Hamilton, Georgia 31811

Hart County Clerk
P.O. Box 128
Hartwell, Georgia 30643

Heard County Clerk
North River St.
Franklin, Georgia 30217

Henry County Clerk
345 Phillips Dr.
McDonough, Georgia
30253-3425

Houston County Clerk
200 Carl Vinson Pkwy.
Warner Robbins, Georgia
31088-5808

Irwin County Clerk
710 N. Irwin Ave.
Ocilla, Georgia
31774-0287

Jackson County Clerk
P.O. Box 68
Jefferson, Georgia 30549

Jasper County Clerk
County Courthouse
Monticello, Georgia 31064

Jeff Davis County Clerk
Jeff Davis St.
Hazlehurst, Georgia 31539

Jefferson County Clerk
P.O. Box 658
Louisville, Georgia
30434-0658

Jenkins County Clerk
P.O. Box 797
Millen, Georgia
30442-0797

Johnson County Clerk
P.O. Box 269
Wrightsville, Georgia
31096-0269

Jones County Clerk
P.O. Box 1359
Gray, Georgia 31032

Lamar County Clerk
327 Thomaston St.
Barnesville, Georgia
30204-1612

Lanier County Clerk
100 W. Main St.
Lakeland, Georgia
31635-1116

Laurens County Clerk
2121 Bellevue Rd.
Dublin, Georgia 31021

Lee County Clerk
P.O. Box 56
Leesburg, Georgia
31763-0056

Liberty County Clerk
Courthouse Square
Hinesville, Georgia 31313

Lincoln County Clerk
P.O. Box 340
Lincolnton, Georgia
30817-0340

Long County Clerk
P.O. Box 426
Ludowici, Georgia 31316

Lowndes County Clerk
P.O. Box 1349
Valdosta, Georgia
31603-1349

Lumpkin County Clerk
99 Courthouse Hill, Suite A
Dahlonega, Georgia 30533

Macon County Clerk
P.O. Box 216
Oglethorpe, Georgia 30168

Madison County Clerk
P.O. Box 147
Danielsville, Georgia
30633-0147

Marion County Clerk
Courthouse Square
Buena Vista, Georgia
31803-0481

McDuffie County Clerk
P.O. Box 28
Thomson, Georgia 30824

McIntosh County Clerk
P.O. Box 453
Darien, Georgia 31305

Meriwether County Clerk
P.O. Box 608
Greenville, Georgia 30222

Miller County Clerk
155 S. 1st St.
Colquitt, Georgia
31737-1284

Mitchell County Clerk
12 Broad St.
Camilla, Georgia 31730

Monroe County Clerk
P.O. Box 817
Forsyth, Georgia
31029-0187

**Montgomery
County Clerk**
P.O. Box 295
Mt. Vernon, Georgia
30445-0295

Morgan County Clerk
141 E. Jefferson St.
Madison, Georgia
30650-1361

Murray County Clerk
3rd Ave.
Chatsworth, Georgia
30705-0023

Muscogee County Clerk
1000 10th St.
Columbus, Georgia
31901-2617

Newton County Clerk
1113 Usher St.
Covington, Georgia
30209-3155

Oconee County Clerk
15 Water St.
Watkinsville, Georgia
30677-0145

Oglethorpe County Clerk
P.O. Box 70
Lexington, Georgia 30648

Paulding County Clerk
116 Main St.
Dallas, Georgia
30132-1441

Peach County Clerk
205 W. Church St.
Ft. Valley, Georgia
31030-0468

Pickens County Clerk
211-1 N. Main St.
Jasper, Georgia
30143-9501

Pierce County Clerk
P.O. Box 646
Blackshear, Georgia 31516

Pike County Clerk
P.O. Box 377
Zebulon, Georgia
30295-0377

Polk County Clerk
100 Prior St. #101
Cedartown, Georgia 30125

Pulaski County Clerk
P.O. Box 29
Hawkinsville, Georgia
31036-0029

Putnam County Clerk
108 S. Madison Ave.
Eatonton, Georgia 31024

Quitman County Clerk
P.O. Box 7
Georgetown, Georgia
31754

Rabun County Clerk
P.O. Box 925
Clayton, Georgia 30525

Randolph County Clerk
Court St.
Cuthbert, Georgia 31740

Richmond County Clerk
530 Greene St.
Augusta, Georgia 30911

Rockdale County Clerk
922 Court St. NE
Conyers, Georgia 30012

Schley County Clerk
P.O. Box 352
Ellaville, Georgia
31806-0352

Screven County Clerk
216 Mims Rd.
Sylvania, Georgia 30467

Seminole County Clerk
P.O. Box 458 County
Courthouse
Donalsonville, Georgia
31745-0458

Spalding County Clerk
132 E. Solomon St.
Griffin, Georgia
30223-3312

Stephens County Clerk
P.O. Box 386
Toccoa, Georgia
30577-0386

Stewart County Clerk
P.O. Box 157
Lumpkin, Georgia
31815-0157

Sumter County Clerk
P.O. Box 246
Americus, Georgia 31709

Talbot County Clerk
P.O. Box 155
Courthouse Square
Talbotton, Georgia
31827-0155

Taliaferro County Clerk
P.O. Box 114
Courthouse Square
Crawfordville, Georgia
30631

Tattnall County Clerk
Main and Brazell Streets
Reidsville, Georgia 30453

Taylor County Clerk
P.O. Box 148
Butler, Georgia 31006

Telfair County Clerk
Courthouse Square
McRae, Georgia 31055

Terrell County Clerk
955 Forrester Dr. SE
Dawson, Georgia
31742-0525

Thomas County Clerk
P.O. Box 1582
Thomasville, Georgia
31799

Tift County Clerk
P.O. Box 826
Tifton, Georgia
31793-0826

Toombs County Clerk
Courthouse Square and
Hwy 280
Lyons, Georgia 30436

Towns County Clerk
P.O. Box 178
Hiawassee, Georgia 30546

Treutlen County Clerk
P.O. Box 88
Soperton, Georgia
30457-0088

Troup County Clerk
900 Dallas St.
LaGrange, Georgia 30241

Twiggs County
101 Magnolia St.
Jeffersonville, Georgia
31044-0202

Union County Clerk
Rural Route 8, Box 8005
Blairsville, Georgia
30512-9808

Upson County Clerk
P.O. Box 889
Thomaston, Georgia 30286

Walker County Clerk
P.O. Box 445
Lafayette, Georgia
30728-0445

Walton County Clerk
Court St. Annex 1
Monroe, Georgia 30655

Ware County Clerk
800 Church St.
Waycross, Georgia
31502-1069

Warren County Clerk
100 Main St.
Warrenton, Georgia 30828-0046

Washington County Clerk
P.O. Box 271
Sandersville, Georgia
31082-0271

Wayne County Clerk
174 N. Brunswick St.
Jesup, Georgia 31545

Webster County Clerk
P.O. Box 29
Preston, Georgia
31824-0029

Wheeler County Clerk
P.O. Box 477
Alamo, Georgia 30411

White County Clerk
1657 S. Main St.
Cleveland, Georgia 30528

Whitfield County Clerk
300 W. Crawford St.
Dalton, Georgia 30722

Wilcox County Clerk
Courthouse Square
Abbeville, Georgia 31001

Wilkes County Clerk
23 E. Court St.
Washington, Georgia
30673-1516

Wilkinson County Clerk
100 Main St.
Irwinton, Georgia 31042

Worth County Clerk
201 N. Main
Sylvester, Georgia
31791-2100

HAWAII
http://www.state.hi.us/

Hawaii County Clerk
25 Aupuni St.
Hilo, Hawaii 96720-4252

Honolulu County Clerk
City Hall
Honolulu, Hawaii
96813-3014

Kauai County Clerk
4396 Rice St.
Lihue, Hawaii 96766-1337

Maui County
200 S. High St.
Wailuku, Hawaii
96793-2155

IDAHO
http://www.state.id.us/

Ada County Clerk
650 Main St.
Boise, Idaho 83702-5960

Adams County Clerk
P.O. Box 48
Council, Idaho 83612-0048

Bannock County Clerk
624 E. Center St., Rm. 211
Pocatello, Idaho
83201-6274

Bear Lake County Clerk
7 E. Center St.
Paris, Idaho 83261

Benewah County Clerk
318 Highland.
St. Maries, Idaho 83861

Bingham County Clerk
501 N. Maple St.
Blackfoot, Idaho 83221

Blaine County Clerk
206 1st Ave., South,
Suite 200
Hailey, Idaho 83333

Boise County Clerk
P.O. Box 157
Idaho City, Idaho
83631-0157

Bonner County Clerk
215 S. 1st Ave.
Sandpoint, Idaho
83664-1305

Bonneville County Clerk
605 N. Capital Ave.
Idaho Falls, Idaho
83402-3582

Boundary County Clerk
315 Kootnal St.
Bonners Ferry, Idaho
83805-0419

Butte County Clerk
P.O. Box 737
Arco, Idaho 83213-0737

Camas County Clerk
P.O. Box 430
Fairfield, Idaho
83327-0430

Canyon County Clerk
1115 Albany St.
Caldwell, Idaho
83605-3542

Caribou County Clerk
159 S. Main St.
Soda Springs, Idaho
83276-1427

Cassia County Clerk
County Courthouse
Burley, Idaho 83318-1862

Clark County Clerk
P.O. Box 205
Dubois, Idaho 83423-0205

Clearwater County Clerk
P.O. Box 586
Orofino, Idaho 83544-0586

Custer County Clerk
P.O. Box 597
Challis, Idaho 83226

Elmore County Clerk
150 S. 4th East
Mountain Home, Idaho
83647

Franklin County Clerk
39 W. Oneida St.
Preston, Idaho 83263-1234

Fremont County Clerk
151 W. 1st North
St. Anthony, Idaho 83445

Gem County Clerk
415 E. Main St.
Emmett, Idaho 83617-3049

Gooding County Clerk
P.O. Box 417
Gooding, Idaho
83330-0417

Idaho County Clerk
320 W. Main St.
Grangeville, Idaho
83530-1948

Jefferson County Clerk
120 N. Clark St.
Rigby, Idaho 83442-1462

Jerome County Clerk
300 N. Lincoln Ave.
Jerome, Idaho 83338

Kootenai County Clerk
501 N. Government Way
Coeur d'Alene, Idaho
83814-2915

Latah County Clerk
522 S. Adams St.
Moscow, Idaho 83843

Lemhi County Clerk
206 Courthouse Dr.
Salmon, Idaho 83467-3943

Lewis County Clerk
510 Oak St.
Nez Perce, Idaho 83543

Lincoln County Clerk
111 W. B St.
Shoshone, Idaho
83352-0800

Madison County Clerk
P.O. Box 389
Rexburg, Idaho
83440-0389

Minidoka County Clerk
715 G St.
Rupert, Idaho 83350-0474

Nez Perce County Clerk
P.O. Box 896
Lewiston, Idaho
83501-0896

Oneida County Clerk
10 Court St.
Malad City, Idaho 83252

Owyhee County Clerk
P.O. Box 128
Murphy, Idaho 83650

Payette County Clerk
1130 Third Ave. N.
Payette, Idaho 83661-2473

Power County Clerk
543 Bannock Ave.
American Falls, Idaho
83211-1200

Shoshone County Clerk
P.O. Box 1049
Wallace, Idaho 83873-1049

Teton County Clerk
89 N. Main
Driggs, Idaho 83422

Twin Falls County Clerk
P.O. Box 126
Twin Falls, Idaho 83303

Valley County Clerk
P.O. Box 737
Cascade, Idaho 83611-0737

**Washington
County Clerk**
P.O. Box 670
Weisor, Idaho 83672-0670

ILLINOIS
http://www.state.il.us/

Adams County Clerk
521 Vermont St.
Quincy, Illinois 62301

Alexander County Clerk
2000 Washington Ave.
Cairo, Illinois 62914

Bond County Clerk
P.O. Box 407
Greenville, Illinois 62246

Boone County Clerk
601 N. Main St.
Belvidere, Illinois 61008

Brown County Clerk
21 W. Court St.
Mt. Sterling, Illinois 62353

Bureau County Clerk
County Courthouse
Princeton, Illinois 61356

Calhoun County Clerk
P.O. Box 187
Hardin, Illinois 62047-0187

Carroll County Clerk
P.O. Box 152
Mt. Carroll, Illinois
61053-0152

Cass County Clerk
100 E. Springfield St.
Virginia, Illinois 62691

Champaign County Clerk
1776 E. Washington St.
Urbana, Illinois 61801

Christian County Clerk
600 N. Main St.
Taylorville, Illinois
62568-0190

Clark County Clerk
501 Archer Ave.
Marshall, Illinois 62441

Clay County Clerk
P.O. Box 160
Louisville, Illinois
62858-0160

Clinton County Clerk
850 Fairfax
Carlyle, Illinois 62231

Coles County Clerk
651 Jackson Ave., Rm. 122
Charleston, Illinois 61920

Cook County Clerk
118 N. Clark St.
Chicago, Illinois 60602

Crawford County Clerk
P.O. Box 602
Robinson, Illinois
62454-0602

**Cumberland
County Clerk**
Courthouse Square
Toledo, Illinois 62468-0146

Dekalb County Clerk
110 E. Sycamore St.
Sycamore, Illinois
60178-1448

DeWitt County Clerk
201 W. Washington St.
Clinton, Illinois 61727

Douglas County Clerk
401 S. Center St.
Tuscola, Illinois
61953-0067

DuPage County Clerk
421 N. Farm Rd.
Wheaton, Illinois
60187-3978

Edgar County Clerk
115 W. Court St., Rm. J
Paris, Illinois 61944

Edwards County Clerk
50 E. Main St.
Albion, Illinois 62806

Effingham County Clerk
P.O. Box 628
Effingham, Illinois
62401-0628

Fayette County Clerk
221 S. 7th St.
Vandalia, Illinois 62471

Ford County Clerk
200 W. State St. Rm. 101
Paxton, Illinois 60957

Franklin County Clerk
202 W. Main St.
Benton, Illinois 62918

Fulton County Clerk
100 N. Main St.
Lewistown, Illinois
61542-1409

Gallatin County Clerk
P.O. Box 550
Shawneetown, Illinois
62984

Greene County Clerk
519 N. Main St.
Carrollton, Illinois 62016

Grundy County Clerk
111 E. Washington St.
Morris, Illinois 60450

Hamilton County Clerk
Courthouse
McLeansboro, Illinois
62859

Hancock County Clerk
Court House
Carthage, Illinois 62321

Hardin County Clerk
Main St.
Elizabethtown, Illinois
62931

Henderson County Clerk
P.O. Box 308
Oquawka, Illinois 61469

Henry County Clerk
100 S. Main St.
Cambridge, Illinois 61238

Iroquois County Clerk
550 S. 10th St.
Watseka, Illinois
60970-1810

Jackson County Clerk
1001 Walnut St.
Murphysbobo, Illinois
62966-2194

Jasper County Clerk
100 W. Jordan St.
Newton, Illinois
62448-1973

Jefferson County Clerk
100 S. 10th St.
Mt. Vernon, Illinois 62864

Jersey County Clerk
210 W. Pearl St.
Jerseyville, Illinois
62052-1675

Jo Daviess County Clerk
330 N. Bench St.
Galena, Illinois 61036

Johnson County Clerk
400 Court Square
Vienna, Illinois 62995

Kane County Clerk
719 S. Batavia Ave.,
Bldg B
Geneva, Illinois
60134-2722

Kankakee County Clerk
189 E. Court St.
Kankakee, Illinois 60901

Kendall County Clerk
110 W. Fox St.
Yorkville, Illinois 60560

Knox County Clerk
200 S. Cherry St.
Galesburg, Illinois
61401-4912

Lake County Clerk
18 N. County St., Rm. 101
Waukegan, Illinois
60085-4364

Lasalle County Clerk
707 E. Etna Rd County
Gov. Ctr.
Ottawa, Illinois
61350-1033

Lawrence County Clerk
County Courthouse
Lawrenceville, Illinois
62439

Lee County Clerk
P.O. Box 329
Dixon, Illinois 61021

Livingston County Clerk
112 W. Madison St.
Pontiac, Illinois 61764

Logan County Clerk
601 Broadway St.
Lincoln, Illinois 62656

Macon County Clerk
141 S. Main
Decatur, Illinois 62523

Macoupin County Clerk
County Courthouse
Carlinville, Illinois 62626

Madison County Clerk
155 N. Main St.
Edwardsville, Illinois
62025

Marion County Clerk
P.O. Box 637
Salem, Illinois 62881-0637

Marshall County Clerk
122 N. Prairie St.
Lacon, Illinois 61540-1216

Mason County Clerk
County Courthouse
100 N. Broadway
Havana, Illinois
62644-0090

Massac County Clerk
P.O. Box 429
Metropolis, Illinois
62960-0429

**McDonough
County Clerk**
County Courthouse
Macomb, Illinois 61455

McHenry County Clerk
2200 N. Seminary Ave.
Woodstock, Illinois 60098

McLean County Clerk
Court House, Rm. 102
Bloomington, Illinois
61702

Menard County Clerk
P.O. Box 456
Petersburg, Illinois 62675

Mercer County Clerk
100 SE 3rd St.
Aledo, Illinois 61231

Monroe County Clerk
Courthouse 100 S. Main St.
Waterloo, Illinois 62298

**Montgomery
County Clerk**
1 Courthouse Square
Hillsboro, Illinois 62049

Morgan County Clerk
300 W. State St.
Jacksonville, Illinois
62650-2061

Moultrie County Clerk
Courthouse
Sullivan, Illinois 61951

Ogle County Clerk
P.O. Box 357
Oregon, Illinois
61061-0357

Peoria County Clerk
324 Main St.
Peoria, Illinois 61602

Perry County Clerk
P.O. Box 438
Pinckneyville, Illinois
62274

Piatt County Clerk
101 W. Washington St.
Monticello, Illinois 61856

Pike County Clerk
Route 36
Pittsfield, Illinois 62363

Pope County Clerk
Courthouse
Golconda, Illinois 62938

Pulaski County Clerk
P.O. Box 218
Mound City, Illinois
62963-0218

Putnam County Clerk
Courthouse
Hennepin, Illinois 61327

Randolph County Clerk
Courthouse
Chester, Illinois 62233

Richland County Clerk
103 W. Main St.
Olney, Illinois 62450

**Rock Island
County Clerk**
1504 3rd Ave.
Rock Island, Illinois 61201

Saline County Clerk
Courthouse
Harrisburg, Illinois 62946

Sangamon County Clerk
200 S. 9th St., Rm. 101
Springfield, Illinois 62701

Schuyler County Clerk
Courthouse
Rushville, Illinois 62681

Scott County Clerk
Courthouse
Winchester, Illinois 62694

Shelby County Clerk
324 E. Main St.
Shelbyville, Illinois 62565

St. Clair County Clerk
10 Public Square
Belleville, Illinois
62220-1623

Stark County Clerk
130 W. Main St.
Toulon, Illinois 61483

Stephenson County Clerk
15 N. Galena Ave.
Freeport, Illinois
61032-4348

Tazewell County Clerk
4th and Court St.
Pekin, Illinois 61554

Union County Clerk
311 W. Market St.
Jonesboro, Illinois 62952

Vermilion County Clerk
6 N. Vermilion St.
Danville, Illinois
61832-5842

Wabash County Clerk
4th and Market St.
Mt. Carmel, Illinois 62863

Warren County Clerk
Courthouse
Monmouth, Illinois 61462

**Washington
County Clerk**
Courthouse
Nashville, Illinois 62263

Wayne County Clerk
300 E. Main St.
Fairfield, Illinois
62837-0187

White County Clerk
Courthouse
Carmi, Illinois 62821

Whiteside County Clerk
200 E. Knox St.
Morrison, Illinois 61270

Will County Clerk
302 N. Chicago St.
Joliet, Illinois 60432

Williamson County Clerk
200 W. Jefferson St.
Marion, Illinois
62959-3061

Winnebago County Clerk
404 Elm St., Rm. 103
Rockford, Illinois 61101

Woodford County Clerk
P.O. Box 38
Eureka, Illinois 61530

INDIANA

http://www.state.in.us/

Adams County Clerk
Adams County Service
Complex
313 W. Jefferson St,
Rm. 314
Decatur, Indiana 46733

Allen County Clerk
One E..Main St.
Ft. Wayne, Indiana
46802-1804

**Bartholomew
County Clerk**
440 Third St., Suite 303
Columbus, Indiana
47201-6798

Benton County Clerk
700 E. 5th St., Suite 15
Fowler, Indiana
47944-1556

Blackford County Clerk
100 N. Jefferson
Hartford City, Indiana
47348

Boone County Clerk
416 W. Camp St.
Lebanon, Indiana
46052-2161

Brown County Clerk
P.O. Box 281
Nashville, Indiana 47448

Carroll County Clerk
Courthouse, 101 W. Main
Delphi, Indiana 46923

Cass County Clerk
200 Court Park, Gov. Bldg
Logansport, Indiana 46947

Clark County Clerk
1216 Akers Ave.
Jeffersonville, Indiana
47130

Clay County Clerk
Courthouse, 609 E.
National Ave.
Brazil, Indiana 47834

Clinton County Clerk
211 N. Jackson St.
Frankfort, Indiana 46041

Crawford County Clerk
306 Oak Hill Circle
English, Indiana 47118

Daviess County Clerk
Courthouse, 200 E. Walnut
Washington, Indiana 47501

Dearborn County Clerk
215-B W. High St.
Lawrenceburg, Indiana
47025

Decatur County Clerk
801 N. Lincoln
Greensburg, Indiana 47240

Dekalb County Clerk
215 E. 9th, Suite 201
Auburn, Indiana 46706

Delaware County Clerk
100 W. Main St.
Muncie, Indiana 47305

Dubois County Clerk
602 Main St.
Jasper, Indiana 47546

Elkhart County Clerk
608 Oakland Ave.
Elkhart, Indiana 46516

Fayette County Clerk
111 W. 4th St.
Connersville, Indiana
47331

Floyd County Clerk
1917 Bono Rd.
New Albany, Indiana
47150

Fountain County Clerk
210 S. Perry St.
Attica, Indiana 47918

Franklin County Clerk
459 Main St.
Brookville, Indiana 47012

Fulton County Clerk
1009 W. 3rd St.
Rochester, Indiana
46975-1546

Gibson County Clerk
Courthouse Annex
800 S. Prince St.
Princeton, Indiana 47670

Grant County Clerk
401 S. Adams St.
Marion, Indiana 46953

Greene County Clerk
Courthouse
Bloomfield, Indiana 47424

Hamilton County Clerk
One Hamilton County Sq.,
Suite 30
Noblesville, Indiana 46060

Hancock County Clerk
9 E. Main St., Rm. 105
Greenfield, Indiana 46140

Harrison County Clerk
245 Atwood St.,
North Wing.
Corydon, Indiana
47112-1333

Hendricks County Clerk
County Gov. Center
355 S. Washington St.
Danville, Indiana 46122

Henry County Clerk
208 S. 12th St.
New Castle, Indiana 47362

Howard County Clerk
120 Fast Mulberry,
Rm. 206
Kokomo, Indiana 46901

Huntington County Clerk
Courthouse, Rm. 205
Huntington, Indiana 46750

Jackson County Clerk
207 N. Pine St.
Seymour, Indiana 47220

Jasper County Clerk
105 W. Kellner Blvd.
Rensselaer, Indiana
47978-2888

Jay County Clerk
120 N. Court St.
Portland, Indiana 47371

Jefferson County Clerk
715 Green Rd.
Madison, Indiana 47250

Jennings County Clerk
P.O. Box 323
Vernon, Indiana 47282

Johnson County Clerk
86 W. Court St.
Franklin, Indiana 46131

Knox County Clerk
624 Broadway St.
Vincennes, Indiana
47591-5338

Kosciusko County Clerk
100 W. Center St.
Warsaw, Indiana
46580-2846

La Grange County Clerk
114 W. Michigan St.
LaGrange, Indiana 46761

La Porte County Clerk
809 State St.
La Porte, Indiana 46350

Lake County Clerk
2293 N. Main St.
Crown Point, Indiana
46307

Lawrence County Clerk
2419 Mitchell Rd.
Bedford, Indiana 47421

Madison County Clerk
206 E. 9th St.
Anderson, Indiana
46016-1538

Marion County Clerk
3838 N. Rural St.
Indianapolis, Indiana
46205

Marshall County Clerk
112 W. Jefferson St.,
Rm. 103
Plymouth, Indiana 46563

Martin County Clerk
P.O. Box 716
Shoals, Indiana 47581

Miami County Clerk
Courthouse, Rm. 110
Peru, Indiana 46970-2231

Monroe County Clerk
119 W. 7th St.
Bloomington, Indiana
47402-0547

**Montgomery
County Clerk**
307 Binford St. - Basement
Crawfordsville, Indiana
47933

Morgan County Clerk
180 S. Main St., Suite 252
Martinsville, Indiana 46151

Newton County Clerk
210 E. State St.
Morocco, Indiana 47963

Noble County Clerk
2090 N. State Rd. 9,
Suite C
Albion, Indiana
46701-1049

Ohio County Clerk
515 Second St.
Rising Sun, Indiana 47040

Orange County Clerk
205 E. Main St.
Paoli, Indiana 47454

Owen County Clerk
Courthouse, First Fl.
Spencer, Indiana 47460

Parke County Clerk
116 W. High St., Rm. 10
Rockville, Indiana 47872

Perry County Clerk
Courthouse Annex
Cannelton, Indiana
47520-1251

Pike County Clerk
801 Main St.
Petersburg, Indiana 47567

Porter County Clerk
155 Indiana Ave., Suite 104
Valparaiso, Indiana 46383

Posey County Clerk
126 E. 3rd St.
Mt.Vernon, Indiana 47620

Pulaski County Clerk
125 S. Riverside Dr.,
Suite 205
Winamac, Indiana 46996

Putnam County Clerk
Courthouse, 4th Fl.
Greencastle, Indiana 46135

Randolph County Clerk
211 S. Main St.
Winchester, Indiana 47394

Ripley County Clerk
107 N. Washington St.
Versailles, Indiana
47042-0177

Rush County Clerk
Courthouse, Rm. 5
Rushville, Indiana 46173

Scott County Clerk
1471 N. Gardner St.
Scottsburg, Indiana 47170

Shelby County Clerk
53 W. Polk St.
Shelbyville, Indiana 46176

Spencer County Clerk
Courthouse, 3rd Fl., Rm. 1
Rockport, Indiana
47635-0012

St. Joseph County Clerk
227 W. Jefferson Blvd.
South Bend, Indiana 46601

Starke County Clerk
Courthouse, 1st Fl.
Main St.
Knox, Indiana 46534

Steuben County Clerk
55 S. Public Square
Angola, Indiana 46703

Sullivan County Clerk
102 N. Section St.
Sullivan, Indiana 47882

**Switzerland
County Clerk**
211 E. Main St.
Vevay, Indiana 47043

Tippecanoe County Clerk
20 N. 3rd St.
Lafayette, Indiana
47901-1211

Tipton County Clerk
1000 S. Main St.
Tipton, Indiana 46072

Union County Clerk
26 W. Union St.
Liberty, Indiana
47353-1350

**Vanderburgh
County Clerk**
One NW Martin Luther
King Blvd
Admin. Bldg., Rm. 127
Evansville, Indiana
47708-1888

Vermillion County Clerk
825 S. Main St.
Newport, Indiana 47966

Vigo County Clerk
201 Cherry St.
Terre Haute, Indiana
47807-2986

Wabash County Clerk
Memorial Hall
89 West Hill St.
Wabash, Indiana
46992-2015

Warren County Clerk
210 S. Perry St.
Attica, Indiana 47918

**Warrick
County Clerk**
215 S. First St.
Boonville, Indiana 47601

**Washington
County Clerk**
35 Public Square
Salem, Indiana 47167

Wayne County Clerk
Admin. Bldg.
401 E. Main St.
Richmond, Indiana
47375-1172

Wells County Clerk
223 W. Washington St.
Bluffton, Indiana 46714

White County Clerk
P.O. Box 838
Monticello, Indiana 47960

Whitley County Clerk
101 W. Market, Suite A
Columbia City, Indiana
46725-2402

IOWA

http://www.state.ia.us/

Adair County Clerk
P.O. Box L
Greenfield, Iowa
50849-1290

Adams County Clerk
Davis and 9th
Corning, Iowa 50841

Allamakee County Clerk
P.O. Box 248
Waukon, Iowa 52172-0248

Appanoose County Clerk
County Courthouse
Centerville, Iowa 52544

Audubon County Clerk
County Courthouse
Audubon, Iowa 50025

Benton County Clerk
100 E. 4th St.
Vinton, Iowa 52349

**Black Hawk
County Clerk**
316 E. 5th St.
Waterloo, Iowa
50703-4712

Boone County Clerk
County Courthouse
Boone, Iowa 50036

Bremer County Clerk
415 E. Bremer Ave.
Waverly, Iowa 50677

Buchanan County Clerk
210 5th Ave. Nebraska
Independence, Iowa 50644

**Buena Vista
County Clerk**
P.O. Box 1186
Storm Lake, Iowa
50588-1186

Butler County Clerk
P.O. Box 325
Allison, Iowa 50602-0307

Calhoun County Clerk
P.O. Box 273
Rockwell City, Iowa 50579

Carroll County Clerk
P.O. Box 867
Carroll, Iowa 51401-0867

Cass County Clerk
7th St. Courthouse
Atlantic, Iowa 50022

Cedar County Clerk
400 Cedar St.
Tipton, Iowa 52772-1752

**Cerro Gordon County
Clerk**
220 N. Washington Ave.
Mason City, Iowa
50401-3254

Cherokee County Clerk
P.O. Box F
Cherokee, Iowa 51012

Chickasaw County Clerk
Prospect St.
New Hampton, Iowa 50659

Clarke County Clerk
117½ S. Main St.
Osceola, Iowa 50213-1299

Clay County Clerk
215 W. 4th St.
Spencer, Iowa 51301-0604

Clayton County Clerk
111 High St.
Elkader, Iowa 52043

Clinton County Clerk
P.O. Box 157
Clinton, Iowa 52732-0157

Crawford County Clerk
P.O. Box 546
Denison, Iowa 51442-0546

Dallas County Clerk
801 Court St.
Adel, Iowa 50003-1447

Davis County Clerk
Courthouse Square
Bloomfield, Iowa
52537-1600

Decatur County Clerk
207 N. Main St.
Leon, Iowa 50144-1647

Delaware County Clerk
P.O. Box 527
Manchester, Iowa
52057-0527

Des Moines County Clerk
513 N. Main St.
Burlington, Iowa
52601-5221

Dickinson County Clerk
18th and Hill County
Courthouse
Spirit Lake, Iowa 51360

Dubuque County Clerk
720 Central Ave.
Dubuque, Iowa
52001-7079

Emmet County Clerk
609 1st Ave. N.
Estherville, Iowa 51334

Fayette County Clerk
Vine St.
West Union, Iowa 52175

Floyd County Clerk
101 S. Main St.
Charles City, Iowa
50616-2756

Franklin County Clerk
12 First Ave. NW
Hampton, Iowa
50441-0026

Fremont County Clerk
Courthouse Square
Sidney, Iowa 51652-0549

Greene County Clerk
County Courthouse
Jefferson, Iowa
50129-2294

Grundy County Clerk
700 G Ave.
Grundy Center, Iowa
50638-1440

Guthrie County Clerk
200 N. 5th St.
Guthrie Center, Iowa
50115-1331

Hamilton County Clerk
County Courthouse
Webster City, Iowa
50595-3158

Hancock County Clerk
855 State St.
Garner, Iowa 50438

Hardin County Clerk
Edgington Ave.
Eldora, Iowa 50627-1741

Harrison County Clerk
113 N. 2nd Ave.
Logan, Iowa 51546-1331

Henry County Clerk
100 E. Washington St.
Mt. Pleasant, Iowa
52641-1931

Howard County Clerk
218 N. Elm St.
Cresco, Iowa 52136-1522

Humboldt County Clerk
County Courthouse
Dakota City, Iowa
50529-9999

Ida County Clerk
401 Moorehead St.
Ida Grove, Iowa
51445-1429

Iowa County Clerk
Court Ave.
Marengo, Iowa 52301

Jackson County Clerk
201 W. Platt St.
Maquoketa, Iowa
52060-2243

Jasper County Clerk
100 1st St.
Newton, Iowa 50208-0666

Jefferson County Clerk
P.O. Box 984
Fairfield, Iowa 52556-0984

Johnson County Clerk
913 S. Dubuque St.
Iowa City, Iowa
52244-1350

Jones County Clerk
High St.
Anamosa, Iowa 52205

Keokuk County Clerk
Courthouse Square
Sigourney, Iowa
52591-1499

Kossuth County Clerk
114 W. State St.
Algona, Iowa 50511-2613

Lee County Clerk
P.O. Box 1443
Ft. Madison, Iowa
52627-1443

Linn County Clerk
50 3rd Ave. Bridge
Cedar Rapids, Iowa
52401-1704

Louisa County Clerk
117 S. Main St.
Wapello, Iowa 52653-1547

Lucas County Clerk
County Courthouse
Chariton, Iowa 50049

Lyon County Clerk
206 S. 2nd Ave.
Rock Rapids, Iowa
51246-1597

Madison County Clerk
P.O. Box 152
Winterset, Iowa
50273-0152

Mahaska County Clerk
P.O. Box 30
Oskaloosa, Iowa
52577-0030

Marion County Clerk
P.O. Box 497
Knoxville, Iowa
50138-0497

Marshall County Clerk
17 E. Main St.
Marshalltown, Iowa
50158-4906

Mills County Clerk
418 Sharp St.
Glenwood, Iowa
51534-1756

Mitchell County Clerk
County Courthouse
Osage, Iowa 50461

Monona County Clerk
610 Iowa Ave.
Onawa, Iowa 51040

Monroe County Clerk
County Courthouse
Albia, Iowa 52531

**Montgomery
County Clerk**
105 Coolbaugh St.
Red Oak, Iowa 51566

Muscatine County Clerk
P.O. Box 327
Muscatine, Iowa
52761-0327

O'Brien County Clerk
155 S. Hayes
Primghar, Iowa 51245

Osceola County Clerk
614 5th Ave.
Sibley, Iowa 51249-1704

Page County Clerk
112 E. Main St.
Clarinda, Iowa 51632-2197

Palo Alto County Clerk
11th and Broadway
Emmetsburg, Iowa 50536

Plymouth County Clerk
3rd Ave. and 2nd St. SE
Le Mars, Iowa 51031

Pocahontas County Clerk
Court Square County
Courthouse
Pocahontas, Iowa 50574

Polk County Clerk
500 Mulberry St., Rm. 304
Des Moines, Iowa
50309-4238

**Pottawattamie
County Clerk**
227 S. 6th St.
Council Bluffs, Iowa 51501

Poweshiek County Clerk
302 E. Main St.
Montezuma, Iowa 50171

Ringgold County Clerk
County Courthouse
Mt. Ayr, Iowa 50854

Sac County Clerk
P.O. Box 368
Sac City, Iowa 50583-0368

Scott County Clerk
416 W. 4th St.
Davenport, Iowa 52801

Shelby County Clerk
P.O. Box 431
Harlan, Iowa 51537-0431

Sioux County Clerk
210 Central Ave. SW
Orange City, Iowa
51041-1751

Story County Clerk
900 6th St.
Nevada, Iowa 50201-2004

Tama County Clerk
County Courthouse
Toledo, Iowa 52342-0306

Taylor County Clerk
County Courthouse
Bedford, Iowa 50833

Union County Clerk
300 N. Pine St.
Creston, Iowa 50801-2430

Van Buren County Clerk
P.O. Box 475
Keosauqua, Iowa
52565-0475

Wapello County Clerk
4th and Court St.
Ottumwa, Iowa
52501-2599

Warren County Clerk
P.O. Box 379
Indianola, Iowa
50125-0379

**Washington
County Clerk**
P.O. Box 391
Washington, Iowa 52353

Wayne County Clerk
P.O. Box 424
Corydon, Iowa 50060-0424

Webster County Clerk
703 Central Ave.
Ft. Dodge, Iowa 50501

Winnebago County Clerk
126 S. Clark St.
Forest City, Iowa
50436-1793

Winneshiek County Clerk
201 W. Main St.
Decorah, Iowa 52101

Woodbury County Clerk
101 Court St.
Sioux City, Iowa
51101-1909

Worth County Clerk
1000 Central Ave.
Northwood, Iowa
50459-1523

Wright County Clerk
P.O. Box 306
Clarion, Iowa 50525-0306

KANSAS

http://www.state.ks.us/

Allen County Clerk
1 North Washington St.
Iola, Kansas 66749-2841

Anderson County Clerk
100 E. 4th Ave.
Garnett, Kansas 66032

Atchison County Clerk
423 N. 5th St.
Atchison, Kansas 66002

Barber County Clerk
120 E. Washington Ave.
Medicine Lodge, Kansas
67104-1421

Barton County Clerk
P.O. Box 1089
Great Bend, Kansas 67530

Bourbon County Clerk
210 S. National Ave.
Fort Scott, Kansas 66701

Brown County Clerk
Courthouse Square
Hiawatha, Kansas 66434

Butler Country Clerk
200 W. Central Ave.
El Dorado, Kansas 67042

Chase County Clerk
P.O. Box 547
Cottonwood Falls, Kansas
66845

**Chautauqua County
Clerk**
215 N. Chautauqua St.
Sedan, Kansas 67361-1326

Cherokee County Clerk
300 E. Maple
Columbus, Kansas
66725-1806

Cheyenne County
P.O. Box 985
St. Francis, Kansas
67756-0985

Clark County Clerk
P.O. Box 886
Ashland, Kansas 67831

Clay County Clerk
P.O. Box 98
Clay Center, Kansas
67432-0098

Cloud County Clerk
811 Washington St.
Concordia, Kansas
66901-3415

Coffey County Clerk
6th and Neosho
Burlington, Kansas 66839

Comanche County Clerk
P.O. Box 397
Coldwater, Kansas
67029-0397

Cowley County Clerk
311 E. 9th Ave.
Winfield, Kansas 67156

Crawford County Clerk
County Courthouse
P.O. Box 249
Girard, Kansas 66743–249

Decatur County Clerk
120 E. Hall
Oberlin, Kansas 67749

Dickinson County Clerk
P.O. Box 248
Abilene, Kansas 67410

Doniphan County Clerk
Main St.
Troy, Kansas 66087

Douglas County Clerk
111 E. 11th St.
Lawrence, Kansas
66044-2912

Edwards County Clerk
312 Massachusetts Ave.
Kinsley, Kansas
67547-1059

Elk County Clerk
P.O. Box 606
Howard, Kansas 67349

Ellis County Clerk
1204 Fort St.
Hays, Kansas 67601-3831

Ellsworth County Clerk
P.O. Box 396
Ellsworth, Kansas
67439-0396

Finney County Clerk
P.O. Box M
Garden City, Kansas
67846-0450

Ford County Clerk
Central and Spruce St.
Dodge City, Kansas 67801

Franklin County Clerk
3rd and Main St.
Ottawa, Kansas 66067

Geary County Clerk
8th and Franklin
Junction City, Kansas
66441

Gove County Clerk
P.O. Box 128
Gove, Kansas 67736-0128

Graham County Clerk
410 N. Pomeroy St.
Hill City, Kansas
67642-1645

Grant County Clerk
108 S. Glenn St.
Ulysses, Kansas
67880-2551

Gray County Clerk
P.O. Box 487
Cimarron, Kansas 67835

Greeley County Clerk
P.O. Box 277
Tribune, Kansas
67879-0277

Greenwood County Clerk
311 N. Main St.
Eureka, Kansas
67045-0268

Hamilton County Clerk
N. Main St.
Syracuse, Kansas 67878

Harper County Clerk
County Courthouse
Anthony, Kansas 67003

Harvey County Clerk
P.O. Box 687
Newton, Kansas 67114

Haskell County Clerk
P.O. Box 518
Sublette, Kansas 67877

Hodgeman County Clerk
P.O. Box 247
Jetmore, Kansas 67854

Jackson County Clerk
Courthouse Square
Holton, Kansas 66436

Jefferson County Clerk
P.O. Box 321
Oskaloosa, Kansas
66066-0321

Jewell County Clerk
307 N. Commercial St.
Mankato, Kansas
66956-2025

Johnson County Clerk
111 South Cherry,
Suite 1200
Olathe, Kansas 66061

Kearny County Clerk
305 N. Main St.
Lakin, Kansas 67860

Kingman County Clerk
130 N. Spruce St.
Kingman, Kansas 67068

Kiowa County Clerk
211 E. Florida Ave.
Greensburg, Kansas
67054-2211

Labette County Clerk
P.O. Box 387
Oswego, Kansas 67356

Lane County Clerk
144 S. Lane
Dighton, Kansas
67839-0788

**Leavenworth
County Clerk**
601 S. Third St.,
Suite 3051
Leavenworth, Kansas
66048

Lincoln County Clerk
216 E. Lincoln Ave.
Lincoln, Kansas 67455

Linn County Clerk
P.O. Box B
Mound City, Kansas
66056-0601

Logan County Clerk
710 W. 2nd St.
Oakley, Kansas
67748-1251

Lyon County Clerk
402 Commercial St.
Emporia, Kansas
66801-4000

Marion County Clerk
Courthouse Square
P.O. Box 219
Marion, Kansas
66861-0219

Marshall County Clerk
1201 Broadway
Marysville, Kansas
66508-1844

McPherson County Clerk
Kansas and Maple St.
McPherson, Kansas
67460-0425

Meade County Clerk
200 N. Fowler St.
Meade, Kansas 67864-0278

Miami County Clerk
120 S. Pearl St.
Paola, Kansas 66071

Mitchell County Clerk
P.O. Box 190
Beloit, Kansas 67420

**Montgomery
County Clerk**
P.O. Box 446
Independence, Kansas
67301

Morris County Clerk
501 W. Main St.
Council Grove, Kansas
66846

Morton County Clerk
P.O. Box 1116
Elkhart, Kansas
67950-1116

Nemaha County Clerk
607 Nemaha St.
Seneca, Kansas 66538

Neosho County Clerk
P.O. Box 237
Erie, Kansas 66733

Ness County Clerk
202 W. Sycamore St.
Ness City, Kansas 67560

Norton County Clerk
Courthouse
Norton, Kansas 67654

Osage County Clerk
717 Topeka Ave.
Lyndon, Kansas 66451

Osborne County Clerk
W. Main St.
Osborne, Kansas 67473

Ottawa County Clerk
307 N. Concord St.
Minneapolis, Kansas 67467

Pawnee County Clerk
715 Broadway
Larned, Kansas
67550-3054

Phillips County Clerk
3rd and State St.
Phillipsburg, Kansas 67661

**Pottawatomie
County Clerk**
P.O. Box 187
Westmoreland, Kansas
66549

Pratt County Clerk
300 S. Ninnescah St.
Pratt, Kansas 67124

Rawlins County Clerk
607 Main St.
Atwood, Kansas
67730-1839

Reno County Clerk
206 W. 1st Ave.
Hutchinson, Kansas
67501-5245

Republic County Clerk
County Courthouse
Route 1
Belleville, Kansas
66935-9801

Rice County Clerk
101 W. Commercial St.
Lyons, Kansas 67554

Riley County Clerk
110 Courthouse Plaza
Manhattan, Kansas
66502-6018

Rooks County Clerk
115 N. Walnut St.
Stockton, Kansas
67669-1663

Rush County Clerk
715 Elm St.
LaCrosse, Kansas 67548

Russell County Clerk
P.O. Box 113
Russell, Kansas 67665

Saline County Clerk
300 W. Ash St.
Salina, Kansas 67401-2335

Scott County Clerk
303 Court St.
Scott City, Kansas
67871-1122

Sedgwick County Clerk
525 N. Main St.
Wichita, Kansas 67203

Seward County Clerk
415 N. Washington Ave.
Liberal, Kansas
67901-3462

Shawnee County Clerk
200 SE 7th St.
Topeka, Kansas
66603-3922

Sheridan County Clerk
P.O. Box 899
Hoxie, Kansas 67740-0899

Sherman County Clerk
813 Broadway
Goodland, Kansas 67735

Smith County Clerk
218 S. Grant St.
Smith Center, Kansas
66967-2708

Stafford County Clerk
209 N. Broadway St.
St. John, Kansas 67576

Stanton County Clerk
P.O. Box 190
Johnson, Kansas 67855

Stevens County Clerk
200 E. 6th St.
Hugoton, Kansas
67951-2652

Sumner County Clerk
500 N. Washington Ave.
Wellington, Kansas
67152-4064

Thomas County Clerk
300 N. Court St.
Colby, Kansas 67701-2439

Trego County Clerk
216 N. Main St.
Wakeeney, Kansas
67672-2102

Wabaunsee County Clerk
215 Kansas St.
Alma, Kansas 66401-9797

Wallace County Clerk
313 Main St.
Sharon Springs, Kansas
67758

Washington County Clerk
214 C St.
Washington, Kansas
66968-1928

Wichita County Clerk
P.O. Box 968
Leoti, Kansas 67861

Wilson County Clerk
615 Madison St.
Fredonia, Kansas 66736

Woodson County Clerk
105 W. Rutledge St.
Yates Center, Kansas 66783

Wyandotte County Clerk
710 N. 7th St.
Kansas City, Kansas
66101-3047

KENTUCKY

http://www.state.ky.us/

Adair County Clerk
425 Public Square
Columbia, Kentucky
42728-1451

Allen County Clerk
P.O. Box 336
Scottsville, Kentucky
42164-0036

Anderson County Clerk
151 S. Main St.
Lawrenceburg, Kentucky
40342-1175

Ballard County Clerk
P.O. Box 145
Wickliffe, Kentucky
42087-0145

Barren County Clerk
103 Courthouse Square
Glasgow, Kentucky
42141-2812

Bath County Clerk
Main St.
Owingsville, Kentucky
40360-0609

Bell County Clerk
P.O. Box 156
Pineville, Kentucky
40977-0156

Boone County Clerk
2950 E. Washington St.
Burlington, Kentucky
41005-0874

Bourbon County Clerk
P.O. Box 312
Paris, Kentucky
40361-0312

Boyd County Clerk
2800 Louisa St.
Catlettsburg, Kentucky
41129-1116

Boyle County Clerk
321 W. Main St., Rm. 123
Danville, Kentucky
40422-1848

Bracken County Clerk
Locus St.
Brooksville, Kentucky
41004-0147

Breathitt County Clerk
1127 Main St.
Jackson, Kentucky
41339-1194

**Breckenridge
County Clerk**
Courthouse Square
Hardinsburg, Kentucky
40143-0538

Bullitt County Clerk
149 N. Walnut St.
Shepherdsville, Kentucky
40165-0006

Butler County Clerk
Courthouse on Main St.
Morgantown, Kentucky
42261

Caldwell County Clerk
100 E. Market St., Rm. 3
Princeton, Kentucky
42445-1675

Calloway County Clerk
101 S. 5th St.
Murray, Kentucky
42071-2569

Campbell County Clerk
340 York St.
Newport, Kentucky 41071

Carlisle County Clerk
West Court St.
Bardwell, Kentucky 42023

Carroll County Clerk
County Courthouse
440 Main St.
Carrollton, Kentucky
41008-1064

Carter County Clerk
Courthouse, Rm. 232
Grayson, Kentucky 41143

Casey County Clerk
Courthouse Square
Liberty, Kentucky 42539

Christian County Clerk
511 S. Main St.
Hopkinsville, Kentucky
42240-2368

Clark County Clerk
34 S. Main St.
Winchester, Kentucky
40391

Clay County Clerk
316 Main St., Suite 143
Manchester, Kentucky
40962-0463

Clinton County Clerk
212 Washington
Albany, Kentucky 42602

Crittenden County Clerk
107 S. Main St.
Marion, Kentucky
42064-1507

**Cumberland
County Clerk**
P.O. Box 275
Burkesville, Kentucky
42717

Daviess County Clerk
212 St. Ann St., Rm. 105
Owensboro, Kentucky
42302-0389

Edmonson County Clerk
Main and Cross St.
Brownsville, Kentucky
42210

Elliott County Clerk
P.O. Box 225
Sandy Hook, Kentucky
41171-0710

Estill County Clerk
130 Main St.
Irvine, Kentucky 40336

Fayette County Clerk
162 W. Main St.
Lexington, Kentucky
40507

Fleming County Clerk
100 Court Square
Flemingsburg, Kentucky
41041

Floyd County Clerk
3rd Ave. Courthouse
Prestonsburg, Kentucky
41653

Franklin County Clerk
P.O. Box 338
Frankfort, Kentucky 40602

Fulton County Clerk
Moulton and Wellington St.
Hickman, Kentucky
42050-0126

Gallatin County Clerk
P.O. Box 616
Warsaw, Kentucky 41095

Garrard County Clerk
Public Square
Lancaster, Kentucky
40444-1057

Grant County Clerk
P.O. Box 469
Courthouse Basement
Williamstown, Kentucky
41097-0469

Graves County Clerk
902 W. Broadway
Mayfield, Kentucky
42066-2021

Grayson County Clerk
10 Public Square
Leitchfield, Kentucky
42754

Green County Clerk
203 W. Court St.
Greensburg, Kentucky
42743-1552

Greenup County Clerk
Courthouse, Rm. 204
Greenup, Kentucky 41144

Hancock County Clerk
County
Administration Bldg.
Hawesville, Kentucky
42348

Hardin County Clerk
14 Public Square
Elizabethtown, Kentucky
42701

Harlan County Clerk
205 Central St.
Harlan, Kentucky 40831

Harrison County Clerk
190 W. Pike St.
Cynthiana, Kentucky
40131

Hart County Clerk
Courthouse, Main St.
Munfordville, Kentucky
42765-0277

Henderson County
P.O. Box 374
Henderson, Kentucky
42420

Henry County Clerk
P.O. Box 615
New Castle, Kentucky
40050

Hickman County Clerk
110 E. Clay St.
Clinton, Kentucky 42031

Hopkins County Clerk
P.O. Box 737
Madisonville, Kentucky
42431

Jackson County Clerk
Courthouse, Rm. 108
McKee, Kentucky 40447

Jefferson County Clerk
527 W. Jefferson St.,
Rm 100
Louisville, Kentucky 40202

Jessamine County Clerk
101 Main St.
Nicholasville, Kentucky
40356

Johnson County Clerk
Courthouse on Court St.
Paintsville, Kentucky
41240

Kenton County
P.O. Box 1109
Covington, Kentucky
41012

Knott County Clerk
P.O. Box 446
Hindman, Kentucky 41822

Knox County Clerk
401 Court Square,
Suite 102
Barbourville, Kentucky
40906-0105

Larue County Clerk
County Courthouse
Hodgenville, Kentucky
42748

Laurel County Clerk
County Courthouse
London, Kentucky 40741

Lawrence County Clerk
122 S. Main Cross St.
Louisa, Kentucky 41230

Lee County Clerk
Courthouse, Rm. 11,
Main St.
Beattyville, Kentucky
41311

Leslie County Clerk
P.O. Box 916
Hyden, Kentucky 41749

Letcher County Clerk
P.O. Box 58
Whitesburg, Kentucky
41858

Lewis County Clerk
P.O. Box 129
Vanceburg, Kentucky
41179-0129

Lincoln County Clerk
102 E. Main St.
Stanford, Kentucky 40484

Livingston County Clerk
P.O. Box 400
Smithland, Kentucky
42081

Logan County Clerk
229 W. 3rd St.
Russellville, Kentucky
42276

Lyon County Clerk
P.O. Box 350
Eddyville, Kentucky
42038-0350

Madison County Clerk
101 W. Main St.
Richmond, Kentucky
40475

Magoffin County Clerk
P.O. Box 530
Salyersville, Kentucky
41465-0530

Marion County Clerk
120 W. Main St.
Lebanon, Kentucky 40033

Marshall County Clerk
1101 Main St.
Benton, Kentucky 42025

Martin County Clerk
P.O. Box 485
Inez, Kentucky 41224-0485

Mason County Clerk
P.O. Box 234
Maysville, Kentucky 41056

McCracken County Clerk
Washington and 7th St.
Paducha, Kentucky 42002

McCreary County Clerk
P.O. Box 699
Whitley City, Kentucky
42653

McLean County Clerk
210 Main St.
Calhoun, Kentucky 42327

Meade County Clerk
Fairway Dr.
Brandenburg, Kentucky
40108-0614

Menifee County Clerk
P.O. Box 123
Frenchburg, Kentucky
40322-0123

Mercer County Clerk
P.O. Box 426
Harrodsburg, Kentucky
40330

Metcalfe County Clerk
P.O. Box 850
Edmonton, Kentucky
42129

Monroe County Clerk
P.O. Box 188
Tompkinsville, Kentucky
42167

**Montgomery County
Clerk**
P.O. Box 414
Mt. Sterling, Kentucky
40353

Morgan County Clerk
505 Prestonsburg St.
West Liberty, Kentucky
41472

**Muhlenberg
County Clerk**
100 S. Main St.
Greenville, Kentucky
42345

Nelson County Clerk
311 E. Stephen Foster Ave.
Bardstown, Kentucky
40004-0312

Nicholas County Clerk
P.O. Box 227
Carlisle, Kentucky 40311

Ohio County Clerk
P.O. Box 85
Hartford, Kentucky 42347

Oldham County Clerk
100 W. Jefferson St.
La Grange, Kentucky
40031

Owen County Clerk
P.O. Box 338
Owenton, Kentucky 40359

Owsley County Clerk
154 Main St.
Booneville, Kentucky
41314

Pendleton County Clerk
P.O. Box 112
Falmouth, Kentucky 41040

Perry County Clerk
P.O. Box 150
Hazard, Kentucky
41701-0150

Pike County Clerk
320 Main St.
Pikeville, Kentucky 41501

Powell County Clerk
P.O. Box 548
Stanton, Kentucky 40380

Pulaski County Clerk
P.O. Box 724
Somerset, Kentucky
42501-0724

Robertson County Clerk
P.O. Box 75
Mt. Olivet, Kentucky
41064

Rockcastle County Clerk
Main St.
Mt. Vernon, Kentucky
40456-0365

Rowan County Clerk
672 E. Main St.
Morehead, Kentucky 40351

Russell County Clerk
P.O. Box 579
Jamestown, Kentucky
42629

Scott County Clerk
101 E. Main St.
Georgetown, Kentucky
40324

Shelby County Clerk
501 Main St.
Shelbyville, Kentucky
40066

Simpson County Clerk
103 W. Cedar
Franklin, Kentucky 42134

Spencer County Clerk
P.O. Box 544
Taylorsville, Kentucky
40071-0544

Taylor County Clerk
203 N. Court St., Suite 5
Campbellsville, Kentucky
42718

Todd County Clerk
P.O. Box 307
Elkton, Kentucky 42220

Trigg County Clerk
P.O. Box 1310
Cadiz, Kentucky 42211

Trimble County Clerk
P.O. Box 262
Bedford, Kentucky 40006

Union County Clerk
Main and Morgan Streets
Morganfield, Kentucky
42437

Warren County Clerk
429 E. 10th St.
Bowling Green, Kentucky
42101-2250

**Washington
County Clerk**
P.O. Box 446
Springfield, Kentucky
40069-0446

Wayne County Clerk
109 Main St.
Monticello, Kentucky
42633-0565

Webster County Clerk
25 Main St.
Dixon, Kentucky 42409

Whitley County Clerk
111 Main St.
Williamsburg, Kentucky
40769

Wolfe County Clerk
P.O. Box 400
Campton, Kentucky
41301-0400

Woodford County Clerk
County Courthouse
Main St.
Versailles, Kentucky 40383

LOUISIANA

http://www.state.la.us/

Acadia Parish Clerk
P.O. Box 1342
Crowley, Louisiana
70527-1342

Allen Parish Clerk
P.O. Box G
Oberlin, Louisiana
70655-2007

Ascension Parish Clerk
P.O. Box 192
Donaldsonville, Louisiana
70346

Assumption Parish Clerk
Martin Luther King Dr.
and Hwy 1
Napoleonville, Louisiana
70390

Avoyelles Parish Clerk
301 N. Main St.
Marksville, Louisiana
71351

Beauregard Parish Clerk
P.O. Box 310
De Ridder, Louisiana
70634-0310

Bienville Parish Clerk
300 Courthouse Square
Arcadia, Louisiana 71001

Bossier Parish Clerk
P.O. Box 369
Benton, Louisiana 71006

Caddo Parish Clerk
501 Texas St.
Shreveport, Louisiana
71101-5401

Calcasieu Parish Clerk
P.O. Box 1030
Lake Charles, Louisiana
70602-1030

Caldwell Parish Clerk
Courthouse
Columbia, Louisiana 71418

Cameron Parish Clerk
P.O. Box 549
Cameron, Louisiana
70631-0549

Catahoula Parish Clerk
P.O. Box 198
Harrisonburg, Louisiana
71340-0198

Claiborne Parish Clerk
Courthouse Square
Homer, Louisiana 71040

Concordia Parish Clerk
P.O. Box 790
Vidalia, Louisiana 71373

DeSoto Parish Clerk
P.O. Box 1206
Mansfield, Louisiana
71052

**East Baton Rouge
Parish Clerk**
222 St. Louis St.
Baton Rouge, Louisiana
70802-5817

East Carroll Parish Clerk
400 1st St.
Lake Providence, Louisiana
71254-2616

**East Feliciana
Parish Clerk**
P.O. Box 599
Clinton, Louisiana 70722

Evangeline Parish Clerk
Court St., 2nd Fl.
Ville Platte, Louisiana
70586

Franklin Parish Clerk
210 Main St.
Winnsboro, Louisiana
71295-2708

Grant Parish Clerk
Courthouse, Main St.
Colfax, Louisiana 71417

Iberia Parish Clerk
300 Iberia St.
New Iberia, Louisiana
70560

Iberville Parish Clerk
P.O. Box 423
Plaquemine, Louisiana
70765

Jackson Parish Clerk
500 E. Courthouse Ave.
Jonesboro, Louisiana
71251

Jefferson Parish Clerk
200 Derbigny St.
3rd Fl. Main Courthouse
Gretna, Louisiana
70054-0010

**Jefferson Davis
Parish Clerk**
P.O. Box 1409
Jennings, Louisiana 70546

Lafayette Parish Clerk
P.O. Box 4508
Lafayette, Louisiana
70502-4508

Lafourche Parish Clerk
209 Green St.
Thibodaux, Louisiana
70302

Lasalle Parish Clerk
P.O. Box 1372
Jena, Louisiana
71342-1372

Lincoln Parish Clerk
100 W. Texas Ave.
Ruston, Louisiana 71270

Livingston Parish Clerk
20180 Iowa St.
Livingston, Louisiana
70754

Madison Parish Clerk
100 N. City St.
Tallulah, Louisiana 71282

Morehouse Parish Clerk
125 E. Madison St.
Bastrop, Louisiana
71221-0509

**Natchitoches
Parish Clerk**
P.O. Box 799
Natchitoches, Louisiana
71458-0799

Orleans Parish Clerk
1300 Perdido St.
New Orleans, Louisiana
70112-2114

Ouachita Parish Clerk
300 St. John St.
Monroe, Louisiana
71201-7326

Plaquemines Parish Clerk
Courthouse
Pointe Ala Hache,
Louisiana 70082

**Pointe Coupee
Parish Clerk**
P.O. Box 86
New Roads, Louisiana
70760-0086

Rapides Parish Clerk
P.O. Box 952
Alexandria, Louisiana
71309-0952

Red River Parish Clerk
615 E. Carroll St.
Coushatta, Louisiana
71019-8731

Richland Parish Clerk
108 Courthouse Square
Rayville, Louisiana 71269

Sabine Parish Clerk
400 Court St.
Many, Louisiana 71449

St. Bernard Parish Clerk
8201 W. Judge Perez Dr.
Chalmette, Louisiana
70043-1611

St. Charles Parish Clerk
P.O. Box 302
Hahnville, Louisiana 70057

St. Helena Parish Clerk
Court Square
Greensburg, Louisiana
70441-0308

St. James Parish Clerk
P.O. Box 106
Convent, Louisiana 70723

**St. John The Baptist
Parish Clerk**
P.O. Box 38
Edgard, Louisiana 70049

St. Landry Parish Clerk
Court and Landry St.
Opelousas, Louisiana
70570

St. Martin Parish Clerk
County Courthouse
St. Martinville, Louisiana
70582-0009

St. Mary Parish Clerk
500 Main St.
Franklin, Louisiana 70538

**St. Tammany
Parish Clerk**
510 E. Boston
Covington, Louisiana
70433-2945

Tangipahoa Parish Clerk
P.O. Box 215
Amite, Louisiana 70422

Tensas Parish Clerk
Courthouse Square
St. Joseph, Louisiana
71366-0078

Terrebonne Parish Clerk
301 Goode St.
Houma, Louisiana
70360-1569

Union Parish Clerk
Main and Bayou St.
Farmerville, Louisiana
71241

Vermilion Parish Clerk
P.O. Box 790
Abbeville, Louisiana
70511-0790

Vernon Parish Clerk
201 S. 3rd St.
Leesville, Louisiana
71496-0040

Washington Parish Clerk
Washington and Main St.
Franklinton, Louisiana
70438-0607

Webster Parish Clerk
410 Main St.
Minden, Louisiana
71055-3325

**West Baton Rouge
Parish Clerk**
P.O. Box 107
Port Allen, Louisiana
70767

**West Carroll
Parish Clerk**
P.O. Box 630
Oak Grove, Louisiana
71263-0630

**West Feliciana
Parish Clerk**
Royal and Prosperity
St. Francisville, Louisiana
70775

Winn Parish Clerk
P.O. Box 951
Winnfield, Louisiana
71483-0951

MAINE

http://www.state.me.us/

**Androscoggin
County Clerk**
2 Turner St.
Auburn, Maine 04210-5953

Arooslook County Clerk
13 Hall St.
Fort Kent, Maine 04730

**Cumberland
County Clerk**
142 Federal St.
Portland, Maine 04101

Franklin County Clerk
38 Main St.
Farmington, Maine 04938

Hancock County Clerk
60 State St.
Ellsworth, Maine
04605-1926

Kennebec County Clerk
95 State St.
Augusta, Maine
04330-5611

Knox County Clerk
P.O. Box 885
Rockland, Maine
04841-0885

Lincoln County Clerk
High St. County
Courthouse
Wiscasset, Maine 04578

Oxford County Clerk
26 Western Ave.
South Paris, Maine
04281-1417

Penobscot County Clerk
97 Hammond St.
Bangor, Maine 04401

Piscataquis County Clerk
51 E. Main St.
Dover-Foxcroft, Maine
04426-1306

Sagadahoc County Clerk
752 High St.
Bath, Maine 04530-2436

Somerset County Clerk
County Courthouse
Skowhegan, Maine
04976-9801

Waldo County Clerk
73 Church St.
Belfast, Maine 04915-1705

**Washington
County Clerk**
P.O. Box 297
Machias, Maine
04654-0297

York County Clerk
Court St.
Alfred, Maine 04002

MARYLAND

http://www.state.md.us/

Allegany County Clerk
3 Pershing St.
Cumberland, Maryland
21502-3043

**Anne Arundel
County Clerk**
44 Calvert St.
Annapolis, Maryland
21401-1930

Baltimore County Clerk
401 Bosley Ave.
Towson, Maryland 21204

**Baltimore City
County Clerk**
6550 Reisterstown Plaza
Baltimore, Maryland
21202-3417

Calvert County Clerk
175 Main St.
Prince Frederick, Maryland
20678

Caroline County Clerk
P.O. Box 207
Denton, Maryland
21629-0207

Carroll County Clerk
225 N. Center St.
Westminster, Maryland
21157-5107

Cecil County Clerk
129 E. Main St., Rm. 108
Elkton, Maryland 21921

Charles County Clerk
P.O. Box B
La Plata, Maryland
20646-0167

Dorchester County Clerk
P.O. Box 26
Cambridge, Maryland
21613-0026

Frederick County Clerk
100 West Patrick St.
Frederick, Maryland 21701

Garrett County Clerk
203 S. Fourth St.
Oakland, Maryland
21550-1535

Harford County Clerk
20 West Courtland St.
Bel Air, Maryland
21014-3833

Howard County Clerk
3430 Courthouse Dr.
Ellicott City, Maryland
21043-4300

Kent County Clerk
Cross St.
Chestertown, Maryland
21620

**Montgomery
County Clerk**
101 Monroe St.
Rockville, Maryland
20850-2540

**Prince George's
County Clerk**
Administration Bldg.
Upper Marlboro, Maryland
20772-3050

**Queen Anne's
County Clerk**
107 N. Liberty St.
Centreville, Maryland
21617

Somerset County Clerk
P.O. Box 99
Princess Anne, Maryland
21853

St. Mary's County Clerk
P.O. Box 316 Peabody St.
Leonardtown, Maryland
20650

Talbot County Clerk
Courthouse
Easton, Maryland 21601

**Washington
County Clerk**
Summit Ave.
Hagerstown, Maryland
21740

Wicomico County Clerk
P.O. Box 198
Salisbury, Maryland 21801

Worcester County Clerk
Courthouse
Snow Hill, Maryland 21863

MASSACHUSETTS

http://www.state.ma.us/

Barnstable County Clerk
Rt. 6A
Barnstable, Massachusetts
02630

Berkshire County Clerk
44 Bank Row
Pittsfield, Massachusetts
01201-6202

Bristol County Clerk
11 Court St.
Taunton, Massachusetts
02780-3223

Dukes County Clerk
81 Main St.
Edgartown, Massachusetts
02539

Essex County Clerk
36 Federal St.
Salem, Massachusetts
01970

Franklin County Clerk
425 Main St.
Greenfield, Massachusetts
01301-3313

Hampden County Clerk
50 State St.
Springfield, Massachusetts
01103-2027

Hampshire County Clerk
33 King St.
Northampton,
Massachusetts 01060-3236

Middlesex County Clerk
208 Cambridge St.
Cambridge, Massachusetts
02141-1202

Nantucket County Clerk
16 Broad St.
Nantucket, Massachusetts
02554-3500

Norfolk County Clerk
649 High St.
Dedham, Massachusetts
02026-1831

Plymouth County Clerk
Russell St.
Plymouth, Massachusetts
02360

Suffolk County Clerk
1 Pemberton Square
Boston, Massachusetts
02108-1706

Worcester County Clerk
2 Main St.
Worcester, Massachusetts
01608-1116

MICHIGAN

http://www.state.mi.us/

Alcona County Clerk
106 Fifth St.
Harrisville, Michigan
48740-9789

Alger County Clerk
101 Court St.
Munising, Michigan
49862-1103

Allegan County Clerk
113 Chestnut St.
Allegan, Michigan
49010-1332

Alpena County Clerk
720 W. Chisholm St.
Alpena, Michigan
49707-2429

Antrim County Clerk
208 E. Cayuga St.
Bellaire, Michigan 49615

Arenac County Clerk
Courthouse
Standish, Michigan 48658

Baraga County Clerk
Courthouse
L'Anse, Michigan
49946-1085

Barry County Clerk
Courthouse
Hastings, Michigan 49058

Bay County Clerk
515 Center Ave.
Bay City, Michigan
48708-5941

Benzie County Clerk
Courthouse
Beulah, Michigan 49617

Berrien County Clerk
701 Main St.
Saint Joseph, Michigan
49085

Branch County Clerk
31 Division St.
Coldwater, Michigan 49036

Calhoun County Clerk
315 W. Green St.
Marshall, Michigan 49068

Cass County Clerk
120 N. Broadway
Cassopolis, Michigan
49031-1302

Charlevoix County Clerk
Courthouse
Charlevoix, Michigan
49720

Cheboygan County Clerk
P.O. Box 70
Cheboygan, Michigan
49721

Chippewa County Clerk
Courthouse
Sault Ste. Marie, Michigan
49783-2183

Clare County Clerk
P.O. Box 438
Harrison, Michigan
48625-0438

Clinton County Clerk
100 E. State St.
St. Johns, Michigan
48879-1571

Crawford County Clerk
200 W. Michigan Ave.
Grayling, Michigan
49738-1745

Delta County Clerk
310 Ludington St.
Escanaba, Michigan
49829-4057

Dickinson County Clerk
P.O. Box 609
Iron Mountain, Michigan
49801

Eaton County Clerk
1045 Independence Blvd
Charlotte, Michigan
48813-1033

Emmet County Clerk
200 Division St.
Petoskey, Michigan 49770

Genesee County Clerk
900 S. Saginaw St.
Flint, Michigan 48502

Gladwin County Clerk
401 W. Cedar
Gladwin, Michigan
48624-2023

Gogebic County Clerk
200 N. Moore St.
Bessemer, Michigan 49911

**Grand Traverse
County Clerk**
400 Boardman
Traverse City, Michigan
49684

Gratiot County Clerk
Courthouse
Ithaca, Michigan 48847

Hillsdale County Clerk
Courthouse
Hillsdale, Michigan 49242

Houghton County Clerk
401 E. Houghton Ave.
Houghton, Michigan
49931-2016

Huron County Clerk
250 E. Huron Ave.
Bad Axe, Michigan 48413

Ingham County Clerk
366 S. Jefferson St.
Mason, Michigan 48854

Ionia County Clerk
Courthouse
Ionia, Michigan 48846

Iosco County Clerk
P.O. Box 838
Tawas City, Michigan
48764-0838

Iron County Clerk
2 South 6th St.
Crystal Falls, Michigan
49920-1413

Isabella County Clerk
200 N. Main St.
Mt. Pleasant, Michigan
48858-2321

Jackson County Clerk
312 S. Jackson
Jackson, Michigan 49201

Kalamazoo County Clerk
201 W. Kalamazoo
Kalamazoo, Michigan
49007-3734

Kalkaska County Clerk
605 N. Birch
Kalkaska, Michigan
49646-9436

Kent County Clerk
300 Monroe, NW
Grand Rapids, Michigan
49503-2206

Keweenaw County Clerk
Courthouse
Eagle River, Michigan
49924

Lake County Clerk
P.O. Box B
Baldwin, Michigan
49304-0902

Lapeer County Clerk
Courthouse
Lapeer, Michigan 48446

Leelanau County Clerk
Courthouse
Leland, Michigan 49654

Lenawee County Clerk
425 N. Main St.
Adrian, Michigan 49221

Livingston County Clerk
200 E. Grand River
Howell, Michigan 48843

Luce County Clerk
East Court St.
Newberry, Michigan 49868

Mackinac County Clerk
100 Marley St.
St. Ignace, Michigan
49781-1457

Macomb County Clerk
40 N. Main
Mt. Clemens, Michigan
48043

Manistee County Clerk
415 Third St.
Manistee, Michigan
49660-1606

Marquette County Clerk
232 W. Baraga Ave.
Marquette, Michigan
49855-4710

Mason County Clerk
Courthouse
Ludington, Michigan
49431

Mecosta County Clerk
400 Elm St.
Big Rapids, Michigan
49307-1849

Menominee County Clerk
Courthouse
Menominee, Michigan
49858

Midland County Clerk
220 W. Ellsworth St.
Midland, Michigan 48640

Missaukee County Clerk
Courthouse
Lake City, Michigan 49651

Monroe County Clerk
106 E. First
Monroe, Michigan
48161-2143

Montcalm County Clerk
211 W. Main St.
Stanton, Michigan 48888

**Montmorency County
Clerk**
P.O. Box 415
Atlanta, Michigan 49709

Muskegon County Clerk
990 Terrace St.
Muskegon, Michigan
49442-3301

Newaygo County Clerk
1087 Newell St.
White Cloud, Michigan
49349

Oakland County Clerk
1200 N. Telegraph Rd.
Pontiac, Michigan
48053-1008

Oceana County Clerk
P.O. Box 153
Hart, Michigan 49420

Ogemaw County Clerk
Courthouse
West Branch, Michigan
48661

Ontonagon County Clerk
725 Greenland Rd.
Ontonagon, Michigan
49953-1423

Osceola County Clerk
301 W. Upton
Reed City, Michigan
49677-1149

Oscoda County Clerk
P.O. Box 399
Mio, Michigan 48647

Otsego County Clerk
225 W. Main St.
Gaylord, Michigan
49735-1348

Ottawa County Clerk
414 Washington St.
Grand Haven, Michigan
49417-1443

**Presque Isle
County Clerk**
151 E. Huron St.
Rogers City, Michigan
49779-1316

**Roscommon
County Clerk**
Courthouse
Roscommon, Michigan
48653

Saginaw County Clerk
111 S. Michigan
Saginaw, Michigan
48602-2019

Sanilac County Clerk
67 W. Sanilac Ave.
Sandusky, Michigan
48471-1060

Schoolcraft County Clerk
300 Walnut St.
Manistique, Michigan
49854-1414

Shiawassee County Clerk
Courthouse
Corunna, Michigan 48817

St. Clair County Clerk
201 McMorran Blvd.
Port Huron, Michigan
48060-4006

St. Joseph County Clerk
P.O. Box 189
Centreville, Michigan
49032-0189

Tuscola County Clerk
440 N. State St.
Caro, Michigan
48723-1555

Van Buren County Clerk
Courthouse
Paw Paw, Michigan
49079-1496

Washtenaw County Clerk
101 E. Huron St.
Ann Arbor, Michigan
48107-8645

Wayne County Clerk
728 City County Bldg.
Detroit, Michigan
48226-3413

Wexford County Clerk
Courthouse
Cadillac, Michigan 49601

MINNESOTA

http://www.state.mn.us/

Aitkin County Clerk
209 2nd St., NW
Aitkin, Minnesota 56431

Anoka County Clerk
325 E. Main St.
Anoka, Minnesota 55303

Becker County Clerk
915 Lake Ave.
Detroit Lakes, Minnesota
56502

Beltrami County Clerk
619 Beltrami Ave. NW
Bemidji, Minnesota 56601

Benton County Clerk
531 Dewey St.
Foley, Minnesota 56329

Big Stone County Clerk
20 SE 2nd St.
Ortonville, Minnesota
56278

Blue Earth County Clerk
P.O. Box 3524
Mankato, Minnesota
56001-4585

Brown County Clerk
P.O. Box 248
New Ulm, Minnesota
56073

Carlton County Clerk
301 Walnut
Carlton, Minnesota 55718

Carver County Clerk
600 E. 4th St.
Chaska, Minnesota 55318

Cass County Clerk
P.O. Box 3000
Walker, Minnesota 56484

Chippewa County Clerk
629 N. 11th St.
Montevideo, Minnesota
56265

Chisago County Clerk
313 N. Main St.
Center City, Minnesota
55012

Clay County Clerk
807 11th St. N.
Moorhead, Minnesota
56561

Clearwater County Clerk
213 Main Ave. N.
Bagley, Minnesota 56621

Cook County Clerk
P.O. Box 1150
Grand Marais, Minnesota
55604

**Cottonwood
County Clerk**
900 Third Ave.
Windom, Minnesota 56101

Crow Wing County Clerk
326 Laurel St.
Brainerd, Minnesota 56401

Dakota County Clerk
1590 W. Highway 55
Hastings, Minnesota 55033

Dodge County Clerk
22 E. Sixth St.
Mantorville, Minnesota
55955

Douglas County Clerk
305 Eighth Ave. W.
Alexandria, Minnesota
56308

Faribault County Clerk
P.O. Box 130
Blue Earth, Minnesota
56013

Fillmore County Clerk
101 Fillmore St.
Preston, Minnesota 55965

Freeborn County Clerk
411 S. Broadway
Albert Lea, Minnesota
56007

Goodhue County Clerk
509 W. Fifth St.
Red Wing, Minnesota
55066

Grant County Clerk
10 Second St. NE
Elbow Lake, Minnesota
56531

Hennepin County Clerk
300 S. Sixth St., 2nd Fl.
Minneapolis, Minnesota
55487-0999

Houston County Clerk
P.O. Box 29
Caledonia, Minnesota
55921

Hubbard County Clerk
Courthouse
Park Rapids, Minnesota
56470

Isanti County Clerk
555 18th Ave. SW
Cambridge, Minnesota
55008

Itasca County Clerk
123 Fourth St. NE
Grand Rapids, Minnesota
55744

Jackson County Clerk
P.O. Box 209
Jackson, Minnesota 56143

Kanabec County Clerk
18 N. Vine
Mora, Minnesota 55051

Kandiyohi County Clerk
400 SW Benson Ave. SW
Willmar, Minnesota 56201

Kittson County Clerk
410 S. Fifth St.
Hallock, Minnesota 56728

**Koochiching
County Clerk**
715 Fourth St.
International Falls,
Minnesota 56649

**Lac qui Parle
County Clerk**
P.O. Box 132
Madison, Minnesota 56256

Lake County Clerk
601 Third Ave.
Two Harbors, Minnesota
55616

**Lake of the Woods
County Clerk**
206 SE Eighth Ave.
Baudette, Minnesota 56623

Le Sueur County Clerk
88 S. Park Ave.
Le Center, Minnesota
56057

Lincoln County Clerk
319 N. Rebecca St.
Ivanhoe, Minnesota 56142

Lyon County Clerk
607 W. Main
Marshall, Minnesota 56258

Mahnomen County Clerk
County Courthouse
Mahnomen, Minnesota
56557

Marshall County Clerk
208 E. Colvin Ave.
Warren, Minnesota 56762

Martin County Clerk
201 Lake Ave.
Fairmont, Minnesota 56031

McLeod County Clerk
P.O. Box 127
Glencoe, Minnesota 55336

Meeker County Clerk
325 N. Sibley Ave.
Litchfield, Minnesota
55355

Mille Lacs County Clerk
635 2nd St. SE
Milaca, Minnesota 56353

Morrison County Clerk
213 First Ave. SE
Little Falls, Minnesota
56345

Mower County Clerk
201 First St. NE
Austin, Minnesota 55912

Murray County Clerk
2500 28th St.
Slayton, Minnesota 56172

Nicollet County Clerk
501 S. Minnesota Ave.
St. Peter, Minnesota 56082

Nobles County Clerk
P.O. Box 757
Worthington, Minnesota
56187

Norman County Clerk
16 E. Third Ave.
Ada, Minnesota 56510

Olmsted County Clerk
151 Fourth St. SE
Rochester, Minnesota
55904

Otter Tail County Clerk
P.O. Box 867
Fergus Falls, Minnesota
56538

Pennington County Clerk
P.O. Box 616
Thief River Falls,
Minnesota 56701

Pine County Clerk
315 Sixth St., Suite 3
Pine City, Minnesota 55063

Pipestone County Clerk
416 S. Hiawatha
Pipestone, Minnesota
56164

Polk County Clerk
P.O. Box 397
Crookston, Minnesota
56716-0397

Pope County Clerk
130 E. Minnesota Ave.
Glenwood, Minnesota
56334

Ramsey County Clerk
555 Cedar St.
St. Paul, Minnesota 55101

Red Lake County Clerk
124 N. Main St.
Red Lake Falls, Minnesota
56750

Redwood County Clerk
P.O. Box 130
Redwood Falls, Minnesota
56283

Renville County Clerk
500 E. DePue
Olivia, Minnesota 56277

Rice County Clerk
320 NW Third St., Suite 10
Faribault, Minnesota 55021

Rock County Clerk
204 E. Brown
Luverne, Minnesota 56156

Roseau County Clerk
606 Fifth Ave. SW, Rm. 20
Roseau, Minnesota 56751

Scott County Clerk
428 S. Holmes St.
Shakopee, Minnesota
55379

Sherburne County Clerk
13880 Highway 10
Elk River, Minnesota
55330

Sibley County Clerk
400 Court Ave.
Gaylord, Minnesota 55334

St. Louis County Clerk
100 N. Fifth Ave. W
Duluth, Minnesota 55801

Stearns County Clerk
705 Courthouse Square,
Rm. 125
St. Cloud, Minnesota
56303

Steele County Clerk
111 E. Main St.
Owatonna, Minnesota
55060

Stevens County Clerk
P.O. Box 530
Morris, Minnesota 56267

Swift County Clerk
301 14th St. N
Benson, Minnesota 56215

Todd County Clerk
215 First Ave. S
Long Prairie, Minnesota
56347

Traverse County Clerk
702 Second Ave. N
Wheaton, Minnesota
56296-0428

Wabasha County Clerk
625 Jefferson Ave.
Wabasha, Minnesota 55981

Wadena County Clerk
P.O. Box 415
Wadena, Minnesota 56482

Waseca County Clerk
307 N. State St.
Waseca, Minnesota 56093

**Washington
County Clerk**
1520 W. Frontage Rd.
Stillwater, Minnesota
55082

Watonwan County Clerk
P.O. Box 518
St. James, Minnesota
56081

Wilkin County Clerk
300 S. Fifth St.
Breckenridge, Minnesota
56520

Winona County Clerk
74 W. Third St.
Winona, Minnesota 55987

Wright County Clerk
10 NW Second St., Rm. 160
Buffalo, Minnesota
55313-1165

**Yellow Medicine
County Clerk**
415 Ninth Ave.
Granite Falls, Minnesota
56241

MISSISSIPPI

http://www.state.ms.us/
Adams County Clerk
115 S. Wall St.
Natchez, Mississippi 39120

Alcorn County Clerk
P.O. Box 112
Corinth, Mississippi 38834

Amite County Clerk
243 W. Main St.
Liberty, Mississippi 39645

Attala County Clerk
230 W. Washington St.
Kosciusko, Mississippi
39090

Benton County Clerk
P.O. Box 218
Ashland, Mississippi
38603-0218

Bolivar County Clerk
200 N. Court St.
Cleveland, Mississippi
38732

Calhoun County Clerk
P.O. Box 8
Pittsboro, Mississippi
38951-0008

Carroll County Clerk
Lexington St.
Carrollton, Mississippi
38917-0291

Chicasaw County Clerk
101 N. Jefferson
Houston, Mississippi 38851

Choctaw County Clerk
112 Quinn St.
Ackerman, Mississippi
39735-0250

Claiborne County Clerk
410 Main St.
Port Gibson, Mississippi
39150

Clark County Clerk
101 S. Archusa Ave.
Quitman, Mississippi
39355

Clay County Clerk
205 Court St.
West Point, Mississippi
39773-0815

Coahoma County Clerk
P.O. Box 98
Clarksdale, Mississippi
38614-0098

Copiah County Clerk
100 Caldwell Dr.
Hazlehurst, Mississippi
39083

Covington County Clerk
101 S. Elm Ave.
Collins, Mississippi 39428

DeSoto County Clerk
Courthouse
Hernando, Mississippi
38632

Forrest County Clerk
641 N. Main St.
Hattiesburg, Mississippi
39403-0951

Franklin County Clerk
Main St. Meadville,
Mississippi 39653

George County Clerk
320 Cox St.
Lucedale, Mississippi
39452

Greene County Clerk
Main St.
Leakesville, Mississippi
39451-0610

Grenada County Clerk
59 Green St.
Grenada, Mississippi
38901-1208

Hancock County Clerk
152 Main St.
Bay St. Louis, Mississippi
39520

Harrison County Clerk
Courthouse
Gulfport, Mississippi
39502

Hinds County Clerk
P.O. Box 686
Jackson, Mississippi
39205-0686

Holmes County Clerk
P.O. Box 239
Lexington, Mississippi
39095-0239

Humphreys County Clerk
102 Castleman St.
Belzoni, Mississippi
39038-0547

Issaquena County Clerk
129 Court St.
Mayersville, Mississippi
39113

Itawamba County Clerk
P.O. Box 776
Fulton, Mississippi 38843

Jackson County Clerk
P.O. Box 998
Pascagoula, Mississippi
39567

Jasper County Clerk
Court St.
Bay Springs, Mississippi
39422

Jefferson County Clerk
307 S. Main St.
Fayette, Mississippi 39069

**Jefferson Davis
County Clerk**
1025 Third St.
Prentiss, Mississippi
39474-1137

Jones County Clerk
415 N. 5th Ave.
Laurel, Mississippi
39441-3968

Kemper County Clerk
Bell St.
De Kalb, Mississippi 39328

Lafayette County Clerk
Town Square
Oxford, Mississippi 38655

Lamar County Clerk
203 Main St.
Purvis, Mississippi 39475

Lauderdale County Clerk
500 Constitution Ave.
Meridian, Mississippi
39302

Lawrence County Clerk
517 E. Broad St.
Monticello, Mississippi
39654-0040

Leake County Clerk
P.O. Box 72
Carthage, Mississippi
39051-0072

Lee County Clerk
200 W. Jefferson St.
Tupelo, Mississippi 38802

Leflore County Clerk
317 W. Market St.
Greenwood, Mississippi
38930

Lincoln County Clerk
300 S. 2nd St.
Brookhaven, Mississippi
39601

Lowndes County Clerk
521 Second Ave. N
Columbus, Mississippi
39701

Madison County Clerk
146 W. Center St.
Canton, Mississippi 39046

Marion County Clerk
250 Broad St. #2
Columbia, Mississippi
39429

Marshall County Clerk
128 E. Van Dorn Ave.
Holly Springs, Mississippi
38635

Monroe County Clerk
201 W. Commerce St.
Aberdeen, Mississippi
39730

**Montgomery
County Clerk**
614 Summit St.
Winona, Mississippi 38967

Neshoba County Clerk
401 Beacon St. #107
Philadelphia, Mississippi
39350-0067

Newton County Clerk
92 W. Broad St.
Decatur, Mississippi 39327

Noxubee County Clerk
505 S. Jefferson St.
Macon, Mississippi 39341

Oktibbeha County Clerk
101 W. Main St.
Starkville, Mississippi
39759

Panola County Clerk
215 S. Pocahontas St.
Batesville, Mississippi
38666

Pearl River County Clerk
200 S. Main St.
Poplarville, Mississippi
39470

Perry County Clerk
Main St.
New Augusta, Mississippi
39462-0198

Pike County Clerk
200 E. Bay St.
Magnolia, Mississippi
39652

Pontotoc County Clerk
11 E. Washington St.
Pontotoc, Mississippi
38863-0209

Prentiss County Clerk
100 N. Main St.
Booneville, Mississippi
38829

Quitman County Clerk
23 Chestnut St.
Marks, Mississippi 38646

Rankin County Clerk
301 E. Government St.
Brandon, Mississippi
39042

Scott County Clerk
100 E. Main St.
Forest, Mississippi 39074

Sharkey County Clerk
400 Locust St.
Rolling Fork, Mississippi
39159-0218

Simpson County Clerk
109 W. Pine Ave.
Mendenhall, Mississippi
39114

Smith County Clerk
123 Main St.
Raleigh, Mississippi 39153

Stone County Clerk
P.O. Drawer 7
Wiggins, Mississippi 39577

Sunflower County Clerk
200 Main St.
Indianola, Mississippi
38751-0988

**Tallahatchie
County Clerk**
1 Court Square
Charleston, Mississippi
38921-0330

Tate County Clerk
201 Ward St.
Senatobia, Mississippi
38668-2616

Tippah County Clerk
Main St.
Ripley, Mississippi 38663

Tishomingo County Clerk
1008 Battleground Dr.
Iuka, Mississippi 38852

Tunica County Clerk
1300 School St. #104
Tunica, Mississippi 38676

Union County Clerk
109 Main St. E
New Albany, Mississippi
38652-0847

Walthall County Clerk
P.O. Box 351
Tylertown, Mississippi
39667-0351

Warren County Clerk
1009 Cherry St.
Vicksburg, Mississippi
39180

**Washington
County Clerk**
900 Washington Ave.
Greenville, Mississippi
38702

Wayne County Clerk
609 Azalea Dr.
Waynesboro, Mississippi
39367

Webster County Clerk
Highway 9N
Walthall, Mississippi 39771

Wilkinson County Clerk
P.O. Box 516
Woodville, Mississippi
39669-0516

Winston County Clerk
115 S. Court Ave.
Louisville, Mississippi
39339-0188

Yalobusha County Clerk
132 Blackmur Dr.
Water Valley, Mississippi
38965

Yazoo County Clerk
211 E. Broadway St.
Yazoo City, Mississippi
39194

MISSOURI

http://www.state.mo.us/

Adair County Clerk
Courthouse
Kirksville, Missouri 63501

Andrew County Clerk
Courthouse
Savannah, Missouri 64485

Atchison County Clerk
40 Washington St.
Rock Port, Missouri 64482

Audrain County Clerk
Courthouse
Mexico, Missouri 65265

Barry County Clerk
Courthouse
Cassville, Missouri 65625

Barton County Clerk
Courthouse
Lamar, Missouri 64759

Bates County Clerk
Courthouse
Butler, Missouri 64730

Benton County Clerk
P.O. Box 1238
Warsaw, Missouri
65355-1238

Bollinger County Clerk
Courthouse
Marble Hill, Missouri
63764

Boone County Clerk
600 E. Broadway
Columbia, Missouri 65201

Buchanan County Clerk
Fifth and Jules
St. Joseph, Missouri 64501

Butler County Clerk
P.O. Box 332
Poplar Bluff, Missouri
63901-0332

Caldwell County Clerk
P.O. Box 67
Kingston, Missouri
64650-0067

Callaway County Clerk
Courthouse
Fulton, Missouri 65251

Camden County Clerk
1 Court Circle
Camdenton, Missouri
65020

**Cape Girardeau
County Clerk**
1 Barton Square
Jackson, Missouri 63755

Carroll County Clerk
Courthouse
Carrollton, Missouri 64633

Carter County Clerk
P.O. Box 517
Van Buren, Missouri
63965-0517

Cass County Clerk
Courthouse
Harrisonville, Missouri
64701

Cedar County Clerk
P.O. Box 158
Stockton, Missouri 65785

Chariton County Clerk
Courthouse
Keytesville, Missouri
65261

Christian County Clerk
Courthouse
Ozark, Missouri 65721

Clark County Clerk
Courthouse
Kahoka, Missouri 63445

Clay County Clerk
P.O. Box 99
Liberty, Missouri 64068

Clinton County Clerk
P.O. Box 245
Plattsburg, Missouri
64477-0245

Cole County Clerk
301 E. High
Jefferson City, Missouri
65101-3208

Cooper County Clerk
P.O. Box 123
Boonville, Missouri
65233-0123

Crawford County Clerk
Courthouse
Steelville, Missouri 65565

Dade County Clerk
Courthouse
Greenfield, Missouri 65661

Dallas County Clerk
P.O. Box 436
Buffalo, Missouri
65622-0436

Daviess County Clerk
Courthouse, 102 N. Main
Gallatin, Missouri 64640

DeKalb County Clerk
P.O. Box 248
Maysville, Missouri
64469-0248

Dent County Clerk
Courthouse
Salem, Missouri
65560-1298

Douglas County Clerk
Courthouse
Ava, Missouri 65608

Dunklin County Clerk
P.O. Box 188
Kennett, Missouri 63857

Franklin County Clerk
P.O. Box 311
Union, Missouri
63084-0311

Gasconade County Clerk
P.O. Box 295
Hermann, Missouri
65041-0295

Gentry County Clerk
Courthouse
Albany, Missouri 64402

Greene County Clerk
940 Boonville
Springfield, Missouri
65802

Grundy County Clerk
700 Main St.
Trenton, Missouri
64683-2063

Harrison County Clerk
Courthouse
Bethany, Missouri 64424

Henry County Clerk
Courthouse
Clinton, Missouri 64735

Hickory County Clerk
Courthouse
Hermitage, Missouri 65668

Holt County Clerk
Courthouse
Oregon, Missouri 64473

Howard County Clerk
Courthouse
Fayette, Missouri 65248

Howell County Clerk
Courthouse
West Plains, Missouri
65775

Iron County Clerk
P.O. Box 42
Ironton, Missouri
63650-0042

Jackson County Clerk
Kansas City, Missouri
64106

Jasper County Clerk
Courthouse
Carthage, Missouri 64836

Jefferson County Clerk
P.O. Box 100
Hillsboro, Missouri
63050-0100

Johnson County Clerk
Courthouse
Warrensburg, Missouri
64093

Knox County Clerk
Courthouse
Edina, Missouri 63537

Laclede County Clerk
Second and Adam Streets
Lebanon, Missouri 65536

Lafayette County Clerk
P.O. Box 357
Lexington, Missouri
64067-0357

Lawrence County Clerk
Courthouse
Mt. Vernon, Missouri
65712

Lewis County Clerk
Courthouse
Monticello, Missouri 63457

Lincoln County Clerk
201 Main St.
Troy, Missouri 63379-1127

Linn County Clerk
Courthouse
Linneus, Missouri 64653

Livingston County Clerk
P.O. Box 803
Chillicothe, Missouri
64601

Macon County Clerk
P.O. Box 382
Macon, Missouri 63552

Madison County Clerk
Court Square
Fredericktown, Missouri
63645

Maries County Clerk
Courthouse
Vienna, Missouri 65582

Marion County Clerk
Courthouse
Palmyra, Missouri 63461

McDonald County Clerk
P.O. Box 665
Pineville, Missouri 64856

Mercer County Clerk
Courthouse
Princeton, Missouri 64673

Miller County Clerk
P.O. Box 12
Tuscumbia, Missouri
65082-0012

Mississippi County Clerk
P.O. Box 304
Charleston, Missouri
63834-0304

Moniteau County Clerk
Courthouse
California, Missouri 65018

Monroe County Clerk
300 N. Main St.
Paris, Missouri 65275-1399

**Montgomery
County Clerk**
211 E. Third
Montgomery City, Missouri
63361-1956

Morgan County Clerk
104 N. Fisher
Versailles, Missouri
65084-1202

**New Madrid
County Clerk**
P.O. Box 68
New Madrid, Missouri
63869

Newton County Clerk
Courthouse
Neosho, Missouri 64850

Nodaway County Clerk
Courthouse
Maryville, Missouri 64468

Oregon County Clerk
Courthouse
Alton, Missouri 65606

Osage County Clerk
P.O. Box 826
Linn, Missouri 65051

Ozark County Clerk
Courthouse
Gainesville, Missouri
65655

Pemiscot County Clerk
Ward Ave.
Caruthersville, Missouri
63830

Perry County Clerk
Courthouse
Perryville, Missouri 63775

Pettis County Clerk
415 S. Ohio
Sedalia, Missouri
65301-4435

Phelps County Clerk
Third and Rolla St.
Rolla, Missouri 65401

Pike County Clerk
115 W. Main
Bowling Green, Missouri
63334

Platte County Clerk
Courthouse
Platte City, Missouri 64079

Polk County Clerk
Courthouse
Bolivar, Missouri 65613

Pulaski County Clerk
Courthouse
Waynesville, Missouri
65583

Putnam County Clerk
Courthouse
Unionville, Missouri 63565

Ralls County Clerk
Courthouse
New London, Missouri
63459-0444

Randolph County Clerk
S. Main St.
Huntsville, Missouri 65259

Ray County Clerk
Courthouse
Richmond, Missouri 64085

Reynolds County Clerk
Courthouse Square
Centerville, Missouri
63633

Ripley County Clerk
Courthouse
Doniphan, Missouri 63935

Saline County Clerk
Courthouse
Marshall, Missouri 65340

Schuyler County Clerk
P.O. Box 187
Lancaster, Missouri
63548-0187

Scotland County Clerk
Courthouse
Memphis, Missouri 63555

Scott County Clerk
Courthouse
Benton, Missouri 63736

Shannon County Clerk
P.O. Box 187
Eminence, Missouri
65466-0187

Shelby County Clerk
P.O. Box 186
Shelbyville, Missouri
63469-0186

St. Charles County Clerk
Third and Jefferson
St. Charles, Missouri
63301

St. Clair County Clerk
P.O. Box 334
Osceola, Missouri 64776

**St. Francois
County Clerk**
Courthouse
Farmington, Missouri
63640

St. Louis County Clerk
111 S. Meramec Ave.,
1st Fl.
Clayton, Missouri
63105-1711

St. Louis City Clerk
634 N. Grand Blvd.
St. Louis City, Missouri
63103-2803

**Ste. Genevieve
County Clerk**
55 S. Third
Ste. Genevieve, Missouri
63670

Stoddard County Clerk
Courthouse
Bloomfield, Missouri
63825

Stone County Clerk
Courthouse
Galena, Missouri 65656

Sullivan County Clerk
Courthouse
Milan, Missouri 63556

Taney County Clerk
Courthouse
Forsyth, Missouri 65653

Texas County Clerk
210 N. Grand
Houston, Missouri
65483-1224

Vernon County Clerk
Courthouse
Nevada, Missouri 64772

Warren County Clerk
116 W. Main
Warrenton, Missouri 63383

**Washington County
Clerk**
102 N. Missouri
Potosi, Missouri 63664

Wayne County Clerk
Courthouse
Greenville, Missouri 63944

Webster County Clerk
P.O. Box 529
Marshfield, Missouri 65706

Worth County Clerk
P.O. Box L
Grant City, Missouri
64456-0530

Wright County Clerk
P.O. Box 98
Hartville, Missouri
65667-0098

MONTANA

http://www.state.mt.us/

Beaverhead County Clerk
2 South Pacific St.
Cluster #3
Dillon, Montana 59725

Big Horn County Clerk
P.O. Drawer H
Hardin, Montana 59034

Blaine County
P.O. Box 278
Chinook, Montana 59523

Broadwater County Clerk
515 Broadway
Townsend, Montana 59644

Carbon County Clerk
P.O. Box 948
Red Lodge, Montana
59068

Carter County Clerk
P.O. Box 315
Ekalaka, Montana
59324-0315

Cascade County Clerk
415 2nd Ave. N., Rm. 203
Great Falls, Montana
59403

Chouteau County Clerk
1308 Franklin
Fort Benton, Montana
59442

Custer County Clerk
1010 Main St.
Miles City, Montana
59301-3419

Daniels County Clerk
P.O. Box 247
Scobey, Montana 59263

Dawson County Clerk
207 W. Bell St.
Glendive, Montana
59330-1616

Deer Lodge County Clerk
800 S. Main
Anaconda, Montana
59711-2999

Fallon County Clerk
10 W. Fallon Ave.
Baker, Montana 59313

Fergus County Clerk
712 W. Main
Lewistown, Montana
59457-2562

Flathead County Clerk
800 S. Main
Kalispell, Montana
59901-5435

Gallatin County Clerk
311 W. Main
Bozeman, Montana
59715-4576

Garfield County Clerk
P.O. Box 7
Jordan, Montana
59337-0007

Glacier County Clerk
512 Main St.
Cut Bank, Montana
59427-3016

Golden Valley County Clerk
107 Kemp
Ryegate, Montana 59074

Granite County Clerk
P.O. Box J
Philipsburg, Montana 59858

Hill County Clerk
Courthouse
Havre, Montana 59501-3999

Jefferson County Clerk
P.O. Box H
Boulder, Montana 59632

Judith Basic County Clerk
Courthouse
Stanford, Montana 59479

Lake County Clerk
106 Fourth Ave.
Polson, Montana 59860-2125

Lewis and Clark County Clerk
316 N. Park
Helena, Montana 59601-5059

Liberty County Clerk
P.O. Box 549
Chester, Montana 59522

Lincoln County Clerk
512 California Ave.
Libby, Montana 59923-1942

Madison County Clerk
110 W. Wallace St.
Virginia City, Montana 59755

McCone County Clerk
P.O. Box 199
Circle, Montana 59215

Meagher County Clerk
P.O. Box 309
White Sulphur Springs, Montana 59645

Mineral County Clerk
P.I. Box 550
Superior, Montana 59872-0550

Missoula County Clerk
Courthouse
Missoula, Montana 59802-4292

Musselshell County Clerk
P.O. Box 686
Roundup, Montana 59072

Park County Clerk
414 E. Callender
Livingston, Montana 59047-2746

Petroleum County Clerk
201 E. Main St.
Winnett, Montana 59087

Phillips County Clerk
314 Second Ave. W.
Malta, Montana 59538

Pondera County Clerk
20 Fourth Ave. SW
Conrad, Montana 59425-2340

Powder River County Clerk
P.O. Box J
Broadus, Montana 59317

Powell County Clerk
409 Missouri
Deer Lodge, Montana 59722-1084

Prairie County Clerk
P.O. Box 125
Terry, Montana 59349-0125

Ravalli County Clerk
Courthouse
Hamilton, Montana 59840

Richland County Clerk
201 W. Main
Sidney, Montana 59270-4035

Roosevelt County Clerk
400 Second Ave. S.
Wolf Point, Montana 59201-1605

Rosebud County Clerk
P.O. Box 48
Forsyth, Montana 59327

Sanders County Clerk
Main St.
Thompson Falls, Montana 59873

Sheridan County Clerk
100 W. Laurel Ave.
Plentywood, Montana 59254-1619

Silver Bow County Clerk
155 W. Granite
Butte, Montana 59701-9256

Stillwater County Clerk
Courthouse
Columbus, Montana 59019

Sweet Grass County Clerk
P.O. Box 460
Big Timber, Montana 59011

Teton County Clerk
P.O. Box 610
Choteau, Montana
59422-0610

Toole County Clerk
226 First St., S.
Shelby, Montana
59474-1920

Treasure County Clerk
P.O. Box 392
Hysham, Montana 59038

Valley County Clerk
501 Court Square, #2
Glasgow, Montana 59230

Wheatland County Clerk
P.O. Box 1903
Harlowton, Montana 59036

Wibaux County Clerk
200 S. Wibaux
Wibaux, Montana 59353

Yellowstone County Clerk
P.O. Box 35001
Billings, Montana
59107-5001

NEBRASKA

http://www.state.ne.us/

Adams County Clerk
500 W. Fifth, Rm. 109
Hastings, Nebraska 68901

Antelope County Clerk
Courthouse
Neligh, Nebraska 68756

Arthur County Clerk
P.O. Box 126
Arthur, Nebraska
69121-0126

Banner County Clerk
P.O. Box 67
Harrisburg, Nebraska
69345-0067

Blaine County Clerk
Courthouse
Brewster, Nebraska 68821

Boone County Clerk
222 S. Fourth St.
Albion, Nebraska
68620-1258

Box Butte County Clerk
510 Box Butte Ave.
Alliance, Nebraska 69301

Boyd County Clerk
Courthouse
Butte, Nebraska 68722

Brown County Clerk
Ainsworth, Nebraska
69210

Buffalo County Clerk
15th and Central Ave.
Kearney, Nebraska 68848

Burt County Clerk
111 N. Thirteenth St.
Tekamah, Nebraska
68061-1043

Butler County Clerk
Courthouse
David City, Nebraska
68632
(402) 367-3091

Cass County Clerk
Fourth and Main St.
Plattsmouth, Nebraska
68048

Cedar County Clerk
101 E. Centre
Hartington, Nebraska
68739

Chase County Clerk
P.O. Box 310
Imperial, Nebraska
69033-0310

Cherry County Clerk
P.O. Box 120
Valentine, Nebraska 69201

Cheyenne County Clerk
Courthouse
Sidney, Nebraska 69162

Clay County Clerk
111 W. Fairfield
Clay Center, Nebraska
68933

Colfax County Clerk
411 E. 11th St.
Schuyler, Nebraska 68661-
1940

Cuming County Clerk
Courthouse
West Point, Nebraska
68788

Custer County Clerk
431 S. Tenth Ave.
Broken Bow, Nebraska
68822-2001

Dakota County Clerk
Courthouse
Dakota City, Nebraska
68731

Dawes County Clerk
Courthouse
Chadron, Nebraska 69337

Dawson County Clerk
P.O. Box 370
Lexington, Nebraska
68850-0370

Deuel County Clerk
Courthouse
Chappell, Nebraska 69129

Dixon County Clerk
Courthouse
Ponca, Nebraska 68770

Dodge County Clerk
435 N. Park
Fremont, Nebraska 68025

Douglas County Clerk
1819 Farnam St., Rm. 402
Omaha, Nebraska 68183

Dundy County Clerk
Courthouse
Benkelman, Nebraska
69021

Fillmore County Clerk
Courthouse
Geneva, Nebraska 68361

Franklin County Clerk
405 15th Ave.
Franklin, Nebraska
68939-1309

Frontier County Clerk
P.O. Box 40
Stockville, Nebraska 69042

Furnas County Clerk
P.O. Box 387
Beaver City, Nebraska
68926-0387

Gage County Clerk
6th and Grant St.
Beatrice, Nebraska 68310

Garden County Clerk
Courthouse
Oshkosh, Nebraska 69154

Garfield County Clerk
P.O. Box 218
Burwell, Nebraska
68823-0218

Gosper County Clerk
P.O. Box 136
Elwood, Nebraska 68937

Grant County Clerk
P.O. Box 128
Hyannis, Nebraska 69350

Greeley County Clerk
P.O. Box 287
Greeley Center, Nebraska
68842-0287

Hall County Clerk
121 S. Pine
Grand Island, Nebraska
68801-6076

Hamilton County Clerk
Courthouse
Auroa, Nebraska 68818

Harlan County Clerk
Courthouse
Alma, Nebraska 68920

Hayes County Clerk
P.O. Box 67
Hayes Center, Nebraska
69032-0067

Hitchcock County Clerk
Courthouse
Trenton, Nebraska 69044

Holt County Clerk
Courthouse
O'Neill, Nebraska 68763

Hooker County Clerk
P.O. Box 184
Mullen, Nebraska
69152-0184

Howard County Clerk
P.O. Box 25
St. Paul, Nebraska
68873-0025

Jefferson County Clerk
411 Fourth St.
Fairbury, Nebraska
68352-2513

Johnson County Clerk
P.O. Box 416
Tecumseh, Nebraska
68450-0416

Kearney County Clerk
Courthouse
Minden, Nebraska 68959

Keith County Clerk
P.O. Box 149
Ogallala, Nebraska
69153-0149

Keya Paha County Clerk
P.O. Box 349
Springview, Nebraska
68778

Kimball County Clerk
114 E. Third St.
Kimball, Nebraska
69145-1401

Knox County Clerk
Courthouse
Center, Nebraska 68724

Lancaster County Clerk
555 Tenth St.
Lincoln, Nebraska
68508-2803

Lincoln County Clerk
Courthouse
North Platte, Nebraska
69101

Logan County Clerk
P.O. Box 8
Stapleton, Nebraska
69163-0008

Loup County Clerk
P.O. Box 187
Taylor, Nebraska
68879-0187

Madison County Clerk
P.O. Box 230
Madison, Nebraska 68748

McPherson County Clerk
P.O. Box 122
Tryon, Nebraska
69167-0122

Merrick County Clerk
P.O. Box 27
Central City, Nebraska
68826-0027

Morrill County Clerk
P.O. Box 610
Bridgeport, Nebraska
69336-0610

Nance County Clerk
Courthouse
Fullerton, Nebraska 68638

Nemaha County Clerk
1824 N. Street
Auburn, Nebraska
68305-2342

Nuckolls County Clerk
Courthouse
Nelson, Nebraska 68961

Otoe County Clerk
P.O. Box 249
Nebraska City, Nebraska
68410

Pawnee County Clerk
P.O. Box 431
Pawnee City, Nebraska
68420-0431

Perkins County Clerk
P.O. Box 156
Grant, Nebraska
69140-0156

Phelps County Clerk
P.O. Box 334
Holdrege, Nebraska
68949-0334

Pierce County Clerk
P.O. Box 218
Pierce, Nebraska
68767-0218

Platte County Clerk
2610 14th St.
Columbus, Nebraska
68601-4929

Polk County Clerk
Courthouse
Osceola, Nebraska 68651

Red Willow County Clerk
500 Norris Ave.
McCook, Nebraska
69001-2006

Richardson County Clerk
1701 Stone St.
Falls City, Nebraska 68355

Rock County Clerk
400 State St.
Bassett, Nebraska
68714-0367

Saline County Clerk
215 Court St.
Wilber, Nebraska
68465-0865

Sarpy County Clerk
1210 Golden Gate Dr.
Papillion, Nebraska
68046-2845

Saunders County Clerk
Chestnut St. Courthouse
Wahoo, Nebraska 68066

Scotts Bluff County Clerk
1825 Tenth St.
Gering, Nebraska
69341-2413

Seward County Clerk
P.O. Box 190
Seward, Nebraska 68434

Sheridan County Clerk
301 E. 2nd St.
Rushville, Nebraska
69360-0039

Sherman County Clerk
P.O. Box 456
Loup City, Nebraska
68853-0456

Sioux County Clerk
Courthouse, Main St.
Harrison, Nebraska 69346

Stanton County Clerk
804 Ivy St.
Stanton, Nebraska 68779

Thayer County Clerk
235 N. 4th St.
Hebron, Nebraska 68370

Thomas County Clerk
P.O. Box 226
Thedford, Nebraska 69166

Thurston County Clerk
106 S. 5th St.
Pender, Nebraska 68047

Valley County Clerk
125 S. 15th St.
Ord, Nebraska 68862-1409

Washington County Clerk
1555 Colfax St.
Blair, Nebraska
68008-2022

Wayne County Clerk
510 N. Pearl St.
Wayne, Nebraska 68787

Webster County Clerk
621 N. Cedar St.
Red Cloud, Nebraska
68970

Wheeler County Clerk
County Courthouse
Bartlett, Nebraska 68622

York County Clerk
510 Lincoln Ave.
York, Nebraska 68467

NEVADA

http://www.state.nv.us/

**Carson City
County Clerk**
885 E. Musser St.
Carson City, Nevada 89701

Churchill County Clerk
190 W. First St.
Fallon, Nevada 89406-3309

Clark County Clerk
625 Shadow Lane
Las Vegas, Nevada 89101

Douglas County Clerk
P.O. Box 218
Minden, Nevada
89423-0218

Elko County Clerk
571 Idaho St.
Elko, Nevada 89801-3770

Esmeralda County Clerk
P.O. Box 547
Goldfield, Nevada
89103-0547

Eureka County Clerk
P.O. Box 677
Eureka, Nevada
89316-0677

Humbolt County Clerk
P.O. Box 352
Winnemucca, Nevada
89445-0352

Lander County Clerk
315 S. Humboldt
Battle Mountain, Nevada
89820-1655

Lincoln County Clerk
1 Main St.
Pioche, Nevada
89043-0090

Lyon County Clerk
31 S. Main St.
Yerington, Nevada
89447-0816

Mineral County Clerk
P.O. Box 1450
Hawthorne, Nevada
89415-1450

Nye County Clerk
P.O. Box 1031
Tonopah, Nevada 89049

Pershing County Clerk
P.O. Box 820
Lovelock, Nevada
89419-0820

Storey County Clerk
P.O. Box D
Virginia City, Nevada
89440-0139

Washoe County Clerk
P.O. Box 11130
Reno, Nevada 89520-0027

White Pine County Clerk
Campton Street
Ely, Nevada 89301

NEW HAMPSHIRE

http://www.state.nh.us/

Belknap County Clerk
P.O. Box 578
Laconia, New Hampshire
03247-0578

Carroll County Clerk
Administration Bldg.
Ossipee, New Hampshire
03864

Cheshire County Clerk
12 Court St.
Keene, New Hampshire
03431-3402

Coos County Clerk
Main Street
Lancaster, New Hampshire
03584

Grafton County Clerk
RR1, Box 65F
North Haverhill, New
Hampshire 03774-9708

**Hillsborough
County Clerk**
19 Temple St.
Nashua, New Hampshire
03060-3444

Merrimack County Clerk
163 N. Main St.
Concord, New Hampshire
03301-5068

**Rockingham
County Clerk**
Rt. 125
Brentwood, New
Hampshire 03830

Strafford County Clerk
P.O. Box 799
Dover, New Hampshire
03820-0799

Sullivan County Clerk
22 Main St.
Newport, New Hampshire
03773-0045

NEW JERSEY

http://www.state.nj.us/

Atlantic County Clerk
5901 Main St.
Mays Landing, New Jersey
08330

Bergen County Clerk
21 Main St.
Hackensack, New Jersey
07601-7017

Burlington County Clerk
49 Rancocas Rd.
Mount Holly, New Jersey
08060-1384

Camden County Clerk
5th and Mickle Blvd.
Camden, New Jersey
08103-4001

Cape May County Clerk
7 N. Main St.
Cape May, New Jersey
08210

**Cumberland
County Clerk**
Broad and Fayette Street
Bridgeton, New Jersey
08302

Essex County Clerk
920 Broad St., Rm. 111
Newark, New Jersey 07101

Gloucester County Clerk
1 N. Broad St.
Woodbury, New Jersey
08096-7376

Hudson County Clerk
595 Newark Ave.
Jersey City, New Jersey
07306-2394

Hunterdon County Clerk
71 Main St.
Flemington, New Jersey
08822

Mercer County Clerk
P.O. Box 8068
Trenton, New Jersey
08650-0068

Middlesex County Clerk
1 John F. Kennedy Square
New Brunswick, New
Jersey 08901

Monmouth County Clerk
Main St.
Freehold, New Jersey
07728-1255

Morris County Clerk
P.O. Box 900
Morristown, New Jersey
07960-0900

Ocean County Clerk
P.O. Box 2191
Toms River, New Jersey
08754

Passaic County Clerk
77 Hamilton St.
Paterson, New Jersey
07505-2018

Salem County Clerk
92 Market St.
Salem City, New Jersey
08079-1913

Somerset County Clerk
P.O. Box 3000
Somerville, New Jersey
08876-1262

Sussex County Clerk
4 Park Place
Newton, New Jersey 07860

Union County Clerk
2 Broad St.
Elizabeth, New Jersey
07201

Warren County Clerk
Rt. 519
Wayne Dumont Jr. Bldg.
Belvidere, New Jersey
07823

NEW MEXICO

http://www.state.nm.us/

Bernalillo County Clerk
One Civic Plaza NW
Albuquerque, New Mexico
87102

Catron County Clerk
P.O. Box 507
Reserve, New Mexico
87830

Chaves County Clerk
401 N. Main St.
Roswell, New Mexico
88201-4726

Cibola County Clerk
515 W. High St.
Grants, New Mexico
87020-2526

Colfax County Clerk
P.O. Box 1498
Raton, New Mexico
87740-1498

Curry County Clerk
700 N. Main St.
Clovis, New Mexico
88102-1168

DeBaca County Clerk
P.O. Box 347
Fort Sumner, New Mexico
88819

Dona Ana County Clerk
251 W. Amador Ave.
Las Cruces, New Mexico
88005

Eddy County Clerk
P.O. Box 1139
Carlsbad, New Mexico
88221-1139

Grant County Clerk
P.O. Box 898
Silver City, New Mexico
88062-0898

Guadalupe County Clerk
420 Parker Ave.
Santa Rosa, New Mexico
88435

Harding County Clerk
P.O. Box 1002
Mosquero, New Mexico
87733-1002

Hidalgo County Clerk
300 S. Shakespeare St.
Lordsburg, New Mexico
88045-1939

Lea County Clerk
P.O. Box 4C
Lovington, New Mexico
88260

Lincoln County Clerk
300 Central Ave.
Carrizozo, New Mexico
88301-0711

Los Alamos County Clerk
2300 Trinity Dr.
Los Alamos, New Mexico
87544-3051

Luna County Clerk
P.O. Box 1838
Deming, New Mexico
88031-1838

McKinley County Clerk
200 W. Hill Ave.
Gallup, New Mexico 87301

Mora County Clerk
P.O. Box 360
Mora, New Mexico 87732

Otero County Clerk
10th And New York Streets
Alamogordo, New Mexico
88310

Quay County Clerk
300 S. 3rd St.
Tucumcari, New Mexico
88401

Rio Arriba County Clerk
P.O. Box 158
Tierra Amarilla, New
Mexico 87575

Roosevelt County Clerk
Courthouse
Portales, New Mexico
88130

San Juan County Clerk
P.O. Box 550
Aztec, New Mexico 87410

San Miguel County Clerk
Courthouse
Las Vegas, New Mexico
87701

Sandoval County Clerk
P.O. Box 40
Bernalillo, New Mexico
87004

Santa Fe County Clerk
P.O. Box 1985
Santa Fe, New Mexico
87504

Sierra County Clerk
300 Date Street
Truth or Consequences,
New Mexico 87901-2362

Socorro County Clerk
131 Court St.
Socorro, New Mexico
87801

Taos County Clerk
P.O. Box 676
Taos, New Mexico 87571

Torrance County Clerk
9th and Allen
Estancia, New Mexico
87016

Union County Clerk
200 Court St.
Clayton, New Mexico
88415-0430

Valencia County Clerk
P.O. Box 1119
Los Lunas, New Mexico
87031

NEW YORK

http://www.state.ny.us/

Albany County Clerk
16 Eagle St.
Albany, New York
12207-1019

Allegany County Clerk
Courthouse
Belmont, New York 14813

Bronx County Clerk
1780 Grand Concourse
Bronx, New York 10457

Broome County Clerk
44 Hawley St.
Binghamton, New York
13901

**Cattaraugus County
Clerk**
303 Court St.
Little Valley, New York
14755-1028

Cayuga County Clerk
160 Genesee St.
Auburn, New York
13021-3424

**Chautauqua
County Clerk**
P.O. Box 292
Mayville, New York
14757-0292

Chemung County Clerk
210 Lake St.
Elmire, New York
14901-3109

Chenango County Clerk
5 Court St.
Norwich, New York 13815

Clinton County Clerk
137 Margaret St.
Plattsburgh, New York
12901-2933

Columbia County Clerk
Allen and Union St.
Courthouse
Hudson, New York 12534

Cortland County Clerk
60 Central Ave.
Cortland, New York
13045-2716

Delaware County Clerk
4 Court St.
Delhi, New York 13753

Dutchess County Clerk
222 Market St.
Poughkeepsie, New York
12601-3222

Erie County Clerk
92 Franklin St.
Buffalo, New York
14202-3904

Essex County Clerk
Court St.
Elizabethtown, New York
12932

Franklin County Clerk
63 W. Main St.
Malone, New York
12953-1817

Fulton County Clerk
County Bldg.
223 W. Main St.
Johnstown, New York
12905-2331

Genesee County Clerk
Main and Court St.
Batavia, New York 14020

Greene County Clerk
388 Main St.
Catskill, New York 12414

Hamilton County Clerk
Office Bldg.
Lake Pleasant, New York
12108

Herkimer County Clerk
P.O. Box 471
Herkimer, New York
13350-0471

Jefferson County Clerk
175 Arsenal St.
Watertown, New York
13601-2522

Kings County Clerk
360 Adams St.
Brooklyn, New York
11201-3712

Lewis County Clerk
7660 State St.
Lowville, New York
13367-1432

Livingston County Clerk
6 Court St.
Geneseo, New York 14454

Madison County Clerk
N. Court St.
Wampsville, New York
13163-0668

Monroe County Clerk
39 W. Main St.
Rochester, New York
14614

**Montgomery
County Clerk**
Broadway
Fonda, New York 12068

Nassau County Clerk
1 West St.
Mineola, New York
11501-4812

**New York City
Vital Records**
One Center Street,
Rm. 252
New York, New York
10007

New York County Clerk
60 Centre St.
New York, New York
10007-1402

Niagara County Clerk
Courthouse
Lockport, New York 14094

Oneida County Clerk
109 Mary St.
Utica, New York
13350-1921

Onondaga County Clerk
421 Montgomery St. #20
Syracuse, New York 13202

Ontario County Clerk
3907 County Rd. 46
Canandaigua, New York
14424

Orange County Clerk
255-275 Main St.
Goshen, New York
10924-1621

Orleans County Clerk
Courthouse Square
Albion, New York
14411-1449

Oswego County Clerk
West Oneida St.
Oswego, New York 13126

Otsego County Clerk
197 Main St.
Cooperstown, New York
13326-1129

Putnam County Clerk
40 Gleneida Ave.
Carmel, New York 10512

Queens County Clerk
88-11 Sutphin Blvd.
Jamaica, New York 11435

Rensselaer County Clerk
1600 7th Ave.
Troy, New York 12180

Richmond County Clerk
18 Richmond Terrace
Staten Island, New York
10301-1935

Rockland County Clerk
27 New Hempstead Rd.
New City, New York 10956

Saratoga County Clerk
40 McMasters St.
Ballston Spa, New York
12020-1908

Schenectady
County Clerk
City Hall, Rm. 107
Jay St.
Schenectady, New York
12305

Schoharie County Clerk
P.O. Box 549
Schoharie, New York
12157-0549

Schuyler County Clerk
105 Ninth St., Box 8
Watkins Glen, New York
14891

Seneca County Clerk
1 DiPronio Dr.
Waterloo, New York 13165

St. Lawrence
County Clerk
Courthouse
Canton, New York 13617

Steuben County Clerk
Courthouse at 3 Pulteney
Square
Bath, New York 14810

Suffolk County Clerk
County Center
Riverhead, New York
11901-3398

Sullivan County Clerk
100 Main St.
Monticello, New York
12701-1160

Tioga County Clerk
16 Court St.
Owego, New York 13827

Tompkins County Clerk
401 Harris B. Dates Dr.
Ithaca, New York 14850

Ulster County Clerk
244 Fair St.
Kingston, New York
12402-1800

Warren County Clerk
Route 9
Lake George, New York
12845

Washington
County Clerk
Upper Broadway
Fort Edward, New York
12828

Wayne County Clerk
9 Pearl St.
Lyons, New York
14489-0131

Westchester
County Clerk
110 Dr. Martin Luther
King Jr. Blvd
White Plains, New York
10601

Wyoming County Clerk
143 N. Main St.
Warsaw, New York
14569-1123

Yates County Clerk
110 Court St.,
County Bldg.
Penn Yan, New York 14527

NORTH CAROLINA

http://www.state.nc.us/

Alamance County Clerk
124 W. Elm St.
Graham, North Carolina
27253

Alexander County Clerk
201 First St. SW, Suite 1
Taylorsville,
North Carolina 28681

Alleghany County Clerk
P.O. Box 186
Sparta, North Carolina
28675

Anson County Clerk
P.O. Box 352
Wadesboro, North Carolina
28170

Ashe County Clerk
P.O. Box 367
Jefferson, North Carolina
28640

Avery County Clerk
P.O. Box 87
Newland, North Carolina
28657-0356

Beaufort County Clerk
P.O. Box 514
Washington,
North Carolina 27889

Bertie County Clerk
P.O. Box 340
Windsor, North Carolina
27983

Bladen County Clerk
P.O. Box 247
Elizabethtown,
North Carolina 28337

Brunswick County Clerk
P.O. Box 87
Bolivia, North Carolina
28422

Buncombe County Clerk
60 Court Plaza
Asheville, North Carolina
28801

Burke County Clerk
P.O. Box 936
Morganton, North Carolina
28655

Cabarrus County Clerk
P.O. Box 707
Concord, North Carolina
28026

Caldwell County Clerk
905 West Ave. NW
Lenoir, North Carolina
28645

Camden County Clerk
P.O. Box 190
Camden, North Carolina
27921

Carteret County Clerk
Courthouse Square
Admin. Bldg.
Beaufort, North Carolina
28516

Caswell County Clerk
P.O. Box 98
Yanceyville,
North Carolina 27379

Catawba County Clerk
P.O. Box 65
Newton, North Carolina
28658

Chatham County Clerk
P.O. Box 756
Pittsboro, North Carolina
27312

Cherokee County Clerk
Cherokee County
Courthouse
Murphy, North Carolina
28906

Chowan County Clerk
P.O. Box 487
Edenton, North Carolina
27932

Clay County Clerk
P.O. Box 118
Hayesville, North Carolina
28904-0118

Cleveland County Clerk
P.O. Box 1210
Shelby, North Carolina
28151-1210

Columbus County Clerk
P.O. Box 1086
Whiteville, North Carolina
28472

Craven County
406 Craven St.
New Bern, North Carolina
28560

**Cumberland
County Clerk**
P.O. Box 2039
Fayetteville,
North Carolina 28301-5749

Currituck County Clerk
P.O. Box 71
Currituck, North Carolina
27929-0039

Dare County Clerk
P.O. Box 70
Manteo, North Carolina
27954

Davidson County Clerk
P.O. Box 464
Lexington, North Carolina
27293

Davie County Clerk
123 S. Main St.
Mocksville, North Carolina
27028

Duplin County Clerk
P.O. Box 970
Kenansville,
North Carolina 28349

Durham County Clerk
414 E. Main St.
Durham, North Carolina
27701

Edgecombe County Clerk
P.O. Box 386
Tarboro, North Carolina
27886

Forsyth County Clerk
P.O. Box 20639
Winston-Salem,
North Carolina 27120

Franklin County Clerk
P.O. Box 545
Louisburg, North Carolina
27549

Gaston County Clerk
P.O. Box 1578
Gastonia, North Carolina
28053

Gates County Clerk
P.O. Box 345
Gatesville, North Carolina
27938

Graham County Clerk
P.O. Box 406
Robbinsville,
North Carolina 28771

Granville County Clerk
P.O. Box 427
Oxford, North Carolina
27565

Greene County Clerk
P.O. Box 68
Snow Hill, North Carolina
28580

Guilford County Clerk
P.O. Box 3427
Greensboro, North Carolina
27402

Halifax County Clerk
P.O. Box 67
Halifax, North Carolina
27839

Harnett County Clerk
729 S. Main St.
Lillington, North Carolina
27546

Haywood County Clerk
Haywood County
Courthouse
Waynesville,
North Carolina 28786

Henderson County Clerk
200 N. Grove St., Suite 129
Hendersonville,
North Carolina 28792

Hertford County Clerk
P.O. Box 36
Winton, North Carolina
27986

Hoke County Clerk
304 N. Main St.
Raeford, North Carolina
28376

Hyde County Clerk
P.O. Box 294
Swan Quarter,
North Carolina 27885-0337

Iredell County Clerk
P.O. Box 904
Statesville, North Carolina
28677-0788

Jackson County Clerk
401 Grindstaff Cove Rd
Sylva, North Carolina
28779

Johnston County Clerk
P.O. Box 118
Smithfield, North Carolina
27577

Jones County Clerk
P.O. Box 189
Trenton, North Carolina
28585

Lee County Clerk
P.O. Box 2040
Sanford, North Carolina
27311

Lenoir County Clerk
P.O. Box 3289
Kinston, North Carolina
28502

Lincoln County Clerk
Lincoln Co. Courthouse
Lincolnton, North Carolina
28092

Macon County Clerk
5 West Main St.
Franklin, North Carolina
28734

Madison County Clerk
P.O. Box 66
Marshall, North Carolina
28753

Martin County Clerk
P.O. Box 348
Williamston,
North Carolina 27892-0668

McDowell County Clerk
1 South Main St.
Marion, North Carolina
28752-1450

**Mecklenburg
County Clerk**
249 Billingsley Rd
Charlotte, North Carolina
28211

Mitchell County Clerk
P.O. Box 82
Bakersville, North Carolina
28705

**Montgomery
County Clerk**
P.O. Box 695
Troy, North Carolina 27371

Moore County Clerk
P.O. Box 1210
Carthage, North Carolina
28327

Nash County Clerk
P.O. Box 974
Nashville, North Carolina
27856

**New Hanover
County Clerk**
316 Princess St., Rm. 216
Wilmington,
North Carolina 28401

**Northampton County
Clerk**
P.O. Box 128
Jackson, North Carolina
27845

Onslow County Clerk
P.O. Box 159, Rm. 107
Jacksonville,
North Carolina 28540

Orange County Clerk
208 S. Cameron St.
Hillsborough,
North Carolina 27278

Pamlico County Clerk
P.O. Box 423
Bayboro, North Carolina
28515

Pasquotank County Clerk
P.O. Box 154
Elizabeth City, North
Carolina 27909

Pender County Clerk
P.O. Box 43
Burgaw, North Carolina
28425

**Perquimans
County Clerk**
P.O. Box 74
Hertford, North Carolina
27944

Person County Clerk
Courthouse Square
Roxboro, North Carolina
27573

Pitt County Clerk
P.O. Box 35
Greenville, North Carolina
27835

Polk County Clerk
P.O. Box 308
Columbus, North Carolina
28722

Randolph County Clerk
P.O. Box 4066
Asheboro, North Carolina
27203

Richmond County Clerk
114 E. Franklin St. #101
Rockingham,
North Carolina 28379

Robeson County Clerk
P.O. Box 22
Lumberton, North Carolina
28358

**Rockingham
County Clerk**
P.O. Box 56
Wentworth, North Carolina
27375

Rowan County Clerk
P.O. Box 2568
Salisbury, North Carolina
28145

Rutherford County Clerk
P.O. Box 551
Rutherfordton,
North Carolina 28139

Sampson County Clerk
P.O. Box 256
Clinton, North Carolina
28328

Scotland County Clerk
P.O. Box 769
Laurinburg, North Carolina
28352

Stanley County Clerk
P.O. Box 97
Albemarle, North Carolina
28002

Stokes County Clerk
P.O. Box 67
Danbury, North Carolina
27016

Surry County Clerk
P.O. Box 303
Dobson, North Carolina
27017

Swain County Clerk
P.O. Box 417
Bryson City,
North Carolina 28713

**Transylvania
County Clerk**
12 East Main St.
Brevard, North Carolina
28712

Tyrrell County Clerk
P.O. Box 449
Columbia, North Carolina
27925

Union County Clerk
P.O. Box 248
Monroe, North Carolina
28111

Vance County Clerk
122 Young St. Courthouse
Henderson, North Carolina
27536-2017

Wake County Clerk
10 Sunnybrook Rd
Raleigh, North Carolina
27620

Warren County Clerk
P.O. Box 506
Warrenton, North Carolina
27589-1929

**Washington
County Clerk**
P.O. Box 1007
Plymouth, North Carolina
27962-1007

Watauga County Clerk
842 W. King St., Suite 9
Boone, North Carolina
28607

Wayne County Clerk
P.O. Box 267
Goldsboro, North Carolina
27533

Wilkes County Clerk
Wilkes County Courthouse
Wilkesboro, North Carolina
28697

Wilson County Clerk
P.O. Box 1728
Wilson, North Carolina
27694

Yadkin County Clerk
P.O. Box 211
Yadkinville, North Carolina
27055

Yancey County Clerk
Courthouse, Rm. 4
Burnsville, North Carolina
28714

NORTH DAKOTA
http://www.state.nd.us/

Adams County Clerk
P.O. Box 469
Hettinger, North Dakota
58639

Barnes County Clerk
P.O. Box 774
Valley City, North Dakota
58072

Benson County Clerk
P.O. Box 213
Minnewaukan, North
Dakota 58351

Billings County Clerk
P.O. Box 138
Medora, North Dakota
58645

Bottineau County Clerk
314 W. 5th St.
Bottineau, North Dakota
58318

Bowman County Clerk
P.O. Box 379
Bowman, North Dakota
58623

Burke County Clerk
P.O. Box 219
Bowbells, North Dakota
58721

Burleigh County Clerk
P.O. Box 1055
Bismarck, North Dakota
58502

Cass County Clerk
P.O. Box 2806
Fargo, North Dakota 58108

Cavalier County Clerk
901 3rd St.
Langdon, North Dakota
58249

Dickey County Clerk
P.O. Box 336
Ellendale, North Dakota
58436

Divide County Clerk
P.O. Box 68
Crosby, North Dakota
58730-0049

Dunn County Clerk
P.O. Box 136
Manning, North Dakota
58642

Eddy County Clerk
524 Central Ave.
New Rockford, North
Dakota 58356-1698

Emmons County Clerk
P.O. Box 905
Linton, North Dakota
58552

Foster County Clerk
P.O. Box 257
Carrington, North Dakota
58421

**Golden Valley
County Clerk**
P.O. Box 9
Beach, North Dakota
58621

**Grand Forks
County Clerk**
P.O. Box 5939
Grand Forks, North Dakota
58201-1477

Grant County Clerk
P.O. Box 258
Carson, North Dakota
58529

Griggs County Clerk
P.O. Box 326
Cooperstown,
North Dakota 58425-0326

Hettinger County Clerk
P.O. Box 668
Mott, North Dakota 58646

Kidder County Clerk
P.O. Box 66
Steele, North Dakota
58482-0110

La Moure County Clerk
P.O. Box 5
La Moure, North Dakota
58458

Logan County Clerk
P.O. Box 6
Napoleon, North Dakota
58561

McHenry County Clerk
P.O. Box 117
Towner, North Dakota
58788

McIntosh County Clerk
P.O. Box 179
Ashley, North Dakota
58413

McKenzie County Clerk
P.O. Box 524
Watford City, North Dakota
58854

McLean County Clerk
P.O. Box 1108
Washburn, North Dakota
58577

Mercer County Clerk
P.O. Box 39
Stanton, North Dakota
58571-0039

Morton County Clerk
210 Second Ave. NW
Mandan, North Dakota
58554-3124

Mountrail County Clerk
P.O. Box 69
Stanley, North Dakota
58784

Nelson County Clerk
P.O. Box 565
Lakota, North Dakota
58344

Oliver County Clerk
P.O. Box 125
Center, North Dakota
58530-0166

Pembina County Clerk
301 Dakota St. W, #6
Cavalier, North Dakota
58220-0160

Pierce County Clerk
240 SE Second St.
Rugby, North Dakota
58368-1830

Ramsey County Clerk
524 4th Ave., #4
Devils Lake, North Dakota
58301-2701

Ransom County Clerk
P.O. Box 626
Lisbon, North Dakota
58054

Renville County Clerk
P.O. Box 68
Mohall, North Dakota
58761-0068

Richland County Clerk
418 Second Ave. North
Wahpeton, North Dakota
58075

Rolette County Clerk
P.O. Box 460
Rolla, North Dakota 58367

Sargent County Clerk
P.O. Box 176
Forman, North Dakota
58032-0098

Sheridan County Clerk
P.O. Box 668
McClusky, North Dakota
58463-0636

Sioux County Clerk
P.O. Box L
Fort Yates, North Dakota
58538

Slope County Clerk
P.O. Box JJ
Amidon, North Dakota
58620-0449

Stark County Clerk
P.O. Box 130
Dickinson, North Dakota
58602-0130

Steele County Clerk
P.O. Box 296
Finley, North Dakota
58230

Stutsman County Clerk
511 Second Ave. SE
Jamestown, North Dakota
58401-4210

Towner County Clerk
P.O. Box 517
Cando, North Dakota
58324

Traill County Clerk
P.O. Box 805
Hillsboro, North Dakota
58045

Walsh County Clerk
600 Cooper Ave.
Grafton, North Dakota
58237-1542

Ward County Clerk
P.O. Box 5005
Minot, North Dakota 58701

Wells County Clerk
P.O. Box 596
Fessenden, North Dakota
58437-0596

Williams County Clerk
P.O. Box 2047
Williston, North Dakota
58802-1246

OHIO

http://www.state.oh.us/

Adams County Clerk
110 West Main
West Union, Ohio
45693-1347

Allen County Clerk
301 N. Main St.
Lima, Ohio 45801-4456

Ashland County Clerk
West 2nd St.
Ashland, Ohio 44805

Ashtabula County Clerk
25 W. Jefferson St.
Jefferson, Ohio
44047-1027

Athens County Clerk
Court and Washington St.
Athens, Ohio 45701-2888

Auglaize County Clerk
214 S. Wagner St.
Wapakoneta, Ohio 45895

Belmont County Clerk
101 Main St.
St. Clairsville, Ohio
43950-1224

Brown County Clerk
Danny L. Pride Courthouse
Georgetown, Ohio 45121

Butler County Clerk
130 High St.
Hamilton, Ohio 45011

Carroll County Clerk
119 Public Square
Carrollton, Ohio 44615

Champaign County Clerk
200 N. Main St.
Urbana, Ohio 43078

Clark County Clerk
529 E. Home Rd.
Springfield, Ohio 45502

Clermont County Clerk
76 South Riverside
Batavia, Ohio 45103-2602

Clinton County Clerk
46 S. South St.
Wilmington, Ohio
45177-2214

**Columbiana
County Clerk**
105 S. Market St.
Lisbon, Ohio 44432-1255

Coshocton County Clerk
349½ Main St.
Coshocton, Ohio
43812-1510

Crawford County Clerk
112 E. Mansfield St.
Bucyrus, Ohio 44820

Cuyahoga County Clerk
1200 Ontario St.
Cleveland, Ohio 44113

Darke County Clerk
4th and Broadway
Greenville, Ohio 45331

Defiance County Clerk
500 Court St.
Defiance, Ohio 43512-2157

Delaware County Clerk
91 N. Sandusky
Delaware, Ohio
43015-1703

Elyria City Clerk
202 Chestnut St.
Elyria, OH 44035

Erie County Clerk
323 Columbus Ave.
Sandusky, Ohio 44870

Fairfield County Clerk
224 E. Main St., Rm. 303
Lancaster, Ohio
43130-3842

Fayette County Clerk
110 East Court
Washington Court House,
Ohio 43160-1355

Franklin County Clerk
181 Washington Blvd.
Columbus, Ohio
43215-4095

Fulton County Clerk
210 S. Fulton
Wauseon, Ohio
43567-1355

Gallia County Clerk
18 Locust St.
Gallipolis, Ohio 45631

Geauga County Clerk
231 Main St.
Chardon, Ohio 44024

Greene County Clerk
45 N. Detroit St.
Xenia, Ohio 45385

Guernsey County Clerk
Wheeling Ave.
Cambridge, Ohio 43725

Hamilton County Clerk
230 East 9th St.
William Howard
Taft Center
Cincinnati, Ohio 45202

Hancock County Clerk
300 S. Main St.
Findlay, Ohio 45840-9039

Hardin County Clerk
Public Square
Kenton, Ohio 43326

Harrison County Clerk
100 W. Market St.
Cadiz, Ohio 43907

Henry County Clerk
660 N. Perry
Napoleon, Ohio
43545-1702

Highland County Clerk
P.O. Box 825
Hillsboro, Ohio
45133-0825

Hocking County Clerk
1 East Main St.
Logan, Ohio 43138-1207

Holmes County Clerk
East Jackson St.
Millersburg, Ohio 44654

Huron County Clerk
2 East Main St.
Norwalk, Ohio 44857

Jackson County Clerk
226 Main St.
Jackson, Ohio 45640

Jefferson County Clerk
301 Market St.
Steubenville, Ohio
43952-2133

Knox County Clerk
106 East High St.
Mount Vernon, Ohio
43050-3453

Lake County Clerk
33 Mill St.
Painesville, Ohio 44077

Lawrence County Clerk
5th and Park Ave.
Ironton, Ohio 45638

Licking County Clerk
20 South 2nd St.
Newark, Ohio 43055-9553

Logan County Clerk
Main and East Columbus
St., 2nd Fl.
Bellefontaine, Ohio
43311-0429

Lorain County Clerk
226 Middle Ave., Admin
Bldg. 4th Fl.
Elyria, Ohio 44035

Lucas County Clerk
635 N. Erie St.
Toledo, Ohio 43624

Madison County Clerk
1 North Main St., Rm. 205
London, Ohio 43140

Mahoning County Clerk
120 Market St.
Youngstown, Ohio
44503-1710

Marion County Clerk
114 N. Main St.
Marion, Ohio 43302-3030

Medina County Clerk
93 Public Square
Medina, Ohio 44256-2205

Meigs County Clerk
144 Butternut Ave.
Pomeroy, Ohio 45769

Mercer County Clerk
101 N. Main St.
Celina, Ohio 45822

Miami County Clerk
201 West Main St.
Troy, Ohio 45373-3239

Monroe County Clerk
101 N. Main St., Rm. 12
Woodsfield, Ohio 43793

**Montgomery
County Clerk**
451 West 3rd St.
Dayton, Ohio 45422

Morgan County Clerk
19 East Main St.
McConnelsville, Ohio
43756-1172

Morrow County Clerk
48 East High St.
Mount Gilead, Ohio 43338

Muskingum County Clerk
401 Main St.
Zanesville, Ohio
43701-3567

Noble County Clerk
County Courthouse
Caldwell, Ohio 43724

Ottawa County Clerk
315 Madison St.
Port Clinton, Ohio
43452-1936

Paulding County Clerk
County Courthouse
Paulding, Ohio 45879

Perry County Clerk
P.O. Box 167
New Lexington, Ohio
43764

Pickaway County Clerk
207 S. Court St.
Circleville, Ohio 43113

Pike County Clerk
100 East Second
Waverly, Ohio 45690-1301

Portage County Clerk
203 West Main St.
Ravenna, Ohio 44266-2761

Preble County Clerk
100 Main St.
Eaton, Ohio 45320

Putnam County Clerk
245 East Main St.
Ottawa, Ohio 45875-1968

Richland County Clerk
50 Park Ave., East
Mansfield, Ohio
44902-1850

Ross County Clerk
425 Chestnut St., #2077
Chillicothe, Ohio
45601-2306

Sandusky County Clerk
100 North Park Ave.
Fremont, Ohio 43420-2454

Scioto County Clerk
602 7th St.
Portsmouth, Ohio
45662-3948

Seneca County Clerk
3140 S. State Route 100
Tiffin, Ohio 44883

Shelby County Clerk
129 East Court St.
Sidney, Ohio 45365

Stark County Clerk
115 Central Plaza North
Canton, Ohio 44702-1290

Summit County Clerk
209 South High St.
Akron, Ohio 44308

Trumbull County Clerk
418 South Main St.
Warren, Ohio 44481-1005

Tuscarawas County Clerk
Public Square
New Philadelphia, Ohio
44663

Union County Clerk
5th and Court St.
Marysville, Ohio 43040

Van Wert County Clerk
121 East Main St.,
2nd Fl.
Van Wert, Ohio 45891

Vinton County Clerk
Courthouse
McArthur, Ohio 45651

Warren County Clerk
320 East Silver St.
Lebanon, Ohio 45036-1816

Washington County Clerk
205 Putnam St.
Marietta, Ohio 45750

Wayne County Clerk
P.O. Box 407
Wooster, Ohio 44691

Williams County Clerk
107 Butler St.
Bryan, Ohio 43506

Wood County Clerk
1 Courthouse Square
Bowling Green, Ohio
43402-2427

Wyandot County Clerk
County Courthouse
Upper Sandusky, Ohio
43351

OKLAHOMA

http://www.state.ok.us/

Adair County Clerk
P.O. Box 169
Stilwell, Oklahoma 74960

Alfalfa County Clerk
300 South Grand
Cherokee, Oklahoma
73728

Atoka County Clerk
201 East Court
Atoka, Oklahoma
74525-2045

Beaver County Clerk
111 West 2nd St.
Beaver, Oklahoma 73932

Beckham County Clerk
P.O. Box 67
Sayre, Oklahoma 73662

Blaine County Clerk
P.O. Box 138
Watonga, Oklahoma 73772

Bryan County Clerk
P.O. Box 1789
Durant, Oklahoma 74702

Caddo County Clerk
P.O. Box 10
Anadarko, Oklahoma
73005

Canadian County Clerk
Courthouse
El Reno, Oklahoma 73036

Carter County Clerk
First and B Street, SW
Ardmore, Oklahoma 73401

Cherokee County Clerk
213 West Delaware
Tahlequah, Oklahoma
74464-3639

Choctaw County Clerk
Choctaw County
Courthouse
Hugo, Oklahoma 74743

Cimarron County Clerk
P.O. Box 788
Boise City, Oklahoma
73933

Cleveland County Clerk
201 South Jones
Norman, Oklahoma 73069

Coal County Clerk
3 North Main St.
Coalgate, Oklahoma
74538-2832

Comanche County Clerk
Courthouse
Lawton, Oklahoma
73501-4326

Cotton County Clerk
301 North Broadway St.
Walters, Oklahoma
73572-1271

Craig County Clerk
301 W. Canadian
Vinita, Oklahoma 74301

Creek County Clerk
222 E. Dewey, Suite 200
Sapulpa, Oklahoma 74066

Custer County Clerk
P.O. Box 300
Arapaho, Oklahoma 73620

Delaware County Clerk
P.O. Box 309
Jay, Oklahoma 74346-0309

Dewey County Clerk
P.O. Box 368
Taloga, Oklahoma
73667-0368

Ellis County Clerk
100 South Washington
Arnett, Oklahoma
73832-0257

Garfield County Clerk
Rm. 101
Enid, Oklahoma 73701

Garvin County Clerk
Courthouse
Pauls Valley, Oklahoma
73075

Grady County Clerk
P.O. Box 1009
Chickasha, Oklahoma
73023-1009

Grant County Clerk
Courthouse
Medford, Oklahoma
73759-1243

Greer County Clerk
Courthouse
Mangum, Oklahoma 73554

Harmon County Clerk
Courthouse
Hollis, Oklahoma 73550

Harper County Clerk
P.O. Box 369
Buffalo, Oklahoma
73834-0369

Haskell County Clerk
202 East Main
Stigler, Oklahoma
74462-2439

Hughes County Clerk
P.O. Box 914
Holdenville, Oklahoma
74848-0914

Jackson County Clerk
Courthouse
Altus, Oklahoma 73521

Jefferson County Clerk
220 North Main St.
Waurika, Oklahoma
73573-2234

Johnston County Clerk
Courthouse
Tishomingo, Oklahoma
73460

Kay County Clerk
Courthouse
Newkirk, Oklahoma 74647

Kingfisher County Clerk
P.O. Box 118
Kingfisher, Oklahoma
73750

Kiowa County Clerk
Courthouse
Hobart, Oklahoma 73651

Latimer County Clerk
109 North Central
Wilburton, Oklahoma
74578-2440

LeFlore County Clerk
P.O. Box 218
Poteau, Oklahoma
74953-0607

Lincoln County Clerk
P.O. Box 126
Chandler, Oklahoma
74834-0126

Logan County Clerk
Courthouse
Guthrie, Oklahoma
73044-4939

Love County Clerk
405 West Main St.
Marietta, Oklahoma
73448-2848

Major County Clerk
East Broadway
Fairview, Oklahoma 73737

Marshall County Clerk
P.O. Box 58
Madill, Oklahoma 73446

Mayes County Clerk
Courthouse
Pryor, Oklahoma 74361

McClain County Clerk
P.O. Box 629
Purcell, Oklahoma 73080

McCurtain County Clerk
P.O.a Box 1078
Idabel, Oklahoma 74745

McIntosh County Clerk
P.O. Box 108
Eufaula, Oklahoma
74432-0108

Murray County Clerk
P.O. Box 240
Sulphur, Oklahoma
73086-0240

Muskogee County Clerk
P.O. Box 2307
Muskogee, Oklahoma
74402-2307

Nobel County Clerk
300 Courthouse Dr. #11
Perry, Oklahoma 73077

Nowata County Clerk
229 North Maple St.
Nowata, Oklahoma
74048-2654

Okfuskee County Clerk
P.O. Box 26
Okemah, Oklahoma
74859-0026

Oklahoma County Clerk
320 NW Robert S. Kerr
Oklahoma City, Oklahoma
73102-3441

Okmulgee County Clerk
P.O. Box 904
Okmulgee, Oklahoma
74447

Osage County Clerk
P.O. Box 87
Pawhuska, Oklahoma
74056-0087

Ottawa County Clerk
Courthouse
Miami, Oklahoma 74354

Pawnee County Clerk
Courthouse
Pawnee, Oklahoma
74058-2568

Payne County Clerk
Sixth and Husband
Stillwater, Oklahoma
74074

Pittsburg County Clerk
Courthouse
McAlester, Oklahoma
74501

Pontotoc County Clerk
P.O. Box 1425
Ada, Oklahoma 74820

**Pottawatomie
County Clerk**
325 N. Broadway
Shawnee, Oklahoma
74801-6919

**Pushmataha
County Clerk**
203 SW Third
Antlers, Oklahoma
74523-3899

Roger Mills County Clerk
P.O. Box 708
Cheyenne, Oklahoma
73628

Rogers County Clerk
219 South Missouri
Claremore, Oklahoma
74017-7832

Seminole County Clerk
Courthouse
Wewoka, Oklahoma 74884

Sequoyah County Clerk
120 East Chickasaw St.
Sallisaw, Oklahoma
74955-4655

Stephens County Clerk
Courthouse
Duncan, Oklahoma 73533

Texas County Clerk
P.O. Box 197
Guymon, Oklahoma
73942-0197

Tillman County Clerk
P.O. Box 992
Frederick, Oklahoma
73542

Tulsa County Clerk
500 South Denver
Tulsa, Oklahoma 74103-3826

Wagoner County Clerk
307 East Cherokee
Wagoner, Oklahoma
74467-4729

Washington County Clerk
420 South Johnstone
Bartlesville, Oklahoma
74003-6605

Washita County Clerk
P.O. Box 380
Cordell, Oklahoma 73632

Woods County Clerk
P.O. Box 386
Alva, Oklahoma 73717

Woodward County Clerk
1600 Main St.
Woodward, Oklahoma
73801-3046

OREGON

http://www.state.or.us/

Baker County Clerk
1995 Third St.
Baker, Oregon 97814-3363

Benton County Clerk
120 NW Fourth St.
Corvallis, Oregon
97330-4728

Clackamas County Clerk
906 Main St.
Oregon City, Oregon 97045

Clatsop County Clerk
749 Commercial
Astoria, Oregon 97103

Columbia County Clerk
Strand St.
St. Helens, Oregon 97051

Coos County Clerk
250 N. Baxter St.
Coquille, Oregon
97423-1899

Crook County Clerk
300 East Third St.
Prineville, Oregon
97754-1949

Curry County Clerk
P.O. Box 746
Gold Beach, Oregon
97444-0746

Deschutes County Clerk
1164 NW Bond
Bend, Oregon 97701-1905

Douglas County Clerk
1036 SE Douglas
Roseburg, Oregon
97470-3317

Gilliam County Clerk
221 S. Oregon St.
Condon, Oregon 97823

Grant County Clerk
200 South Canyon Blvd.
Canyon City, Oregon
97820

Harney County Clerk
450 North Buena Vista
Burns, Oregon 97720

Hood River County Clerk
309 State St.
Hood River, Oregon 97031

Jackson County Clerk
10 South Oakdale
Medford, Oregon
97501-2952

Jefferson County Clerk
66 South East D St.
Madras, Oregon
97741-1707

Josephine County Clerk
North West Sixth and C
Grants Pass, Oregon 97526

Klamath County Clerk
316 Main St.
Klamath Falls, Oregon
97601-6347

Lake County Clerk
513 Center St.
Lakeview, Oregon
97630-1539

Lane County Clerk
125 East Eighth Ave.
Eugene, Oregon
97401-2922

Lincoln County Clerk
225 West Olive St.
Newport, Oregon
97365-3811

Linn County Clerk
P.O. Box 100
Albany, Oregon
97321-0031

Malheur County Clerk
251 B Street West
Vale, Oregon 97918-0130

Marion County Clerk
Courthouse
Salem, Oregon 97301

Morrow County Clerk
P.O. Box 338
Heppner, Oregon
97836-0338

Multnomah County Clerk
426 SW Stark, 2nd Fl.
Portland, Oregon 97204

Polk County Clerk
850 Main Street
Dallas, Oregon 97338-3116

Sherman County Clerk
P.O. Box 365
Moro, Oregon 97039-0365

Tillamook County Clerk
201 Laurel Ave.
Tillamook, Oregon
97141-2394

Umatilla County Clerk
216 SE Fourth Ave.
Pendleton, Oregon
97801-2500

Union County Clerk
1100 L Ave.
La Grande, Oregon
97850-2121

Wallowa County Clerk
101 South River St.
Enterprise, Oregon
97828-0170

Wasco County Clerk
5th and Washington
The Dalles, Oregon 97058

**Washington
County Clerk**
155 North First Ave.
Hillsboro, Oregon
97124-3002

Wheeler County Clerk
P.O. Box 327
Fossil, Oregon 97830-0327

Yamhill County Clerk
5th and Evans
McMinnville, Oregon
97128

PENNSYLVANIA
http://www.state.pa.us/

Adams County Clerk
111 Baltimore St.
Gettysburg, Pennsylvania
17325-2312

Allegheny County Clerk
414 Grant St.
Pittsburgh, Pennsylvania
15219

Armstrong County Clerk
Market St.
Kittanning, Pennsylvania
16201

Beaver County Clerk
Courthouse
Beaver, Pennsylvania
15009

Bedford County Clerk
203 S. Juliana St.
Bedford, Pennsylvania
15522-1714

Berks County Clerk
633 Court St.
Reading, Pennsylvania
19601

Blair County Clerk
423 Allegheny St.
Hollidaysburg,
Pennsylvania 16648-2022

Bradford County Clerk
301 Main St.
Towanda, Pennsylvania
18848-1824

Bucks County Clerk
Main and Court St.
Doylestown, Pennsylvania
18901

Butler County Clerk
South Main St.
Butler, Pennsylvania 16001

Cambria County Clerk
200 South Center St.
P.O. Box 298
Ebensburg, Pennsylvania
15931

Cameron County Clerk
20 East 5th St.
Emporium, Pennsylvania
15834

Carbon County Clerk
P.O. Box 129 Courthouse
Jim Thorpe, Pennsylvania
18229

Centre County Clerk
Willowbank Bldg.
Bellefonte, Pennsylvania
16823

Chester County Clerk
601 Westtown Rd.,
Suite 080
West Chester, Pennsylvania
19380-0990

Clarion County Clerk
Main Street
Clarion, Pennsylvania
16214

Clearfield County Clerk
2 Market St.
Clearfield, Pennsylvania
16830-2404

Clinton County Clerk
County Courthouse
Lock Haven, Pennsylvania
17745

Columbia County Clerk
35 West Main St.
Bloomsburg, Pennsylvania
17815-1702

Crawford County Clerk
903 Diamond Park
Meadville, Pennsylvania
16335-2677

**Cumberland
County Clerk**
Hanover St.
Carlisle, Pennsylvania
17013

Dauphin County Clerk
Front and Market Street
Harrisburg, Pennsylvania
17101-2012

Delaware County Clerk
West Front St.
Media, Pennsylvania 19063

Elk County Clerk
P.O. Box 314
Ridgeway, Pennsylvania
15853

Erie County Clerk
140 West Sixth St.
Erie, Pennsylvania
16501-1011

Fayette County Clerk
61 East Main St.
Uniontown, Pennsylvania
15401-3514

Forest County Clerk
P.O. Box 423
Tionesta, Pennsylvania
16353

Franklin County Clerk
157 Lincoln Way, East
Chambersburg,
Pennsylvania 17201-2211

Fulton County Clerk
North Second St.
McConnellsburg,
Pennsylvania 17233

Greene County Clerk
93 East High St.
Waynesburg, Pennsylvania
15370

**Huntingdon
County Clerk**
223 Penn St.
Huntingdon, Pennsylvania
16652

Indiana County Clerk
825 Philadelphia
Indiana, Pennsylvania
15701-3934

Jefferson County Clerk
155 Jefferson Place
Brookville, Pennsylvania
15825-1236

Juniata County Clerk
P.O. Box 68
Miffintown, Pennsylvania
17059-0068

**Lackawanna
County Clerk**
Vital Statistics Office
100 Lackawanna Ave.
Scranton, Pennsylvania
18503

Lancaster County Clerk
50 North Duke St.
Lancaster, Pennsylvania
17603

Lawrence County Clerk
101 S. Mercer St.
New Castle, Pennsylvania
16101

Lebanon County Clerk
400 South Eighth St.
Lebanon, Pennsylvania
17042-6794

Lehigh County Clerk
455 Hamilton St.
Allentown, Pennsylvania
18105

Luzerne County Clerk
200 North River St.
Wilkes-Barre, Pennsylvania
18702-2685

Lycoming County Clerk
48 West Third St.
Williamsport, Pennsylvania
17701-6519

McKean County Clerk
P.O. Box 202
Smethport, Pennsylvania
16749

Mercer County Clerk
South Diamond St.
Mercer, Pennsylvania
16137

Mifflin County Clerk
20 North Wayne St.
Lewistown, Pennsylvania
17044-1770

Monroe County Clerk
Courthouse Square
Stroudsburg, Pennsylvania
18360

Montgomery County Clerk
P.O. Box 311
Norristown, Pennsylvania
19404

Montour County Clerk
29 Mill St.
Danville, Pennsylvania
17821-1945

Northampton County Clerk
7th and Washington St.
Easton, Pennsylvania
18042-7401

Northumberland County Clerk
2nd and Market St.
Sunbury, Pennsylvania
17801

Perry County Clerk
P.O. Box 37
New Bloomfield,
Pennsylvania 17068

Philadelphia County Clerk
3101 Market St. First Fl.
Philadelphia, Pennsylvania
19104

Pike County Clerk
506 Broad St.
Milford, Pennsylvania
18337-1511

Potter County Clerk
1 East Second St.
Coudersport, Pennsylvania
16915

Schuylkill County Clerk
N. 2nd St. and Laurel Blvd.
Pottsville, Pennsylvania
17901

Snyder County Clerk
11 West Market St.
Middleburg, Pennsylvania
17842

Somerset County Clerk
111 E. Union St.
Somerset, Pennsylvania
15501

Sullivan County Clerk
Main and Muncy
Laporte, Pennsylvania
18626

Susquehanna County Clerk
Courthouse
Montrose, Pennsylvania
18801

Tioga County Clerk
116-188 Main St.
Wellsboro, Pennsylvania
16901-1410

Union County Clerk
103 South 2nd St.
Lewisburg, Pennsylvania
17837-1903

Venango County Clerk
Liberty and 12th Street
Franklin, Pennsylvania
16323

Warren County Clerk
204 Fourth St.
Warren, Pennsylvania
16365-2318

Washington County Clerk
100 West Beau St.
Washington, Pennsylvania
15301-4402

Wayne County Clerk
925 Court St.
Honesdale, Pennsylvania
18431-9517

Westmoreland County Clerk
Westmoreland
County Court House
Main St.
Greensburg, Pennsylvania
15601-2405

Wyoming County Clerk
Courthouse Square
Tunkhannock,
Pennsylvania 18657-1216

York County Clerk
28 East Market St.
York, Pennsylvania
17401-1501

RHODE ISLAND
http://www.state.ri.us/

Bristol County Clerk
1 Dorrance Plaza
Bristol, Rhode Island
02809

Kent County Clerk
222 Quaker Lane
East Greenwich, Rhode
Island 02818

Newport County Clerk
Washington Square
Newport, Rhode Island
02840

Providence County Clerk
250 Benefit
Providence, Rhode Island
02903-2719

**Washington
County Clerk**
4800 Tower Hill Rd.
Wakefield, Rhode Island
02879

SOUTH CAROLINA

http://www.state.sc.us/

Abbeville County Clerk
P.O. Box 99
Abbeville, South Carolina
29620-0099

Aiken County Clerk
P.O. Box 583
Aiken, South Carolina
29802-0583

Allendale County Clerk
P.O. Box 126
Allendale, South Carolina
29810-0126

Anderson County Clerk
220 McGee Rd.
Anderson, South Carolina
29625

Bamberg County Clerk
P.O. Box 150
Bamberg, South Carolina
29003-0150

Barnwell County Clerk
P.O. Box 723
Barnwell, South Carolina
29812-0723

Beaufort County Clerk
Courthouse
Beaufort, South Carolina
29901

Berkeley County Clerk
223 North Live Oak Dr.
Moncks Corner,
South Carolina 29461-2331

Calhoun County Clerk
302 S. Railroad Ave.
St. Matthews,
South Carolina 29135-1452

Charleston County Clerk
4050 Bridgeview Dr.
North Charleston,
South Carolina 29405

Cherokee County Clerk
P.O. Box 866
Gaffney, South Carolina
26342

Chester County Clerk
P.O. Box 580
Chester, South Carolina
29706-0580

**Chesterfield
County Clerk**
P.O. Box 529
Chesterfield,
South Carolina 29709-0529

Clarendon County Clerk
P.O. Box E
Manning, South Carolina
29102-0136

Colleton County Clerk
P.O. Box 620
Walterboro, South Carolina
29488-0620

Darlington County Clerk
Courthouse
Darlington, South Carolina
29532-3213

Dillon County Clerk
P.O. Box 1220
Dillon, South Carolina
29536-1220

Dorchester County Clerk
101 Ridge St.
St. George, South Carolina
29477-2443

Edgefield County Clerk
215 Jeter St.
Edgefield, South Carolina
29824-1133

Fairfield County Clerk
P.O. Box 236
Winnsboro, South Carolina
29180-0236

Florence County Clerk
180 North Irby St.
Florence, South Carolina
29501-3456

**Georgetown
County Clerk**
715 Prince St.
Georgetown,
South Carolina 29440-3631

Greenville County Clerk
P.O. Box 2507
Greenville, South Carolina
29602

Greenwood County Clerk
528 Monument
Greenwood, South Carolina
29646-2643

Hampton County Clerk
P.O. Box 7
Hampton, South Carolina
29924-0007

Horry County Clerk
P.O. Box 288
Conway, South Carolina
29528-0288

Jasper County Clerk
P.O. Box 248
Ridgeland, South Carolina
29936-0248

Kershaw County Clerk
Courthouse
Camden, South Carolina
29020

Lancaster County Clerk
P.O. Box 1809
Lancaster, South Carolina
29720

Laurens County Clerk
P.O. Box 287
Laurens, South Carolina
29360-0287

Lee County Clerk
Courthouse Square
Bishopville, South Carolina
29010

Lexington County Clerk
Courthouse
Lexington, South Carolina
29072

Marion County Clerk
P.O. Box 295
Marion, South Carolina
29571-0295

Marlboro County Clerk
P.O. Box 996
Bennettsville,
South Carolina 29512-0996

**McCormick
County Clerk**
P.O. Box 86
McCormick,
South Carolina 28735

Newberry County Clerk
P.O. Box 278
Newberry, South Carolina
29108-0278

Oconee County Clerk
P.O. Box 158
Walhalla, South Carolina
29691-0158

**Orangeburg
County Clerk**
P.O. Box 100
Orangeburg,
South Carolina 29116-0100

Pickens County Clerk
P.O. Box 215
Pickens, South Carolina
29671-0215

Richland County Clerk
1701 Main St.
Columbia, South Carolina
29201-2833

Saluda County Clerk
Courthouse Square
Saluda, South Carolina
29138-1444

**Spartanburg
County Clerk**
180 Magnolia St.
Spartanburg,
South Carolina 29306

Sumter County Clerk
141 North Main St.
Sumter, South Carolina
29150-4965

Union County Clerk
P.O. Box G
Union, South Carolina
29379-0200

**Williamsburg
County Clerk**
203 North Brooks
Kingstree, South Carolina
29556

York County Clerk
P.O. Box 649
York, South Carolina
29745-0649

SOUTH DAKOTA

http://www.state.sd.us/

Aurora County Clerk
Courthouse
Plankinton, South Dakota
57368

Beadle County Clerk
Courthouse
Huron, South Dakota
57350

Bennett County Clerk
Main St.
Martin, South Dakota
57551

**Bon Homme
County Clerk**
Courthouse
Tyndall, South Dakota
57066

Brookings County Clerk
314 Sixth Ave.
Brookings, South Dakota
57006-2041

Brown County Clerk
111 South East First Ave.
Aberdeen, South Dakota
57401-4203

Brule County Clerk
300 South Courtland
Chamberlain, South Dakota
57325-1508

Buffalo County Clerk
Courthouse
Gann Valley, South Dakota
57341-0148

Butte County Clerk
Courthouse
Belle Fourche,
South Dakota 57717

Campbell County Clerk
P.O. Box 146
Mound City, South Dakota
57646

**Charles Mix
County Clerk**
Courthouse
Lake Andes, South Dakota
57356

Clark County Clerk
Courthouse
Clark, South Dakota 57225

Clay County Clerk
P.O. Box 403
Vermillion, South Dakota
57069-0403

Codington County Clerk
Courthouse
Watertown, South Dakota
57201

Corson County Clerk
200 First St. East
McIntosh, South Dakota
57641

Custer County Clerk
420 SW Mount Rushmore
Custer, South Dakota
57730-1934

Davison County Clerk
200 East 4th Ave.
Mitchell, South Dakota
57301-2631

Day County Clerk
710 West First St.
Webster, South Dakota
57274

Deuel County Clerk
P.O. Box 125
Clear Lake, South Dakota
57226

Dewey County Clerk
Courthouse
Timber Lake, South Dakota
57656

Douglas County Clerk
Courthouse
Armour, South Dakota
57313

Edmunds County Clerk
Courthouse
Ipswich, South Dakota
57451

Fall River County Clerk
906 North River St.
Hot Springs, South Dakota
57747-1387

Faulk County Clerk
Courthouse
Faulkton, South Dakota
57438

Grant County Clerk
210 East Fifth Ave.
Milbank, South Dakota
57252-2433

Gregory County Clerk
Courthouse
Burke, South Dakota 57523

Haakon County Clerk
Courthouse
Philip, South Dakota 57567

Hamlin County Clerk
Courthouse
Hayti, South Dakota 57241

Hand County Clerk
415 West First Ave.
Miller, South Dakota
57362-1346

Hanson County Clerk
Courthouse
Alexandria, South Dakota
57311

Harding County Clerk
Courthouse
Buffalo, South Dakota
57720

Hughes County Clerk
104 E. Capital
Pierre, South Dakota
57501-2563

Hutchinson County Clerk
Courthouse
Olivet, South Dakota
57052

Hyde County Clerk
P.O. Box 306
Highmore, South Dakota
57345-0306

Jackson County Clerk
Courthouse
Kadoka, South Dakota
57543

Jerauld County Clerk
Courthouse
Wessington Springs,
South Dakota 57382

Jones County Clerk
Courthouse
Murdo, South Dakota
57559

Kingsbury County Clerk
Courthouse
De Smet, South Dakota
57231

Lake County Clerk
P.O. Box 447
Madison, South Dakota
57042-0447

Lawrence County Clerk
644 Main St.
Deadwood, South Dakota
57732-1124

Lincoln County Clerk
100 East Fifth St.
Canton, South Dakota
57013-1732

Lyman County Clerk
Courthouse
Kennebec, South Dakota
57544

Marshall County Clerk
Courthouse
Britton, South Dakota
57430

McCook County Clerk
Courthouse
Salem, South Dakota
57058

McPherson County Clerk
P.O. Box L
Leola, South Dakota 57456

Meade County Clerk
1425 Sherman St.
Sturgis, South Dakota
57785-1452

Mellette County Clerk
P.O. Box C
White River, South Dakota
57579

Miner County Clerk
Courthouse
Howard, South Dakota
57349

Minnehaha County Clerk
415 N. Dakota Ave.
Sioux Falls, South Dakota
57102-0192

Moody County Clerk
P.O. Box 152
Flandreau, South Dakota
57028

Pennington County Clerk
P.O. Box 230
Rapid City, South Dakota
57709-0230

Perkins County Clerk
Courthouse
Bison, South Dakota 57620

Potter County Clerk
201 South Exene
Gettysburg, South Dakota
57442-1521

Roberts County Clerk
411 Second Ave. East
Sisseton, South Dakota
57262-1403

Sanborn County Clerk
Courthouse
Woonsocket, South Dakota
57385

Shannon County Clerk
906 North St.
Hot Springs, South Dakota
57747-1387

Spink County Clerk
210 East Seventh Ave.
Redfield, South Dakota
57469-1266

Stanley County Clerk
Courthouse
Fort Pierre, South Dakota
57532

Sully County Clerk
Courthouse
Onida, South Dakota 57564

Todd County Clerk
200 East Third St.
(c/o Tripp County)
Winner, South Dakota
57580-1806

Tripp County Clerk
200 East Third St.
Winner, South Dakota
57580-1806

Turner County Clerk
Main St.
Parker, South Dakota
57053

Union County Clerk
P.O. Box 757
Elk Point, South Dakota
57025-0757

Walworth County Clerk
P.O. Box 199
Selby, South Dakota
57472-0199

Yankton County Clerk
P.O. Box 155
Yankton, South Dakota
57078-0137

Ziebach County Clerk
Main St.
Dupree, South Dakota
57623

TENNESSEE
http://www.state.tn.us/

Anderson County Clerk
100 N. Main St.
Clinton, Tennessee 37716

Bedford County Clerk
104 Northside Square
Shelbyville, Tennessee
37160

Benton County Clerk
3 East Court Square, #101
Camden, Tennessee 38320

Bledsoe County Clerk
P.O. Box 149
Pikeville, Tennessee 37367

Blount County Clerk
345 Court St.
Maryville, Tennessee
37804

Bradley County Clerk
P.O. Box 46
Cleveland, Tennessee
37364-0046

Campbell County Clerk
195 Kentucky St.
Jacksboro, Tennessee
37757

Cannon County Clerk
Public Square
Woodbury, Tennessee
37190

Carroll County Clerk
P.O. Box 110
Huntingdon, Tennessee
38344-0110

Carter County Clerk
801 East Elk Ave.
Elizabethton, Tennessee
37643

Cheatham County Clerk
100 Public Square
Ashland City, Tennessee
37015-1711

Chester County Clerk
133 East Main St.
Henderson, Tennessee
38340

Claiborne County Clerk
1740 Main St., Suite 201
Tazewell, Tennessee 37879

Clay County Clerk
100 Courthouse Square
Celina, Tennessee 38551

Cocke County Clerk
111 Court Ave.
Newport, Tennessee 37821

Coffee County Clerk
300 Hillsboro Blvd
Manchester, Tennessee
37355

Crockett County Clerk
Courthouse
Alamo, Tennessee 38001

**Cumberland
County Clerk**
Main St.
Crossville, Tennessee
38555-9428

Davidson County Clerk
311 23rd Ave. North
Nashville, Tennessee 37203

Decatur County Clerk
P.O. Box 488
Decaturville, Tennessee
38329-0488

DeKalb County Clerk
County Courthouse,
Rm. 205
Smithville, Tennessee
37166

Dickson County Clerk
4 Court Square
Charlotte, Tennessee 37036

Dyer County Clerk
P.O. Box 1360
Dyersburg, Tennessee
38025-1360

Fayette County Clerk
P.O. Box 218
Somerville, Tennessee
38068-0218

Fentress County Clerk
Main St.
Jamestown, Tennessee
38556

Franklin County Clerk
1 South Jefferson St.
Winchester, Tennessee
37398

Gibson County Clerk
P.O. Box 228
Trenton, Tennessee 38382

Giles County Clerk
P.O. Box 678
Madison and First St.
Pulaski, Tennessee
38478-0678

Grainger County Clerk
Highway 11 West
Rutledge, Tennessee 37861

Greene County Clerk
Courthouse
Greeneville, Tennessee
37743

Grundy County Clerk
Hwy 56
Altamont, Tennessee 37301

Hamblen County Clerk
511 West Second N St.
Morristown, Tennessee
37814-3964

Hamilton County Clerk
625 Georgia Ave. #201
Chattanooga, Tennessee
37402

Hancock County Clerk
Main St.
Sneedville, Tennessee
37869

Hardeman County Clerk
100 N. Main
Bolivar, Tennessee
38008-2322

Hardin County Clerk
601 Main St.
Savannah, Tennessee 38372

Hawkins County Clerk
150 Washington St.
Rogersville, Tennessee
37857

Haywood County Clerk
100 N. Washington
Brownsville, Tennessee
38012-2557

Henderson County Clerk
17 Monroe St.
Lexington, Tennessee
38351

Henry County Clerk
100 W. Washington St.
Paris, Tennessee 38242

Hickman County Clerk
101 College St.
Centerville, Tennessee
37033

Houston County Clerk
100 Main St.
Erin, Tennessee 37061

Humphreys County Clerk
102 Thompson St. #2
Waverly, Tennessee 37185

Jackson County Clerk
101 E. Hull Ave.
Gainesboro, Tennessee
38562

Jefferson County Clerk
204 W. Main St.
Dandridge, Tennessee
37725

Johnson County Clerk
222 Main St.
Mountain City, Tennessee
37683-1612

Knox County Clerk
140 Dameron Ave.
Knoxville, Tennessee
37917-6413

Lake County Clerk
Church St.
Tiptonville, Tennessee
38079

Lauderdale County Clerk
Courthouse
Ripley, Tennessee 38063

Lawrence County Clerk
Courthouse
Lawrenceburg, Tennessee
38464

Lewis County Clerk
110 N. Park St.
Hohenwald, Tennessee
38462

Lincoln County Clerk
112 Main St. South
Fayetteville, Tennessee
37334

Loudon County Clerk
101 Mulberry St.
Loudon, Tennessee 37774

Macon County Clerk
104 Courthouse
Lafayette, Tennessee 37083

Madison County Clerk
Courthouse
Jackson, Tennessee 38301

Marion County Clerk
1 Courthouse Square
Jasper, Tennessee 37347

Marshall County Clerk
207 Marshall County
Courthouse
Lewisburg, Tennessee
37091

Maury County Clerk
Public Square
Columbia, Tennessee
38401

McMinn County Clerk
6 West Madison Ave.
Athens, Tennessee 37303

McNairy County Clerk
Courthouse
Selmer, Tennessee 38375

Meigs County Clerk
P.O. Box 218
Decatur, Tennessee
37322-0218

Monroe County Clerk
103 College St.
Madisonville, Tennessee
37354

**Montgomery County
Clerk**
Courthouse
Clarksville, Tennessee
37042

Moore County Clerk
P.O. Box 206
Lynchburg, Tennessee
37352

Morgan County Clerk
415 N. Kingston St.
Wartburg, Tennessee 37887

Obion County Clerk
Courthouse
Union City, Tennessee
37261

Overton County Clerk
317 East University St.
Livingston, Tennessee
38570

Perry County Clerk
P.O. Box 16
Linden, Tennessee
37096-0016

Pickett County Clerk
1 Courthouse Square
Byrdstown, Tennessee
38549

Polk County Clerk
Hwy 411
Benton, Tennessee 37307

Putnam County Clerk
29 Washington
Cookeville, Tennessee
38501

Rhea County Clerk
1475 Market St.
Dayton, Tennessee 37321

Roane County Clerk
200 W. Race St.
Kingston, Tennessee 37763

Robertson County Clerk
101 5th Ave. W
Springfield, Tennessee
37172

Rutherford County Clerk
26 N. Public Square
Murfreesboro, Tennessee
37130

Scott County Clerk
P.O. Box 69
Huntsville, Tennessee
37756

Sequatchie County Clerk
308 Cherry St.
Dunlap, Tennessee 37327

Sevier County Clerk
125 Court Ave. #202
Sevierville, Tennessee
37862

Shelby County Clerk
814 Jefferson Ave.
Memphis, Tennessee 38105

Smith County Clerk
211 Main St. North
Carthage, Tennessee 37030

Steward County Clerk
P.O. Box 67
Dover, Tennessee
37058-0067

Sullivan County Clerk
3411 Highway 126
Blountville, Tennessee
37617

Sumner County Clerk
155 East Main St.
Gallatin, Tennessee 37066

Tipton County Clerk
P.O. Box 528
Covington, Tennessee
38019-0528

Trousdale County Clerk
200 East Main St. #2
Hartsville, Tennessee
37074

Unicoi County Clerk
100 N. Main Ave.
Erwin, Tennessee
37650-0340

Union County Clerk
901 Main St.
Maynardville, Tennessee
37807-0395

Van Buren County Clerk
Courthouse Square
Spencer, Tennessee
38585-0126

Warren County Clerk
Courthouse
McMinnville, Tennessee
37110

**Washington
County Clerk**
Courthouse
Jonesboro, Tennessee
37659

Wayne County Clerk
P.O. Box 185
Waynesboro, Tennessee
38485

Weakley County Clerk
P.O. Box 587
Dresden, Tennessee 38225

White County Clerk
1 E. Bockman Way
Sparta, Tennessee 38583

Williamson County Clerk
1320 W. Main St.
Franklin, Tennessee 37064

Wilson County Clerk
228 E. Main St.
Lebanon, Tennessee 37087

TEXAS

http://www.state.tx.us/

Anderson County Clerk
500 N. Church St.
Palestine, Texas 75801

Andrews County Clerk
P.O. Box 727
Andrews, Texas 79714

Angelina County Clerk
P.O. Box 908
Lufkin, Texas 75902-0908

Aransas County Clerk
301 Live Oak
Rockport, Texas
78382-2744

Archer County Clerk
P.O. Box 458
Archer City, Texas 76351

Armstrong County Clerk
P.O. Box 309
Claude, Texas 79019-0309

Atascosa County Clerk
Circle Dr.
Jourdanton, Texas 78026

Austin County Clerk
1 East Main
Bellville, Texas
77418-1521

Bailey County Clerk
P.O. Box 735
Muleshoe, Texas
79347-0735

Bandera County Clerk
Courthouse
Bandera, Texas 78003

Bastrop County Clerk
803 Pine St.
Bastrop, Texas 78602-0577

Baylor County Clerk
Courthouse
Seymour, Texas 76380

Bee County Clerk
105 West Corpus Christi
Beeville, Texas 78102-5627

Bell County Clerk
Courthouse
Belton, Texas 76513

Bexar County Clerk
Courthouse
San Antonio, Texas
78285-5100

Blanco County Clerk
P.O. Box 65
Johnson City, Texas
78636-0065

Borden County Clerk
P.O. Box 124
Gail, Texas 79738

Bosque County Clerk
P.O. Box 617
Meridian, Texas
76665-0617

Bowie County Clerk
Courthouse
New Boston, Texas 75570

Brazoria County Clerk
P.O. Box D
Angleton, Texas
77515-1504

Brazos County Clerk
300 East 26th St. #314
Bryan, Texas 77803

Brewster County Clerk
P.O. Box 119
Alpine, Texas 79831

Briscoe County Clerk
P.O. Box 375
Silverton, Texas
79257-0375

Brooks County Clerk
Courthouse
Falfurrias, Texas 78355

Brown County Clerk
200 South Broadway
Brownwood, Texas
76801-3136

Burleson County Clerk
P.O. Box 57
Caldwell, Texas 77836

Burnet County Clerk
220 S. Pierce St.
Burnet, Texas 78611-3136

Caldwell County Clerk
Courthouse
Lockhart, Texas 78644

Calhoun County Clerk
211 South Ann
Port Lavaca, Texas
77979-4249

Callahan County Clerk
Courthouse
Baird, Texas 79504

Cameron County Clerk
964 East Harrison St.
Brownsville, Texas 78520

Camp County Clerk
126 Church St.
Pittsburg, Texas
75686-1346

Carson County Clerk
P.O. Box 487
Panhandle, Texas
79068-0487

Cass County Clerk
P.O. Box 468
Linden, Texas 75563-0468

Castro County Clerk
100 East Bedford
Dimmitt, Texas
79027-2643

Chambers County Clerk
P.O. Box 728
Anahuac, Texas
77514-0728

Cherokee County Clerk
Courthouse
Rusk, Texas 75785

Childress County Clerk
P.O. Box 4
Childress, Texas
79201-3755

Clay County Clerk
P.O. Box 548
Henrietta, Texas
76365-0548

Cochran County Clerk
Courthouse
Morton, Texas 79346

Coke County Clerk
P.O. Box 150
Robert Lee, Texas
76945-0150

Coleman County Clerk
P.O. Box 591
Coleman, Texas
76834-0591

Collin County Clerk
Courthouse
McKinney, Texas
75069-5655

**Collingsworth County
Clerk**
Courthouse
Wellington, Texas
79095-3037

Colorado County Clerk
P.O. Box 68
Columbus, Texas 78934

Comal County Clerk
100 Main Plaza, Suite 104
New Braunfels, Texas
78130

Comanche County Clerk
Courthouse
Comanche, Texas
76442-3264

Concho County Clerk
Courthouse
Paint Rock, Texas 76866

Cooke County Clerk
Courthouse
Gainesville, Texas 76240

Coryell County Clerk
Main St.
Gatesville, Texas 76528

Cottle County Clerk
P.O. Box 717
Paducah, Texas 79248

Crane County Clerk
P.O. Box 578
Crane, Texas 79731-0578

Crockett County Clerk
P.O. Box C
Ozona, Texas 76943-2502

Crosby County Clerk
Courthouse
Crosbyton, Texas
79322-2503

Culberson County Clerk
P.O. Box 158
Van Horn, Texas
79855-0158

Dallam County Clerk
P.O. Box 1352
Dalhart, Texas 79002-1352

Dallas County Clerk
509 Main St.
Dallas, Texas 75202-3507

Dawson County Clerk
P.O. Box 1268
Lamesa, Texas 79331-1268

De Witt County Clerk
307 N. Gonzales St.
Cuero, Texas 77954-2970

Deaf Smith County Clerk
Courthouse
Hereford, Texas
79045-5515

Delta County Clerk
200 West Dallas Ave.
Cooper, Texas 75432-1726

Denton County Clerk
P.O. Box 2187
Denton, Texas 76202-2187

Dickens County Clerk
Courthouse
Dickens, Texas 79229

Dimmit County Clerk
103 N. Fifth St.
Carrizo Springs, Texas
78834-3101

Donley County Clerk
Courthouse
Clarendon, Texas
79226-2020

Duval County Clerk
Courthouse
San Diego, Texas 78384

Eastland County Clerk
P.O. Box 110
Eastland, Texas
76448-0110

Ector County Clerk
Courthouse
Odessa, Texas 79763

Edwards County Clerk
P.O. Box 184
Rocksprings, Texas
78880-0184

El Paso County Clerk
500 East San Antonio
El Paso, Texas 79901-2421

Ellis County Clerk
Courthouse
Waxahachie, Texas
75165-3759

Erath County Clerk
Courthouse
Stephenville, Texas
76401-4219

Falls County Clerk
P.O. Box 458
Marlin, Texas 76661-0458

Fannin County Clerk
Courthouse
Bonham, Texas 75418

Fayette County Clerk
151 N. Washington St.
La Grange, Texas 78945

Fisher County Clerk
Courthouse
Roby, Texas 79543

Floyd County Clerk
P.O. Box 476
Floydada, Texas
79235-0476

Foard County Clerk
P.O. Box 539
Crowell, Texas 79227

Fort Bend County Clerk
301 Jackson
Richmond, Texas 77469

Franklin County Clerk
P.O. Box 68
Mount Vernon, Texas
75457-0068

Freestone County Clerk
P.O. Box 1017
Fairfield, Texas
75840-1017

Frio County Clerk
P.O. Box X
Pearsall, Texas 78061-1423

Gaines County Clerk
Courthouse
Seminole, Texas
79360-4341

Galveston County Clerk
P.O. Box 2450
Galveston, Texas 77553

Garza County Clerk
Courthouse
Post, Texas 79356-3242

Gillespie County Clerk
P.O. Box 551
Fredericksburg, Texas
78624-0551

Glasscock County Clerk
P.O. Box 190
Garden City, Texas
79739-0190

Goliad County Clerk
P.O. Box 5
Goliad, Texas 77963-0005

Gonzales County Clerk
Courthouse
Gonzales, Texas 78629

Gray County Clerk
200 N. Russell St.
Pampa, Texas 79065-6442

Grayson County Clerk
100 West Houston
Sherman, Texas 75090

Gregg County Clerk
P.O. Box 3049
Longview, Texas
75606-3049

Grimes County Clerk
P.O. Box 209
Anderson, Texas 77830

Guadalupe County Clerk
Courthouse
Seguin, Texas 78155-5727

Hale County Clerk
P.O. Box 710
Plainview, Texas
79073-0710

Hall County Clerk
Courthouse
Memphis, Texas
79245-3341

Hamilton County Clerk
Courthouse
Hamilton, Texas 76531

Hansford County Clerk
P.O. Box 367
Spearman, Texas
79081-0367

Hardeman County Clerk
Courthouse
Quanah, Texas 79252

Hardin County Clerk
P.O. Box 38
Kountze, Texas
77625-0038

Harris County Clerk
1001 Preston, 4th Fl.
Houston, Texas 77251

Harrison County Clerk
Courthouse
Marshall, Texas 75671

Hartley County Clerk
P.O. Box 22
Channing, Texas
79018-0022

Haskell County Clerk
P.O. Box 905
Haskell, Texas 79521

Hays County Clerk
Courthouse
San Marcos, Texas 78666

Hemphill County Clerk
P.O. Box 867
Canadian, Texas
79014-0867

Henderson County Clerk
Courthouse
Athens, Texas 75751

Hidalgo County Clerk
P.O. Box 58
Edinburg, Texas
78540-0058

Hill County Clerk
P.O. Box 398
Hillsboro, Texas
76645-0398

Hockley County Clerk
Courthouse
Levelland, Texas
79336-4529

Hood County Clerk
P.O. Box 339
Granbury, Texas
76048-0339

Hopkins County Clerk
P.O. Box 288
Sulphur Springs, Texas
75482-0288

Houston County Clerk
Courthouse
Crockett, Texas 75835

Howard County Clerk
P.O. Box 1468
Big Spring, Texas
79721-1468

Hudspeth County Clerk
Courthouse
Sierra Blanca, Texas 79851

Hunt County Clerk
P.O. Box 1316
Greenville, Texas
75401-1316

Hutchinson County Clerk
P.O. Box F
Stinnett, Texas 79083-0526

Irion County Clerk
Courthouse
Mertzon, Texas 76941

Jack County Clerk
100 Main St.
Jacksboro, Texas
76056-1746

Jackson County Clerk
115 West. Main St.
Edna, Texas 77957-2733

Jasper County Clerk
Courthouse
Jasper, Texas 75951

Jeff Davis County Clerk
P.O. Box 398
Fort Davis, Texas
79734-0398

Jefferson County Clerk
P.O. Box 1151
Beaumont, Texas 77704

Jim Hogg County Clerk
102 East Tilley
Hebbronville, Texas
78361-3554

Jim Wells County Clerk
Courthouse
Alice, Texas 78332-4845

Johnson County Clerk
Courthouse
Cleburne, Texas 76031

Jones County Clerk
P.O. Box 552
Anson, Texas 79501-0552

Karnes County Clerk
Courthouse
Karnes City, Texas
78118-2959

Kaufman County Clerk
Courthouse
Kaufman, Texas 75142

Kendall County Clerk
Courthouse
Boerne, Texas 78006

Kenedy County Clerk
P.O. Box 7
Sarita, TX 78385-0007

Kent County Clerk
P.O. Box 9
Jayton, Texas 79528-0009

Kerr County Clerk
700 Main Street
Kerrville, Texas 78028

Kimble County Clerk
501 Main St.
Junction, Texas
76849-4763

King County Clerk
Courthouse
Guthrie, Texas 79236

Kinney County Clerk
P.O. Box 9
Brackettville, Texas
78832-0009

Kleberg County Clerk
P.O. Box 1327
Kingsville, Texas
78364-1327

Knox County Clerk
County House
Benjamin, Texas 79505

La Salle County Clerk
P.O. Box 340
Cotulla, Texas 78014-0340

Lamar County Clerk
119 North Main
Paris, Texas 75460-4265

Lamb County Clerk
Courthouse
Littlefiled, Texas 79339

Lampasas County Clerk
P.O. Box 231
Lampasas, Texas
76550-0231

Lavaca County Clerk
Courthouse
Hallettsville, Texas 77964

Lee County Clerk
P.O. Box 419
Giddings, Texas
78942-0419

Leon County Clerk
P.O. Box 98
Centerville, Texas
75833-0098

Liberty County Clerk
1923 Sam Huston
Liberty, Texas 77575-4815

Limestone County Clerk
200 West State St.
Groesbeck, Texas
76642-1702

Lipscomb County Clerk
Courthouse
Lipscomb, Texas 79056

Live Oak County Clerk
P.O. Box 280
George West, Texas
78022-0280

Llano County Clerk
801 Ford, Rm. 101
Llano, Texas 78643

Loving County Clerk
Courthouse
Mentone, Texas 79754

Lubbock County Clerk
P.O. Box 10536
Lubbock, Texas 79408

Lynn County Clerk
Courthouse
Tahoka, Texas 79373

Madison County Clerk
101 West Main
Madisonville, Texas 77864

Marion County Clerk
P.O. Box F
Jefferson, Texas
75657-0420

Martin County Clerk
Courthouse
Stanton, Texas 79782

Mason County Clerk
P.O. Box 702
Mason, Texas 76856-0702

Matagorda County Clerk
1700 Seventh Street
Bay City, Texas
77414-5034

Maverick County Clerk
Courthouse
Eagle Pass, Texas 78853

McCulloch County Clerk
Courthouse
Brady, Texas 76825

McLennan County Clerk
225 W. Waco Dr.
Waco, Texas 76707

McMullen County Clerk
P.O. Box 235
Tilden, Texas 78072-0235

Medina County Clerk
Courthouse
Hondo, Texas 78861

Menard County Clerk
Courthouse
Menard, Texas 76659

Midland County Clerk
P.O. Box 211
Midland, Texas
79702-0211

Milam County Clerk
100 South Fannin
Cameron, Texas
76520-4216

Mills County Clerk
P.O. Box 646
Goldthwaite, Texas
76844-0646

Mitchell County Clerk
P.O. Box 1166
Colorado City, Texas
79512-1166

Montague County Clerk
P.O. Box 77
Montague, Texas
76251-0077

**Montgomery
County Clerk**
301 N. Main, Suite 128
Conroe, Texas 77301-2637

Moore County Clerk
P.O. Box 396
Dumas, Texas 79029-0396

Morris County Clerk
500 Broadnax St.
Daingerfield, Texas
75638-1304

Motley County Clerk
County Clerk
Matador, Texas 79224

Nacogdoches
County Clerk
101 West Main St.
Nacogdoches, Texas
75961-5119

Navarro County Clerk
300 West Third Ave.
Corsicana, Texas 75110

Newton County Clerk
P.O. Box 484
Newton, Texas 75966-0484

Nolan County Clerk
P.O. Box 98
Sweetwater, Texas 79556

Nueces County Clerk
901 Leopard
Corpus Christi, Texas
78401-3606

Ochiltree County Clerk
511 South Main St.
Perryton, Texas
79070-3154

Oldham County Clerk
P.O. Box 469
Vega, Texas 79092-0469

Orange County Clerk
801 Division St.
Orange, Texas 77630-6321

Palo Pinto County Clerk
Courthouse
Palo Pinto, Texas 76072

Panola County Clerk
Rm. 201
Carthage, Texas 75633

Parker County Clerk
1112 Santa Fe Dr.
Weatherford, Texas
76086-5827

Parmer County Clerk
P.O. Box 356
Farwell, Texas 79325-0356

Pecos County Clerk
103 West Callahan St.
Fort Stockton, Texas
79735-7101

Polk County Clerk
101 Church St. West
Livingston, Texas
77351-3201

Potter County Clerk
511 South Taylor
Amarillo, Texas
79101-2437

Presidio Country Clerk
P.O. Box 789
Marfa, Texas 79843-0789

Rains County Clerk
P.O. Box 187
Emory, Texas 75440-0187

Randall County Clerk
P.O. Box 660
Canyon, Texas 79015-0660

Reagan County Clerk
P.O. Box 100
Big Lake, Texas
76932-0100

Real County Clerk
P.O. Box 656
Leakey, Texas 78873-0656

Red River County Clerk
400 North Walnut St.
Clarksville, Texas 75426

Reeves County Clerk
P.O. Box 867
Pecos, Texas 79772-0867

Refugio County Clerk
P.O. Box 704
Refugio, Texas 78377-0704

Roberts County Clerk
P.O. Box 477
Miami, Texas 79059-0477

Robertson County Clerk
P.O. Box L
Franklin, Texas
77856-0300

Rockwall County Clerk
Courthouse
Rockwall, Texas 75087

Runnels County Clerk
P.O. Box 189
Ballinger, Texas
76821-0189

Rusk County Clerk
P.O. Box 758
Henderson, Texas
75653-0758

Sabine County Clerk
Courthouse
Hemphill, Texas 75948

San Augustine
County Clerk
106 Courthouse
San Augustine, Texas
75972

San Jacinto County Clerk
P.O. Box 669
Coldspring, Texas 77331

San Patricio
County Clerk
P.O. Box 578
Sinton, Texas 78387-0578

San Saba County Clerk
Courthouse
San Saba, Texas 76877

Schleicher County Clerk
Courthouse
Eldorado, Texas 76936

Scurry County Clerk
Courthouse
Snyder, Texas 79549

Shackelford
County Clerk
P.O. Box 247
Albany, Texas 76430-0247

Shelby County Clerk
P.O. Box 1987
Center, Texas 75935-1987

Sherman County Clerk
P.O. Box 270
Stratford, Texas
79084-0270

Smith County Clerk
100 N. Broadway
Tyler, Texas 75710-1018

Somervell County Clerk
P.O. Box 1098
Glen Rose, Texas
76043-1098

Starr County Clerk
Britton Ave.
Rio Grande City, Texas
78582

Stephens County Clerk
Courthouse
Breckenridge, Texas 76024

Sterling County Clerk
P.O. Box 55
Sterling City, Texas
76951-0055

Stonewall County Clerk
P.O. Box P
Aspermont, Texas
79502-0914

Sutton County Clerk
P.O. Box 481
Sonora, Texas 76950-0481

Swisher County Clerk
Courthouse
Tulia, Texas 79088-2245

Tarrant County Clerk
100 E. Weatherford St.
Fort Worth, Texas 76196

Taylor County Clerk
Courthouse
Abilene, Texas 79608

Terrell County Clerk
P.O. Box 410
Sanderson, Texas
79848-0410

Terry County Clerk
Courthouse
Brownfield, Texas
79316-4328

Throckmorton
County Clerk
P.O. Box 309
Throckmorton, Texas
76083-0309

Titus County Clerk
Courthouse
Mount Pleasant, Texas
75455

Tom Green County Clerk
112 West Beauregard
San Angelo, Texas
76903-5850

Travis County Clerk
1000 Guadalupe
Austin, Texas 78701-2336

Trinity County Clerk
P.O. Box 456
Groveton, Texas
75845-0456

Tyler County Clerk
100 Courthouse
Woodville, Texas
75979-5245

Upshur County Clerk
Courthouse
Gilmer, Texas 75644

Upton County Clerk
P.O. Box 465
Rankin, Texas 79778-0465

Uvalde County Clerk
P.O. Box 284
Uvalde, Texas 78802-0284

Val Verde County Clerk
P.O. Box 1267
Del Rio, Texas 78841-1267

Van Zandt County Clerk
P.O. Box 515
Canton, Texas 75103-0515

Victoria County Clerk
115 North Bridge
Victoria, Texas 77901-6513

Walker County Clerk
1100 University
Huntsville, Texas
77340-4631

Waller County Clerk
836 Austin St.
Hempstead, Texas
77445-4667

Ward County Clerk
Courthouse
Monahans, Texas 79756

**Washington
County Clerk**
P.O. Box K
Brenham, Texas
77833-0609

Webb County Clerk
204 McPherson Dr.
Laredo, Texas 78041-2712

Wharton County Clerk
P.O. Box 69
Wharton, Texas 77488

Wheeler County Clerk
P.O. Box 465
Wheeler, Texas
79096-0465

Wichita County Clerk
P.O. Box 1679
Wichita Falls, Texas
76307-1679

Wilbarger County Clerk
1700 Wilbarger Street
Vernon, Texas 76384-4742

Willacy County Clerk
Courthouse
Raymondville, Texas
78580-3533

Williamson County Clerk
P.O. Box 18
Georgetown, Texas
78627-0018

Wilson County Clerk
P.O. Box 27
Floresville, Texas
78114-0027

Winkler County Clerk
P.O. Box 1007
Kermit, Texas 79745-1007

Wise County Clerk
P.O. Box 359
Decatur, Texas 76234-0359

Wood County Clerk
P.O. Box 338
Quitman, Texas
75783-0338

Yoakum County Clerk
P.O. Box 309
Plains, Texas 79355-0309

Young County Clerk
P.O. Box 218
Graham, Texas 76046-0218

Zapata County Clerk
Courthouse
Zapata, Texas 78076

Zavala County Clerk
Courthouse
Crystal City, Texas
78839-3547

UTAH

http://www.state.ut.us/

Beaver County Clerk
105 East Center
Beaver, Utah 84713

Box Elder County Clerk
1 South Main St.
Brigham City, Utah
84302-2548

Cache County Clerk
655 East 1300 North
Logan, Utah 84341

Carbon County Clerk
120 E. Main St.
Price, Utah 84501

Daggett County Clerk
95 North 1st W.
Manila, Utah 84046

Davis County Clerk
28 East State St.
Farmington, Utah 84025

Duchesne County Clerk
P.O. Box 270
Duchesne, Utah 84021

Emery County Clerk
95 East Main St.
Castle Dale, Utah 84513

Garfield County Clerk
55 S. Main St.
Panguitch, Utah 84759

Grand County Clerk
125 East Center St.
Moab, Utah 84532

Iron County Clerk
68 South 100 East
Parowan, Utah 84761

Juab County Clerk
160 N. Main St.
Nephi, Utah 84648

Kane County Clerk
76 N. Main St.
Kanab, Utah 84741

Millard County Clerk
765 S. Highway 99
Fillmore, Utah 84631

Morgan County Clerk
48 W. Young St.
Morgan, Utah 84050

Piute County Clerk
21 N. Main St.
Junction, Utah 84740

Rich County Clerk
20 S. Main St.
Randolph, Utah 84064

Salt Lake County Clerk
610 S. 200 E.
Salt Lake City, Utah 84111

San Juan County Clerk
117 S. Main St.
Monticello, Utah 84535

Sanpete County Clerk
160 N. Main
Manti, Utah 84642-1266

Sevier County Clerk
250 N. Main
Richfield, Utah
84701-2158

Summit County Clerk
P.O. Box 128
Coalville, Utah 84017

Tooele County Clerk
47 South Main
Tooele, Utah 84074

Uintah County Clerk
147 E. Main St.
Vernal, Utah 84078

Utah County Clerk
589 S. State St.
Provo, Utah 84606

Wasatch County Clerk
25 N. Main St.
Heber City, Utah 84032

**Washington County
Clerk**
197 East Tabernacle St.
St. George, Utah 84770

Wayne County Clerk
18 South Main
Loa, Utah 84747

Weber County Clerk
2549 Washington Blvd,
Suite 320
Ogden, Utah 84401

VERMONT

http://www.state.vt.us/

Addison County Clerk
5 Court St.
Middlebury, Vermont
05753-1405

Bennington County Clerk
207 South St.
Bennington, Vermont
05201

Caledonia County Clerk
27 Main St.
St. Johnsbury, Vermont
05819-2637

Chittenden County Clerk
175 Main St.
Burlington, Vermont
05401-8310

Essex County Clerk
Courthouse
Guildhall, Vermont 05905

Franklin County Clerk
Church St.
St. Albans, Vermont 05478

Grand Isle County Clerk
P.O. Box 7
North Hero, Vermont
05474-0007

Lamoille County Clerk
P.O. Box 303
Hyde Park, Vermont
05655-0303

Orange County Clerk
Courthouse
Chelsea, Vermont 05038

Orleans County Clerk
P.O. Box 787
Newport, Vermont
05855-0787

Rutland County Clerk
83 Center St.
Rutland, Vermont
05701-4017

**Washington
County Clerk**
P.O. Box 426
Montpelier, Vermont
05602-0426

Windham County Clerk
P.O. Box 207
Newfane, Vermont
05345-0207

Windsor County Clerk
12 The Green
Woodstock, Vermont
05091-1212

VIRGINIA

http://www.state.va.us/

Accomack County Clerk
Courthouse
Accomack, Virginia 23301

Albemarle County Clerk
401 McIntire Rd.
Charlottesville, Virginia
22901-4579

Alleghany County Clerk
Main Street
Covington, Virginia 24426

Amelia County Clerk
Courthouse
Amelia Court House,
Virginia 23002

Amherst County Clerk
100 E. St.
Amherst, Virginia 24521

**Appomattox
County Clerk**
P.O. Box 672
Appomattox, Virginia
24522-0672

Arlington County Clerk
1400 N. Courthouse Rd.
Arlington, Virginia
22201-2622

Augusta County Clerk
6 East Johnson St.
Staunton, Virginia 24401-
4301

Bath County Clerk
P.O. Box 180
Warm Springs, Virginia
24484-0180

Bedford County Clerk
201 East Main St.
Bedford, Virginia 24623

Bland County Clerk
P.O. Box 295
Bland, Virginia 24315-0295

Botetourt County Clerk
P.O. Box 219
Fincastle, Virginia 24090

Brunswick County Clerk
P.O. Box 399
Lawrenceville, Virginia
23868-0399

Buchanan County Clerk
P.O. Box 950
Grundy, Virginia
24614-0950

**Buckingham
County Clerk**
P.O. Box 252
Buckingham, Virginia
23921-0252

Campbell County Clerk
P.O. Box 7
Rustburg, Virginia 24588

Caroline County Clerk
Courthouse
Bowling Green, Virginia
22427

Carrol County Clerk
P.O. Box 515
Hillsville, Virginia
24343-0515

Charles County Clerk
P.O. Box 128
Charles City, Virginia
23030-0128

Charlotte County Clerk
P.O. Box 38
Charlotte Court House,
Virginia 23923

**Chesterfield
County Clerk**
P.O. Box 40
Chesterfield, Virginia
23832-0040

**City of Alexandria
County Clerk**
301 King St.
Alexandria, Virginia 22313

**City of Fredericksburg
County Clerk**
P.O. Box 7447
Fredericksburg, Virginia
22404-7447

**City of Martinsville
County Clerk**
P.O. Box 1112
Martinsville, Virginia
24114

**City of Petersburg
County Clerk**
Union and Tabb St.
Petersburg, Virginia 23803

**City of Richmond
Vital Records**
109 Governor St.
Richmond, Virginia 23219

**City of Roanoke Vital
Records**
515 8th St. SW
Richmond, Virginia
24016-3529

**City of Salem
County Clerk**
P.O. Box 869
Salem, Virginia
24153-0869

**City of Virginia Beach
County Clerk**
Municipal Center,
Building 1
Virginia Beach, Virginia
23456

Clarke County Clerk
P.O. Box 189
Berryville, Virginia
22611-0189

Craig County Clerk
P.O. Box 185
New Castle, Virginia 24127

Culpeper County Clerk
Courthouse
Culpeper, Virginia 22701

**Cumberland
County Clerk**
P.O. Box 77
Cumberland, Virginia
23040-0077

Dickenson County Clerk
P.O. Box 190
Clintwood, Virginia 24228

Dinwiddie County Clerk
14103 Boydton Plank Rd.
Dinwiddie, Virginia
23841-2511

Emporia County Clerk
201 N. Main Street
Emporia, Virginia 23817

Essex County Clerk
P.O. Box 445
Tappahannock, Virginia
22560-0445

Fairfax County Clerk
4110 Chain Bridge Rd.
Fairfax, Virginia 22030

Fauquier County Clerk
40 Culpeper St.
Warrenton, Virginia 22186

Floyd County Clerk
Courthouse
Floyd, Virginia 24091

Fluvanna County Clerk
Courthouse
Palmyra, Virginia 22963

Franklin County Clerk
Courthouse Building
Rocky Mount, Virginia
24151

Frederick County Clerk
5 North Kent St.
Winchester, Virginia 22601

Giles County Clerk
120 North Main St.
Pearisburg, Virginia
24134-1625

Gloucester County Clerk
P.O. Box 329
Gloucester, Virginia 23061-
0329

Goochland County Clerk
P.O. Box 10
Goochland, Virginia
23063-0010

Grayson County Clerk
129 Davis St.
Independence, Virginia
24348-9602

Greene County Clerk
P.O. Box 386
Stanardsville, Virginia
22973-0386

Greensville County Clerk
337 S. Main St.
Emporia, Virginia
23847-2027

Halifax County Clerk
P.O. Box 786
Halifax, Virginia
24558-0786

Hanover County Clerk
Courthouse
Hanover, Virginia 23069

**Henrico (East) County
Health Dept.**
3810 Nine Mile Rd.
Richmond, Virginia 23223

**Henrico (West) County
Health Dept.**
8600 Dixon Powers Dr.
Richmond, Virginia 23273

Henry County Clerk
Courthouse
Martinsville, Virginia
24114

Highland County Clerk
P.O. Box 190
Monterey, Virginia 24465

**Isle of Wight
County Clerk**
Courthouse
Isle of Wight, Virginia
23397

James County Clerk
114 Stanley Dr.
Williamsburg, Virginia
23185-2538

**King and Queen
County Clerk**
Courthouse
King and Queen
Courthouse, Virginia 23085

**King George County
Clerk**
P.O. Box 105
King George, Virginia
22485

**King William
County Clerk**
P.O. Box 215
King William, Virginia
23086

Lancaster County Clerk
P.O. Box 125
Lancaster, Virginia 22503

Lee County Clerk
Courthouse
Jonesville, Virginia 24263

Loudoun County Clerk
P.O. Box 550
Leesburg, Virginia
22075-0550

Louisa County Clerk
P.O. Box 160
Louisa, Virginia
23093-0160

Lunenburg County Clerk
Courthouse
Lunenburg, Virginia 23952

Madison County Clerk
Main St.
Madison, Virginia 22727

Mathews County Clerk
Court St.
Mathews, Virginia 23109

**Mecklenburg
County Clerk**
P.O. Box 307
Boydton, Virginia
23917-0207

Middlesex County Clerk
Courthouse
Saluda, Virginia 23149

**Montgomery
County Clerk**
P.O. Box 6126
Christiansburg, Virginia
24068-6126

Nelson County Clerk
Courthouse
Lovingston, Virginia 22949

New Kent County Clerk
P.O. Box 98
New Kent, Virginia
23124-0050

**Northampton
County Clerk**
Courthouse
Eastville, Virginia 23347

**Northumberland
County Clerk**
Courthouse
Heathsville, Virginia 22473

Nottoway County Clerk
Courthouse
Nottoway, Virginia 23955

Orange County Clerk
P.O. Box 230
Orange, Virginia 22960

Page County Clerk
101 South Court St.
Luray, Virginia 22835-1224

Patrick County Clerk
P.O. Box 148
Stuart, Virginia 24171-0148

Pittsylvania County Clerk
P.O. Box 31
Chatham, Virginia
24531-0031

Powhatan County Clerk
3834 Old Buckingham Rd.
Powhatan, Virginia
23139-7019

**Prince Edward
County Clerk**
P.O. Box 304
Farmville, Virginia
23901-0304

**Prince George
County Clerk**
P.O. Box 68
Prince George, Virginia
23875-0068

**Prince William
County Clerk**
P.O. Box 191
Prince William, Virginia
22192

Pulaski County Clerk
Third St.
Pulaski, Virginia 24301

**Rappahannock
County Clerk**
P.O. Box 116
Washington, Virginia
22747-0116

Richmond County Clerk
Court St.
Warsaw, Virginia 22572

Roanoke County Clerk
P.O. Box 1126
Salem, Virginia
24153-1126

Rockbridge County Clerk
Courthouse Square
Lexington, Virginia 24450

**Rockingham
County Clerk**
Circuit Court Square
Harrisonburg, Virginia
22801

Russell County Clerk
P.O. Box 435
Lebanon, Virginia 24266

Scott County Clerk
P.O. Box 665
Gate City, Virginia
24251-0665

**Shenandoah
County Clerk**
P.O. Box 406
Woodstock, Virginia
22664-0406

Smyth County Clerk
P.O. Box 1025
Marion, Virginia
24354-1025

**Southampton
County Clerk**
Courthouse
Courtland, Virginia 23837

**Spotsylvania
County Clerk**
P.O. Box 99
Spotsylvania, Virginia
22553-0099

Stafford County Clerk
P.O. Box 339
Stafford, Virginia
22554-0339

Suffolk County Clerk
441 Market St.
Suffolk, Virginia
23434-5237

Surry County Clerk
P.O. Box 65
Surry, Virginia 23883-0065

Sussex County Clerk
P.O. Box 1337
Sussex, Virginia
23884-0337

Tazewell County Clerk
P.O. Box 958
Tazewell, Virginia 24651

Warren County Clerk
1 East Main St.
Front Royal, Virginia
22630

**Washington
County Clerk**
111 North Court St.
Abingdon, Virginia 24210

**Westmoreland
County Clerk**
P.O. Box 467
Montross, Virginia
22520-0467

Wise County Clerk
P.O. Box 570
Wise, Virginia 24293-0570

Wythe County Clerk
P.O. Box 440
Wytheville, Virginia
24382-0440

York County Clerk
P.O. Box 532
Yorktown, Virginia
23690-0532

WASHINGTON

http://www.state.va.us/

Adams County Clerk
210 West Broadway
Ritzville, Washington
99169-1860

Asotin County Clerk
135 2nd St.
Asotin, Washington 99402

Benton County Clerk
P.O. Box 190
Prosser, Washington
99350-0190

Chelan County Clerk
P.O. Box 3025
Wenatchee, Washington
98801-0403

Clallam County Clerk
223 East 4th St.
Port Angeles, Washington
98362-3098

Clark County Clerk
1200 Franklin St.
Vancouver, Washington
98660-2872

Columbia County Clerk
341 East Main St.
Dayton, Washington
99328-1361

Cowlitz County Clerk
312 SW First St.
Kelso, Washington
98626-1724

Douglas County Clerk
P.O. Box 516
Waterville, Washington
98858-0516

Ferry County Clerk
P.O. Box 498
Republic, Washington
99166-0498

Franklin County Clerk
1016 N. Fourth Ave.
Pasco, Washington
99301-3706

Garfield County Clerk
P.O. Box 915
Pomeroy, Washington
99347-0915

Grant County Clerk
P.O. Box 37
Ephrata, Washington
98823-0037

**Grays Harbor
County Clerk**
102 W. Broadway, Rm. 203
Montesano, Washington
98563

Island County Clerk
P.O. Box 1317
Coupeville, Washington
98239-1317

Jefferson County Clerk
P.O. Box 1220
Port Townsend,
Washington 98368

King County Clerk
500 4th Ave. Admin Bldg,
Rm. 214
Seattle, Washington 98104

Kitsap County Clerk
614 Division St.
Port Orchard, Washington
98366-4614

Kittitas County Clerk
205 West Fifth Ave.
Ellensburg, Washington
98926-2887

Klickitat County Clerk
205 South Columbus
Goldendale, Washington
98620-9286

Lewis County Clerk
344 West Main
Chehalis, Washington
98532-1922

Lincoln County Clerk
450 Logan St.
Davenport, Washington
99122-9501

Mason County Clerk
Fourth and Alder
Shelton, Washington 98584

Okanogan County Clerk
P.O. Box 72
Okanogan, Washington
98840-0072

Pacific County Clerk
P.O. Box 67
South Bend, Washington
98586-0067

**Pend Oreille
County Clerk**
P.O. Box 5000
Newport, Washington
99156-5000

Pierce County Clerk
3629 South D St.
Tacoma, Washington 98408

San Juan County Clerk
Courthouse
Friday Harbor, Washington
98250

Skagit County Clerk
P.O. Box 837
Mt. Vernon, Washington
98273-0837

Skamania County Clerk
P.O. Box 790
Stevenson, Washington
98648-0790

Snohomish County Clerk
3000 Rockefeller
Everett, Washington 98201

Spokane County Clerk
1101 W. College Ave.
Spokane, Washington
99210

Stevens County Auditor
215 South Oak St.
Colville, Washington 99114

Thurston County Clerk
2000 Lakeridge SW
Olympia, Washington
98502-6045

**Wahkiakum
County Clerk**
P.O. Box 116
Cathlamet, Washington
98612-0116

**Walla Walla County
Clerk**
315 West Main St.
Walla Walla, Washington
99362-2838

Whatcom County Clerk
311 Grand Ave.
Bellingham, Washington
98225-4038

Whitman County Clerk
P.O. Box 390
Colfax, Washington
99111-0390

Yakima County Clerk
Second and East B St.
Yakima, Washington 98901

WEST VIRGINIA
http://www.state.wv.us/

Barbour County Clerk
P.O. Box 310
Philippi, West Virginia
26416-0310

Berkeley County Clerk
100 West King St.
Martinsburg, West Virginia
25401-3210

Boone County Clerk
Boone County Courthouse
Madison, West Virginia
25130

Braxton County Clerk
P.O. Box 486
Sutton, West Virginia
26601-0486

Brooke County Clerk
632 Main St.
Wellsburg, West Virginia
26070

Cabell County Clerk
Courthouse
Huntington, West Virginia
25701

Calhoun County Clerk
P.O. Box 230
Grantsville, West Virginia
26147

Clay County Clerk
P.O. Box 190
Clay, West Virginia 25043

Doddridge County Clerk
118 East Court St.
West Union, West Virginia
26456

Fayette County Clerk
Courthouse
Fayetteville, West Virginia
25840

Gilmer County Clerk
Courthouse
Glenville, West Virginia
26351

Grant County Clerk
5 Highland Ave.
Petersburg, West Virginia
26847-1705

Greenbrier County Clerk
P.O. Box 506
Lewisburg, West Virginia
24901-0506

Hampshire County Clerk
Courthouse
Romney, West Virginia
26757

Hancock County Clerk
P.O. Box 367
New Cumberland,
West Virginia 26047

Hardy County Clerk
P.O. Box 540
Moorefield, West Virginia
26836-0540

Harrison County Clerk
301 West Main
Clarksburg, West Virginia
26301-2909

Jackson County Clerk
Courthouse
Ripley, West Virginia
25271

Jefferson County Clerk
Courthouse
Charles Town,
West Virginia 25414

Kanawha County Clerk
P.O. Box 3226
Charleston, West Virginia
25332-3226

Lewis County Clerk
P.O. Box 87
Weston, West Virginia
26452-0087

Lincoln County Clerk
Courthouse
Hamlin, West Virginia
25523

Logan County Clerk
Courthouse
Logan, West Virginia
25601

Marion County Clerk
Courthouse
Fairmont, West Virginia
26554

Marshall County Clerk
P.O. Box 459
Moundsville, West Virginia
26041-0459

Mason County Clerk
Courthouse
Point Pleasant,
West Virginia 25550

Mcdowell County Clerk
P.O. Box 967
Welch, West Virginia
24801-0967

Mercer County Clerk
Courthouse Square
Princeton, West Virginia
24740

Mineral County Clerk
150 Armstrong St.
Keyser, West Virginia
26726-0250

Mingo County Clerk
P.O. Box 1197
Williamson, West Virginia
25661-1197

**Monongalia
County Clerk**
Courthouse
Morgantown, West Virginia
26505

Monroe County Clerk
Courthouse
Union, West Virginia
24983

Morgan County Clerk
Fairfax St.
Berkeley Springs,
West Virginia 25411

Nicholas County Clerk
Courthouse
Summersville,
West Virginia 26651

Ohio County Clerk
1500 Chapline St., Rm. 205
Wheeling, West Virginia
26003-3553

Pendleton County Clerk
Courthouse
Franklin, West Virginia
26807

Pleasants County Clerk
Courthouse
St. Marys, West Virginia
26170

Pocahontas County Clerk
900C Tenth Ave.
Marlinton, West Virginia
24954-1333

Preston County Clerk
101 West Main
Kingwood, West Virginia
26537-1121

Putnam County Clerk
P.O. Box 508
Winfield, West Virginia
25213-0508

Raleigh County Clerk
Courthouse
Beckley, West Virginia
25801

Randolph County Clerk
Courthouse
Elkins, West Virginia
26241

Ritchie County Clerk
115 East Main St.
Harrisville, West Virginia
26362

Roane County Clerk
P.O. Box 69
Spencer, West Virginia
25276

Summers County Clerk
P.O. Box 97
Hinton, West Virginia
25951-0097

Taylor County Clerk
Courthouse
Grafton, West Virginia
26354

Tucker County Clerk
Courthouse
Parsons, West Virginia
26287

Tyler County Clerk
P.O. Box 66
Middlebourne,
West Virginia 26149-0066

Upshur County Clerk
Courthouse
Buckhannon, West Virginia
26201

Wayne County Clerk
Courthouse
Wayne, West Virginia
25570

Webster County Clerk
Courthouse
Webster Springs,
West Virginia 26268

Wetzel County Clerk
P.O. Box 156
New Martinsville,
West Virginia 26155-0156

Wirt County Clerk
P.O. Box 53
Elizabeth, West Virginia
26143-0053

Wood County Clerk
Courthouse
Parkersburg, West Virginia
26101

Wyoming County Clerk
P.O. Box 309
Pineville, West Virginia
24874-0309

WISCONSIN

http://www.state.wi.us/

Adams County Clerk
402 N. Main St.
Friendship, Wisconsin
53934-9375

Ashland County Clerk
201 Main St. W.
Ashland, Wisconsin
54806-1652

Barron County Clerk
330 E. LaSalle Ave.
Barron, Wisconsin
54812-1540

Bayfield County Clerk
117 E. 5th St.
Washburn, Wisconsin
54891-9464

Brown County Clerk
305 E. Walnut St.
Green Bay, Wisconsin
54301-5027

Buffalo County Clerk
407 S. 2nd St.
Alma, Wisconsin 54610

Burnett County Clerk
7410 County Rd K #103
Siren, Wisconsin 54872

Calumet County Clerk
206 Court St.
Chilton, Wisconsin
53014-1127

Chippewa County Clerk
711 N. Bridge St.
Chippewa Falls, Wisconsin
54729

Clark County Clerk
P.O. Box 384
Neillsville, Wisconsin
54456

Columbia County Clerk
400 Dewitt St.
Portage, Wisconsin 53821

Crawford County Clerk
220 N. Beaumont Rd.
Prairie Du Chien,
Wisconsin 53821

Dane County Clerk
P.O. Box 1438
Madison, Wisconsin 53701

Dodge County Clerk
127 E. Oak St.
Juneau, Wisconsin 53039

Door County Clerk
421 Nebraska St.
Sturgeon Bay, Wisconsin
54235

Douglas County Clerk
1313 Belknap St.
Superior, Wisconsin 54880

Dunn County Clerk
800 Wilson Ave.
Menomonie, Wisconsin
54751

Eau Claire County Clerk
721 Oxford Ave.
Eau Claire, Wisconsin
54703-5481

Florence County Clerk
501 Lake Ave.
Florence, Wisconsin 54121

**Fond du Lac
County Clerk**
160 S. Macy St.
Fond du Lac, Wisconsin
54936

Forest County Clerk
200 E. Madison St.
Crandon, Wisconsin
54520-1415

Grant County Clerk
130 West Maple St.
Lancaster, Wisconsin
53813-1625

Green County Clerk
1016 16th Ave.
Monroe, Wisconsin
53566-1702

Green Lake County Clerk
492 Hill St.
Green Lake, Wisconsin
54941

Iowa County Clerk
222 North Iowa St.
Dodgeville, Wisconsin
53533-1557

Iron County Clerk
300 Taconite St.
Hurley, Wisconsin
54534-1546

Jackson County Clerk
307 Main St.
Black River Falls,
Wisconsin 54615-1756

Jefferson County Clerk
320 Main St.
Jefferson, Wisconsin 53549

Juneau County Clerk
220 E. State St.
Mauston, Wisconsin
53948-1398

Kenosha County Clerk
1010 56th St.
Kenosha, Wisconsin
53140-3738

Kewaunee County Clerk
613 Dodge St.
Kewaunee, Wisconsin
54216-1322

LaCrosse County Clerk
400 4th St. N.
LaCrosse, Wisconsin
54601-3227

Lafayette County Clerk
626 Main St.
Darlington, Wisconsin
53530-1397

Langlade County Clerk
800 Clairmont St.
Antigo, Wisconsin
54409-1947

Lincoln County Clerk
1110 East Main St.
Merrill, Wisconsin
54452-2554

Manitowoc County Clerk
1010 S. 8th St.
Manitowoc, Wisconsin
54221

Marathon County Clerk
500 Forest St.
Wausau, Wisconsin 54403

Marinette County Clerk
1926 Hall Ave.
Marinette, Wisconsin
54143-1717

Marquette County Clerk
77 W. Park St.
Montello, Wisconsin 53949

Menominee County Clerk
Courthouse Lane
Keshena, Wisconsin 54135

Milwaukee County Clerk
Courthouse Annex
907 N. 10th St.
Milwaukee, Wisconsin
53233

Monroe County Clerk
202 South K St., Rm. 2
Sparta, Wisconsin
54656-2187

Oconto County Clerk
301 Washington St.
Oconto, Wisconsin 54153

Oneida County Clerk
1 Courthouse Square
Rhinelander, Wisconsin
54501

Outagamie County Clerk
410 South Walnut St.
Appleton, Wisconsin
54911-5936

Ozaukee County Clerk
121 West Main St.
Port Washington,
Wisconsin 53074-1813

Pepin County Clerk
740 7th Ave. W.
Durand, Wisconsin
54736-1635

Pierce County Clerk
414 W. Main St.
Ellsworth, Wisconsin
54011-0119

Polk County Clerk
100 Polk County Plaza
Balsam Lake, Wisconsin
54810-9071

Portage County Clerk
1516 Church St.
Stevens Point, Wisconsin
54481-3501

Price County Clerk
104 S. Eyder Ave. #205
Phillips, Wisconsin
54555-1342

Racine County Clerk
730 Wisconsin Ave.
Racine, Wisconsin
53403-1238

Richland County Clerk
181 W. Seminary St.
Richland Center, Wisconsin
53581-2356

Rock County Clerk
51 South Main St.
Janesville, Wisconsin
53545-3951

Rusk County Clerk
311 Miner Ave. E.
Ladysmith, Wisconsin
54848-1862

Sauk County Clerk
505 Broadway St.
Baraboo, Wisconsin
53913-2401

Sawyer County Clerk
P.O. Box 273
Hayward, Wisconsin
54843-0273

Shawano County Clerk
311 N. Main St.
Shawano, Wisconsin
54166-2145

Sheboygan County Clerk
615 N. 6th St.
Sheboygan, Wisconsin
53081-4612

St. Croix County Clerk
1101 Carmichael Rd.
Hudson, Wisconsin
54016-7708

Taylor County Clerk
224 S. 2nd St.
Medford, Wisconsin
54451-1811

**Trempealeau
County Clerk**
36245 Main St.
Whitehall, Wisconsin
54773

Vernon County Clerk
400 Court House Square St.
Viroqua, Wisconsin
54665-1555

Vilas County Clerk
P.O. Box 369
Eagle River, Wisconsin
54521-0369

Walworth County Clerk
100 W. Walworth St.
Elkhorn, Wisconsin
53121-1769

Washburn County Clerk
10 West 4th Ave.
Shell Lake, Wisconsin
54871

**Washington
County Clerk**
432 E. Washington St.
West Bend, Wisconsin
53095-2530

Waukesha County Clerk
1320 Pewaukee Rd.
Waukesha, Wisconsin
53188-3870

Waupaca County Clerk
109 South Main
Waupaca, Wisconsin 54981

Waushara County Clerk
209 S. Saint Marie
Wautoma, Wisconsin
54982

Winnebago County Clerk
415 Jackson St.
Oshkosh, Wisconsin
54901-4751

Wood County Clerk
400 Market St.
Wisconsin Rapids,
Wisconsin 54494-4868

WYOMING

http://www.state.wy.us/

Albany County Clerk
Courthouse
Laramie, Wyoming
82070-3836

Big Horn County Clerk
Courthouse
Basin, Wyoming 82410

Campbell County Clerk
500 South Gillette Ave.
Gillette, Wyoming
82716-4239

Carbon County Clerk
Fifth and Spruce
Rawlins, Wyoming 82301

Converse County Clerk
P.O. Box 990
Douglas, Wyoming
82633-0990

Crook County Clerk
P.O. Box 37
Sundance, Wyoming
82729-0037

Fremont County Clerk
P.O. Box CC
Lander, Wyoming 82520

Goshen County Clerk
P.O. Box 160
Torrington, Wyoming
82240

Hot Springs County Clerk
Courthouse
Thermopolis, Wyoming
82443-2729

Johnson County Clerk
76 North Main
Buffalo, Wyoming
82834-1847

Laramie County Clerk
1902 Carey Ave.
Cheyenne, Wyoming 82001

Lincoln County Clerk
Courthouse
Kemmerer, Wyoming
83101-3141

Natrona County Clerk
200 North Center
Casper, Wyoming
82601-1949

Niobrara County Clerk
P.O. Box 420
Lusk, Wyoming 82225

Park County Clerk
P.O. Box 160
Cody, Wyoming
82414-0160

Platte County Clerk
P.O. Box 728
Wheatland, Wyoming
82201-0728

Sheridan County Clerk
224 S. Main St.
Sheridan, Wyoming
82801-4855

Sublette County Clerk
21 South Tyler St.
Pinedale, Wyoming 82941

Sweetwater County Clerk
P.O. Box 730
Green River, Wyoming
82935-0730

Teton County Clerk
P.O. Box 1727
Jackson, Wyoming
83001-1727

Uinta County Clerk
225 Ninth St.
Evanston, Wyoming
82930-3415

Washakie County Clerk
P.O. Box 260
Worland, Wyoming
82401-0260

Weston County Clerk
1 West Main
Newcastle, Wyoming
82701-2106

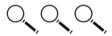

Another Book from Joseph Culligan

"*1,789,200* women were battered by their boyfriends within a recent reporting period." —Bureau of Justice statistic

JOSEPH CULLIGAN

Licensed Private Investigator, and author of YOU CAN FIND ANYBODY!

WHEN IN DOUBT, CHECK HIM' OUT

A Woman's Survival Guide

Updated Annually

$19.95 • Tradepaper • ISBN: 1-58872-001-2
Available from your local bookstore or library

This Book May Answer These Questions . . .

How much alimony does he pay?
How much child support does he pay?
What assets does he own?
Does his divorce file say he beat his wife?
Has he ever been arrested?

And much, much more!

". . . arms women with the information they need to conduct an inexpensive background check on just about any man who has aroused their suspicion." — *Chicago Tribune*

". . . why shouldn't someone check out the person she plans to spend the next 50 years with?" — *Detroit Free Press*

"This book is quite an eye-opener. Clearly, this sort of protective research can save women from all manner of traumatic or dangerous situations." — *American Library Association*

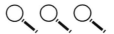

Joseph Culligan Investigative Camp Exclusive Weekend Programs

Be one of the select few to spend a weekend with Joe Culligan and his colleagues as they share all of their professional secrets. Joe Culligan's Investigative Camps are open to a very limited number of people and will be held in some of the most beautiful hotels in the world. Come learn the tricks of the trade from one of the most sought-after P.I.'s in the world.

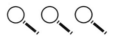

Joe Culligan Investigative Camp

You will learn:

- how to perform surveillance and place concealed cameras;

- forensic locksmithing, including thumbprint and retina scans;

- how to obtain and use high-tech spy equipment (it's not justfor the CIA anymore);

- secrets from the best computer wizards around;

- how to create your own lock-picking tools . . .

. . . and many more of Joseph Culligan's exclusive secrets!

For more information, visit
www.josephculligan.com or **www.Jodere.com**.

NOTES